HOLLYWOOD
Remains to Be Seen

HOLLYWOOD
Remains to Be Seen

A GUIDE TO THE MOVIE STARS' FINAL HOMES

Mark J. Masek

Cumberland House
Nashville, Tennessee

Published by Cumberland House Publishing, Inc., 431 Harding Industrial Drive, Nashville, TN 37211
www.cumberlandhouse.com

Cover design: Unlikely Suburban Design
Cover photos: Mark Masek
Interior design: Mary Sanford

Library of Congress Cataloging-in-Publication Data
Masek, Mark J., 1953-
   Hollywood remains to be seen : a guide to the movie stars' final homes / Mark J. Masek.
     p. cm.
   Includes bibliographical references and index.
   ISBN 1-58182-245-6 (pbk. : alk. paper)
   1. Motion picture actors and actresses—Tombs—California—Los Angeles—Directories.   I. Title.
 PN1998.2 .M38 2001
 791.43'028'092279494--dc21

                                        2001047276

Printed in the United States of America
1 2 3 4 5 6 7—06 05 04 03 02 01

Then, last week, as it must to all men, death came to Charles Foster Kane.

—CITIZEN KANE (1941), Screenplay by
Herman Mankiewicz and Orson Welles

~

You know something, George? I think we're dead.

—Marion Kerby (Constance Bennett) to George Kerby (Cary Grant)
in TOPPER (1937), Screenplay by Eric Hatch, Jack Jevne, and Eddie Moran

CONTENTS

ACKNOWLEDGMENTS

Special thanks to all who helped with the preparation of this book, particularly my wife, Theresa Norton Masek, for her valuable assistance and enthusiasm. Without her, this book could never have been written. For more than two years, she tolerated my research excursions to cemeteries and libraries, listened to my endless stories of celebrity and cemetery trivia, edited the early drafts, and supported me in every way possible. Simple thanks aren't nearly enough.

I would also like to thank my parents, Glenn and Helen Masek, for their support and assistance, as well as everyone else who was forced, coerced, or otherwise begged to read portions of this work in progress and provide valuable input and suggestions, including Ray Norton, Patrick Norton, Terry Masek, and Rick Masek.

Thanks also to Lisa Reitzel, my fellow grave-hound, who accompanied me on many of my cemetery excursions.

And thanks to Ron Pitkin at Cumberland House, for his faith and support.

INTRODUCTION

What's the one place in Hollywood where you're guaranteed the chance to get "up close and personal" with real celebrities and legends of the entertainment industry? Strange as it may seem, cemeteries are becoming one of the most popular destinations for Hollywood tourists and film fans who want to visit the final and permanent homes of the rich, famous, and passed-on.

But why do fans want to see the plot of earth or marble vault that houses a celebrity's earthly remains? What's the attraction to seeing a celebrity's name etched in granite or printed in bronze, along with the dates of their birth and death?

You might just as easily ask, Why do fans pay to buy a map, or be driven by the busload past the homes where celebrities haven't lived for years, if they ever lived there at all? Why do fans spend thousands, even millions of dollars to buy items of celebrity memorabilia? Simply put, we are fascinated by celebrity, and our fascination is growing.

In late 1999, an auction house in New York City put an assortment of Marilyn Monroe's personal possessions up for sale, including clothing, jewelry, and household items. The dress she wore on May 19, 1962, when she sang "Happy Birthday" to President John F. Kennedy at Madison Square Garden was sold for $1,267,500; a cardigan sweater she wore in a series of photographs taken shortly before her death sold for $167,500; three pairs of denim blue jeans she wore in the 1954 film *River of No Return* were purchased by designer Tommy Hilfiger for $42,550; and a pair of leather boots she wore in her last film, *The Misfits* (1961), went for $85,000. Before the auction, the memorabilia went on a national promotional tour, and more than 28,000 people paid $95 just to buy a catalog of the items up for sale.

If fans are still so interested in Monroe, nearly forty years after her death, that they're willing to pay $240,000 for one of her makeup cases, $130,000 for her driver's license, or $21,850 for one of her plaster floor lamps, it only makes sense that they'd be interested in visiting her final resting place. She may have owned a lot of lamps, but she's buried in only one location. And, in fact,

Monroe's crypt at Westwood Memorial Park is one of the most popular celebrity graves in Los Angeles. Hundreds of fans, many of them who weren't even born when Monroe died, visit her grave every day to pay their respects, leave flowers and notes, and pose for pictures in front of the small bronze plaque with her name on it. Hundreds of fans show up every year for a memorial service on the anniversary of her death, just as they do at Hollywood Forever Cemetery on the anniversary of the death of silent-film star Rudolph Valentino.

Visiting the graves of celebrities also gives fans some insight into the celebrity's personality and how he or she wished to be remembered. Some celebrities left detailed instructions in their wills with directions on how and where they wanted to be buried, and set aside enough money to pay for the lavish funeral services and memorials. Some celebrities, like Douglas Fairbanks Sr. and Al Jolson, were laid to rest in elaborate and majestic settings, complete with marble pillars, huge reflecting pools and fountains, cascading waterfalls, and statues of themselves. Perhaps they just wanted to make sure they would never be forgotten.

For many celebrities, their final resting places are a major part of their history and legend—the mysterious "Lady in Black" who visits Valentino's crypt every year on the anniversary of his death, or ex-husband Joe DiMaggio making arrangements for the delivery of six red roses to Monroe's crypt three times a week for twenty years.

Some celebrities are buried in more humble settings in remote locations, with small grave markers or no markers at all. Cremated remains are scattered in a favorite location. In some cases, the remains have even been moved to discourage visits from fans or tourists.

But fans still seek them out. At any time on a typical weekend afternoon, you can usually find a dozen or more people strolling through tiny Westwood Memorial Park, which probably has more well-known names per acre than any cemetery in the world. They walk up and down the rows of graves or among the wall crypts, looking for a particular name, or just any famous name. They signal to each other when they find something of interest, they gather to read the inscription on the grave marker, then they continue their quest. Some fans leave flowers, photographs, or other items.

Hubert Eaton, the man who revolutionized the cemetery business and transformed Forest Lawn in Glendale into perhaps the most famous cemetery in the world, identified what he called the "Memorial Impulse"—the desire by all people to be remembered after death. (Ironically, Forest Lawn is one of the strictest cemeteries about identifying celebrity graves, and it strongly discourages visits from fans. Many celebrities interred there are in locations inaccessible to the public.)

There are probably as many reasons to visit a celebrity's grave as there are visitors. Most visitors, I hope, are simply fans who want to pay their respects to someone who has brought them joy. Perhaps it's just an opportunity to spend some time in quiet, peaceful surroundings. Or, since we're all going to end up there eventually, perhaps it's a way for us to face and prepare for our own death.

Whatever the reason, however, before you go traipsing off through cemeteries, a few words of etiquette and advice are in order. Remember, for many people, cemeteries are sacred grounds where the mortal remains of their loved ones are buried. Whenever you are in any cemetery, be as polite, respectful, and courteous as you would be in a stranger's home or a place of worship. Also, it's likely that a burial service will be in progress when you visit. At some of the larger cemeteries, perhaps even several services. You will also likely encounter people who are paying their respects to departed loved ones. They might not know and most likely couldn't care less that an Academy Award–winning actor is buried a few feet away. Remember the last funeral service you attended for a friend or family member. You wouldn't want to look up and see a bunch of loud, raucous people rambling over the nearby graves. Try to dress appropriately and be as quiet, discreet, and considerate as possible. Since most of the cemeteries are privately owned, you may be asked to leave.

Many cemeteries have gates where you'll be asked to stop and state your purpose before you enter. Try not to look too much like a tourist. Hide the camera (and this book) in the back seat, and tell them solemnly that you're "here for a visit," and you shouldn't have any problems. Just don't mention who you're there to visit. Many cemeteries also have maps of the grounds available at the main entrance.

And cemeteries aren't the place to be looking for souvenirs, either. As tempting as it might be, don't take any flowers, dirt, or chips of marble from the grave of your favorite celebrity. If you really need a lasting memory, a discreetly snapped photograph should be enough.

This book is not intended to be the complete and definitive list of everyone who's buried in every cemetery around southern California. This is a guide to the specific highlights of selected cemeteries in and around Los Angeles. You may be looking for the grave of a favorite performer or celebrity, or you may be visiting the area and want to spend an hour or two at a particular cemetery. This book will tell you a little about the history of the cemetery and guide you to the final resting places of its most famous residents.

For some of the larger and more star-studded cemeteries, like Forest Lawn–Glendale and Hollywood Forever, I've offered several smaller tours, either arranged for a particular area of the cemetery, or special "theme tours." When you visit a cemetery, stop in the office first and ask for a map of the grounds. Even though the directions and descriptions in this book should be adequate to help you find what you're looking for, it never hurts to have a little extra information. Most cemeteries are divided into sections, either by letter, name, or both. In most cases, the names of the sections are printed on the curb along the roadway. The specific lots are usually identified by number, and the numbers can be found on small, round cement markers. It wouldn't hurt to bring along a small compass, either. The directions may tell you to walk northwest, or turn south, and a compass will help make certain that you're heading in the right direction.

Also, in many cases, there is some disagreement about the date of a celebrity's birth. For some, it may have been an attempt to shave a few years off and appear younger. For others, they may have started the lie at a young age to appear older. Either way, for the purposes of this book, the accepted birth date will be the date inscribed on the tombstone or grave marker.

R.I.P.
(Read in Peace)

Mark Masek
Pasadena, California

HOLLYWOOD
Remains to Be Seen

Forest Lawn Memorial Park–Glendale

~

1712 South Glendale Avenue
Glendale, California 91205

~ HISTORY

Hubert Eaton, born in Missouri in 1881, started his career as a mining engineer in Nevada, but found his fame and fortune in the ground in California. In 1912, Eaton arrived in Tropico—now part of Glendale—to take a job selling plots in a struggling, six-year-old, twelve-acre graveyard called Forest Lawn. The only structure on the property was a tiny, dilapidated gardener's shack. Shortly after he started working at the cemetery, Eaton came up with the then-radical idea of "pre-need" sales of plots and monuments and, within a year, sales at Forest Lawn were up 250 percent. In less than five years, Forest Lawn had increased to fifty-five acres and Eaton was offered a job as manager of the property.

According to the Forest Lawn legend, Eaton stood on a hilltop overlooking the property on New Year's Day, 1917, and had a vision. While Forest Lawn was still a traditional cemetery—drab and dreary with large monuments over the graves— Eaton came up with the ingenious idea of a "memorial park" with no "unsightly" tombstones, and a philosophy of cemeteries depicting a beginning and a celebration of life, rather than an ending. Eventually, Eaton's revolutionary ideas transformed Forest Lawn into a lush, beautifully landscaped, 300-acre cemetery with more than 300,000 permanent residents, and forever changed the look of cemeteries across the country.

Depending on which version of the story you believe, Eaton was either a visionary genius who transformed the American cemetery into a true garden of memories and a place to celebrate life and honor the dearly departed, or a cunning opportunist who planned and built a near-monopolistic mortuary empire that continues to rake in millions of dollars each year thanks to huge profit markups on cemetery plots, coffins, funeral services, flowers, and every other aspect of the death business.

Eaton wrote "The Builder's Creed," which is literally carved in stone and displayed on a massive wall at both Forest Lawn–Glendale and Forest Lawn–Hollywood Hills. The Creed outlines Eaton's dream for Forest Lawn:

> I shall endeavor to build Forest Lawn as different, as unlike other cemeteries as sunshine is unlike darkness, as Eternal Life is unlike death. I shall try to build at Forest Lawn a great park, devoid of misshapen monuments and other customary signs of earthly death, but filled with towering trees, sweeping lawns, splashing fountains, singing birds, beautiful statuary, cheerful flowers, noble memorial architecture with interiors full of light and color, and redolent of the world's best history and romances. I believe these things educate and uplift a community.
>
> Forest Lawn shall become a place where lovers new and old shall love to stroll and watch the sunset's glow, planning for the future or reminiscing of the past; a place where artists study and sketch; where school teachers bring happy children to see the things they read of in books; where little churches invite, triumphant in the knowledge that from their pulpits only words of love can be spoken; where memorialization of loved ones in sculptured marble and pictorial glass shall be encouraged but controlled by acknowledged artists; a place where the sorrowing will be soothed and strengthened because it will be God's garden.

Eaton also expanded the range of services offered by the cemetery. Despite vigorous opposition from local undertakers, Forest Lawn opened the first mortuary within a cemetery in 1934. By adding the mortuary, coffin salesroom, crematorium, church, and florist shop on the Forest Lawn property, Eaton created a one-stop burial shop. The grounds also contain a museum and gift shop. The sign in front of Forest Lawn, which once read, "A place for the living to enjoy," now lists the available services, and reminds potential customers that "one call makes all arrangements."

Eaton's dream may seem noble and inspirational, but the current reality at Forest Lawn is very different. Although Eaton's idyllic vision is a place where "lovers old and new" can "stroll and watch the sunset's glow," the official guidelines for visitors, printed on the back of the cemetery map, state, "Loitering is prohibited. Persons other than property owners and relatives and friends of deceased persons interred or to be interred in the Forest Lawn Memorial Parks should not linger or 'hang around' on the grounds or in the buildings." So you'd better stroll quickly. And if you're going to watch that sunset's glow, you better do it while you're moving.

One may also look at Eaton's dream of a cemetery "devoid of misshapen monuments," where lawn sculpture is "encouraged but controlled," and see a more practical dream of a cemetery with ground-level grave markers where the grass can be more efficiently and quickly cut with a large mower.

The rules also prohibit any photography inside any buildings, and "no commercial or professional photography is allowed under any circumstances without the express written consent of Forest Lawn"—which is why there are no photographs of the Forest Lawn grounds in this book. Currently, however, in keeping with the letter, if not the spirit, of Eaton's "Builder's Creed," artists' sketching is *not* expressly prohibited, provided the artist sketches quickly and does not loiter. If you absolutely need a photograph of one of the Forest Lawn statue reproductions or stained-glass windows, those items are readily available at the cemetery gift shop, located in the "museum" at the northern edge of the property, where visitors can also choose from among a wide variety of souvenirs, including post cards, magnets, small bells, souvenir spoons, and letter openers, all printed with the Forest Lawn name.

In *The American Way of Death Revisited,* a scathing exposé of the American funeral industry, Jessica Mitford devotes an entire chapter to Eaton and Forest Lawn. Though she acknowledges that Eaton "has probably had more influence on trends in the modern cemetery industry than any other human being," she also comments on the "vulgarity" of Forest Lawn and notes that "much of the Forest Lawn statuary looks like the sort of thing one might win in a shooting gallery."

Forest Lawn will not identify the locations of any of its celebrity graves. In fact, it's been reported that if any Forest Lawn employee points out a grave location, he or she will be fired on the spot. Most of the cemetery's massive Great Mausoleum, which is prominently featured in much of its promotional literature, is closed to the public. Many of the memorial gardens are surrounded by high walls, with warning signs on the doors that state, "Admittance to these private memorial gardens is restricted to those possessing a Golden Key of Memory, given to each owner at the time of purchase." The garden doors also include a sign stating that a key is required to exit, but this apparently refers only to visitors, not those interred there.

In a city where celebrity is the only really important currency, Forest Lawn–Glendale is still at the top of the cemetery "A List." Unfortunately, Forest Lawn has become a cranky, ill-tempered old celebrity, eager to enjoy the glamour and fortune, but not at all willing to do anything for fans who have made its fame a reality. But, after all, Forest Lawn is a privately owned, commercial facility, not a public park, so its owners can do whatever they want. And if you don't follow their rules, you will be asked to leave, or possibly even be arrested for trespassing. Even though many celebrity grave-hunters consider getting kicked out of Forest Lawn as sort of a rite of passage, even a badge of honor, you'll still be better off if you follow the rules.

∼ DIRECTIONS

From the south, take the Golden State Freeway (5) to the exit at Los Feliz Boulevard. Take Los Feliz east about a mile to Glendale Avenue, then south on Glendale Avenue about 400 yards to the main entrance. From the north, take the Ventura Freeway (134) to the Glendale Avenue exit, then south on Glendale Avenue about two miles to the main cemetery entrance.

∼ HOURS

The grounds are open from 8 A.M. to 6 P.M., the Great Mausoleum is open from 9 A.M. to 4:30 P.M. (admission is restricted), the flower shop is open from 8 A.M. to 5 P.M., and the mortuary is open from 8 A.M. to 9 P.M.

∼

The Tour

Forest Lawn–Glendale is so large that it would take more than a day just to see the highlights. To make the visit more manageable, we've divided the cemetery into four separate tours—the Grounds, the Freedom Mausoleum, the Great Mausoleum, and the *Wizard of Oz* Tour. At the main entrance, stop at the information booth and ask for a map of the grounds, which includes a listing of all the sections and buildings on the property (as well as a list of rules for visitors).

Tour I: The Grounds

From the main entrance off Glendale Avenue, follow the main road toward the Wee Kirk O' the Heather Church—where Ronald Reagan married his first wife, actress Jane Wyman, in 1940. On a hill directly west of the church, in the Wee Kirk Churchyard Section, is a large family monument, topped by a bronze statue of a kneeling archer protecting a woman and two small children. Drive around to the west side of the hill. Walk up the hill to the statue of the archer, and walk in the direction the archer is pointing. About forty-five feet away, in the sixth row of graves, you'll find the final resting place of actor James Maitland Stewart, best known to film fans around the world simply as **Jimmy Stewart (1908–1997).**

During his sixty-year career, Stewart appeared in more than one hundred films, from light comedies and drama to Westerns and action-adventure, even musicals, and became one of the most popular and beloved performers both among his fans and within the entertainment industry. With his gangly good looks, thoughtful drawl, and overriding sense of small-town decency, Stewart could bring depth and complexity to any role, even though, as most film critics point out, he wasn't really playing a character—he was just being himself.

Born in Indiana, Pennsylvania, Stewart attended Princeton University, receiving a degree in architecture in 1932, but he was still not sure what he would do with the rest of his life. He had been a member of a theatrical club at the university, and after graduation he decided to pursue an acting career rather than accept a scholarship for a master's degree in architecture. Stewart went to New York City and appeared in several plays on and off Broadway. He was paid fifty dollars for his film debut in a comedy short titled *Art Trouble* (1934), starring Shemp Howard, better known as one of the Three Stooges. His first role in a feature-length film was playing a newspaper reporter, ironically named Shorty given Stewart's lanky physique, in *The Murder Man* (1935), starring Spencer Tracy.

Stewart appeared in more than two dozen films over the next four years, playing a wide range of characters, from a murder suspect in *After the Thin Man* (1936), to singing and dancing with Eleanor Powell in *Born to Dance* (1936). Stewart also appeared in *Wife vs. Secretary* (1936), *Small Town Girl* (1936), *Navy Blue and Gold* (1937), *The Last Gangster* (1937), *The Shopworn Angel* (1938), *Vivacious Lady* (1938), and *You Can't Take It With You* (1938), Stewart's first film with director Frank Capra.

Stewart became a major film star with his performance as a naively heroic young senator, Jefferson Smith, in Capra's *Mr. Smith Goes to Washington* (1939), for which Stewart received his first of five nominations for the Academy Award as Best Actor. The same year, Stewart appeared in his first Western, playing the gun-shy marshal who tamed a town—and Marlene Dietrich—in *Destry Rides Again* (1939). For his performance in *The Philadelphia Story* (1940), costarring Cary Grant and Katharine Hepburn, Stewart was again nominated for an Academy Award. When he won the Best Actor statuette, he sent the Oscar back home to Pennsylvania where it remained on display in the window of his father's hardware store for many years.

Stewart was the first Hollywood star to enlist in the military for World War II, joining nearly a year before the attack on Pearl Harbor. He was initially refused entry into the U.S. Air Force because he weighed five pounds less than the 148-pound minimum requirement, but Stewart convinced the recruiting officer to ignore the weight requirement. Stewart's war record included twenty-five combat missions in Europe as a command pilot. He rose to the rank of colonel—the highest-ranking actor in military history—and earned the Air Medal, the Distinguished Flying Cross, the Croix de Guerre, and seven battle stars. In 1959, while serving in the Air Force Reserves, Stewart became a brigadier general, and the Indiana County Airport in his hometown was renamed the Jimmy Stewart Airport. He retired from the Reserves in 1968.

When Stewart was first sent to Europe to fly bombing missions, his father gave him a letter in which he wrote, "Jim, I'm banking on the enclosed copy of the 91st Psalm. The thing that takes the place of fear and worry is the promise of these words. I am staking my faith in these words. I feel sure that God will lead you through this mad experience. . . . God bless you and keep you. I love you more than I can tell you. Dad." Stewart carried the letter with him for the rest of his life, and the words from the psalm that his father gave him are written on his grave marker: "For He shall give his angels charge over thee to keep thee in all thy ways."

When he returned from the war in 1945, Stewart discovered that many studios wanted to hire him, but they wanted him for war films, to capitalize on his war record and reputation, which Stewart did not want to do. Instead, he went to work for Capra on *It's a Wonderful Life* (1946), the classic holiday film about a man from a small town who doesn't feel that his life has had any purpose, and the wingless angel who shows him how much he has touched the lives of those around him. Stewart's performance earned him another Academy Award nomination.

Stewart continued to play a wide range of characters, including the suspicious teacher in Alfred Hitchcock's *Rope* (1948); the crusading reporter who frees an innocent man in *Call Northside 777* (1948); Monty Stratton, the Chicago White Sox pitcher who returned to the mound after losing a leg, in *The Stratton Story* (1949); a circus clown wanted for murder in *The Greatest Show on Earth* (1952); a cold-blooded bounty hunter in *The Naked Spur* (1953); a voyeuristic photographer-turned-sleuth in Hitchcock's *Rear Window* (1954); the beloved Big Band leader in *The Glenn Miller Story* (1954); Stewart's boyhood hero, Charles Lindbergh, in *The Spirit of St. Louis* (1957); the obsessive romantic in Hitchcock's *Vertigo* (1958); a cynical marshal in *Two Rode Together* (1961); and a lawyer trying to bring civilization to a lawless Western town in *The Man Who Shot Liberty Valance* (1962). Stewart also received Academy Award nominations for his performances as the eccentric tippler Elwood P. Dowd in *Harvey* (1950), and the easygoing but slick defense attorney in *Anatomy of a Murder* (1959).

In 1971, Stewart played a college professor in a television series, *The Jimmy Stewart Show,* which lasted one season. In 1973, he returned to television in another short-lived series, *Hawkins,* playing a shrewd country lawyer. In 1980, the American Film Institute awarded Stewart its eighth Life Achievement Award, and in 1984 the Academy of Motion Picture Arts and Sciences awarded him a Lifetime Achievement Award, "for his fifty years of memorable performances, and for his high ideals both on and off the screen." The following year, Stewart received the Presidential Medal of Freedom, the nation's highest civilian honor.

When Stewart died in 1997, President Bill Clinton said, "America lost a national treasure. Jimmy Stewart was a great actor, a gentleman, and a patriot." In 1998, the American Film Institute released its list of "100 Greatest American Movies," in commemoration of the first 100 years of American cinema. The list contains five films starring Stewart—*Mr. Smith Goes to Washington, The Philadelphia Story, It's a Wonderful Life, Rear Window,* and *Vertigo.*

Stewart typically portrayed the soft-spoken, slow-speaking guy next door, a common man of honor and dignity, just trying to do the right thing, often in the face of overwhelming opposition. So it seems appropriate that, when so many of the celebrities at Forest Lawn–Glendale are hidden in inaccessible mausoleums or padlocked gardens, Stewart's grave is out in the middle of an open lawn, close to the main entrance, in an easy location for fans and friends to pay their respects.

Buried next to Stewart is his wife, Gloria Hatrick Stewart (1918–1994). Her grave marker contains the inscription "In our most loving memories, she will always be with us. She made life better." In an industry where people change spouses as often as they change hairstyles, the Stewarts were married for nearly forty-five years—one of the most enduring marriages in the history of Hollywood.

Gloria Stewart had two children from a previous marriage—Ronald and Michael. In 1951, the Stewarts had twin daughters, Judy and Kelly. On June 8, 1969, Ronald, a lieutenant in the U.S. Marine Corps, was killed in Vietnam while leading a reconnaissance patrol in Quang Tri province. He was eleven days shy of his twenty-fifth birthday. Ronald Walsh McLean is buried next to his mother. Despite their public prominence, the Stewarts were quiet and private in their mourning. Shortly after Ronald's death, a Pentagon representative visited the Stewarts and suggested publicizing their son's heroic death, perhaps as a way to help offset some of the public criticism of the Nixon administration's policy in Vietnam. The Stewarts were intensely opposed to the idea, and the Pentagon representative was quickly asked to leave their home. When a television network suggested a film based on Ronald's life, the Stewarts didn't even respond to the idea.

Stewart was born May 20, 1908, in Indiana, Pennsylvania.
He died July 2, 1997, in Los Angeles.

After you leave the Stewarts' graves, continue on the road behind the Wee Kirk O' the Heather Church until you see the Cathedral Slope Section on your left. Continue around the hill in the center of the Cathedral Slope Section and stop just as the road starts to straighten out on the other side.

In the Cathedral Slope Section, on the eastern slope of the hill, about seventy-five feet from the road, in Section 1675, you'll find the grave of one of the most honored persons in the history of the Academy Awards—costume designer **Edith Head (1897–1981).** Her grave is in front of the tall pine tree closest to the top of the hill.

In the early 1920s, Head taught art and French classes at the Hollywood School for Girls. She also took art classes herself, specializing in landscapes. When she saw a classified advertisement for a sketch artist to assist the head designer at Paramount Studios, Head applied for the job and was hired. In 1938, she became the first woman ever appointed chief designer at a major film studio.

From 1948 to 1977, Head received thirty-six nominations and eight Academy Awards for individual achievement. After her first nomination for *The Emperor Waltz* (1948), Head was nominated for an Academy Award for nineteen consecutive years until 1966, winning seven times. In some years, when the Academy gave out awards for costume design in both color and black-and-white films, she was nominated twice. In 1950, she won in both categories, for *Samson and Delilah* in the color category, and for *All About Eve* in black and white. Head also won Oscars for her work on *The Heiress* (1949), *A Place in the Sun* (1951), *Roman Holiday* (1953), *Sabrina* (1954), *The Facts of*

Life (1960), and *The Sting* (1973). Head is the most honored costume designer, and the most honored woman, in the history of the Academy Awards.

With more than 1,100 screen credits, Head worked on some of the best known and most critically acclaimed films in history, including *Double Indemnity* (1944), *Sunset Boulevard* (1950), *Shane* (1953), *War of the Worlds* (1953), *White Christmas* (1954), *The Man Who Shot Liberty Valance* (1962), *The Birds* (1963), and *Butch Cassidy and the Sundance Kid* (1969). She dressed everyone from Clara Bow to Paul Newman, from Fred Astaire to Jerry Lewis, from Marilyn Monroe to Elvis Presley.

Her grave marker reads, "Edith Head Ihnen—Beloved Wife, Friend, Artist." She is buried next to her husband, Wiard Ihnen (1897–1979), a set designer and art director who won two Academy Awards himself, for art direction on *Wilson* (1944) and *Blood on the Sun* (1945).

Edith Head was born October 28, 1897, in San Bernardino, California. She died October 24, 1981, in Los Angeles.

Southeast of Head's grave, across the road in the Everlasting Love Section, right next to the curb in Plot 814, is the grave of actress **Carole Landis (1919–1948).**

Landis moved to California from the Midwest in 1934, and found work as a hula dancer and a Big Band singer in San Francisco. After signing a studio contract with Warner Bros., she appeared in more than twenty films in 1937 and 1938, including *A Star Is Born* with Janet Gaynor and Fredric March, and *A Day at the Races* with the Marx Brothers. But Landis usually played bit parts—cashiers, hatcheck girls, secretaries, and party guests.

Her big break came when director Hal Roach cast her with Victor Mature in *One Million Years B.C.* (1940). She followed that with *Turnabout* (1941), costarring with Adolph Menjou, and *I Wake Up Screaming* (1941), with Mature and Betty Grable. Landis continued to star in small films, while the best roles in the biggest films were given to the more established Hollywood stars of the day.

Landis toured extensively with the USO during World War II, helping to sell War Bonds and entertaining the troops, both in the United States and overseas. She wrote about her experiences in a best-selling book, titled *Four Jills in a Jeep,* and also starred in the film version of the book, playing herself.

In the late 1940s, with her fourth marriage ending in divorce, Landis had slipped back to playing supporting roles in smaller films. She was eventually dropped by 20th Century-Fox and was involved in a fairly well-publicized affair with married actor Rex Harrison. When Harrison decided to end the relationship, and with her career slumping, Landis committed suicide by taking an overdose of sleeping pills in 1948. Though only twenty-nine when she died, Landis was a talented singer, dancer, and actress who could handle both dramatic and comedic roles. She appeared in more than fifty films.

Carole Landis was born Frances Lillian Mary Ridste on January 1, 1919, in Fairchild, Wisconsin. She died July 5, 1948, in Pacific Palisades, California.

Continue on the road, heading northeast, toward the Triumphant Faith Terraces at the northeast edge of the cemetery property. When you reach the Terraces, turn right. On the left side, in the Triumphant Faith Terraces Section, look for a huge blue-and-white sculpture marking the graves of Frederick Llewellyn (1917–1999) and Jane E. Llewellyn (1919–1990). Frederick Llewellyn succeeded his uncle, Hubert Eaton, as CEO of Forest Lawn when Eaton died in 1966. Llewellyn served in that position until he retired in 1987 and his son, John F. Llewellyn, succeeded him as Forest Lawn's CEO. Jane Llewellyn served as director of the Forest Lawn museum from 1967 until her death. Eaton and most of the rest of his family are buried in the Great Mausoleum.

Directly across the road from the Llewellyns' memorial is a white statue of a family atop a white sarcophagus. Directly to the left of that sarcophagus, right next to the sidewalk, is the grave of six-time Emmy nominee and two-time winner **Ted Knight (1923–1986)**, best known as the pompous, inept television news anchor Ted Baxter on *The Mary Tyler Moore Show*, which ran from 1970 to 1977. The last episode of the series featured new management taking over the fictional television station and firing everyone but Baxter.

Knight made his film debut in a brief, non-speaking role as a prison guard in Alfred Hitchcock's *Psycho* (1960). Knight appeared in small, often uncredited roles in several films during the 1960s, including *Two Rode Together* (1961), *Swingin' Along* (1961), *The Candidate* (1964), *Blindfold* (1965), and *Countdown* (1968). Knight also made guest appearances in dozens of television series in the 1960s, including *The Wild, Wild West; Bonanza; The Virginian; Combat!; The Invaders; Outer Limits; The Twilight Zone; Get Smart; The Fugitive; The F.B.I.; Gomer Pyle, U.S.M.C.;* and *Gunsmoke.*

In 1970, Knight was cast as Ted Baxter, the news anchor for fictional television station WJM-TV in *The Mary Tyler Moore Show*. Knight was nominated for an Emmy Award as Best Supporting Actor in a Comedy Series each year from 1972 through 1977, winning in 1973 and 1976. After the series ended, Knight appeared in the short-lived television series *The Ted Knight Show* in 1978, then starred as cartoonist Henry Rush in *Too Close for Comfort* from 1980 to 1985. Knight also appeared as Judge Smails in *Caddyshack* (1980).

As Ted Baxter, Knight would often say, "Hi, guys," whenever he entered a room. His grave marker includes the phrase "Bye, guy." It also includes the theatrical masks of comedy and tragedy.

Knight was born Thaddeus Wladyslaw Konopka on December 7, 1923, in Terryville, Connecticut. He died August 26, 1986, in Los Angeles.

On the opposite side of the statue of the family, about fifteen feet away, in the fourth row from the sidewalk, you'll find the grave of actor **Robert Alda (1914–1986).** Born Alphonso D'Abruzzo, Alda created his professional name by combining the first two letters of his first name with the first two letters of his last name.

Alda started his career as a vaudeville singer and dancer and made his film debut in what remained his most memorable performance, as composer George Gershwin in *Rhapsody in Blue* (1945). Over the next few years, Alda appeared in supporting roles in several films, including *Cloak and Dagger* (1946), *The Beast With Five Fingers* (1946), and *Tarzan and the Slave Girl* (1950). During this time, Alda also hosted several television game shows and regularly appeared in plays on Broadway, including *Harbor Lights, What Makes Sammy Run,* and *Guys and Dolls,* for which he won the Tony Award in 1951 for Best Actor in a Musical for his performance as Sky Masterson.

In the early 1960s, Alda moved to Italy and appeared in Italian films for the next fifteen years. He returned to the United States and made guest appearances on dozens of television shows, including *Mission: Impossible, The Dukes of Hazzard, The Incredible Hulk, The Facts of Life, Wonder Woman, Quincy, Ironside, The Rockford Files, Kojak, Here's Lucy, Fantasy Island, Laverne & Shirley,* and two appearances on *M*A*S*H,* the long-running sitcom that starred Alda's son, Alan Alda.

Alda was born Alphonso Giuseppe Giovanni Roberto D'Abruzzo on February 26, 1914, in New York City. He died May 3, 1986, in Los Angeles.

Continue on the road, with the Triumphant Faith Terraces on your left, and look for a sign marking the Court of the Christus on the left. The court features an eleven-foot-high white marble statue of Jesus Christ. On the left side of the Court of the Christus is a gateway to the Garden of Remembrance. Walk about two hundred feet, through the first section of the garden, into the next section. About fifty feet into the second section, along the low wall on the left, you'll find the grave of actress **Merle Oberon (1917–1979).**

Throughout her film career, Oberon claimed she was born in Tasmania, with birth dates ranging from 1904 to 1917. Near the end of her life, Oberon admitted that she was actually born in Calcutta, India, the daughter of a racially mixed marriage between her Anglo-Indian mother and white Australian father. When she was a teenager, Oberon moved to London, called herself Queenie O'Brien or Queenie Thompson, and appeared in small roles in several British films, including *Men of Tomorrow* (1933) and *The Private Life of Henry VIII* (1933), in which she played Anne Boleyn. After she appeared as Lady Marguerite Blakeney in *The Scarlet Pimpernel* (1934), Oberon came to Hollywood, and capitalized on her exotic beauty.

Oberon's performance in *The Dark Angel* (1935) won her an Academy Award nomination as Best Actress. She also appeared in *These Three* (1936), *Over the Moon* (1937), and *The Divorce of Lady X* (1938), and perhaps her best-known performance was in *Wuthering Heights* (1939), costarring with Laurence Olivier. Oberon was a busy actress in the 1940s, appearing in *That Uncertain Feeling* (1941), *The Lodger* (1944), *A Song to Remember* (1945), *Temptation* (1946), and *Berlin Express* (1948), but she never matched her early success.

Oberon's nephew, Michael Korda, told Oberon's story in a thinly veiled novel called *Queenie*, the story of a woman born in Calcutta who claims she was born in Tasmania to hide her racial origins, and reaches the brink of Hollywood stardom. The novel was made into a film in 1987.

Oberon married her fourth husband, Robert Wolders, in 1975. The name on her grave marker identifies her as Merle Oberon Wolders.

Oberon was born Estelle Merle O'Brien Thompson on
February 19, 1917 (some sources say 1911), in Calcutta, India.
She died November 23, 1979, in Malibu, California.

Almost directly opposite Oberon's grave, next to the tall wall on the right side, you'll find the grave of **Terry Alan Kath (1946–1978),** one of the founding members of the jazz-rock group Chicago, who accidentally shot and killed himself when the group was at the height of its fame.

Kath, a singer, prolific songwriter, and gifted guitarist, grew up in a musical household in Chicago. In 1966, Kath and some friends from DePaul University—Peter Cetera, Robert Lamm, Walter Parazaider, Danny Seraphine, Walt Perry, James Pankow, and Lee Loughnane—formed a band called the Missing Links, with a sound that combined rock, jazz, and blues music. When Jimi Hendrix saw the band perform in Los Angeles in 1968, he reportedly told one of the band members, "Your guitar player (Kath) is better than me." The band changed its name to Chicago Transit Authority and released their first album in April 1969, featuring their first hit, "Does Anybody Really Know What Time It Is?" The album peaked at number seventeen on the *Billboard* charts, but it remained on the charts for more than three years, making it the longest-running album by a rock group up to that time.

The following year, the band shortened its name to Chicago. They released a string of chart-topping albums in the early 1970s, with hits including "Colour My World," "25 or 6 to 4," "Make Me Smile," "Saturday in the Park," "Feelin' Stronger Every Day," "Just You 'n' Me," "Wishing You Were Here," "Old Days," "(I've Been) Searchin' So Long," and "If You Leave Me Now," which was the first Chicago song to hit the top of the *Billboard* charts. In 1976, Chicago won a Grammy Award for Best Pop Vocal Performance by a Duo, Group or Chorus for "If You Leave Me Now."

On January 23, 1978, a few days before his thirty-second birthday, Kath and his wife, Camelia, were at a party at the home of a band technician in Woodland Hills, California. Kath, an avid gun collector, brought two handguns with him, and at the end of the party he pulled out the guns and began to play with them. He pointed one of the guns at his head and pulled the trigger, but the gun was empty. Kath picked up the other gun and, when he was asked to stop playing with the weapons, he uttered his last words—"Don't worry, it's not loaded"—pointed the gun at his head, and pulled the trigger. Unfortunately, he was wrong, and he died instantly. Kath's funeral was attended by hundreds of fellow musicians and fans, including then–California governor Jerry Brown.

After Kath's death, Chicago considered breaking up, but did not. The group's next album included the first song they recorded after Kath's death, a tribute to him called "Alive Again." The band has changed personnel several times since Kath's death and, more than thirty years after they started, they're still going strong. In terms of album sales, Chicago has been one of the most popular and enduring American bands of all time.

Kath was born January 31, 1946, in Chicago, Illinois.
He died January 23, 1978, in Woodland Hills, California.

Walk up the stairs to the right of Kath's grave to a smaller, elevated section. In the center of that section, along the wall behind Kath's grave, you'll find the grave of the creator of the cartoon characters Rocky and Bullwinkle, **Jay T. Ward (1920–1989).**

Ward graduated from Harvard University and was attending the University of California in Berkeley, with plans to open a real estate office, when he was hit by a lumber truck while walking near his home. During his long convalescence, Ward reconsidered his career plans and started working on what would become his first animation success—*Crusader Rabbit,* which debuted on television in 1950. *Rocky and His Friends* followed in 1959, followed by *The Bullwinkle Show* in 1961, *Fractured Flickers* in 1963, *Hoppity Hooper* in 1964, *George of the Jungle* in 1967, *and The Dudley Do-Right Show* in 1969.

The *Rocky* series introduced Bullwinkle, the dim-witted moose, and his pal, Rocket J. "Rocky" Squirrel, along with Boris Badenov, Natasha Fatale, Dudley Do-Right, Snidely Whiplash, Mr. Peabody and Sherman, Tom Slick, and many other characters. Ward's animation style was to keep the scenes simple, limit the character movement, and focus on the writing. His primary direction to his writers was that the stories and the dialogue should make him laugh. And although Bullwinkle, Rocky, and all their costars certainly appeal to children, the intelligent, witty writing, wordplay, puns, and references to popular culture make the cartoons a favorite among adults, too.

Ward's characters have also been revived recently in several live-action films, including *George of the Jungle* (1997), *Dudley Do-Right* (1999), and *The Adventures of Rocky and Bullwinkle* (2000).

Ward's grave marker identifies him as "Our Big Dad."

Ward was born J. Troplong Ward on September 20, 1920, in San
Francisco, California. He died October 12, 1989, in Los Angeles.

On the opposite side of the Court of the Christus is the locked door leading to the Gardens of Memory. A sign on the door reads, "Admittance to these private memorial gardens is restricted to those possessing a Golden Key of Memory, given to each owner at the time of purchase."

Inside the Gardens of Memory are the graves of actresses **Mary Pickford (1893–1979)** and **Judy Canova (1916–1983)**, actors **Warner Baxter (1891–1951)** and **Humphrey Bogart (1899–1957)**, and directors **Sam Wood (1883–1949)** and **Victor McLaglen (1886–1959)**.

Continue on the road, past a life-size replica of Michelangelo's *David*. Poor David has had a difficult life at the cemetery. The original version of the statue wasn't quite an exact replica of the statue as it appears in Florence, Italy. The Forest Lawn version was clad in a fig leaf, and it was destroyed in an earthquake in 1971. The head and feet from that statue can be seen in the Forest Lawn museum. When the statue was replaced with a new version a decade later, without the fig leaf, the cemetery received complaints about the full-frontal nudity, and the statue was temporarily removed. For the moment, anyway, David is back on his pedestal, without the fig leaf.

Turn right at the first road past David, and stop about fifty feet past the turn when you see a large, spreading pine tree on your left, in the Eventide Section. Walk about forty feet southeast of that pine tree, perpendicular to the road, to Plot 2998, and you'll find the grave of producer and director **William Wyler (1902–1981)**.

Wyler was a distant cousin of Carl Laemmle, the founder of Universal Pictures, and he got his start writing and directing two-reel Westerns for Universal in 1925. After directing dozens of shorts for Universal, Wyler gradually moved to feature-length films in the early 1930s, including *Hell's Heroes* (1930), *A House Divided* (1931), and *The Gay Deception* (1935). Wyler received his first of twelve Academy Award nominations as Best Director for *Dodsworth* (1936). Wyler was also nominated for directing *Wuthering Heights* (1939), *The Letter* (1940), *The Little Foxes* (1941), *The Heiress* (1949), *Detective Story* (1951), *Roman Holiday* (1953), *Friendly Persuasion* (1956), and *The Collector* (1965). Wyler won the award for directing *Mrs. Miniver* (1942), *The Best Years of Our Lives* (1946), and *Ben-Hur* (1959). In 1966, Wyler won the Irving G. Thalberg Memorial Award, and in 1976, he was given the Life Achievement Award by the American Film Institute.

Wyler was born July 1, 1902, in Mulhouse, France.
He died July 27, 1981, in Los Angeles.

————————————

Go back to the pine tree, and walk about one hundred feet south, down the hill, and in Plot 2896 you'll find the grave of director **Ernst Lubitsch (1892–1947).**

Lubitsch started his career as a performer in Germany, appearing in high school plays. In 1911, he joined the Deutsches Theater, and the following year, he took a job as a handyman at the Bioscope studios in Berlin and quickly began to appear in films. Lubitsch became a successful comedian and started to write and direct his own films. By 1918, Lubitsch had given up performing to concentrate on writing and directing.

Lubitsch came to the United States in 1922 at the request of actress Mary Pickford, who wanted him to direct her in *Dorothy Vernon of Haddon Hall* (1924). After reading the script, Lubitsch decided against that project, and instead directed Pickford in *Rosita* (1923). The film was critically acclaimed, and it launched Lubitsch's long and successful career. Lubitsch's films were known for their sophisticated and witty looks at American society and psychology, and his deft handling of these issues was known as the "Lubitsch Touch."

Lubitsch was nominated three times for the Academy Award as Best Director, for *The Patriot* (1928), *The Love Parade* (1929), and *Heaven Can Wait* (1943). Although he never won, he did receive a special Academy Award in 1947, "for his distinguished contributions to the art of the motion picture." Lubitsch's other films include *Trouble in Paradise* (1932), *One Hour With You* (1932), *If I Had a Million* (1932), *Design for Living* (1933), *The Merry Widow* (1934), *Ninotchka* (1939), *The Shop Around the Corner* (1940), *That Uncertain Feeling* (1941), *To Be or Not to Be* (1942), *A Royal Scandal* (1945), and *Cluny Brown* (1946).

Lubitsch was born January 28, 1892, in Berlin, Germany.
He died November 30, 1947, in Los Angeles.

Go back to the road and continue heading northwest, with the Eventide Section on your left. At the end of the section, turn left, then left again, heading back toward the southeast. You'll have the Eventide Section on your left, and the Graceland Section on your right. Continue for a few hundred feet, and look for a large, spreading pine tree on your right, next to a trash can in the shape of a tree stump. The word *Graceland* is also stenciled on the curb at that spot. From that point, walk about 140 feet down the hill, toward another large pine tree. Next to that tree, in Plot 5905, you'll find the grave of actor **Robert**

Young (1907–1998), best known for his television roles in *Father Knows Best* and *Marcus Welby, M.D.*

Throughout his career, Young played characters who were wholesome, charming, soft-spoken, and decent but rarely got the girl in the end. MGM studio chief Louis B. Mayer once said that Young had "no sex appeal." But Young's relatively bland characters were popular in supporting roles in more than one hundred films during his sixty-year career.

Born in Chicago, Young moved to California at an early age, and began appearing in stage plays. His film debut was a small role in *It Is the Law* (1924), but his first significant roles were in *The Black Camel* (1931), starring Warner Oland and Bela Lugosi, and *The Sin of Madelon Claudet* (1931), starring Helen Hayes and Lewis Stone. Young was a busy actor after that, appearing in dozens of films in the 1930s and 1940s, usually in supporting roles, including *Strange Interlude* (1932), *Tugboat Annie* (1933), *Spitfire* (1934), *Secret Agent* (1936), *Stowaway* (1936), *Northwest Passage* (1940), *Western Union* (1941), *Lady Be Good* (1941), *Claudia* (1943), *The Canterville Ghost* (1944), and *Crossfire* (1947).

In 1949, Young starred as Jim Anderson, the wholesome and decent father in the radio program *Father Knows Best*. After five years on radio, the show moved to television in 1954, as viewers watched Young and his television family face the crises of jobs, dating, and other familiar family traumas. *Father Knows Best* ran until 1962 and continues to live on in syndication. From 1969 to 1976, Young starred as wholesome and decent Dr. Welby in the television series *Marcus Welby, M.D.* For the 1970–71 season, it was the top-rated show on television, according to the Nielsen Media Research ratings. Young was nominated for an Emmy Award in 1956 for his role in *Father Knows Best,* and he was nominated for the Golden Globe Award as Best Actor in a Television Drama for five consecutive years for *Marcus Welby, M.D.,* from 1970 to 1974. He won only once, in 1972.

In his later years, Young revealed that his public image was a direct contrast to his private life, which included a thirty-year battle with alcoholism and depression, resulting in a suicide attempt in 1991. After he discovered that he was suffering from a chemical imbalance, Young began to speak publicly about the issues and problems related to alcohol and depression, and his personal struggles. In appreciation for the help he was given by a psychiatrist in Illinois, Young made a donation to the Franciscan Medical Center in East Moline, Illinois, to open the Robert Young Center for Community Mental Health.

Young is buried next to his wife, Elizabeth Louise Henderson Young (1910–1994). They were married for sixty-one years, from 1933 until her death.

Young was born Robert George Young on February 22, 1907,
in Chicago, Illinois. He died July 21, 1998,
in Westlake Village, California.

Continue a few hundred feet farther down the road, and look for a large pine tree on the right, leaning over the road. Next to the pine tree the word *Graceland* is stenciled on the curb. About twenty feet before you reach the tree, and about fifteen feet from the road, in Plot 1565, you'll find the grave of actor **Dwight Frye (1899–1943)**, who made a career of playing wild-eyed lunatics, crazed hunchbacks, deranged villagers, and mad scientists' assistants in classic horror films of the 1930s and early 1940s. Frye appeared in *Dracula* (1931), *Frankenstein* (1931), *The Invisible Man* (1933), and *The Bride of Frankenstein* (1935), as well as three more films in the *Frankenstein* series.

As a youngster, Frye received training in voice and piano and was heading toward a career as a musician. But Frye was drawn to the theater, and he began performing in small traveling theater companies. He ended up on Broadway, where he was a popular and successful actor, appearing in comedies and musicals, including a play titled *The Devil in the Cheese* in 1926, which costarred Bela Lugosi.

Frye made his film debut in a small role as a wedding guest in *The Night Bird* (1928), then appeared in two crime dramas in 1930, *The Doorway to Hell* and *Man to Man*. Frye next appeared in *Dracula* (1931) as Renfield, the real-estate agent who visits the castle of Count Dracula and becomes the vampire's first victim, as Renfield is transformed into a wild-eyed, bug-eating lunatic, and Dracula's slave. Frye's performance was so memorable, he quickly became typecast in roles as lunatics and psychopaths.

After *Dracula*, Frye appeared in *The Maltese Falcon* (1931), the first filmed version of Dashiel Hammett's classic detective story, then returned to horror films as Fritz, the demented, hunchbacked laboratory assistant in *Frankenstein* (1931). Frye played similar roles in *The Vampire Bat* (1933), *The Circus Queen Murder* (1933), *The Bride of Frankenstein* (1935), *The Great Impersonation* (1935), *The Man Who Found Himself* (1937), *Son of Frankenstein* (1939), *The Ghost of Frankenstein* (1942), *Frankenstein Meets the Wolf Man* (1943), and *Dead Men Walk* (1943).

Despite his long list of horror credits, Frye did fight against the typecasting and played small roles in other kinds of films, including *The Western Code* (1932), *Attorney for the Defense* (1932), *Florida Special* (1936), *Something to Sing About* (1937), *Fast Company* (1938), and *The Son of Monte Cristo* (1940). He often returned to the stage, where he had more of an opportunity to play more varied roles, although he did revive the role of Renfield in a stage version of *Dracula*.

In early 1943, with his opportunities in film dwindling, Frye went to work as a draftsman and tool designer at an aircraft manufacturing company in Los Angeles. A few months later, he was offered a significant role in a filmed biography of President Woodrow Wilson, and it looked as if Frye's film career might be on the rebound. Unfortunately, Frye suffered from heart problems, and because he was a devout Christian Scientist, he refused any medical help. On November 7, 1943, three days before filming was scheduled to begin on *Wilson*, Frye suffered a fatal heart attack while riding on a crowded bus in Hollywood with his wife and young son. He was forty-four.

Frye was born Dwight Iliff Fry on February 22, 1899, in Salina, Kansas. He died November 7, 1943, in Los Angeles.

Continue a few hundred feet farther down the road, until you see another tree stump–shaped trash can on the left. About fifty feet before the trash can, right next to the curb and a tree in the Eventide Section, Plot 3741, you'll find the grave of another performer best known for her work in horror films, Russian actress **Maria Ouspenskaya (1887–1949),** who played Maleva, the mysterious gypsy fortuneteller who warns Lon Chaney Jr. about his future in *The Wolf Man* (1941).

Born in Russia, Ouspenskaya studied singing at the Warsaw Conservatory and acting at Adasheff's School of the Drama in Moscow, later joining the Moscow Art Theatre, where she worked under the direction of Konstantin Stanislavski, creator of the famous Stanislavski method of acting. Ouspenskaya came to the United States in 1922 and remained here when the Moscow Art Theatre returned to Russia. She became a successful Broadway actress and founded the School of Dramatic Art in New York City in 1929.

In an effort to earn enough money to keep her acting school open, Ouspenskaya came to Hollywood, making her American screen debut in *Dodsworth* (1936), for which she was nominated for an Academy Award for Best Supporting Actress. Ouspenskaya, with her thick Slavic accent, usually portrayed foreign aristocracy or immigrant grandmothers. She also appeared in *Love Affair* (1939)—for which she was again nominated as Best Supporting Actress—*Judge Hardy and Son* (1939), *The Rains Came* (1939), *The Mortal Storm* (1940), *Dr. Ehrlich's Magic Bullet* (1940), *Waterloo Bridge* (1940), *The Shanghai Gesture* (1941), *Kings Row* (1943), and *Tarzan and the Amazons* (1945).

In *The Wolf Man* (1941), Ouspenskaya played the mother of Bela Lugosi, the werewolf who bites Lon Chaney Jr. and turns him into a werewolf. She played the same character in *Frankenstein Meets the Wolf Man* (1943).

Ouspenskaya was severely injured in a fire in her Los Angeles apartment in 1949. She died three days later. Her grave marker identifies her as "Our Beloved Madam."

Ouspenskaya was born July 29, 1887 (some sources say 1876 or 1897), in Tula, Russia. She died December 3, 1949, in Los Angeles.

Down the hill from the Eventide Section, midway between that section and the Great Mausoleum, you'll find the Vale of Memory Section. At the north-west corner of that section, you'll find another tree stump–shaped trash can. About two hundred feet south of that can is a tall pine tree, and about fifty feet north of that pine tree, in Plot 2086, you'll find the grave of actor **Wallace Beery (1885–1949).** The husky, gravel-voiced Beery, often described as having a face like a fist, was an unlikely candidate for a leading man, but he appeared in more than two hundred films and was one of the most popular film stars of the 1930s.

In 1902, the sixteen-year-old Beery joined the Ringling Bros. circus as an assistant to the elephant trainer. Two years later, he left the circus after a leopard clawed his arm and went to New York City, where he found work singing in variety shows. Beery then went to Hollywood and made his film debut in *Mr. Dippy Dipped* (1913). Beery appeared in a series of short musicals and comedies, including several films in the *Sweedie* series, in which Beery dressed as a female Swedish maid. Beery also directed many of these early films. Beery costarred with Gloria Swanson in one of her first film appearances, in *Sweedie Goes to College* (1915). Beery and Swanson were married in 1916, but divorced two tempestuous years later.

By the early 1920s, Beery had given up his maid's outfit to appear in action and adventure films, including *The Last of the Mohicans* (1920), *The Four*

Horsemen of the Apocalypse (1921), *Robin Hood* (1922), *Richard the Lion-Hearted* (1923), *The Three Ages* (1923), *The Sea Hawk* (1924), *The Lost World* (1925), *The Devil's Cargo* (1925), *Pony Express* (1925), and *Beggars of Life* (1928). When sound films became popular, Beery developed his screen persona as the gruff, burly, tough guy, but with a lovable, sensitive side. He costarred with Marie Dressler in *Min and Bill* (1930) and followed that with one of his most famous roles, as the ex–boxing champ trying to raise his son, Dink, played by Jackie Cooper, in *The Champ* (1931). For his performance, Beery was the co-winner of the Academy Award for Best Actor, sharing the honor with Frederic March. Beery also starred in *The Christmas Party* (1931), *Grand Hotel* (1932), *Flesh* (1932), *Dinner at Eight* (1933), *The Bowery* (1933), *Tugboat Annie* (1933), *Viva Villa!* (1934), *Treasure Island* (1934), *China Seas* (1935), *Ah, Wilderness!* (1935), *Barnacle Bill* (1941), and *Bad Bascomb* (1946).

On Beery's grave marker is a facsimile of his signature, and the epitaph "No man is indispensable, but some are irreplaceable."

Beery was born Wallace Fitzgerald Beery on April 1, 1885, in Kansas City, Missouri. He died April 15, 1949, in Los Angeles.

Between the Vale of Memory Section and the Great Mausoleum is the Sunrise Slope Section. In the Sunrise Slope Section, directly behind the main section of the mausoleum, is a large memorial featuring a classical statue of a father and mother and their three young children, with the youngest child perched happily on the father's shoulder. The memorial contains the remains of wide-mouthed comedian **Joe E. Brown (1891–1973).**

In 1902, the ten-year-old Brown left home—with the blessing of his parents—and joined the circus. Brown became part of a tumbling act called "The Five Marvelous Ashtons," touring the country and performing with circuses and in vaudeville theaters. Brown added comedy to the act, and he became a popular burlesque and Broadway performer in the early 1920s. Despite his talent as a comedian, Brown's film debut in *The Circus Kid* (1928) featured him in a serious role as a lion tamer. Brown had more success in his early comedies and musicals, including *Sally* (1929), *Hold Everything* (1930), *Maybe It's Love* (1930), *Top Speed* (1930), *The Tenderfoot* (1932), and *A Midsummer Night's Dream* (1935). A former semiprofessional baseball player, Brown was able to show off his athletic talents in *Fireman, Save My Child* (1932), *Elmer the Great* (1933), and *Alibi Ike* (1935). In his contract with Warner Bros. studios, Brown insisted on a clause that would allow him to organize a baseball team at the studio, and he would play whenever he had the chance.

Brown was known for his rubbery face, large mouth, and ear-splitting yell. After Brown left Warner Bros. in 1937, he appeared in a long string of low-budget, relatively unsuccessful comedies. On October 8, 1942, Brown's son, Capt. Don Evan Brown of the U.S. Army Air Force, was killed in the crash of a military training plane. Brown subsequently announced his retirement from films in 1943 and focused his energy on entertaining U.S. troops around the world. Inspired by the response he received, Brown returned to films with a serious role as a small-town minister in *The Tender Years* (1947). His next film role was as Cap'n Andy Hawks in *Show Boat* (1951). Brown appeared often on radio and television throughout the 1950s, and he capped his career with one of his most memorable and popular roles as Osgood Fielding III, the millionaire who pursues Jack Lemmon in *Some Like It Hot* (1959).

The memorial where Brown is buried was originally built for his son. Brown is buried with his wife, Kathryn M. Brown (1892–1977), whom he married in 1915. Also buried in the memorial are the Browns' adopted son, producer and studio executive Mitchell J. "Mike" Frankovich (1909–1992), and his wife, actress Binnie Barnes Frankovich (1903–1998). In the center of the memorial, just below the statue, is a small plaque that appears to be a family crest. In the center of the plaque is the mask of a clown, with "The Joe E. Browns" written across the top, and "We Laugh to Win" written across the bottom.

In his biography, *Laughter Is a Wonderful Thing*, Brown wrote that he was born in 1892, and most biographical references to him cite that as his birth year. On the memorial, however, the year is listed as 1891.

Brown was born Joseph Evan Brown on July 28, 1891 (some sources say 1892), in Holgate, Ohio. He died July 6, 1973, in Los Angeles.

About 350 feet north of Brown's memorial, and about fifteen feet from the road, in the Sunrise Slope Section, Plot 72, you'll find the grave of director and comedian **Charley Chase (1893–1940).**

Chase appeared in vaudeville and musical comedy productions before joining Mack Sennett's Keystone studios in 1914. He costarred in dozens of comedy shorts, including *Tillie's Punctured Romance* (1914), *The Rounders* (1914), *Mabel's Busy Day* (1914), *Peanuts and Bullets* (1915), *Chased into Love*

(1917), and *Ship Ahoy* (1919). Chase also directed many of the comedies, usually under his real name, Charles Parrott.

In 1921, Chase joined the Hal Roach studios as a director. Three years later, he switched back to acting, usually in supporting roles as the dapper but shy man-about-town, or the meek, henpecked husband. Either as a director or costar, Chase worked with most of the top film comedians of the era, including Charlie Chaplin, Roscoe "Fatty" Arbuckle, Mabel Normand, Ford Sterling, and Stan Laurel and Oliver Hardy. When sound films became popular in the early 1930s, Chase showed that he had a beautiful singing voice, which he often demonstrated in his films. Chase also appeared as an obnoxious conventioneer in one of Laurel and Hardy's best feature films, *Sons of the Desert* (1933).

In 1937, Chase moved to Columbia studios, where he directed some of the Three Stooges shorts, and continued to appear in comedy shorts himself.

Chase is buried next to his wife, BeBe Eltinge Chase (1888–1948).

Chase was born Charles Parrott on October 20, 1893, in Baltimore, Maryland. He died June 20, 1940, in Los Angeles.

Up the hill from Chase's grave, next to the mausoleum, you can see a large white stone memorial, with a kneeling angel on each side. This memorial marks the grave of evangelist **Aimee Semple McPherson (1890–1944)**, founder and pastor of the Angelus Temple in Los Angeles, and the first nationally known religious broadcaster.

From an early age in her hometown of Ontario, Canada, McPherson demonstrated her talents as a public speaker and debater, though she considered herself a staunch atheist. In 1908, McPherson was converted to a religious life when she married a young traveling evangelist named Robert Semple. On the way to preach the gospel in China, McPherson and Semple stopped in England, and McPherson delivered her first sermon in London's Albert Hall.

Shortly after the couple arrived in China in 1910, Semple contracted malaria and dysentery and died. McPherson and her daughter returned to the United States, where she met and married a young accountant named Harold McPherson in 1912. A year later, McPherson gave birth to her second child, a boy. McPherson continued her religious work, teaching Bible classes and giving sermons. She returned to Ontario and began praying and preaching on the streets. When McPherson began to attract larger and larger crowds, she started touring and preaching across the United States and Canada. In 1919, McPherson and her family settled in Los Angeles, and she purchased property near Echo Park and built a 5,300-seat auditorium, which she named the Angelus Temple. The $1.5 million facility, paid for entirely by donations from her followers, opened in 1923 as the home of the International Church of the Foursquare Gospel (ICFG).

McPherson's theatrical services at the Angelus Temple, complete with a full orchestra, attracted thousands of followers. Using large choirs, colorful costumes, and elaborate sets to draw people to her church, McPherson, usually clad in flowing white robes with a large cross around her neck, provided a popular religious alternative to stage plays and vaudeville. In early 1924, McPherson launched radio station KFSG (which stood for "Kall Foursquare Gospel"), which broadcast the Sunday services from the temple. The following year, she opened the Lighthouse of International Foursquare Evangelism (LIFE) Bible College. In May 1926, as she was building her evangelical dynasty, "Sister Aimee," as she was known, went for a swim in the ocean near Venice, California—and disappeared. The initial assumption was that she had drowned. But several days later, McPherson's mother said she had received a ransom note, demanding $500,000 for the evangelist's safe return. More than a month after she disappeared, McPherson was found wandering in a small town in Mexico and was brought back to Los Angeles.

McPherson said she had been kidnapped by two people named Steve and Rose, tortured, and held in a shack in the desert. When her kidnappers left her alone, McPherson said she was able to cut the ropes that held her with the jagged edge of a tin can and escape. Many law enforcement officials, however, didn't believe McPherson's story, and no one was ever charged with her kidnapping. A few months later, stories began to surface that McPherson was having an affair with a former KFSG radio engineer. Rather than being held against her will in the desert, according to the stories, McPherson had actually run off with the engineer to Carmel, California, where McPherson could escape her fame for a few weeks.

After a six-week grand jury investigation, McPherson and her mother were charged with criminal conspiracy for making up the kidnapping story. When some witnesses changed their stories, however, the charges were dropped before the case came to trial. But McPherson couldn't avoid controversy. In 1931, long divorced from her second husband, McPherson eloped with choir singer David Hutton, which upset many of her followers. Their marriage lasted less than three years. McPherson and her mother also battled publicly over the management of the Angelus Temple, and they eventually stopped speaking to each other. Charges also surfaced concerning improper use of the millions of dollars in donations received by the temple.

Throughout the 1930s, McPherson continued her ministry. She opened a soup kitchen, which fed thousands during the depression, and preached more than twenty sermons each week. By the early 1940s, McPherson's physical and emotional health began to decline, and she began to take tranquilizers and sedatives to help her sleep. On September 27, 1944, while on a preaching tour in Oakland, California, McPherson apparently took too many of the sedatives and died. The cause of her death was determined to be an "accidental overdose."

McPherson's body lay in the Angelus Temple for three days, to allow mourners to pay their respects. More than ten thousand mourners crowded into the temple after waiting for hours in long lines, and later they gathered at Forest Lawn for McPherson's memorial services. Sixteen pallbearers were needed to carry her 1,200-pound bronze casket about two hundred feet from the road up the hill to its final resting place, on what would have been McPherson's fifty-fourth birthday. Blocks were set up every few feet so they could set the casket down and rest. When she was buried, the name on the memorial said simply "McPherson." Later, it was changed to include her full name. In her will, McPherson left only $10 to her mother, $2,000 to her daughter, and control of the Angelus Temple and the International Church of the Foursquare Gospel to her son, Rolf.

More than fifty years after McPherson's death, under Rolf McPherson's guidance, the International Church of the Foursquare Gospel continues to grow and prosper, and radio station KFSG is still on the air in Los Angeles, at 96.3 FM, and continues to broadcast services from the Angelus Temple. As of December 31, 1999, according to the ICFG, there were 1,836 Foursquare churches in the United States, with more than 233,000 members. Elsewhere in the world, there were more than 24,300 churches in 106 countries, ministering to more than 3 million members.

McPherson was born Aimee Elizabeth Kennedy on October 9, 1890, in Salford, Ontario, Canada. She died September 27, 1944, in Oakland, California.

About 500 feet north of McPherson's grave and about 275 feet from the road, in the middle of a small grove of tall pine trees, in Plot 3105, you'll find the grave of **William Demarest (1892–1983),** a veteran character actor in more than 150 films, but perhaps best remembered for his role as Uncle Charley in the 1960s television series *My Three Sons.*

Demarest was a vaudeville performer and professional boxer who made his film debut in *When the Wife's Away* (1926). He appeared in supporting roles in several silent films, including a small role in *The Jazz Singer* (1927), starring Al Jolson. Ironically, Demarest also appeared in *The Jolson Story* (1946), for which he received his only Academy Award nomination, for Best Supporting Actor.

Demarest typically played tough-guy roles, including police officers, hard-boiled reporters, crusty ministers, bartenders, and army officers. Demarest was also a favorite actor of director Preston Sturges, appearing in ten of Sturges's films—*Diamond Jim* (1935), *Easy Living* (1937), *Christmas in July* (1940), *The Great McGinty* (1940), *The Lady Eve* (1941), *The Palm Beach Story* (1942), *Sullivan's Travels* (1942), *The Great Moment* (1944), *Hail the Conquering Hero* (1944), and *The Miracle of Morgan's Creek* (1944).

From 1965 to 1972, Demarest appeared as Uncle Charley on *My Three Sons,* taking over the role of the gruff housekeeper after the death of William Frawley.

Demarest is buried next to his mother, Minnie Demarest (1859–1929), and his brother, actor Ruben "Rube" Demarest (1886–1962). His grave marker identifies Demarest as "Carl Wm. Demarest."

Demarest was born Carl William Demarest on February 27, 1892, in St. Paul, Minnesota. He died December 28, 1983, in Palm Springs, California.

Head back toward the Wee Kirk O' the Heather Church, near the main entrance. As you approach the church, with the Whispering Pines Section on your left, stop near the exit road from the church parking area. Look for the number "321" stenciled on the curb in the Whispering Pines Section. There is a hill in the center of the Whispering Pines Section, and the number is roughly at the highest point of the hill. About 100 feet southwest of that point, look for a small white marble bench. Walk along the same row of grave markers that the bench is in, toward the main entrance of the cemetery. About 125 feet away, in Plot 1141, you'll find the grave of Academy Award–winning director **Michael Curtiz (1886–1962).**

Curtiz was an actor and accomplished director in his native Hungary. In

1919, when the Communist regime nationalized the Hungarian film industry, Curtiz sought political refuge in Austria and Germany, where he continued to direct. He came to Hollywood in 1926, quickly becoming a successful director for Warner Bros. studios.

Despite his legendary battles with actor Humphrey Bogart, Curtiz won the Academy Award as Best Director for *Casablanca* (1942). He was also nominated for *Four Daughters* (1938), *Angels With Dirty Faces* (1938), and *Yankee Doodle Dandy* (1942). Curtiz directed many of the tough, gritty films produced by Warner Bros. in the 1930s and 1940s, including *20,000 Years in Sing Sing* (1932), *Captain Blood* (1935), *The Walking Dead* (1936), *The Sea Hawk* (1940), *The Sea Wolf* (1941), *Passage to Marseille* (1944), *Mildred Pierce* (1945), *Flamingo Road* (1949), and *Young Man With a Horn* (1950).

But he could also direct lighter fare, including *White Christmas* (1954), *Night and Day* (1946), *Life With Father* (1947), *Trouble Along the Way* (1953), *We're No Angels* (1955), and *The Adventures of Huckleberry Finn* (1960). He even directed Elvis Presley in *King Creole* (1958).

Curtiz was well known for controlling his actors and crew with an iron fist, and he often got into heated arguments on the set with anyone who would cross him. Curtiz was also legendary for his problems with the English language. While directing *The Charge of the Light Brigade* (1936), which starred, among others, David Niven, Curtiz wanted riderless horses in the background during the final charge, so he called out, "Bring on the empty horses!" That comment became the title of Niven's autobiography.

Curtiz was born Mihali Kertész Kaminer on December 24, 1886, in Budapest, Hungary. He died April 10, 1962, in Los Angeles.

From Curtiz's grave, walk six rows up, toward the crest of the hill. Turn left and walk about ten feet, to Plot 1066, and you'll find the grave of popular comedian and master of the "double take," **Jack Oakie (1903–1978).**

Oakie was raised in Oklahoma, and took his name from the common nickname for residents of that state. He moved to New York City, attended business school, and worked as a telephone clerk at a brokerage house on Wall Street. After performing in a company show, he was encouraged to turn professional, and he made his stage debut as a dancer on Broadway in George M. Cohan's *Little Nellie Kelly* in 1922. Oakie made his film debut the following year, with a small role in *His Children's Children* (1923). Oakie worked steadily through the 1920s and 1930s, often in supporting roles as the slow-witted, happy-go-lucky buffoon, in films including *Million Dollar Legs* (1932), *If I Had a Million* (1932), *The Eagle and the Hawk* (1933), *Alice in Wonderland* (1933), *The Call of the Wild* (1935), *The Toast of New York* (1937), and *The Affairs of Annabel* (1938). Though he played primarily supporting roles in comedies and musicals, he generally stole every scene he was in.

Oakie is perhaps best remembered for his performance as Napaloni, the dictator of Bacteria, in Charlie Chaplin's *The Great Dictator* (1940). Oakie's performance, a stinging parody of Italian dictator Benito Mussolini, won him his only Academy Award nomination, as Best Supporting Actor. Oakie went into semiretirement in the early 1960s but continued to make guest appearances on television.

Oakie's grave marker identifies him as "Lewis Delaney Offield, also known as Jack Oakie," with this epitaph: "In a simple double-take, thou hast more than voice e'er spake; When you hear laughter that wonderful sound, you know that Jack Oakie's around."

Oakie was born Lewis Delaney Offield on November 12, 1903, in Sedalia, Missouri. He died January 23, 1978, in Northridge, California.

From Oakie's grave, you can see the main gates of the cemetery on Glendale Avenue. Walk about fifty feet toward the gates, then turn left and walk about ten feet. There, in Plot 986, you'll find the grave of the silent screen's King of the Cowboys, **Tom Mix (1880–1940).**

Mix was a bartender and part-time sheriff in Dewey, Oklahoma, when he joined a traveling Wild West show. The show often provided horses and riders for Westerns, and Mix made his screen debut in *Ranch Life in the Great Southwest* (1910). Mix appeared in more than a hundred short Westerns over the next few years, many of which he also produced and directed. In 1917, Mix joined Fox studios and quickly became the most popular cowboy star of the silent screen, with action-packed films combining folksy humor and daredevil stunts. Riding his horse, Tony, Mix performed many of his own stunts and was often injured as a result.

With the growing popularity of sound films in the late 1920s, Mix left the screen to tour with the Ringling Bros. Circus. He made a handful of films in the early 1930s.

Mix was killed in an automobile accident in Arizona. He was buried in a silver coffin with his distinctive "TM" brand on the side, wearing a belt buckle that spelled out his name in diamonds. The "TM" brand also appears on his grave marker, along with a facsimile of his signature.

Mix was born Thomas Hezikiah Mix on January 6, 1880, in
Mix Run, Pennsylvania. He died October 12, 1940,
in Florence, Arizona.

From Mix's grave, walk another hundred feet toward the main cemetery gates, then one row over to the left. There, in Plot 984, you'll find the grave of actor **Edward Everett Horton (1886–1970)**, who played supporting roles in dozens of musicals and comedies from the 1920s to the 1940s, and later narrated the Fractured Fairy Tales segments on *The Bullwinkle Show,* from 1959 until his death.

Horton made his stage debut as a singer and dancer while still a student at Columbia University. He made his screen debut in *Too Much Business* (1922), and later appeared in more than 120 films, usually as a jittery fuss-budget in comedies and musicals, including *The Front Page* (1931), *Lost Horizon* (1937), *Holiday* (1938), *Here Comes Mr. Jordan* (1941), and *Arsenic and Old Lace* (1944).

Horton provided comic relief in three films with Fred Astaire and Ginger Rogers—*The Gay Divorcee* (1934), *Top Hat* (1935), and *Shall We Dance?* (1937). Horton was also a favorite of director Ernst Lubitsch, appearing in *Trouble in Paradise* (1932), *Design for Living* (1933), *The Merry Widow* (1934), *Angel* (1937), and *Bluebeard's Eighth Wife* (1938).

At the end of his career, in the late 1960s, the Ivy League–educated Horton became strangely popular portraying Native American characters in television sitcoms, appearing as Roaring Chicken in the *F Troop* series, and as Chief Screaming Eagle in the *Batman* series.

Horton is buried next to his mother, Isabella Diack Horton (1859–1961), and his sister, Hannabelle Horton Grant (1890–1992).

Horton was born March 18, 1886, in Brooklyn, New York.
He died September 29, 1970, in Encino, California.

From Horton's grave, walk south, nine rows down the other side of the hill, then turn left and walk about 120 feet. There, in Plot 724, you'll find the grave of actor **Alan Hale Sr. (1892–1950).**

After his initial career choice as an opera singer didn't work out, Hale came to Hollywood. He first found work as an actor in supporting roles and directing films for Cecil B. De Mille. Hale made his screen debut in *The Cowboy and the Lady* (1911), and played supporting roles in dozens of silent films.

The burly, jovial Hale appeared in most of the popular adventure films produced by Warner Bros. studios in the 1930s and 1940s, often appearing with his offscreen friend Errol Flynn. Flynn and Hale appeared in thirteen films together, including *The Prince and the Pauper* (1937), *The Adventures of Robin Hood* (1938), *The Sisters* (1939), *The Private Lives of Elizabeth and Essex* (1939), *Dodge City* (1939), *The Sea Hawk* (1940), *Santa Fe Trail* (1940), *Virginia City* (1940), *Footsteps in the Dark* (1942), *Gentleman Jim* (1942), *Desperate Journey* (1942), *Thank Your Lucky Stars* (1943), and *The Adventures of Don Juan* (1948).

Hale also appeared in *It Happened One Night* (1934), *Of Human Bondage* (1934), *The Lost Patrol* (1934), *Great Expectations* (1934), *Stella Dallas* (1937), *The Man in the Iron Mask* (1939), *They Drive by Night* (1940), *The Strawberry Blonde* (1941), *Destination Tokyo* (1943), and *Night and Day* (1946).

Hale's grave marker contains a facsimile of his signature. He is buried next to his wife, Gretchen Hartman Hale (1897–1979).

Hale is the father of Alan Hale Jr., best known as the Skipper on the 1960s television series *Gilligan's Island.*

Hale was born Rufus Alan McKahan on February 10, 1892, in Washington, D.C. He died January 22, 1950, in Los Angeles.

Tour 2: The Freedom Mausoleum and Surrounding Area

Although the Great Mausoleum is closed to the public, the Freedom Mausoleum at the eastern corner of the cemetery is open. Enter through the main entrance off the Court of Freedom, on the west side of the building. Just inside the door, turn right down the first hallway, and stop at the first corridor on your left, the Sanctuary of Heritage. A large chain blocks the entrance to the Sanctuary of Heritage, but the chain is easily removed in case you want a closer look at the crypts.

In the second column from the entrance, in the second space up from the floor, you'll find the crypt containing **Clara Bow (1907–1965)**, popular film star of the 1920s and America's first real sex symbol, best known as the "It Girl."

Bow grew up in a household of poverty, violence, and mental illness. She escaped her circumstances by entering her photo in a movie magazine contest and winning the top prize: the chance to appear in a small role in the film *Beyond the Rainbow* (1922). Bow's acting was considered so amateurish that her scenes were cut before the film was released. When she became a star a few years later, however, her scenes were restored to the film.

Despite her difficult beginning, Bow worked steadily in films through the 1920s, typically playing supporting roles in films that were described as "domestic melodramas," with an occasional comedy. A partial list of Bow's film credits provides a pretty good idea of the kind of film she specialized in: *Enemies of Women* (1923), *Grit* (1924), *Poisoned Paradise* (1924), *Daughters of Pleasure* (1924), *Empty Hearts* (1924), *Helen's Babies* (1924), *This Woman* (1924), *The Adventurous Sex* (1925), *Eve's Lover* (1925), *Lawful Cheaters* (1925), *Parisian Love* (1925), *Kiss Me Again* (1925), *Free to Love* (1925), *My Lady's Lips* (1925), *Two Can Play* (1926), and *Mantrap* (1926).

Bow had become the symbol for the Roaring '20s and the flapper age—an attractive, vibrant, liberated woman with boundless energy, bobbed hair, "bee-stung" lips, and flashing eyes. Bow also became a symbol for the growing sexual liberation of the era.

The film that defined Bow's career was *It* (1927), in which she played a lowly shopgirl with designs on the wealthy storeowner. In an effort to make him notice her, Bow's character dates the storeowner's best friend, and her plan works. In the film, Bow was a woman who saw what she wanted and did whatever it took to get it. From then on, Bow was known as the "It Girl," with "it" usually meaning sex appeal. Bow also appeared in *Wings* (1927), which won the first Academy Award as Best Picture. Bow continued to appear in films as the often-wild woman who knows what she wants and gets it, including *Get Your Man* (1927), *The Fleet's In* (1928), *The Wild Party* (1929), *Dangerous Curves* (1929), *Her Wedding Night* (1930), *No Limit* (1931), and *Call Her Savage* (1932). When sound films became popular in the early 1930s, Bow's thick Brooklyn accent was a severe handicap. Her last film was *Hoopla* (1933).

Bow married cowboy actor Rex Bell in 1931, and she devoted her time to raising their two children. But she was also the continuing focus of wild rumors about her previous romantic affairs, including one involving the entire University of Southern California football team. Bow's former secretary sold her story to the tabloids, telling wild tales of Bow's frequent and enthusiastic sexual trysts with dozens of Hollywood suitors.

Bow retired from films in 1933, when she was just twenty-six years old, and went to live with Bell on his Walking Box Ranch, west of Searchlight,

Nevada. For the rest of her life, Bow fought a series of personal struggles, including a weight problem and growing mental instability. In her later years, she was often confined to a sanatorium, and she never returned to show business. "Being a sex symbol is a heavy load to carry," Bow once said. In her final years, Bow moved back to Los Angeles, where she lived as a virtual recluse. She died alone, suffering a heart attack while watching a Gary Cooper Western on television.

Bow's crypt marker identifies her as "Hollywood's 'It' Girl."

Bow was born Clara Gordon Bow on July 29, 1907 (some sources say 1905), in Brooklyn, New York. She died September 27, 1965, in Los Angeles.

Bow is buried with her husband, actor **Rex Bell (1903–1962)**. A tall, handsome former college football player at the University of Iowa, Bell made his film debut in *The Cowboy Kid* (1928). He appeared in nearly fifty films over the next fifteen years, primarily low-budget Westerns. Bell retired from films in the early 1940s, moved to Nevada, and operated a store in Las Vegas. In 1954, he was elected lieutenant governor of the state, and in 1958 he made an unsuccessful bid for the governor's office.

Bell's last film appearance was a small, uncredited part in *The Misfits* (1961), starring Clark Gable and Marilyn Monroe. While campaigning again for governor in 1962, Bell suffered a heart attack and died.

Bell was born George Francis Beldam on October 16, 1903, in Chicago, Illinois. He died July 4, 1962, in Las Vegas, Nevada.

Directly above Bow and Bell is the crypt containing the remains of actor **Alan Ladd (1913–1964).**

Ladd worked an assortment of odd jobs around Hollywood before finding work as a handyman on the Warner Bros. lot. He made his screen debut in a small role in *Tom Brown of Culver* (1932), and appeared in small roles in dozens of minor films throughout the 1930s, typically playing college students, soldiers, sailors, and friends of the featured actors. His early screen appearances included uncredited roles as one of the beasts in *Island of Lost Souls* (1933) and a pipe-smoking reporter in *Citizen Kane* (1941). The short—five-foot-five—fair-haired, unemotional Ladd was not considered a leading-man type of actor, and he may have remained in supporting roles if not for the persistence of his agent, former actress Sue Carol, who became Ladd's wife in 1942. Carol helped Ladd land the role of cold-blooded killer Philip Raven in *This Gun for Hire* (1942), costarring with Veronica Lake. Ladd's detached coolness made him a perfect match for Lake, and they were paired in six more films during the 1940s, including *The Glass Key* (1942), *The Blue Dahlia* (1946), and *Saigon* (1948).

Ladd's best-known role was as the mysterious gunfighter who wants to hang up his six-shooters but is forced to defend a homesteading family in *Shane* (1953). Ladd's icy coolness, punctuated by two-fisted action, made him a favorite among film fans, who apparently didn't mind that Ladd was often several inches shorter than his costars. Though never nominated for an Academy Award, Ladd was named the Most Popular Male Star in the Photoplay Awards in 1953, as voted by the readers of *Photoplay* magazine. The following year, he won a Golden Globe Award as World Film Favorite.

Ladd continued starring in action-packed films throughout the 1950s, including *The Red Beret* (1953), *Hell Below Zero* (1954), *Saskatchewan* (1954), *Hell on Frisco Bay* (1955), *The Proud Rebel* (1958), *The Badlanders* (1958), and *One Foot in Hell* (1960), but he was never able to match his earlier successes. In November 1962, Ladd was seriously injured in what was officially described as an "accidental" self-inflicted gunshot wound to his chest. Just over a year later, he died of an overdose of sedatives mixed with alcohol at the age of fifty.

Ladd's final film appearance was in *The Carpetbaggers* (1964), which was released several months after his death.

Ladd's three children have all been involved in the film industry. Ladd's oldest son, Alan Ladd Jr., is a successful film producer and studio executive. His youngest son, David Ladd, is an actor, producer, and former husband of actress Cheryl Ladd. And his daughter, Alana Ladd, appeared in three Westerns in the early 1960s, two of which starred her father. The third was *Young Guns of Texas* (1962), which starred several children of more-famous acting parents.

In front of Ladd's crypt is a small bust of the actor, dressed in his *Shane* costume.

Ladd was born Alan Walbridge Ladd on September 3, 1913, in Hot Springs, Arkansas. He died January 29, 1964, in Palm Springs, California.

Ladd is buried with his second wife, actress and talent agent **Sue Carol Ladd (1907–1982)**. Carol appeared in twenty-five films from 1927 to 1937, typically in supporting roles. After she retired from performing, she became a talent agent and is credited with discovering, among others, Alan Ladd, who became her fourth husband in 1942.

Carol was born Evelyn Lederer on October 30, 1907, in Chicago, Illinois. She died February 4, 1982, in Los Angeles.

One space above and one space to the left of the Ladds is the crypt of actress and singer **Jeanette MacDonald (1907–1965).**

MacDonald started her entertainment career as a dancer, and she was a successful Broadway chorus girl while she was still a teenager. She was brought to Hollywood by director Ernst Lubitsch, and she made her screen debut in *The Love Parade* (1929), costarring with Maurice Chevalier. MacDonald starred in a rapid succession of successful musicals through the early 1930s, including *The Vagabond King* (1930), *Monte Carlo* (1930), *Let's Go Native* (1930), *Oh, For a Man* (1930), and *Love Me Tonight* (1932). Lubitsch, Chevalier, and MacDonald were teamed again in *The Merry Widow* (1935).

MacDonald was first paired with singer Nelson Eddy in *Naughty Marietta* (1935), the story of a French princess who escapes an arranged marriage and finds true love with a dashing sea captain. The film was a tremendous box-office success, and was nominated for an Academy Award as Best Picture. And, of course, that meant more Eddy-MacDonald pairings, beginning with *Rose-Marie* (1936)—perhaps their best-known film together, certainly their most remembered and most-often parodied, featuring Eddy in the uniform of a Canadian Mountie, singing "Indian Love Call" with MacDonald. Eddy and MacDonald, now billed as "America's Singing Sweethearts," continued with *Maytime* (1937), *Sweethearts* (1938), *The Girl of the Golden West* (1938), *New Moon* (1940), *Bitter Sweet* (1940), and their final film together, *I Married an Angel* (1942). In between her films with Eddy, MacDonald costarred with Clark Gable and Spencer Tracy in *San Francisco* (1936).

Both Eddy's and MacDonald's careers slumped after they separated, and MacDonald was dropped by MGM studios. She wasn't seen onscreen again until *Three Daring Daughters* (1948) and *The Sun Comes Up* (1949), which was her final film appearance. MacDonald went into semiretirement, appearing occasionally on television, in concerts, and occasionally onstage in various musicals. Her final public appearance was singing "Ah, Sweet Mystery of Life" at the funeral of MGM studio chief Louis B. Mayer in 1957.

MacDonald was born Jeanette Anna MacDonald on June 18, 1907 (some sources say 1901 or 1903), in Philadelphia, Pennsylvania. She died January 14, 1965, in Houston, Texas.

Buried with MacDonald is her husband, actor **Gene Raymond (1908–1998).**

Raymond was a child performer onstage, and by the time he was a teenager he was a Broadway veteran. In Hollywood, he typically played the romantic lead in minor films, or supporting roles in major films. Raymond made his screen debut in *Personal Maid* (1931), costarred with Clark Gable and Jean Harlow in *Red Dust* (1932), with Bette Davis in *Ex-Lady* (1933), with Fred Astaire and Ginger Rogers in *Flying Down to Rio* (1933), and with Joan Crawford in *Sadie McKee* (1934).

MacDonald and Raymond were married in 1937 and appeared in *Smilin' Through* (1941), their only film together. By the mid-1940s, with MacDonald's career winding down, Raymond began to appear less onscreen as the couple traveled and were active in the Hollywood social scene. Raymond appeared as the host and panelist on several television series during the late 1950s. His final film appearances were in *I'd Rather Be Rich* (1964) and *The Best Man* (1964).

Raymond was born Raymond Guion on August 13, 1908, in New York City. He died May 2, 1998, in Los Angeles.

Directly above MacDonald and Raymond is the crypt of velvet-voiced singer and jazz pianist **Nat "King" Cole (1919–1965).**

Cole was the son of a Baptist minister, and he started his musical career when he was twelve years old, playing the organ in his father's church in Chicago. Two years later, he formed a fourteen-piece band called the Royal Dukes. A few years after that, his publicist put an aluminum foil crown on Cole's head and gave him the nickname "King" Cole. In 1939, Cole formed the King Cole Trio, and they performed throughout the United States and Europe, including a command performance before Queen Elizabeth II.

Cole and his band made their film debut in the musical *Pistol Packin' Mama* (1943) and appeared in several other films in the 1940s and 1950s. In

1950, Cole's recording of "Mona Lisa" became a number one hit. Cole sold more than 50 million records during his career, including "That Ain't Right," "Sweet Lorraine," "Ramblin' Rose," "Sweet Georgia Brown," and "Straighten Up and Fly Right," which he also wrote. In 1956, Cole became the first black performer to have his own television show.

Cole also appeared in *The Blue Gardenia* (1953), *Kiss Me Deadly* (1955), *The Scarlet Hour* (1956), *Istanbul* (1957), *China Gate* (1957), and *St. Louis Blues* (1958). Cole's last film appearance was in *Cat Ballou* (1965).

Cole is the father of singer Natalie Cole.

Cole was born Nathaniel Adams Coles on March 17, 1919, in Montgomery, Alabama. He died February 15, 1965, in Santa Monica, California.

One space down and one space to the left of MacDonald and Raymond is the crypt of married comedians **George Burns (1896–1996)** and **Gracie Allen (1902–1964)**.

Burns began performing in vaudeville as a member of a children's singing quartet. He later tried his hand at comedy and was performing with a partner when he met Allen in 1922. Allen, the daughter of vaudeville performers, also started on the stage at a young age, teaming with her sister in a musical act. Burns and Allen first performed together in 1922, with Allen setting up the jokes and Burns delivering the punch lines. But Burns immediately noticed that his partner was getting all the laughs, so the act was revised with Burns as the straight man, and Allen as his ditzy, scatterbrained partner. Within a few years, Burns and Allen were one of the top acts in vaudeville. They were married in 1926.

They made their film debut in a series of comedy shorts, and their feature debut in *The Big Broadcast* (1932). After a lengthy and successful career in radio, Burns and Allen debuted *The Burns and Allen Show* on television in 1950, and it was a top-rated show for the next eight years, nominated for Emmy Awards as the best comedy show from 1952 to 1955. Allen also received Emmy nominations from 1955 to 1957. When Allen decided to retire in 1958, Burns attempted a solo career in television and nightclubs, but he had little success.

Allen died in 1964, and Burns was out of the spotlight for more than a decade. He returned to play a cantankerous old ex–vaudeville star in Neil Simon's *The Sunshine Boys* (1975), costarring with Walter Matthau. (Burns was not the first choice for the role, however. He replaced Jack Benny, who died shortly before production was to begin.) For his performance, Burns won the Academy Award as Best Supporting Actor, and launched the next phase of his career. Burns next played the title role in *Oh, God!* (1977), as well as two sequels—*Oh, God! Book Two* (1980) and *Oh, God! You Devil* (1984). He also appeared as Mr. Kite in *Sgt. Pepper's Lonely Hearts Club Band* (1978), *Just You and Me, Kid* (1979), *Going in Style* (1979), *Two of a Kind* (1982), and *18 Again!* (1988).

Burns continued to perform in nightclubs and on television. When asked if he ever planned to retire, Burns would respond, "I'm going to stay in show business until I'm the only one left." Burns died a few weeks after his one-hundredth birthday.

After Allen's death, Burns visited her crypt at Forest Lawn at least once a month for the rest of his life. Their crypt contains the simple inscription, "Together Again."

Allen was born Grace Ethel Cecile Rosalie Allen on July 26, 1902, in San Francisco, California. She died August 27, 1964, in Los Angeles.

Burns was born Nathan Birnbaum on January 20, 1896, in New York City. He died March 9, 1996, in Los Angeles.

Head back toward the main entrance of the Freedom Mausoleum. Just past the entrance, on the left side, you'll see the Columbarium of Victory. Inside, on the far wall, about six feet to the right of the statue in the center of the wall, and about eight feet up from the floor, you'll find a plaque marking the remains of singer and actress **Dorothy Dandridge (1922–1965).**

Dandridge's mother and grandmother were both actresses, and she first performed at the age of four, teaming with her sister in a song-and-dance act called "The Wonder Children." After gaining fame as a singer, Dandridge made her screen debut in a small role in *A Day at the Races* (1937), starring the Marx Brothers. After appearing in supporting roles in films throughout the 1940s, Dandridge achieved stardom with starring roles in *Carmen Jones* (1954), *Island in the Sun* (1957), and *Porgy and Bess* (1959). For her performance in *Carmen Jones,* Dandridge became the first black actress to be nominated for an Academy Award as Best Actress. She was also the first black woman to appear on the cover of *Life* magazine.

Dandridge spent most of her career fighting against racial prejudice. Though an extremely talented singer and actress, Dandridge was still unable to find suitable starring roles in films, and she often returned to singing in nightclubs and hotels—even though many of the hotels would hire her to perform, but would not allow her to stay in the hotel as a guest. Her last film appearance was in *The Murder Men* (1961).

Dandridge was found dead in her West Hollywood apartment in 1965, the victim of a barbiturate overdose at forty-two years old.

Dandridge is buried with her mother, actress Ruby Dandridge (1900–1987), who appeared in films including *Never a Dull Moment* (1943), *Cabin in the Sky* (1943), *Saratoga Trunk* (1945), *Dead Reckoning* (1946), and *A Hole in the Head* (1959).

Halle Berry starred in a film based on Dandridge's life, *Introducing Dorothy Dandridge* (1999).

Dandridge was born Dorothy Jean Dandridge on November 9, 1922, in Cleveland, Ohio. She died September 8, 1965, in West Hollywood, California.

Between the Columbarium of Victory and the main entrance to the mausoleum is a stairway leading down to the Patriots' Terrace and the Independence Terrace. Go down the stairs and turn right to the main hallway, the Corridor of Patriots. Turn left in that corridor and look for the Sanctuary of Gratitude, on the left. In that corridor, on the right side, in the third column from the right and the fourth space up from the floor, you'll find the crypt of actor **Francis X. Bushman (1883–1966),** identified as "King of the Movies."

Bushman was a handsome man with a sturdy physique—before becoming an actor, he worked as a sculptor's model. After working onstage for many years, Bushman made his film debut in 1911, appearing in eighteen films that year, mostly short dramas. By the time Bushman joined Metro Pictures Corporation in 1916, he had already appeared in well over one hundred films, mostly dramas and romances, and he was quickly becoming the most popular film star among young fans. He was known as the "Handsomest Man in Movies." But much of his popularity faded when his female admirers discovered that Bushman was secretly married to actress Beverly Bayne, his costar in *Romeo and Juliet* (1916) and many other films.

Bushman's most famous role was as Messala in *Ben-Hur* (1925), with Ramon Novarro in the title role. By the late 1920s, Bushman's salary was estimated at more than a million dollars per year, but his fortune was wiped out in the stock market crash of 1929. Bushman's film career was virtually over in the early 1930s, and he supported himself by appearing on radio soap operas. He also appeared in small roles in *The Bad and the Beautiful* (1952), *Sabrina* (1954), and his last film, *The Ghost in the Invisible Bikini* (1966).

Bushman was born Francis Xavier Bushman on January 10, 1883, in Baltimore, Maryland. He died August 23, 1966, in Pacific Palisades, California.

Head back down the Corridor of Patriots, past the hallway leading to the stairs, and look for the Sanctuary of Worship on your right. On the right side of that corridor, in the second column from the right and the sixth space up from the floor, you'll find the crypt of comedian **Chico Marx (1887–1961)**, the "Italian" member of the Marx Brothers comedy team.

Chico was the oldest of the Marx Brothers but the last to join the act. Chico's younger brothers—Groucho, Harpo, Gummo, and Zeppo—had been performing a musical comedy act under various names by the time Chico joined them. Chico was originally called "Chicko" because of his reputation as a woman-chaser. When the "k" was accidentally left out in a printed program for the act, Chico kept the revised spelling, but his nickname is properly pronounced "Chick-o," not the more common, but incorrect pronunciation, "Cheek-o."

In the early days of the act, Chico was the business manager who secured for the Marx Brothers their first international booking in London, their first Broadway show, and their film contract at MGM studios. Later, Gummo took over management of the act. As successful as Chico was as a show business manager, he was just as unsuccessful as a gambler. Chico was famous for visiting horseracing tracks and hosting card games at the studio, and he almost always lost.

By 1924, the four Marx Brothers—Groucho, Chico, Harpo, and Zeppo—were a hit on Broadway with their musical comedy show, *I'll Say She Is*. They followed that with two more Broadway hits—*The Cocoanuts* and *Animal Crackers*. When talking pictures were introduced in the late 1920s, studios came to Broadway looking for comedians, and the Marxes were signed by Paramount Pictures to appear in the filmed version of *The Cocoanuts* (1929), which they worked on during the day while appearing onstage in *Animal Crackers* every evening.

The Marx Brothers also filmed *Animal Crackers* (1930), followed by *Monkey Business* (1931), *Horse Feathers* (1932), and two films that most Marx Brothers fans agree are the brothers' best work—*Duck Soup* (1933) and *A Night at the Opera* (1935), which was their first film at MGM studios. *A Night at the Opera* was also the brothers' first film without Zeppo. The three remaining Marx Brothers—Groucho, Harpo, and Chico—made five more films at MGM: *A Day at the Races* (1937), *Room Service* (1938), *At the Circus* (1939), *Go West* (1940), and *The Big Store* (1941). After taking several years off, they returned to the screen in *A Night in Casablanca* (1946) and *Love Happy* (1950)—which is perhaps less significant as the Marx Brothers' final film together than it is as one of the first film appearances of Marilyn Monroe. Chico's role in these films was typically as the scheming con artist, usually assisted by Harpo. And, in just about every film, he found the opportunity to play the piano in his unique, "finger-pointing" style.

After the Marx Brothers stopped appearing together in films, Chico continued working, partly to pay off his gambling debts. He was the host of *The College Bowl* television series in 1950, and he also appeared in *The Story of Mankind* (1957) and several television series in the late 1950s.

Just before Chico died in 1961, he said to his daughter, Maxine, "Put in my coffin a deck of cards, a mashie niblick (golf club), and a pretty blonde." Chico's funeral services were held on October 13, 1961, in the Wee Kirk O' the Heather chapel at Forest Lawn. Although Chico wasn't much of a religious person, his family hired a rabbi to officiate at the services. The rabbi had never met Chico, and gave a generic eulogy, except for one comment. Maxine Marx had asked the rabbi to say that her father was "the least malicious man that ever lived." However the rabbi mistakenly said that Chico was "the least mischievous man in the world." Those who truly knew Chico knew how far from the truth that comment was. After the rabbi's eulogy, Harpo leaned over to Maxine and said, "When I go, do me a favor and hire a mime."

Marx was born Leonard Marx on March 22, 1887, in New York City. He died October 11, 1961, in Los Angeles.

Directly across the Corridor of Patriots, in the Sanctuary of Brotherhood, on the left side, in the third column from the left, the third space up from the floor, you'll find the crypt of the non-performing Marx Brother, **Gummo Marx (1893–1977).**

Actually, Gummo and his older brother, Groucho, were the first performers among the brothers, in an act called "The Three Nightingales," with singer Janie O'Reilly. The name and performers in the act changed over the years, as more brothers were added and the focus changed from music to comedy. But Gummo was never entirely comfortable as a performer. He would get extremely nervous, stutter, and often forget his lines while onstage. When Gummo—who was given his nickname because he wore gum-soled shoes— left the act to join the army, he was replaced onstage by his younger brother, Zeppo. After World War I, Gummo went into business selling dresses and cloth, but he later returned to show business as a partner in a talent agency, and he managed the Marx Brothers for many years.

Marx is buried next to his wife, Helen Marx (1907–1976).

Marx was born Milton Marx on October 23, 1893, in New York City. He died April 21, 1977, in Palm Springs, California.

Farther down the Corridor of Patriots, look for the Sanctuary of Liberation on the right. On the left side of that corridor, in the fourth column from the left, the first space up from the floor, you'll find the crypt of the wild-haired member of the Three Stooges, **Larry Fine (1902–1975).**

Fine started performing at an early age, dancing for relatives when he was just two years old. When Fine's arm was severely burned with acid when he was a child, the doctor recommended violin lessons as therapy for the damaged muscles. Although Fine eventually became an accomplished violinist and learned to play other instruments—he later occasionally played in the Three Stooges films—he still had dreams of becoming a comedian. Through his teen years, Fine played the violin in local amateur contests, and also earned money as a boxer.

In 1921, Fine landed a job with a small entertainment troupe. He played the violin, danced, and told jokes. Also on the bill were Mabel and Loretta Haney, two sisters who joined with Fine in a comedy act called "The Haney Sisters and Fine." The trio performed together in vaudeville theaters across the United States and Canada. In 1925, at the Rainbow Gardens in Chicago, Ted Healy and Moe and Shemp Howard saw their act. At the time, Healy and the Howards were popular vaudeville performers, known as "Ted Healy and his Stooges," which consisted of Healy telling jokes from the stage while the Howard brothers heckled him from the audience. Shemp Howard was planning to leave the act to pursue a career as a solo performer, so Healy invited

Fine to replace him. Healy offered Fine a salary of $90 per week, and an extra $10 if he got rid of his violin. Fine joined the act, and Shemp Howard decided not to leave after all. They appeared in a string of successful Broadway shows before heading west to Hollywood to make two-reel comedies. (Fine didn't completely turn his back on his former partners, however. He married Mabel Haney in 1927.)

After their first film, *From Soup to Nuts*, was made in 1930, Shemp left the act and was replaced by another Howard brother, Jerome—better known as Curly. After appearing in ten films with Healy, Fine and the Howards left the act in 1934 to strike out on their own, going to work for Columbia Pictures. The Three Stooges, as they were now known, made nearly 200 two-reelers for Columbia, and they were among the most popular and most profitable film performers of the 1930s, 1940s, and 1950s, though they were never able to convince Columbia to allow them to star in a feature-length film.

When Curly suffered a stroke in 1946, Shemp rejoined the act until his death in 1955. Shemp was briefly replaced by Joe Besser, then Curly Joe DeRita.

Among the Stooges, Fine was often the forgotten man in the middle. While Moe Howard was the leader of the group, and either Curly or Shemp handled the most outlandish physical comedy, Fine's performances were often limited to being the target of Moe's violent attacks, or simply reacting to the situations around him. Ironically, Fine was generally considered to be the most talented actor among the Stooges.

After leaving Columbia in 1958, the Stooges finally had the opportunity to appear in their first feature-length film—*Have Rocket, Will Travel* (1959). They followed that with *Snow White and the Three Stooges* (1961), *The Three Stooges Meet Hercules* (1962), *The Three Stooges Go Around the World in a Daze* (1963), and *The Outlaws Is Coming* (1965). The Stooges also appeared in bit parts in *Four for Texas* (1963), a Western starring Dean Martin and Frank Sinatra, and *It's a Mad Mad Mad Mad World* (1963).

The final Three Stooges film was *Kook's Tour* (1970), which featured the Stooges and their dog on a camping trip. During the final days of filming, Fine suffered a stroke and was unable to complete the film. Director Norman Maurer attempted to salvage the film by adding additional scenes without Fine and narration by Moe Howard. The film was finally released on video in 1999.

Offscreen, Fine was known as a friendly and gregarious man. He often hosted large parties at his home, and he enjoyed betting on horses.

Consequently, he didn't save much of the meager salary he earned. In fact, Fine was almost forced into bankruptcy when Columbia terminated the Three Stooges comedies in 1958.

Fine is buried next to his wife, Mabel Haney Fine (1904–1967). They were married from 1927 until her death. Next to Mabel Fine is their son, John Joseph Fine (1936–1961), who was killed in an automobile accident.

Fine was born Louis Feinberg on October 5, 1902, in Philadelphia, Pennsylvania. He died January 24, 1975, in Woodland Hills, California.

Outside the Freedom Mausoleum, just north of the main entrance, is a small, unmarked, gated courtyard with a tiny statue of a young girl in the corner. On the wall, behind the statue and hidden behind a row of bushes, is the plaque marking the grave of pioneering animator, studio executive, and the most honored person in the history of the Academy Awards, **Walt Disney (1901–1966).**

After serving briefly as a Red Cross ambulance driver in France during the closing months of World War I, Disney returned to the United States and enrolled in the Kansas City Art Institute, where he met fellow animator Ub Iwerks. They created a series of cartoons called *Newman's Laugh-O-Grams* for the Newman theater chain. Disney came to Hollywood in 1923 and partnered with his brother, Roy, and Iwerks to produce a series combining live action with animation, called *Alice in Cartoonland.* In 1927, Disney and Iwerks started their *Oswald the Lucky Rabbit* cartoon series, and the following year they created the character that may be the most recognized figure around the world—Mickey Mouse. (Disney originally wanted to call the character Mortimer Mouse, but his wife urged him to use the name Mickey.)

There are two versions of the story of Mickey's birth. One is that Disney was inspired by a friendly mouse who visited him at his drawing board. The other, less heartwarming version is that the Disney brothers and Iwerks were trying to think of a new cartoon character to replace Oswald. Someone suggested a cat, but there were already several cartoon cats. The next suggestion was a mouse and, when they couldn't think of any other cartoon mouses, they settled on that. Mickey Mouse made his film debut in *Plane Crazy* (1928), which featured Mickey, inspired by Charles Lindbergh's recent flight from New York to Paris, building a plane to take his girlfriend, Minnie, for a ride. Mickey and Minnie's next film, *Gallopin' Gaucho* (1928), featured their visit to a can-tina and Mickey's battle with a cat. Mickey's third film, *Steamboat Willie* (1928), was the first animated film with synchronized sound, and it featured Disney himself providing Mickey's high-pitched voice. Rather than just using sound to give his characters voices, however, Disney incorporated sound as a major part of the cartoon. For example, when a goat eats the sheet music for *Turkey in the Straw*, Minnie cranks the goat's tail, and it plays the tune. Mickey and Minnie also use various animals to create an orchestra. *Steamboat Willie* was a huge success for Disney, and he later added sound to Mickey's first two films.

With Disney and Iwerks sharing the writing and directing duties, Mickey and Minnie appeared in dozens of comedy shorts during the next few years, with their growing collection of friends, including Donald Duck, who first appeared in 1934; Goofy; and Pluto. In 1932, Disney received his first Academy Award, a special Oscar for creating Mickey Mouse.

With Mickey's popularity growing, Disney's operation was forced to grow to keep up with the demand for more cartoons. Disney also created the *Silly Symphonies* cartoon series, in which the action on the screen is synchronized to match a prerecorded soundtrack, rather than the other way around. The first in the series was *The Skeleton Dance* (1929), and the best-known and most successful was *The Three Little Pigs* (1933). Disney also launched a new cartoon innovation—color—with *Flowers and Trees* (1932), which won Disney his second Academy Award and his first in the competitive field of Best Cartoon Short.

In addition to supplying Mickey's voice for the first twenty years of his cartoon life, Disney also provided the inspiration for much of Mickey's personality. Like Disney, and unlike most other cartoon characters, Mickey wasn't particularly funny. He didn't make funny faces or say funny things. The humor in the Mickey Mouse cartoons usually came from the situations, and from Mickey's unswerving determination to accomplish his goal, despite any obstacles that might get in his way, including the hot-tempered Donald Duck, the witless Goofy, and the clumsy Pluto.

The growth of Mickey Mouse as an enterprise started in 1930, when Disney was offered $300 to put Mickey's image on a school notebook. Also in 1930, Mickey started to appear in a daily newspaper comic strip, keeping the cartoon mouse in the eyes and minds of the buying public. At the same time, the Disney studio was turning out a new cartoon short every three to four weeks. From that point on, Disney character merchandise became a major source of income for the Disney studio, fueled by the new shorts and comic strip.

In 1934, Disney took another risk and started work on the first feature-length animated film—*Snow White and the Seven Dwarfs* (1937), a musical classic that remains popular after more than sixty years. Disney's *Fantasia* (1940) was a controversial attempt to use animation to interpret various pieces of classical music. It is now also recognized as a film classic. Disney added animated documentaries to his repertoire with *New Spirit* (1942), which featured Donald Duck's misadventures filling out his income tax forms to help explain the federal tax system. It earned Disney his first Academy Award nomination in the Best Documentary category. Live-action documentaries were added with *Victory Through Air Power* (1943), nature documentaries with *Seal Island* (1948), and action films with *Treasure Island* (1950).

In 1954, Disney came to television with a weekly anthology series, originally called *Disneyland*, but best known as *The Wonderful World of Disney*. Disney himself hosted the show from 1954 until 1966. In the 1950s, Disney phased out the cartoon shorts and focused on the other film departments. But Mickey Mouse wasn't out of a job. In 1955, Disney opened his Disneyland theme park in Anaheim, California, a 160-acre fantasy-amusement park, with Mickey as the official host and ambassador. Disneyland, which has undergone numerous expansions over the years, remains one of the world's top tourist attractions. *The Mickey Mouse Club* also debuted on television in 1955, launching the acting careers of original Mouseketeers Annette Funicello, Paul Petersen, and Johnny Crawford. In recent years, Britney Spears, Christina Aguilera, and Keri Russell all wore the mouse ears as members of *The New Mickey Mouse Club* cast.

In addition to the Disney film studio, the growing Disney empire includes Walt Disney World, which opened in Florida in 1971; Tokyo Disneyland, which opened in 1983; and EuroDisney, which opened in France in 1992.

During his career, Disney received sixty-four individual Academy Award nominations and won twenty-six times—both all-time records. Most of Disney's nominations and awards were for cartoon shorts, but he also won four awards for Best Documentary. In 1941, Disney won the prestigious Irving G. Thalberg Memorial Award, which honors "creative producers whose bodies of work reflect a consistently high quality of motion picture production." Perhaps an even more amazing statistic is that from 1931 to 1962, Disney was nominated for at least one Academy Award every year but one—1940. The year after that incredible string of nominations finally ended, Disney won his first and only Best Picture award for *Mary Poppins* (1963).

The area in front of Disney's grave is often full of flowers and small plastic figurines of his most famous characters, Mickey Mouse and Donald Duck, left behind by visitors. Perhaps partially due to the fact that Disney's grave is hidden and difficult to find, rumors sprang up after his death that his body had been cryogenically frozen and hidden somewhere, perhaps even at Disneyland. Another fact that encouraged the rumors was that Disney's will didn't include any instructions or provisions for a funeral or burial. However, about a year after his death, Disney's estate made a payment of more than $40,000 to Forest Lawn for the burial space and memorial plaque.

Buried with Disney are his wife, Lillian Bounds Disney (1988–1997), and his son-in-law, Robert B. Brown. The plaque also includes the name of his daughter, Sharon M. Disney Brown Lund (1936–1993), with the notation "ashes scattered in paradise." The plaque contains space for a total of eight names. Disney's parents, Elias Disney (1859–1941) and Flora Disney (1868–1938), are buried in Forest Lawn's Great Mausoleum.

> Disney was born Walter Elias Disney on December 1, 1901, in Chicago, Illinois. He died December 15, 1966, in Los Angeles.

Walk out through the courtyard in front of the Freedom Mausoleum, past a large statue of a World War I soldier, and turn right into the Garden of Everlasting Peace, a small, walled courtyard. As soon as you enter through the gate, turn right. In the corner of the garden is a smaller private garden, with the name "Tracy" on the wall. This is the grave of the man often referred to as the "actor's actor," **Spencer Tracy (1900–1967).**

Tracy originally studied for the priesthood, but he quit school to join the U.S. Navy, serving in World War I. He returned home after the war, and while attending classes at Ripon College in Wisconsin he landed the lead role in a school play, *The Truth*. His experience in that play convinced him to pursue acting as a career. Tracy enrolled at the American Academy of Dramatic Arts in New York City and landed his first role on Broadway as a robot in *R.U.R.* Director John Ford saw Tracy on Broadway in *The Last Mile*, and brought him to Hollywood to star in *Up the River* (1930), a prison drama. Tracy appeared in a series of tough-guy roles in crime and prison films for the next few years, including *Quick Millions* (1931), *Young America* (1932), *Society Girl* (1932), *20,000 Years in Sing Sing* (1932), *The Mad Game* (1933), *Looking for Trouble* (1934), *Bottoms Up* (1934), *The Murder Man* (1935), *Whipsaw* (1935), and *Riffraff* (1935).

Perhaps using his seminary training, Tracy played a priest for the first time in *San Francisco* (1936), costarring Clark Gable and Jeanette MacDonald, and received the first of his nine Academy Award nominations as Best Actor. Tracy won the award the following year for his performance in *Captains Courageous* (1937)—though the Oscar statuette he received identified him as "Dick Tracy." The next year, Tracy put the priest's collar back on for *Boys Town* (1938) and won another Academy Award for his performance as Father Flanagan. Tracy was the first actor to win the award in consecutive years—a feat that would not be repeated until Tom Hanks won for *Philadelphia* (1992) and *Forrest Gump* (1993). Tracy was also nominated for *Father of the Bride* (1950), *Bad Day at Black Rock* (1955), *The Old Man and the Sea* (1958), *Inherit the Wind* (1960), *Judgment at Nuremberg* (1961), and *Guess Who's Coming to Dinner* (1967).

For decades, Tracy was a favorite among film fans, who admired his straightforward sincerity, self-effacing humor, and seemingly effortless acting style. Tracy said the only rules of acting were, "Come to work on time, know your lines, and don't bump into the other actors." Despite his apparent simplicity, other actors still point to Tracy as their model. Even Laurence Olivier said, "I've learned more about acting from watching Tracy than in any other way. He has great truth in everything he does."

Onscreen "truth" aside, Tracy is also known for a long-term "openly secret" relationship with actress Katharine Hepburn, which began when they met while making *Keeper of the Flame* (1942). At the time, however, Tracy was married to a former stage actress, Louise Treadwell. Both Tracy and his wife were devout Catholics and did not believe in divorce, so they remained married, even though Tracy continued his relationship with Hepburn for twenty-five years, until his death in 1967. Tracy and Hepburn appeared in nine films together, including *Woman of the Year* (1942), *Without Love* (1945), *The Sea of Grass* (1947), *State of the Union* (1948), *Adam's Rib* (1949), *Pat and Mike* (1952), *Desk Set* (1957), and *Guess Who's Coming to Dinner* (1967). Critics point to the onscreen relationship between Tracy and Hepburn as the first real representation of a strong, independent woman and a strong, independent man relating to each other as equals.

Like the actor, Tracy's grave marker is plain, direct, and to the point, without any unnecessary frills or embellishments. It says, simply, "Tracy."

Tracy was born Spencer Bonaventure Tracy on April 5, 1900, in Milwaukee, Wisconsin. He died June 10, 1967, in Los Angeles.

Along the northern wall of the garden, behind a large tree and in front of a small statue of a woman, is the grave of actor **Errol Flynn (1909–1959).**

Flynn's onscreen image of a wild, fun-loving, hard-drinking, woman-chasing rogue was more than just an image. Flynn was the son of a respected Australian biologist. He attended some of the finest schools in Australia and England and was expelled from most of them for his misbehavior. Flynn's adventurous spirit took him around the world in a variety of jobs before he was offered the role of Fletcher Christian in an Australian film, *In the Wake of the Bounty* (1933). Flynn returned to England, performed onstage, and next appeared onscreen in *Murder at Monte Carlo* (1934), which was produced by Warner Bros. London studio. Flynn was brought to Hollywood, where he played the title role in *Captain Blood* (1935), the first in a series of swash-buckling adventure films, including *The Charge of the Light Brigade* (1936), *The Adventures of Robin Hood* (1938), and *The Sea Hawk* (1940). Flynn also brought his action-packed, reckless style to Westerns and war films, including *Another Dawn* (1937), *The Dawn Patrol* (1938), *Dodge City* (1939), *Virginia City* (1940), *Sante Fe Trail* (1940), *Dive Bomber* (1941), *They Died With Their Boots On* (1941), and *Operation Burma!* (1945). Ironically, when Flynn attempted to enlist in the military during World War II, he was classified 4F and was turned down by every branch of the service due to a heart defect and previous cases of malaria and tuberculosis.

In the early 1940s, two teenage girls accused Flynn of statutory rape in separate incidents. After a highly publicized trial, Flynn was found not guilty, which led to the popular expression "in like Flynn." Rather than ending his career, the rape charges seemed to enhance Flynn's reputation, particularly when rumors began to surface that the charges may have been part of an extortion scheme against several movie executives. By the end of the decade, Flynn's years of hard living were taking a physical toll, and his best swash-buckling days were certainly behind him. He attempted more serious, dramatic roles in films including *Cry Wolf* (1947), *Silver River* (1948), and *That Forsyte Woman* (1949), but with little success.

In the early 1950s, Flynn spent several years in Europe, returning to Hollywood to play an aging alcoholic—perhaps a bit of real-life typecasting—in Hemingway's *The Sun Also Rises* (1957). He played similar roles in *Too Much Too Soon* (1958) and *The Roots of Heaven* (1958). With favorable reviews in those films, Flynn seemed to be building a new career when he died of a heart attack in Canada in 1959, in the arms of a teenage lover. Flynn's friends reportedly slipped six bottles of whiskey into his coffin before he was buried.

Flynn's grave marker contains the inscription "In memory of our father from his loving children."

Flynn was born Errol Leslie Thomson Flynn on June 20, 1909, in Hobart, Tasmania. He died October 14, 1959, in Vancouver, British Columbia, Canada.

At the far western end of the garden, next to the sidewalk and about twelve feet in front of a statue of a nude woman kneeling next to two doves, in Plot 5492, is the grave of the "Lone Ranger," actor **Clayton Moore (1914–1999).**

Moore started his career as a circus acrobat and aerialist and performed at the 1934 World's Fair in Chicago. Moore then went to New York City, where he worked as a model. In 1938, Moore headed to Hollywood, where he worked as an extra and a stuntman in films, primarily Westerns. In the early 1940s, Moore began to appear in larger roles in films, including *The Son of Monte Cristo* (1940), *Perils of Nyoka* (1942), *Black Dragons* (1942), *The Crimson Ghost* (1946), *Jesse James Rides Again* (1947), *Marshal of Amarillo* (1948), and *Sheriff of Wichita* (1949). In 1949, Moore donned the mask of *The Lone Ranger* in the long-running television series. His faithful Indian companion, Tonto, was played by Jay Silverheels. For three years, until 1952, Moore played the masked rider of the plains, upholding the law and decency with his apparently endless supply of silver bullets, the thunder of hoofbeats, and a hearty, "Hi Yo, Silver!" Moore was fired in a salary dispute in 1952 and John Hart played the ranger for the 1952–53 television season. Moore was brought back in 1954 and continued as the ranger until the series ended in 1957, after 169 episodes. Moore also played the role in two feature-length films—*The Lone Ranger* (1956) and *The Lone Ranger and the Lost City of Gold* (1958).

For the next twenty years, Moore made personal appearances as the Lone Ranger, urging a new generation of young fans to follow the "Lone Ranger Creed" of good behavior. In 1979, the Wrather Corp., which owned *The Lone Ranger* television series and the rights to the character, obtained a court order to stop Moore from appearing in public dressed as the Lone Ranger, specifically prohibiting him from wearing the character's signature mask. The Wrather Corp. intended to produce a new *Lone Ranger* film, and they didn't want fans to be confused. Instead, fans were incensed about the treatment of Moore and circulated petitions to allow him to wear the mask again. Moore continued to make appearances, however, wearing wraparound sunglasses instead. When Wrather's film, *The Legend of the Lone Ranger* (1981), starring Klinton

Spilsbury, was released, it was a huge critical and commercial failure. The Wrather Corp. gave in to public pressure in 1984 and allowed Moore to wear the mask again. When Moore died in 1999, the company arranged for the saddle Moore used as the Lone Ranger to be displayed at his memorial service.

Moore was so closely identified with the Lone Ranger that his star on the Hollywood Walk of Fame identifies him as "Clayton Moore—The Lone Ranger." It's the only star on the famous walk that includes both the name of a performer and a character.

Moore is buried next to his first wife, Sally Angela Moore (1912–1986).

Moore was born Jack Carlton Moore on September 14, 1914
(some sources say 1908), in Chicago, Illinois.
He died December 28, 1999, in Los Angeles.

Outside the Garden of Everlasting Peace, in the center of the Court of Freedom, is a twenty-by-thirty-foot mosaic of John Trumbull's painting *The Signing of the Declaration of Independence.* On both sides of the mosaic are gated and locked Gardens of Honor, open only to those possessing the Forest Lawn "Golden Key of Memory." Inside these gardens are the remains of actor and singer **Sammy Davis Jr. (1925–1990),** actors **Robert Taylor (1911–1969)** and **Dick Powell (1904–1963),** actress **Joan Blondell (1906–1979),** directors **Mervyn LeRoy (1900–1987)** and **George Cukor (1899–1983),** and producer **Samuel Goldwyn (1882–1974).**

At the western end of the Court of Freedom is an eighteen-foot-tall bronze and marble statue titled *The Republic,* by Daniel Chester French, the sculptor who created the statue of Abraham Lincoln in the Lincoln Memorial in Washington, D.C. To the left of the statue is a large plaque marking the grave of legendary baseball player, manager, and personality **Casey Stengel (1890–1975).**

In a baseball career that spanned six decades, Stengel was one of the most successful managers in the history of the game, setting records during his term as manager of the New York Yankees in the 1950s. But Stengel is equally famous for his colorful personality, offbeat antics, and a personal style of language that became known as "Stengelese."

Stengel made his major-league debut in 1912 as an outfielder with the Brooklyn Dodgers. His nickname was inspired by both his hometown—Kansas City, or "K.C."—and the popularity of the poem "Casey at the Bat." Stengel played for fourteen seasons for six different National League teams, retiring after the 1925 season with a career batting average of .284. During his playing career, Stengel was often among the league leaders in home runs, batting average, and several other categories. Stengel's first year as a manager was 1934, when he guided the Brooklyn Dodgers to a sixth-place finish. During his first nine years as a manager, Stengel's teams never finished higher than fifth place. But in 1949, Stengel was hired to manage the New York Yankees, and he immediately guided them to an incredible five consecutive World Series championships. Stengel managed the Yankees until 1960 and, in twelve seasons under Stengel, the Yankees won the World Series seven times, won the American League pennant three times, finished second once, and finished third once.

In 1962, Stengel was hired to manage the expansion New York Mets in their first season, and the team set a record by losing 120 games. Stengel managed the Mets for four seasons, but the team never won more than 53 games in a season, and never finished higher than tenth place. Stengel retired after the 1965 season. Even including the lowly Mets, the teams that Stengel managed won 1,905 games while losing 1,842, for a .508 winning percentage. Stengel was elected to the Baseball Hall of Fame in 1966.

The plaque next to Stengel's grave features his image and one of his famous quotes: "There comes a time in every man's life, and I've had plenty of them." Stengel is buried next to his wife, Edna M. Lawson Stengel (1894–1978). They were married on August 18, 1924.

Stengel was born Charles Dillon Stengel on July 30, 1890, in Kansas City, Missouri. He died September 29, 1975, in Glendale, California.

Between Stengel's plaque and the road, in the second row from the curb, in Plot 7065, is the grave of song-and-dance man **Dan Dailey (1915–1978)**.

Dailey started his show business career performing as a child in minstrel shows. After working an assortment of jobs, he ended up on Broadway in 1937, playing a small part in *Babes in Arms*. After playing the lead role in *Stars in Your Eyes* in 1939, he was brought to Hollywood and made his film debut in *The Mortal Storm* (1940). Dailey was building an impressive career as a supporting actor when he entered the military during World War II, and he was absent from the screen from 1942 to 1947. When he returned from the service, he became a leading actor, most often in show business biographies and musicals, including *Mother Wore Tights* (1947), *You Were Meant for Me* (1948),

When My Baby Smiles at Me (1948), *My Blue Heaven* (1950), *There's No Business Like Show Business* (1954), *It's Always Fair Weather* (1955), and *The Best Things in Life Are Free* (1956). Dailey also portrayed baseball pitcher Jerome "Dizzy" Dean in *The Pride of St. Louis* (1952). From the late 1950s on, Dailey appeared primarily onstage or on television, appearing in the series *The Four Just Men* in 1959, *The Governor and J. J.* from 1969 to 1970, and *Faraday and Company* from 1973 to 1974.

Dailey was nominated for an Academy Award as Best Actor for his performance in *When My Baby Smiles at Me*. In 1970, he won a Golden Globe Award as Best Television Actor in a Musical or Comedy for his performance in *The Governor and J. J.*

Dailey's grave marker includes the epitaph "Beloved by many."

Dailey was born Daniel James Dailey Jr. on December 14, 1915 (some sources say 1913 or 1914), in New York City. He died October 16, 1978, in Los Angeles.

Across the street from the Freedom Mausoleum is the small Dedication Section. About ten feet northeast of a tall tree in the center of the Dedication Section, in Plot 4404, you'll find the grave of **Joe Besser (1907–1988)**, who spent two years as one of the Three Stooges.

Besser began his performing career as a comedian in vaudeville and on Broadway. He made his film debut in a two-reel comedy short titled *Cuckoorancho* (1938). He appeared in supporting roles in several comedies, musicals, and dramas in the 1940s and early 1950s, including *Africa Screams* (1949), with Bud Abbott and Lou Costello. Besser also starred in several comedy shorts in the early 1950s produced at Columbia—the same studio that produced the Three Stooges shorts, and often with the same directors and costars who appeared with the Stooges. In 1952, Besser joined the cast of *The Abbott and Costello Show* on television as Stinky Jones. Besser was also a frequent guest on the Jack Benny, Fred Allen, Eddie Cantor, and Milton Berle radio shows.

Besser joined the Three Stooges in 1956, after Shemp Howard died. Besser appeared in sixteen films as one of the Stooges, from 1956 to 1958. Although the Stooges were known for their slapstick, almost violent type of comedy, Besser joined the group only after being assured that he would not be the target of any physical abuse. Besser's signature phrases with the Stooges were "Oooh, you crazy!" and "Not so hard!" which he uttered whenever he was lightly tapped by fellow Stooges Moe Howard or Larry Fine. When Besser left the group in 1958, reportedly to be with his ailing wife, he was replaced by Joe DeRita, who was known as Curly-Joe.

Some critics claim that Besser, with his impish grin and childlike, delicate manner, wasn't a good match for the Stooges. But Besser was a popular and successful comedian before and after his time with the group. When his Stooge days were over, Besser joined the cast of *The Joey Bishop Show* in 1962, playing Mr. Jillson, the apartment building superintendent, until the show was canceled in 1965. Besser also appeared in supporting roles in dozens of films and television series through the early 1970s.

Besser's grave marker reads, "He brought the world love and laughter." He is buried next to his wife, Ernestine Besser (1900–1989).

Besser was born August 12, 1907, in St. Louis, Missouri. He died March 1, 1988, in Los Angeles.

Tour 3: The Great Mausoleum

Head back toward the main entrance of the cemetery and look for the Great Mausoleum, a massive, Gothic building made of gray stone near the center of the cemetery property. At the southern edge of the Great Mausoleum, near the parking area, is a statue of a young boy riding a goat down a steep slope while waving a dead bird over his head. The statue marks the grave of Danish-born actor **Jean Hersholt (1886–1956).**

Though most people only recognize Hersholt for the Humanitarian Award that is presented in his honor each year at the Academy Awards, he was also a popular actor who appeared in more than one hundred films. Hersholt's parents, Henry and Claire Hersholt, were both popular Danish actors. Hersholt appeared in stage plays throughout Scandinavia before coming to the United States in 1914, and making his film debut in a small role in *The Disciple* (1915), a Western starring William S. Hart.

Hersholt appeared in scores of films during the next fifteen years, usually in supporting roles. Because of his Scandinavian accent, Hersholt's opportunities became more limited with sound films, but he continued to appear in character roles, typically playing the kindly country doctor. Among his best-known films, Hersholt appeared in *Greed* (1925), *The Student Prince in Old Heidelberg* (1927), *The Sin of Madelon Claudet* (1931), *Private Lives* (1931),

The Beast of the City (1932), *Emma* (1932), *Grand Hotel* (1932), *Dinner at Eight* (1933), *The Country Doctor* (1936), *Seventh Heaven* (1937), *Heidi* (1937), in which he played Shirley Temple's grandfather, and *Alexander's Ragtime Band* (1938). Hersholt also portrayed Dr. Paul Christian in a long-running radio series and six films in the early 1940s.

Offscreen, Hersholt was one of the founders of the Motion Picture Relief Fund, and he served as president of the Academy of Motion Picture Arts and Sciences. Hersholt also helped create the Motion Picture and Television Country House and Hospital. He was also known for translating the works of Hans Christian Andersen, and the statue above his grave is inspired by one of Andersen's fairy tales.

After Hersholt's death, the Academy of Motion Picture Arts and Sciences instituted the Jean Hersholt Humanitarian Award in 1956, which is presented to members of the film industry to recognize outstanding humanitarian achievements. Winners have included Bob Hope, Gregory Peck, Martha Raye, George Jessel, Frank Sinatra, Danny Kaye, Audrey Hepburn, Elizabeth Taylor, Paul Newman, and Quincy Jones.

Hersholt is buried with his wife, Via Anderson Hersholt (1892–1983), whom he married in 1914, and their son, Allan E. Hersholt (1914–1990). Hersholt's nephew is actor Leslie Nielsen.

Hersholt was born July 12, 1886, in Copenhagen, Denmark. He died June 2, 1956, in Los Angeles.

The doors to the Great Mausoleum are all locked, and visitors must ring a buzzer and tell an employee who they are visiting. Visitors aren't allowed to just wander through the massive building. Though I would never recommend such a thing, a devious person might find a door in the Great Mausoleum with glass panels, peek in, and find a name on one of the crypts. Then they could go to a door on the other side of the Great Mausoleum, ring the buzzer, and tell the employee they want to visit their dear, departed Aunt Edna or Uncle Harry, or whatever name they saw. But, again, that would be a devious and deceitful thing to do, and I would never recommend it. And always remember that you're on private property, not a public park. If you're caught trespassing in forbidden areas or breaking any of the other many cemetery rules, you could be asked to leave, or even arrested. Forest Lawn employees are known for having absolutely no sense of humor when it comes to things like that.

Although the majority of the Great Mausoleum is off-limits to the general public, visitors are allowed in the Memorial Terrace entrance to see the Last Supper stained-glass window. Although most of the corridors and hallways in the area around the window are roped off, and security guards and closed-circuit video cameras help to make sure visitors don't "accidentally" wander off into the wrong areas, there are several notable crypts you can see in the Last Supper window area.

As you enter the Great Mausoleum—after being warned against taking photographs or going into any roped-off areas—you'll walk down a long hallway. When you reach the main area of that section of the Mausoleum, you'll see about 150 chairs set up on your left, in the Memorial Court of Honor, facing the Last Supper window. Instead of heading toward the chairs, however, turn right. The first corridor on your right, behind a low gate, is the Sanctuary of Benediction. Although you can't go past the gate, you can look down the corridor. The first alcove on the left side of the corridor, with the name "Skelton" over the entryway, contains the remains of comedian **Red Skelton (1913–1997).**

Though best remembered as the host of comedy and variety television series that ran for twenty years, from 1951 to 1971, Skelton's entertainment career spanned more than seventy years and included radio, film, television, and stage performances. In later years, Skelton was a popular artist, specializing in oil paintings of clowns.

Skelton was the son of a former circus clown and a cleaning woman, and grew up in dire poverty in Indiana. By the age of seven, Skelton was singing in the streets for pennies to help support his family. Two years later, when Skelton saw comedian Ed Wynn at a vaudeville show, he decided to become an entertainer, and he left home to join a traveling medicine show. Skelton performed throughout the Midwest, eventually working as a clown in the Haggen and Wallenbach Circus—the same circus where his father once worked. In 1937, Skelton first performed his famous "donut dunking" routine, which was his interpretation of the ways different types of people dunked donuts. With the success of that routine, Skelton began performing at larger theaters throughout the United States with his act that featured pantomime and a wide variety of characters.

Skelton made his film debut in *Having Wonderful Time* (1938), starring Ginger Rogers, Douglas Fairbanks Jr., and Lucille Ball. Skelton's first starring role was in *Whistling in the Dark* (1940), in which he played a radio crime-show host who becomes involved in a real-life crime. He also starred in two sequels to that film—*Whistling in Dixie* (1942) and *Whistling in Brooklyn*

(1943). Skelton starred in a series of popular comedies in the 1940s, including *Panama Hattie* (1942), *I Dood It* (1943), *Du Barry Was a Lady* (1943), *The Show-Off* (1946), *Merton of the Movies* (1947), *The Fuller Brush Man* (1948), *A Southern Yankee* (1948), *The Yellow Cab Man* (1950), *Three Little Words* (1950), and *Watch the Birdie* (1951).

In 1951, *The Red Skelton Show* premiered on NBC as a comedy and variety show, usually showcasing Skelton and his many characters, including Clem Kadiddlehopper, Freddie the Freeloader, Willie Lump Lump, Sheriff Dead-Eye, Bolivar Shagnasty, San Fernando Red, Cauliflower McPugg, Junior the Mean Widdle Kid, and the seagulls Gertrude and Heathcliffe. In 1952, Skelton won an Emmy Award as Best Comedian and *The Red Skelton Show* won an Emmy as Best Comedy Show. Skelton's show eventually moved to CBS and remained popular throughout its entire twenty-year run.

After his television show ended in 1971, Skelton continued to tour the country in live performances, and he was an active supporter of various children's charities.

Skelton was born Richard Bernard Skelton on July 18, 1913 (some sources say 1910), in Vincennes, Indiana. He died September 17, 1997, in Rancho Mirage, California.

In the alcove next to Skelton, with the name "Grauman" over the entryway, are the remains of legendary Hollywood theater owner **Sid Grauman (1879–1950).**

Grauman went to Alaska with his father in 1898 to search for gold. They didn't find any gold, but Grauman found a career when he opened a successful movie theater in the Yukon. He moved to San Francisco a few years later, and by 1915 he owned several theaters in northern California and one in New York. In the early 1920s, he opened four theaters in Los Angeles—the Million Dollar, the Rialto, the Metropolitan, and the Egyptian. In May 1927, Grauman opened his most famous theater, the Chinese, on Hollywood Boulevard. In addition to being a businessman, Grauman was also a showman in the P. T. Barnum mold. Grauman's theaters were all lavish and impressive movie palaces, usually decorated around a specific theme. Grauman is also credited with being the first to place huge searchlights in front of his theaters to attract attention during film premieres.

Grauman's Chinese Theater, which is still one of the most popular tourist attractions in Hollywood, is best known for its collection of celebrity handprints and footprints. There are several versions of the story of how Grauman started to feature the imprints in the concrete in front of his theater. The most popular is that actress Norma Talmadge accidentally stepped in wet cement during construction of the theater, and Grauman decided to display her footprint in front of the theater. The concrete slabs include imprints from nearly two hundred of the biggest names in the film industry, and ceremonies are still held when new celebrities are immortalized in stone. In addition to hands and feet, some celebrities have left imprints of more famous body parts or props, including Jimmy Durante's nose, Betty Grable's leg, John Barrymore's profile, and George Burns's cigar. More than two million visitors walk among the concrete slabs every year.

The theater was owned by several corporations until 1973, when it was purchased by Ted Mann and renamed "Mann's Chinese Theater." In 2000, the Mann Theaters chain went bankrupt, and the Chinese Theater is currently owned by the Paramount and Warner Bros. studios.

Grauman appeared as himself in small roles in several films, including *Hollywood* (1923), *Mad About Music* (1938), *Star Dust* (1940), and *Dancing in the Dark* (1949). Grauman was also one of the thirty-six founders of the Academy of Motion Picture Arts and Sciences.

Grauman was born Sidney Patrick Grauman on March 17, 1879, in Indianapolis, Indiana. He died March 5, 1950, in Los Angeles.

Almost at the end of the Sanctuary of Benediction, in the last alcove visible on the left side, are the remains of the first "Blonde Bombshell," actress **Jean Harlow (1911–1937).**

Harlow was the daughter of a successful dentist in Kansas City, Missouri. At the age of sixteen she eloped with a businessman and moved to Los Angeles, where she worked as an extra, making her film debut in *Why Is a Plumber?* (1927). Harlow appeared in small roles in several films over the next few years, including three Laurel and Hardy comedies in 1929—*Liberty, Double Whoopee,* and *Bacon Grabbers.* Harlow's photograph was used in two more films starring the comedy team, once in the role of their mother in *Brats* (1930), and again as Oliver Hardy's girlfriend, Jeanie-Weenie, in *Beau Hunks* (1931). Harlow also had a small role in Charlie Chaplin's *City Lights* (1931).

Harlow's big break came when Howard Hughes cast her in his World War I aviation epic, *Hell's Angels* (1930). Hughes began the film in 1927 as a silent film, with a Swedish actress starring as the woman who comes between two brothers. But, with sound films becoming more popular, *Hell's Angels* became a talkie, and Hughes had to find an English-speaking actress to play the role. With her sultry and steamy performance, Harlow became a star. Harlow next appeared in *Platinum Blonde* (1931) and costarred with James Cagney in *The Public Enemy* (1931), with Spencer Tracy in *Goldie* (1931), and with Clark Gable in *Red Dust* (1932).

Harlow brought a sense of sexual energy to the screen that was magnified when film magazines and publicists began to report some of the more interesting and racy details of her personal life—she posed for nude photographs shot in Griffith Park, she never wore underwear, she always slept in the nude, she rubbed ice on her breasts before shooting a scene, she bleached her pubic hair, and she wrote a novel that was so sexually explicit that MGM studio executives destroyed every copy before it could be published.

Harlow also made headlines in 1932 when she married Paul Bern, a screenwriter, producer, director, and assistant to Irving Thalberg at MGM studios. Two months after the forty-two-year-old, bookish Bern married the twenty-one-year-old Harlow, he was found dead in their Beverly Hills home. After a lengthy investigation, Bern's death was ruled a suicide. (For more on Bern, see Chapter 14.) A year after Bern's death, Harlow married cinematographer Harold Rosson, who was sixteen years her senior. They were divorced two years later, when Harlow accused Rosson of "mental cruelty" for reading in bed and depriving her of sleep.

Harlow may have reached her onscreen sexual pinnacle in *The Red-Headed Woman* (1932), as a girl from the wrong side of the tracks who uses her physical charms to get what she wants from her married boss, a millionaire businessman, and just about any other man she encounters. When the film was banned in England, it only served to make Harlow more popular. But in the early 1930s, with the newly instituted Motion Picture Production Code enforcing strict rules of conduct and behavior in films, Harlow had to tone down her act. She switched to more elegant and sophisticated dramas, and also displayed her impressive comedic talents in films such as *Dinner at Eight* (1933), *Bombshell* (1933), *China Seas* (1935), *Wife vs. Secretary* (1936), *Libeled Lady* (1936), and *Riffraff* (1936).

While making *Saratoga* (1937), her sixth film with Gable, Harlow collapsed on the set and was sent home to rest. It turned out, however, that she was suffering from several severe medical problems, including an inflamed gallbladder, failing kidneys, and a bladder infection. Her kidney problems may have been the result of scarlet fever, which she contracted as a teenager. She died June 7, 1937, at age twenty-six, of cerebral edema and uremic poisoning, which is caused by a buildup of waste products in the blood. After Harlow's sudden death in the prime of her career, rumors began to spread about the cause. Some of the most often repeated stories were that Harlow's mother's religious beliefs kept her from calling a doctor, Harlow was poisoned from toxic chemicals in her hair dye, or that she was injured during a botched abortion.

Harlow's funeral, held two days after her death in the Wee Kirk O' the Heather chapel at Forest Lawn, was the biggest, most spectacular funeral service Hollywood had ever seen. More than 250 invited guests crowded into the small chapel, including Gable, Tracy, Carole Lombard, Norma Shearer, William Powell, Lionel Barrymore, and the Marx Brothers. An estimated $15,000 worth of floral tributes surrounded Harlow's coffin, and MGM studio security guards assisted cemetery staff, Glendale police, and state police in keeping fans outside the cemetery gates. The brief funeral services started with Jeanette MacDonald singing "Indian Love Call," one of Harlow's favorite songs, and ended with Nelson Eddy singing "Ah, Sweet Mystery of Life."

At the time of her death, Harlow was engaged to Powell, who was at her bedside when she died. Powell purchased the alcove where Harlow's body is buried for a reported $30,000, with three available burial spaces. The alcove also contains the body of Harlow's mother, Jean Harlow Carpenter Bello (1889–1958), in an unmarked crypt. The third space is unoccupied.

Like many celebrities who die young, Harlow has remained frozen in time and enduring in popularity. Her life story has been told in several films, including two made in 1965, both titled *Harlow,* one starring Carol Lynley and the other starring Carol Baker. Lindsay Bloom, a former Miss USA, played Harlow in *Hughes and Harlow: Angels in Hell* (1977). Marilyn Monroe was considering the lead in *The Jean Harlow Story* when she died in 1962. And Harlow was also reportedly the model for the character of Catwoman in the Batman comic books.

Harlow's crypt is inscribed with the words "Our Baby."

Harlow was born Harlean Carpenter on March 3, 1911, in Kansas City, Missouri. She died June 7, 1937, in Los Angeles.

Beyond Harlow's alcove, along the back wall of the Sanctuary of Benediction, to the left of the stained-glass window, is the crypt containing the remains of producer **Irving Thalberg (1899–1936).** (Thalberg's crypt is not visible from behind the gate.)

Thalberg was a sickly child. He was born with a heart condition and plagued with an assortment of ailments throughout his life. He was an extremely intelligent and studious child, but when doctors told him he would probably not live to see thirty, he decided to skip college and went to work for a family friend, Carl Laemmle, founder of Universal Pictures.

Thalberg was Laemmle's personal secretary and later became the twenty-year-old head of production at the studio, where his success earned him the nickname "The Boy Wonder." But the relationship between Laemmle and Thalberg soured, reportedly when Thalberg rejected a suggestion that he marry Laemmle's daughter, Rosabelle. Laemmle was known for hiring relatives, and perhaps he just wanted to make Thalberg part of his family. (For more on Laemmle, see Chapter 10.)

In 1923, Thalberg went to work for Louis B. Mayer as his vice president and head of production. The following year, Mayer's studio merged with Metro Pictures Corp. and the Goldwyn Company to form Metro-Goldwyn-Mayer, with Thalberg as vice president and chief of production for the huge entertainment company. Mayer and Thalberg built a film empire at MGM, beginning with their first epic production, *Ben-Hur* (1925), starring Ramon Novarro and Francis X. Bushman and filmed partially on location in Italy.

Thalberg was known for his ability to get the best performances out of temperamental directors and performers and for his meticulous attention to detail and quality. As Thalberg began to get more credit for the success of MGM productions, Mayer began to resent his production chief, and the two often clashed. Thalberg even threatened to leave MGM several times. Thalberg, however, avoided accepting any honors for the films he produced, and his name never appeared in the film credits. "Credit you give yourself is not worth having," he said.

During his tenure at MGM, Thalberg supervised the production of *The Unholy Three* (1930), *Mata Hari* (1931), *Rasputin and the Empress* (1932), *Grand Hotel* (1932), *Tarzan the Ape Man* (1932), *The Barretts of Wimpole Street* (1934), *The Merry Widow* (1934), *Mutiny on the Bounty* (1935), *A Night at the Opera* (1935), *A Day at the Races* (1937), and *The Good Earth* (1937), among many others.

During a Christmas party in 1932, Thalberg suffered a severe heart attack. He took an extended vacation in Europe to recuperate. When he returned, he discovered that most of his authority and influence at MGM had been taken away. He died of pneumonia in 1936, a few months after his thirty-seventh birthday. The following year, the Academy of Motion Picture Arts and Sciences instituted the Irving G. Thalberg Memorial Award, which is presented each year at the Academy Award ceremonies and honors "creative producers whose bodies of work reflect a consistently high quality of motion picture production." The award is a bronze sculpture of Thalberg's head, on a black marble base. The award has been won by Darryl F. Zanuck, David O. Selznick, Walt Disney, Samuel Goldwyn, Cecil B. De Mille, George Stevens, Jack Warner, Stanley Kramer, William Wyler, Alfred Hitchcock, Ingmar Bergman, Steven Spielberg, George Lucas, and Clint Eastwood, among others.

Thalberg is generally thought to be the inspiration for the studio executive in F. Scott Fitzgerald's novel *The Last Tycoon*. Thalberg was also one of the thirty-six founders of the Academy of Motion Picture Arts and Sciences.

Thalberg's crypt contains the inscription "My Sweetheart Forever."

> *Thalberg was born Irving Grant Thalberg on May 30, 1899, in Brooklyn, New York. He died September 14, 1936, in Santa Monica, California.*

Buried with Thalberg is his wife, actress **Norma Shearer (1900–1983).**

Shearer's mother brought her to New York City in 1920, with hopes of getting her work on Broadway in the Ziegfeld Follies. But Florenz Ziegfeld turned her down and Shearer found work as a model and playing bit parts in films. Producer Irving Thalberg was impressed by her performance in *The Stealers* (1920), and he brought her to Hollywood and signed her to a contract at MGM studios in 1923.

Shearer and Thalberg were married in 1927, and having a husband who was chief of production at the studio certainly didn't hurt Shearer's career. She was, however, a talented actress in her own right, and she was nominated six times for the Academy Award as Best Actress, for *Their Own Desire* (1929), *The Divorcee* (1930), *A Free Soul* (1931), *The Barretts of Wimpole Street* (1934), *Romeo and Juliet* (1936), and *Marie Antoinette* (1938). She won the award for her performance in *The Divorcee*. Shearer relied heavily on Thalberg's advice and assistance, and she appeared in a variety of films, from comedy to drama, while he was at MGM.

After Thalberg died in 1936, Shearer made some questionable career decisions, including turning down the role of Scarlett O'Hara in *Gone With the Wind* (1939) and the title role in *Mrs. Miniver* (1942). Those roles were played by Vivien Leigh and Greer Garson, respectively, and both won Academy Awards for their performances. Instead, Shearer appeared in less-memorable films, including *Idiot's Delight* (1939), *Escape* (1940), *We Were Dancing* (1942), and *Her Cardboard Lover* (1942), which was her final screen appearance.

Shearer married ski instructor Martin Arrouge in 1942. The name on the front of her crypt identifies her as Norma Arrouge.

> *Shearer was born Edith Norma Shearer on August 10, 1902*
> *(some sources say 1900), in Montreal, Quebec, Canada. She died*
> *June 12, 1983, in Woodland Hills, California.*

On the right side of the Sanctuary of Benediction, in about the center of the hallway, the third space up from the floor, is the crypt containing the remains of actress **Marie Dressler (1871–1934).**

Dressler was an unlikely star—stocky and homely, with a wide face. But, in the early 1930s, when Jean Harlow, Joan Crawford, Greta Garbo, and Mae West were the glamour queens of the screen, Dressler was the top box-office attraction for four years in a row. Dressler was equally adept at comedic or tragic roles, and she could easily bring a laugh to the audience one minute, and a tear the next.

At fourteen, Dressler, the daughter of a music teacher, joined a theater company. She was an established stage star by the time she was twenty, appearing on Broadway and throughout the vaudeville circuit in light opera, dramas, and comedies. She starred in *Tillie's Nightmare,* which was adapted for film by Mack Sennett and re-titled *Tillie's Punctured Romance* (1914). Starring Dressler with Charlie Chaplin, Mabel Normand, and Mack Swain, it was the first full-length comedy feature film. Dressler starred in two more films in the *Tillie* series, and several other silent comedies.

Dressler's active role in a labor dispute in 1917 left her blacklisted from films for ten years. She returned with a small part in *The Joy Girl* (1927), and she worked steadily after that, appearing primarily in comedies, usually in supporting roles. Dressler costarred with Garbo and Charles Bickford in *Anna Christie* (1930), and with Wallace Beery in perhaps her best-known performance, *Min and Bill* (1930). It was for the latter that Dressler won the Academy Award as Best Actress for her role as the owner of a dockside dive who battles with her fishing boat captain boyfriend and tries to protect a young girl from her alcoholic mother. Dressler received another Best Actress nomination for her role in *Emma* (1932). Dressler and Beery were teamed again in *Tugboat Annie* (1933). Dressler's final screen appearance was in the star-studded *Dinner at Eight* (1933). The film ends with a memorable exchange between Jean Harlow and Dressler, in which Harlow says she's just read a book that predicts "machinery is going to take the place of every profession." Dressler looks Harlow up and down and responds, "Oh, my dear, that's something you need never worry about."

Dressler was born Leila Marie Koerber on November 9, 1871
(some sources say 1868 or 1869), in Cobourg, Ontario, Canada.
She died July 28, 1934, in Santa Barbara, California.

Continue past the Sanctuary of Benediction, away from the Last Supper window. Just past a stairway (which is roped off), on the right side, you'll find the Columbarium of Memory, which contains a large number of cremated remains and is also roped off to prevent entry.

The Columbarium of Memory contains the remains of silent-film actress **Theda Bara (1890–1955)**, actor **Jack Carson (1910–1963)**, composer **Dimitri Tiomkin (1899–1979)**, director **James Whale (1893–1957),** and two of the three Andrews Sisters—**La Verne (1916–1967)** and **Maxene (1916–1995).**

As you walk back up toward the Last Supper window, on the right side, you'll see a corridor labeled Columbarium of Prayer, with a warning sign stating that this is a "Restricted Area, Property Owners Only." Just past that sign, on the left, is the Sanctuary of Trust. A few feet farther down that hallway are the crypts containing the remains of actor **Clark Gable (1901–1960)**, with his third wife, actress **Carole Lombard (1908–1942)**, on one side of him, and his fifth wife, Kathleen "Kay" Gable (1916–1983), on the other side. Buried next to Lombard is her mother, Elizabeth K. Peters (1876–1942), who was killed in the same plane crash that claimed the life of her daughter. At the far end of the Sanctuary of Trust, to the left of a stained-glass window, is an alcove containing the crypt of producer **David O. Selznick (1902–1965).**

Back in the main Memorial Court of Honor, continue walking toward the Last Supper window. Just before you reach the window, on your right, you'll see a large alcove containing the crypt of **Hubert Eaton (1881–1966)**, the "Builder" who made Forest Lawn an internationally known cemetery and a model for cemeteries around the world. Buried with Eaton are his wife, Anna Munger Eaton (1885–1960); his father, James Rodolphus Eaton (1834–1897); his mother, Martha Elizabeth Eaton (1843–1926); his sister, Mable Eaton Llewellyn (1887–1975); Mable's daughter, Elizabeth Llewellyn (1914–1998);

Eaton's cousin, Joseph H. Eaton (1873–1942); and Joseph's son, Bourne Goodridge Eaton (1909–1957).

In the event that you just happen to be inside any other part of the Great Mausoleum, beyond the ropes, the gates, and the signs, paying your respects to a legitimate loved one, and you have the opportunity to wander around the place, here are the locations of some other popular residents:

In the Hall of Inspiration, Columbarium of Nativity, comedian **W. C. Fields (1880–1946)**. Despite Fields's oft-repeated comment that he wanted his grave marker to read, "On the whole, I'd rather be in Philadelphia," his crypt contains only his name and the dates of his birth and death.

In the Begonia Corridor, silent-film comedians **Harold Lloyd (1893–1971)** and **Ben Turpin (1869–1940)**.

In the Columbarium of the Dawn, comedian **Ed Wynn (1886–1966)** and his son, actor **Keenan Wynn (1916–1986)**. Ed Wynn's crypt contains the inscription "Dear God: Thanks," followed by his signature.

In the Sanctuary of Sacred Promise, actor **William "Hopalong Cassidy" Boyd (1895–1972)**.

In the Columbarium of Sanctuary, actor **Robert Cummings (1910–1990)**.

Tour 4: The *Wizard of Oz* Tour

Although none of the four main stars of the 1939 film—Judy Garland, Ray Bolger, Jack Haley, and Bert Lahr—are buried here, there are enough people with ties to either the film or the stars to make for an interesting *Oz* tour. Judy Garland is buried in Ferncliff Cemetery in Hartsdale, New York, but her father, mother, and second husband, director Vincente Minnelli, are all buried in Forest Lawn–Glendale.

The *Oz* tour starts just inside the main gates of the cemetery on Glendale Avenue. Turn right just past the main cemetery offices—a large English Tudor–style building that houses the cemetery offices, mortuary, and flower shop. When you get past the buildings on your right, you're in one of the oldest sections of Forest Lawn–Glendale. Turn left at the first road, between Section B and Section D. Follow the road as it curves to the right, with Section B on your right, until you see Section G on your left. Just off the road in the middle of Section G is a large gravestone with the name "Baum" on it. This is the final resting place of the man who wrote the *Oz* books, **L. Frank Baum (1856–1919),** and his wife, Maud Gage Baum (1861–1953). Ten other members of the Baum family are also buried around this monument.

Baum attempted several businesses in his life, including publisher, newspaper editor, and storeowner, but he was most successful as a dreamer and a writer. Although best remembered for the fourteen books he wrote about the wonderful world of Oz, Baum also wrote many other books for children and adults under a series of pen names, including Floyd Akers, Laura Bancroft, John Estes Cooke, Captain Hugh Fitzgerald, Suzanne Metcalf, Shuyler Staunton, and Edith Van Dyne.

Baum was born Lyman Frank Baum on May 15, 1856, in Chittenango, New York. He died May 6, 1919, in Los Angeles.

Turn left on the first road past Section G and head east, toward the Great Mausoleum. Continue past the mausoleum, until Section M is on your right, and the Acacia Section is on your left. Stop just past the Acacia Garden. In Section M, about 250 feet from the eastern edge of the cemetery, about 50 feet off the road, in the eighth row, Plot 508, you'll find the grave of **Frank A. Gumm (1886–1935)**, Judy Garland's father.

Frank Gumm and his wife, Ethel, were former vaudeville performers who bought a theater and settled in Grand Rapids, South Dakota. They had three daughters—Mary Jane, born in 1915 and nicknamed Susie; Dorothy Virginia, born in 1917 and nicknamed Jimmie; and Frances Ethel, born in 1922 and nicknamed Baby. The three girls, known as the Gumm Sisters, performed a song-and-dance act at various theaters and social functions in Grand Rapids. In 1926, the Gumm family moved to Lancaster, California, where Frank bought the local theater. The girls took dancing and acting lessons, and Ethel Gumm worked as the girls' agent and manager. Within a few years, the Gumm Sisters were popular performers on local radio shows in the Los Angeles area. In 1934, Ethel took her daughters to Chicago to perform at the World's Fair. While in Chicago, they appeared at the Oriental Theatre with headliner George Jessel. Jessel heard laughter in the audience when he introduced the Gumm Sisters, so he suggested that the girls change their name to the Garland Sisters. The youngest Gumm sister, now twelve years old, decided it was time to drop her "Baby" nickname, and took the name Judy Garland.

In 1935, Susie married and Jimmie decided she no longer wanted to perform, which broke up the Garland Sisters act. Ethel pushed Judy toward a movie career, arranging auditions for her at nearly every studio in Hollywood. In September 1935, Judy Garland was signed by MGM studios, with a starting salary of $100 per week and a seven-year option. Two months after Judy signed her contract, Frank Gumm died of a massive cerebral hemorrhage on November 17, 1935—Ethel's thirty-ninth birthday. Four years later, on the anniversary of his death, Ethel Gumm married Will Gilmore, and daughter Judy was shocked that her mother selected that day to re-marry. Ethel and Will Gilmore were divorced less than four years later.

On the other side of the road, about three hundred feet directly behind the Acacia Garden and about fifty feet behind the Lullabyland statue, in Plot 5146, is the grave of **Ethel M. Gilmore (1896–1953),** Judy Garland's mother.

Turn around and head back on the same route, stopping at the Great Mausoleum. Access to the mausoleum is limited to friends and family members visiting a specific loved one. But, in the event that you somehow find yourself inside, in the Columbarium of Security, Niche 17230, you'll find the remains of **Clara Blandick (1881–1962),** who played Dorothy's "Auntie Em" Gale. She worked for only a week on *The Wizard of Oz* and was paid $750.

Blandick was a character actress who appeared in more than 115 films from 1914 to 1950, usually playing a sensible servant or a no-nonsense aunt, including *Gentleman Jim* (1942), with Errol Flynn; *Heaven Can Wait* (1943), with Don Ameche and Gene Tierney; and *Life With Father* (1947), with William Powell, Irene Dunne, and Elizabeth Taylor. Blandick also played Aunt Polly in the 1930 version of *Tom Sawyer*, with Jackie Coogan in the title role, and she appeared in *The Adventures of Huckleberry Finn* (1939) with Mickey Rooney.

In 1962, the eighty-year-old Blandick had been in poor health for several years, suffering from severe arthritis and failing vision. After attending church on Palm Sunday, April 15, 1962, she returned home, dressed up in her best outfit, and surrounded herself with favorite photos and memorabilia. She then took an overdose of sleeping pills and pulled a plastic bag over her head.

Blandick was born June 4, 1881, on an American ship sailing near Hong Kong. She died April 15, 1962, in Los Angeles.

Also in the Great Mausoleum, in the Columbarium of Inspiration, Niche 14639, are the remains of **Charles Grapewin (1869–1956),** who played Dorothy's uncle Henry Gale.

Like Blandick, Grapewin was a veteran actor who appeared in nearly one hundred films from 1900 to 1951, typically playing the grizzled old gentleman in Westerns and murder mysteries. Grapewin appeared in *Torch Singer* (1933), with Claudette Colbert; *The Petrified Forest* (1936), with Humphrey Bogart and

Bette Davis; and *Captains Courageous* (1937), with Spencer Tracy and Freddie Bartholomew. He also played Grandpa Joad in *The Grapes of Wrath* (1940), with Henry Fonda, and he was Inspector Queen in seven installments of the *Ellery Queen* mystery series in the early 1940s.

Like Blandick, Grapewin worked for only a week on *The Wizard of Oz* and was paid $750.

Charles Grapewin was born December 20, 1869, in Xenia, Ohio.
He died February 2, 1956, in Corona, California.

Back outside the Mausoleum, head north on the road that runs east of the building, between the Sunrise Slope Section and the Vale of Memory Section. Just before the road curves to the right, in the second row on the left, about ten feet from the road, in Plot 2148, you'll find the grave of **Mitchell J. Lewis (1880–1956).**

Lewis was a busy contract actor at MGM studios, appearing in 160 films from 1914 to 1955. He usually played supporting roles in MGM dramas, including the first version of *Ben-Hur* (1925), with Ramon Novarro and Francis X. Bushman; Cecil B. De Mille's *The Squaw Man* (1931), with Warner Baxter and Lupe Velez; *The Count of Monte Cristo* (1934), with Robert Donat; *A Tale of Two Cities* (1935), with Ronald Colman and Basil Rathbone; *Go West* (1940), with the Marx Brothers; and *Meet John Doe* (1941), with Gary Cooper and Barbara Stanwyck. But perhaps his most famous role was as Captain of the Winkie Guards in *The Wizard of Oz*, in which he informs Dorothy (Judy Garland), after she splashes water on the Wicked Witch of the West (Margaret Hamilton), "She's dead. You've killed her." And then, "Hail to Dorothy! The Wicked Witch is dead!"

Mitchell J. Lewis was born June 26, 1880, in Syracuse, New York.
He died August 24, 1956, in Woodland Hills, California.

Go back to the northeast edge of the cemetery, to the Triumphant Faith Terraces Section. At the northwest edge of that section, look for the huge blue-and-white sculpture marking the graves of Frederick Llewellyn (1917–1999) and Jane E. Llewellyn (1919–1990). Walk about halfway from the curb to the Llewellyn crypt, then turn right. Walk about two hundred feet, stopping in the middle of the second short set of stairs. There, on the left, in a small private garden, you'll find the grave of director **Vincente Minnelli (1903–1986),** the husband of *Wizard of Oz* star Judy Garland, and the father of actress and singer Liza Minnelli.

At the age of three, Minnelli was performing with his family in the Minnelli Brothers Dramatic Tent Show. As a teenager, he worked as a stage manager and costume designer for a chain of theaters in Chicago. Minnelli then worked as a set designer and costumer on Broadway before joining the Radio City Music Hall in New York City. After directing several productions, Minnelli was hired by MGM studios and made his debut as assistant director on *Panama Hattie* (1942), starring Red Skelton and Ann Sothern. Minnelli next directed Skelton in *I Dood It* (1943) before moving to musicals with *Cabin in the Sky* (1943) and *Meet Me in St. Louis* (1944), starring Judy Garland. Minnelli quickly developed a trademark style—the lavish, colorful MGM musical, filled with sweeping visual scope.

Minnelli and Judy Garland were married in 1945 and had one child, Liza, who was born in 1946. The couple divorced in 1951.

Minnelli remained at MGM for most of his career, directing primarily musicals, including *The Band Wagon* (1953), *Brigadoon* (1954), *Kismet* (1955), and *Bells Are Ringing* (1960), as well as dramas and comedies, including *The Clock* (1945), *Father of the Bride* (1950), *The Bad and the Beautiful* (1952), *Lust for Life* (1956), and *Some Came Running* (1958). Minnelli was nominated for an Academy Award as Best Director for *An American in Paris* (1951), and he won the award for *Gigi* (1958).

Minnelli's grave marker includes this epitaph: "Beloved father and husband, weaver of dreams, you filled our hearts with love, you touched our souls, you made this world more beautiful. Our lives were enriched by knowing you, you are missed, our best beloved."

Minnelli was born Lester Anthony Minnelli on February 28, 1903, in Chicago, Illinois. He died July 25, 1986, in Beverly Hills, California.

The four-legged star of *The Wizard of Oz*, Dorothy's little dog, Toto, was owned and trained by Carl Spitz, who died in 1976 and is buried in the Great Mausoleum, in the Iris Columbarium. Spitz was a popular animal trainer in Hollywood, perhaps best known as the owner and trainer of Buck, the St. Bernard in *The Call of the Wild* (1935), starring Clark Gable and Loretta Young.

But whatever happened to Toto? Unfortunately, there is no known grave marker or memorial for this cute and spunky little canine. Toto was a shy, four-year-old Cairn terrier whose real name was **Terry (1934–1945)**. Even though Toto was referred to as "he" in the film, Terry was really a "she." When Spitz was given the assignment of finding a dog to play Toto, he brought Terry in to audition for the part. Terry got the part and she—or Spitz—was paid a salary of $125 per week for her work in the film.

Terry was actually quite a busy actress in the years before and after *Oz*, appearing with some of the top actors of the day. She made her film debut as Rags in *Bright Eyes* (1934), starring Shirley Temple. Terry also appeared in *Ready for Love* (1934), starring Ida Lupino; *The Dark Angel* (1935), starring Fredric March and Merle Oberon; *Fury* (1936), starring Spencer Tracy; *The Buccaneer* (1938), also starring Fredric March; *Barefoot Boy* (1938); *Son of the Navy* (1940); *Calling Philo Vance* (1940); *Bad Little Angel* (1940); and *Twin Beds* (1942), starring George Brent and Joan Bennett.

There have been several stories about Terry's eventual fate. Terry was eleven years old when she died in 1945. Despite rumors that Terry's stuffed remains were auctioned off in 1996, *Oz* aficionados suggest that the most likely story is that when Terry died, she was buried near the kennel in the backyard of Spitz's home on Riverside Drive in the San Fernando Valley. Years later, Spitz's property was sold to the city of Los Angeles, and the Ventura Freeway was built over it, so it's likely that thousands of motorists are driving over Terry's remains every day. And if a stuffed dog from *The Wizard of Oz* was sold at auction, it was probably a stand-in pooch who filled in for Terry after she was accidentally stepped on by one of the Witch's guardsmen and injured during filming.

2

Forest Lawn Memorial Park–Hollywood Hills

~

6300 Forest Lawn Drive
Los Angeles, California 90068

~ HISTORY

After the incredible success of Forest Lawn's original location in Glendale, Hubert Eaton purchased a four-hundred-acre site for a second cemetery in 1944, adjacent to Griffith Park in Los Angeles, overlooking the San Fernando Valley. Eaton outbid both a residential developer and the city of Los Angeles, which wanted the property to expand Griffith Park.

Since the property had been zoned for residential use, Forest Lawn went to the Los Angeles City Planning Commission in 1946 to request permission to open a cemetery on the site. Thousands of area residents signed petitions against the use of the land as a cemetery, and several city commissions, the Hollywood Chamber of Commerce, and the mayor of Los Angeles also opposed the cemetery plan, for various reasons. The most emotional plea came from residents, who feared that runoff from the property would contaminate an underground reservoir that provided drinking water for more than 300,000 city residents. Experts testified that chemicals used in embalming fluids might leak into the water supply, and the Planning Commission denied Forest Lawn's request to open a cemetery.

Forest Lawn submitted the request to the commission again in 1948 and was again denied. This time, Tina Griffith, the widow of Col. Griffith J. Griffith, who donated the three-thousand-acre parcel that became Griffith Park, requested that the city oppose "any development adjoining the park which might depreciate its value as a great public recreation ground." The cemetery operators then went directly to the Los Angeles City Council, which voted 10-3 in March 1948 to allow the cemetery to open. While opponents considered their options, including placing the question on the ballot for a public vote, Forest Lawn took advantage of a state law to end any possible reversal of the council's decision. The law stated that if six bodies were legally buried on any site, that site would immediately and forever become a cemetery.

Within minutes of the council's vote, Forest Lawn employees buried six bodies on the property, and a cemetery spokesman announced that the land had officially, legally, and irreversibly been converted to a cemetery, and Forest Lawn was open for business.

Interestingly enough, decades before Forest Lawn bought the property, the Hollywood Hills location was the site of another bit of Hollywood history: The battle scenes in D. W. Griffith's Civil War epic, *The Birth of a Nation* (1915), were filmed here. The location currently overlooks the Warner Bros. and Disney studios.

While the Forest Lawn cemetery in Glendale has an obvious religious theme, the Hollywood Hills location is more focused on American history, including an exact replica of Boston's Old North Church. At the southeast corner of the cemetery is the Hall of Liberty, which contains the Liberty Museum and the Museum of Mexican History. A sixty-foot-high statue of George Washington stands in the nearby Court of Liberty, which also includes the 162-foot-long Birth of Liberty mosaic, depicting twenty-five scenes from the country's early history. In front of the mosaic is a statue of Thomas Jefferson. The nearby Lincoln Terrace features a statue of the sixteenth president, as well as a mosaic depicting scenes from his life.

As at the Glendale location, the rules at Forest Lawn–Hollywood Hills prohibit loitering, commercial photography, and refreshments on the grounds or in the buildings. But, in general, Forest Lawn–Hollywood Hills is a little bit friendlier than its Glendale counterpart. No, the employees still won't point out the location of a celebrity's grave, but at least there aren't any inaccessible mausoleums or private gardens that require a "Golden Key of Memory" for admission.

Forest Lawn–Hollywood Hills contains the final remains of some of the greatest, most inventive, and most influential comedy performers in entertainment history, including Buster Keaton, Stan Laurel, Lucille Ball, Ernie Kovacs, Ozzie and Harriet Nelson, Freddie Prinze, Marty Feldman, and animators Walter Lantz and Tex Avery, giving the cemetery both historical and hysterical themes.

The Forest Lawn empire also includes three other cemetery locations in southern California—Covina, Cypress, and Long Beach.

~ DIRECTIONS

From downtown Los Angeles, take the Hollywood Freeway (101) north to Barham Boulevard. Take Barham north about a mile to Forest Lawn Drive and turn right. The cemetery gates are about a mile down Forest Lawn Drive, on the right. Or take the Golden State Freeway (5) north, then west on the Ventura Freeway (134), and exit about a mile and a half down at Forest Lawn Drive. The cemetery gates are on Forest Lawn Drive, about a mile from the Ventura Freeway, on the left.

~ HOURS

The cemetery grounds are open every day from 8 A.M. to 5 P.M. (8 A.M. to 6 P.M. during daylight-savings time). The mortuary building and flower shop are open from 8 A.M. to 9 P.M., and the Hall of Liberty is open from 10 A.M. to 4:15 P.M.

~

The Tour

Pick up a map of the cemetery grounds at the information booth near the main entrance off Forest Lawn Drive. From that point, head straight back to the southeast corner of the cemetery, following the signs to the Hall of Liberty. Stop and park on the road between the Old North Church and the statue of George Washington.

Walk up toward the Washington statue. Just before you reach the first set of steps, turn right. About fifteen feet from the sidewalk, in front of a low brick wall, in Plot 5512, you'll find the simple grave marker of "The Great Stone Face," one of Hollywood's most creative and physically inventive comedians, **Buster Keaton (1895–1966).**

Keaton earned his nickname at an early age, when the six-month-old tot tumbled unharmed down a flight of stairs at a boarding house for vaudeville entertainers. (The story that Keaton got his nickname from magician Harry Houdini is probably more legend than fact.) That set the stage for Keaton's lifetime of acrobatic daredevil antics.

Keaton's parents were vaudeville comedians, and he joined their act when he was three years old. The act, called the Three Keatons, consisted of the parents trying to discipline a mischievous child, with Buster being tossed around the stage, even into the orchestra pit. Even at a young age, Keaton was so skilled at physical comedy and possessed such a keen sense of comic timing that many audience members were convinced that he was actually an adult midget.

By the age of twenty-one, Keaton was an established vaudeville star, and he decided to try his talents in films in New York City. He made his screen debut in *The Butcher Boy* (1917), which was written by, directed by, and costarred Roscoe "Fatty" Arbuckle, who became Keaton's lifelong friend. Keaton and Arbuckle appeared in dozens of comedy shorts over the next few years. In 1920, Keaton came to Hollywood, and released his first feature-length film, *The Saphead* (1920), which established Keaton as a comedy star. He followed that with *One Week* (1920), in which Keaton attempts to construct a house from a do-it-yourself kit. Many fans consider this film to be Keaton's first masterpiece. In 1921, Keaton married actress Natalie Talmadge, of the famous Talmadge sisters, who appeared in several of his films.

Keaton excelled at physical, acrobatic stunts, and he was also a pioneer in the use of multiple-exposure visual effects, dream sequences, and other photography tricks. For the next several years, Keaton wrote, directed, and starred in a series of films that have become silent comedy classics—*The Boat* (1921), *The Playhouse* (1921), *The Blacksmith* (1922), *Cops* (1922), *The Electric House* (1922), *The Paleface* (1922), *The Three Ages* (1923), *Our Hospitality* (1923), *The Balloonatic* (1923), *The Navigator* (1924), *Sherlock, Jr.* (1924), *Seven Chances* (1925), *The Battling Butler* (1926), *College* (1927), *The General* (1927), *The Cameraman* (1928), *Steamboat Bill, Jr.* (1928), and *Spite Marriage* (1929).

The films typically portray Keaton, with his trademark porkpie hat and expressionless face, battling some insurmountable adversity. As a director, Keaton was a perfectionist who would never take a shortcut or cheat the audience out of a laugh. For example, in *The Three Ages*, he played a caveman fighting with a huge opponent. One scene calls for his foe to throw a large rock at him, and for Keaton to swing his club like a baseball bat, sending the rock back and hitting the other caveman. Rather than film each action separately and edit them together, Keaton used a wide continuous shot with both actors and filmed seventy-six takes of the scene until he finally got what he wanted.

By the early 1930s, Keaton's physical health was deteriorating—in part because of the many injuries he had received during his performances—as was his mental health, due to battles with alcohol and a second failed marriage. After spending time in a psychiatric clinic, Keaton returned to films in smaller roles, and also as a writer and assistant director. After success in several stage appearances, Keaton's career as a performer was revived in the late 1940s. Notable was Keaton's performance in *Limelight* (1952), the only film in which Keaton and Charlie Chaplin appeared together. Keaton also appeared in *It's a Mad Mad Mad Mad World* (1963) and three teen beach movies—

Pajama Party (1964), *How to Stuff a Wild Bikini* (1965), and *Beach Blanket Bingo* (1965). Keaton was also the technical adviser on his biography, *The Buster Keaton Story* (1957), which starred Donald O'Connor.

In 1960, Keaton received an honorary Academy Award, "for his unique talents which brought immortal comedies to the screen."

Keaton was born Joseph Frank Keaton VI on October 4, 1895, in Piqua, Kansas. He died February 1, 1966, in Los Angeles.

On the opposite side of the sidewalk, about seventy-five feet to the left, in Plot 5400, you'll find the grave of goggle-eyed comedian and writer **Marty Feldman (1934–1982).**

Feldman, the son of Russian immigrants, hoped for a career as a jazz trumpeter, but poor reviews turned him to comedy, where he first worked as a writer for the BBC in the 1950s and early 1960s. Feldman wrote and performed in three television series in England, working with fellow comedians who would later form the Monty Python's Flying Circus troupe. Feldman knew he could get laughs just by appearing onstage, and he took full advantage of his unique looks. (His nose had been repeatedly broken in boxing matches, and his bulging eyes were the result of a hyperactive thyroid and a botched operation following a car accident.)

Feldman first appeared on television in the United States on the *Dean Martin Presents the Golddiggers* show in 1970. In 1972, he hosted *The Marty Feldman Comedy Machine*, then appeared as Igor, the hunchbacked assistant in *Young Frankenstein* (1974). Feldman also appeared in *The Adventures of Sherlock Holmes' Smarter Brother* (1975), *Silent Movie* (1976), *The Last Remake of Beau Geste* (1977), and *In God We Tru$t* (1980).

Feldman was filming his final scenes for *Yellowbeard* (1983) in Mexico City when he died of a heart attack as the result of food poisoning from eating tainted shellfish. He was forty-eight years old.

Feldman's grave marker contains this epitaph: "He made us laugh, he took my pain away, I love you, Lauretta." Feldman and Lauretta Sullivan were married in 1959.

Feldman was born July 8, 1934 (some sources say 1933), in London, England. He died December 2, 1982, in Mexico City, Mexico.

Return to the sidewalk and walk up to the statue of Washington. Turn left at the statue and walk into a small courtyard area, surrounded by a low wall. In the first courtyard, you'll see a statue of a woman with two small children on the right (south) side. About twenty feet to the left of that statue, next to Plot 5281, you'll find the grave of actor and game-show host **Bert Convy (1933–1991).**

Convy made his film debut in the Western *Gunman's Walk* (1958), starring Van Heflin and Tab Hunter. He also appeared in *A Bucket of Blood* (1959), *Susan Slade* (1961), *Semi-Tough* (1978), *Hero at Large* (1980), and *The Cannonball Run* (1981). But Convy is best known as a contestant and host of such television game shows as *Win, Lose or Draw, Super Password, Tattletales, What's My Line, Love Thy Neighbor,* and *The Match Game.*

Convy's grave marker includes this optimistic epitaph: "His star will shine forever."

Convy was born June 23, 1933, in St. Louis, Missouri. He died July 15, 1991, in Los Angeles.

Continue east into the next walled courtyard area, then turn right. Walk up a few steps into the next courtyard, turn left, and walk into the last walled courtyard before you reach the road. About twenty feet into this courtyard and about eight feet to the right of the sidewalk, in Plot 1265, you'll see a most unusual "grave" marker. The names on the marker are Penn and Teller, and the marker includes a playing card—the three of clubs—and the inscription "Is this your card?" Penn and Teller, a popular and often bizarre magic team, had the marker made as the payoff for "The Eternal Card Trick" from their book *How to Play in Traffic.* And it's one of the few examples that show that the people who run Forest Lawn might actually have a sense of humor. Although the marker is identified as a "cenotaph," technically it isn't. A cenotaph is a memorial marker placed in honor of a person who is buried elsewhere, not a memorial to a playing card.

(Lest you think that Forest Lawn management has no sense of humor at all, there's a crypt in the Sanctuary of Beloved Memories, in the Courts of Remembrance area, with the epitaph "Illegitimi non carbodundum." The phrase is pseudo-Latin, and translates roughly as "Don't let the bastards grind you down." Although "illegitimi" sounds like it could be the Latin word for illegitimate child, or bastard, it's not really the correct word, and Carbodundum is a trademarked name for silicone carbide, a commercial grinding substance invented at the end of the nineteenth century. The phrase is actually a popular slogan often seen in business offices, military posts, and taverns, and it is more accurately described as "fake Latin.")

On the opposite side of the sidewalk, in the northwest corner of the courtyard, you'll see the name "Savalas" on the wall. In front of this marker, in Plot 1281, you'll find the grave of actor **Telly Savalas (1922–1994)**, best known as the star of the 1970s television detective series *Kojak*.

After serving in World War II, Savalas joined the Information Services section of the U.S. State Department, then went to work for ABC News, where he won a Peabody Award for his work on the *Voice of America* series.

Savalas was nearly forty years old when he started his acting career, first on television, then in films. He made his screen debut in *Mad Dog Coll* (1961). The following year, he was nominated for an Academy Award as Best Supporting Actor for his role as a prison inmate in *Birdman of Alcatraz* (1962). Savalas played soldiers, tough guys, and cold-hearted villains in a series of action, crime, and war films, including *Cape Fear* (1962), *Battle of the Bulge* (1965), *Beau Geste* (1966), *The Dirty Dozen* (1967), *Kelly's Heroes* (1970), and the title role in *Pancho Villa* (1972). He also played James Bond's archenemy, Ernst Blofeld, in *On Her Majesty's Secret Service* (1969), starring George Lazenby as Bond.

In 1973, Savalas starred as New York City police detective Theo Kojak in the *Kojak* television series, which ran for six years. Kojak, with his ever-present lollipop and "Who loves ya, baby?" catchphrase, became a fan favorite, and Savalas also appeared in several made-for-television films as the Kojak character, the last in 1990.

Savalas's grave includes a quote from Aristotle: "The hour of departure has arrived, and we go our ways—I to die and you to live. Which is better, God only knows."

Savalas was born Aristotle Savalas on January 21, 1922
(some sources say 1923 or 1924), in Garden City, New York.
He died January 22, 1994, in Los Angeles.

Head back west, toward the George Washington statue. You'll pass through a few courtyards and archways until you're directly behind the statue. At that point, turn left, toward the huge Birth of Liberty mosaic on the wall of the Hall of Liberty. On a low wall to the right of the sidewalk you'll see a plaque marking the grave of half of the most successful comedy team in film history, **Stan Laurel (1890–1965).**

Laurel was the son of an actor and theater manager in England, and he started working on music hall stages as a teenager. He toured the United States with Fred Karno's vaudeville troupe in 1910, along with fellow performer Charlie Chaplin. When the Karno company toured the United States again in 1917, Laurel stayed and made his film debut in *Nuts in May* (1917). Laurel appeared in dozens of silent comedy shorts over the next few years, including starring in a parody of Rudolph Valentino's popular bullfighter film, *Blood and Sand* (1922), titled *Mud and Sand* (1922), in which Laurel's character is named Rhubarb Vaselino. Later that year, Laurel starred as a man accused of dognapping in *Lucky Dog* (1922). Playing a bit part as a masked bandit in the film was another young comedian named Oliver Hardy. It was their first screen appearance together.

The pair didn't work together again until *Forty-Five Minutes From Hollywood* (1926). Though Hardy and Laurel appeared in several more films together, it wasn't until Hal Roach formally paired them as a comedy team that the "Laurel and Hardy" characters emerged—the Mutt and Jeff pair, in suits and bowler hats, full of dignity and self-importance, set to take on the world. The only problem is, they always lose. Their most successful and popular films typically begin with a minor mishap, usually caused by Laurel, that escalates into a full-blown crisis, often with cataclysmic results. But, throughout the ordeal, they are always innocent, simple, and unswervingly dedicated to each other.

Though the Laurel and Hardy characters evolved slowly, *Do Detectives Think?* (1927) is generally accepted as the first official "Laurel and Hardy" film. The pair were masters at every form of comedy, from broad physical humor and slapstick, to verbal sparring, to more subtle humor. Audiences would laugh just as hard at the pair being chased down a flight of stairs by a runaway piano as they would at Hardy's delicate "slow burn" after yet another of Laurel's well-intentioned but misguided efforts. Few other comedians were as successful in so many different ways. Laurel's character, the feather-brained member of the team, would typically scratch his head, blink his eyes, and sob at the first sign of trouble, while the exasperated Hardy would exclaim, "Well, here's another fine mess you've gotten me into!"

While Laurel seemed to be the less intelligent member of the screen duo, offscreen he was the more creative, often writing many of the team's comedy routines.

Laurel and Hardy entered into sound films without missing a beat or losing any of their comedic genius. In fact, their verbal exchanges became the more memorable parts of their films. The duo also progressed from two-reel comedies to full-length features, even though they won an Academy Award in 1932 for *The Music Box,* the first Oscar presented for a live-action short comedy. *The Music Box* was the simple story of Laurel and Hardy trying to haul a piano up a lengthy flight of stairs. The stairs are still there, virtually unchanged, at 923 North Vendome Street, near Del Monte Drive in the Silver Lake neighborhood of Los Angeles. The stairs are a popular spot for Laurel and Hardy fans, and a commemorative plaque identifies the location.

Laurel and Hardy were at their creative and popular peak in the 1930s, with films like *Pardon Us* (1931), *Beau Hunks* (1931), *Towed in a Hole* (1932), *The Devil's Brother* (1933), *Busy Bodies* (1933), *Sons of the Desert* (1933), *Them Thar Hills* (1934), *Tit for Tat* (1935), *Way Out West* (1937), *Swiss Miss* (1938), and *Block Heads* (1938). In the 1940s, Laurel and Hardy continued to work, but their advancing ages necessitated a slower pace and less physical comedy. Laurel and Hardy's last film together was *Utopia* (1950). In 1960, three years after Hardy's death, Laurel was given an honorary Academy Award, "for his creative pioneering in the field of cinema comedy."

"If any of you cry at my funeral," Laurel once said, "I'll never speak to you again." The plaque above Laurel's grave identifies him as, "A master of comedy. His genius in the art of humor brought gladness to the world he loved." Laurel is buried with his seventh wife, Ida Kitaeva Laurel, whom he married in 1946. She died in 1980.

Laurel was born Arthur Stanley Jefferson on June 16, 1890, in Ulverston, England. He died February 23, 1965, in Santa Monica, California.

Continue walking south toward the Liberty mosaic. As you reach the mosaic, on your left you'll see a statue of Thomas Jefferson, the third president of the United States. Turn right, and walk across the road, into the Lincoln Terrace area. Follow the sidewalk up toward the seventeen-foot-high statue of our sixteenth president. Just past the first small set of stairs, on the left side about six feet from the sidewalk, in Plot 4596, you'll find the grave of actor George Savalas (1924–1985), who appeared as Detective Stavros on his brother Telly's *Kojak* television series from 1973 to 1978.

Just past the second set of stairs, on the left, about ten feet from the sidewalk, in Plot 4545, you'll find the grave of **Scatman Crothers (1910–1986)**, the shiny-headed actor with the wide smile, best known as the ghostly bartender in *The Shining* (1980), and as Louie the trash collector in the television series *Chico and the Man* from 1974 to 1978.

Performing since the age of fourteen, Crothers sang and played guitar and drums in a jazz band throughout the Midwest. He came to California in the late 1940s and made his film debut in *East of Sumatra* (1953), for which he also provided the musical score. Crothers also appeared in supporting roles in *The Patsy* (1964), *Hello, Dolly!* (1969), *The Great White Hope* (1970), *Lady Sings the Blues* (1972), *The King of Marvin Gardens* (1972), *The Fortune* (1975), *One Flew Over the Cuckoo's Nest* (1975), and *The Shootist* (1976).

Crothers also provided the voices for numerous cartoon characters in the 1970s and 1980s and guest-starred in dozens of television series in the 1980s. Crothers received his nickname from his talent at "scat singing," the technique of improvising nonsense lyrics to jazz melodies.

Crothers is buried with his wife, Helen M. Crothers (1918–1997).

Crothers was born Benjamin Sherman Crothers on May 23, 1910, in Terre Haute, Indiana. He died November 22, 1986, in Van Nuys, California.

Just past the third set of stairs, on the left, about twenty feet from the sidewalk and right next to a small tree, in Plot 4448, you'll find the grave of actor and director **William Conrad (1920–1994)**, who was the original radio voice of Marshal Matt Dillon on the *Gunsmoke* radio show, and later appeared on television as the overweight private investigator in the *Cannon* series from 1971 to 1976.

Conrad, a former trumpet player and fighter pilot in World War II, made his screen debut in *The Killers* (1946), starring Burt Lancaster and Ava Gardner. He next appeared in a series of supporting roles, usually playing cold-blooded criminals or police detectives, in films including *Body and Soul* (1947), *Sorry, Wrong Number* (1948), *The Milkman* (1950), *Cry Danger* (1951), *The Desert Song* (1953), and *The Naked Jungle* (1954).

Conrad was the radio voice of Marshal Matt Dillon on *Gunsmoke* from 1949 to 1960. He wanted to play the role when *Gunsmoke* came to television in 1955, but the producers didn't think his thinning hair, round face, and hefty physique matched their idea of a Western hero, so James Arness got the part. Conrad did star in several television series, however, including *Cannon* from 1971 to 1976, *Nero Wolfe* in 1981, and *Jake and the Fatman* from 1987 to 1992.

With his rich, authoritative baritone voice, Conrad also narrated several television series, including *The Fugitive* from 1963 to 1967, *The Invaders* from 1967 to 1968, *Tales of the Unexpected* in 1977, and *How the West Was Won* from 1978 to 1979. Conrad also narrated segments of *The Bullwinkle Show* from 1961 to 1973 and guest-starred on several television drama series in the 1980s. He was inducted into the Radio Hall of Fame in 1997.

> *Conrad was born William Cann on September 27, 1920, in Louisville, Kentucky. He died February 11, 1994, in North Hollywood, California.*

Drive back toward the main entrance of the cemetery, turn right at the four-way stop, and head to the Courts of Remembrance, a large garden mausoleum with aboveground crypts and columbaria in the northeast corner of the cemetery. Park on the west side of the courts, next to the Remembrance Section. As you approach the Courts of Remembrance from the west, you'll see two large, white sarcophagi on each side of the main walkway, both topped by a statue of a woman. The sarcophagus on the left contains the remains of one of the most honored actresses in film history, often described as the "First Lady of the American Screen," **Bette Davis (1908–1989).**

After taking acting classes in New York City, where she was a classmate of Lucille Ball, Davis made her stage debut in *The Earth Between* in 1923 and first appeared on Broadway in *Broken Dishes* in 1929. Davis came to Hollywood and made her film debut in *Bad Sister* (1931), which also featured a young actor named Humphrey Bogart. After seeing her performance, Universal studios chief Carl Laemmle said Davis "has about as much sex appeal as Slim Summerville," a lanky comedian who also appeared in the film. But the strong-willed Davis persisted, leaving Universal to work for Warner Bros. After a series of powerful performances in *The Man Who Played God* (1932), *20,000 Years in Sing Sing* (1932), *Three on a Match* (1932), *Cabin in the Cotton* (1932), and *Ex-Lady* (1933), Davis received the first of her eleven Academy Award nominations for Best Actress for her performance in *Of Human Bondage* (1934). She won the award for *Dangerous* (1935) and *Jezebel* (1938). After these successes, as well as her acclaimed performance in *The Petrified Forest* (1936), Davis began to demand more substantial roles. When Warner Bros. didn't provide suitable material, Davis refused a role and threatened to work in Europe, even though she was still under contract at the studio. Davis, who was gaining a reputation as a difficult and temperamental actress, unsuccessfully sued Warner Bros. to break her contract. But in the end, the studio began to offer her better parts in better films.

Davis was the undisputed queen of Hollywood from the late 1930s to the late 1940s, with Academy Award–nominated performances in *Dark Victory* (1939), *The Letter* (1940), *The Little Foxes* (1941), *Now, Voyager* (1942), and *Mr. Skeffington* (1944), as well as *All This, and Heaven, Too* (1940), *The Man Who Came to Dinner* (1942), *In This Our Life* (1942), *Watch on the Rhine* (1943), and *The Corn Is Green* (1945).

By the late 1940s, it was assumed that Davis's career had peaked. But her performance as fading Broadway legend Margo Channing in *All About Eve* (1950)—a last-minute replacement for the ailing Claudette Colbert—revived her career and won her yet another Academy Award nomination. In another role that mirrored her life, Davis received another nomination for her performance as a fading actress in *The Star* (1952). After appearing in a handful of minor films in the 1950s, Davis resurrected her career yet again in *Whatever Happened to Baby Jane?* (1962), in which she played a demented former child star who is forced to take care of her invalid sister, played by Joan Crawford. What happened offscreen was probably much more interesting than what happened onscreen, as Davis and Crawford were in the midst of a long-running, very personal, and vicious feud. Crawford's husband, the former CEO of Pepsi, died shortly before the filming began, and Crawford was still a member of the company's board of directors, so Davis had a Coca-Cola machine installed on the set. But Crawford got some revenge by putting lead weights in her pockets for a scene in which Davis had to drag her across the floor. Despite the turmoil, Davis received her final Academy Award nomination for her performance in the film.

In 1977, Davis was the first woman to receive the American Film Institute's Life Achievement Award. She was on the way home from receiving yet another lifetime achievement award, at the San Sebastian Film Festival in Spain, when she died in Paris in 1989.

Shortly before her death, Davis told an interviewer, "You know what they'll write on my tombstone? 'She did it the hard way.'"

And they did.

Buried along with Davis are her mother, Ruth Favor Davis (1885–1961), and her sister, Barbara Davis Berry (1909–1979).

Davis was born Ruth Elizabeth Davis on April 5, 1908, in Lowell, Massachusetts. She died October 6, 1989, in Paris, France.

Continue into the main entrance of the courtyard, past the Davis sarcophagus. Just inside the courtyard area, turn right. About fifty feet from the walkway, on the right, in the third space up from the ground, you'll find the crypt of actor **Charles Laughton (1899–1962),** best known for his role as Captain Bligh, doing battle with Clark Gable's Fletcher Christian in *Mutiny on the Bounty* (1935).

The roly-poly, thick-lipped Laughton was a former hotel clerk who started performing onstage in London in the 1920s. He also appeared in several silent comedies, where he met actress Elsa Lanchester, whom he married in 1929. Laughton came to the United States to appear in the play *Payment Deferred*, then he went to Hollywood to appear in the film version of the play in 1932. The following year, Laughton won the Academy Award as Best Actor for his performance in *The Private Life of Henry VIII* (1933).

Laughton played a wide range of characters, from butlers to kings, from killers to judges, and everything in between. He was particularly memorable as a pouty Nero in *The Sign of the Cross* (1932), the evil Dr. Moreau in *The Island of Lost Souls* (1932), and Quasimodo the bell-ringer in *The Hunchback of Notre Dame* (1939). Laughton showed off his comedic skills as a proper British butler transplanted into the American West in *Ruggles of Red Gap* (1935). Laughton also appeared in *The Canterville Ghost* (1944), *Captain Kidd* (1945), *The Big Clock* (1948), *Witness for the Prosecution* (1957), and *Spartacus* (1960). His last film was *Advice and Consent* (1962).

Laughton was born July 1, 1899, in Yorkshire, England. He died December 15, 1962, in Los Angeles.

Go back to the main walkway and continue on into the courtyard area, heading toward a large statue of Christ framed by an archway. Just before you pass through the archway, on the right, about ten feet from the walkway, you'll see another large sarcophagus topped by a statue of a woman. This tomb contains the remains of pianist **Liberace (1919–1987).**

Known for his extravagant stage costumes and candelabra-topped piano, Liberace first displayed his musical talents when he learned to play the piano by ear when he was only four years old. As a teenager, he was a soloist with the Chicago Symphony Orchestra. After touring in nightclubs and concert halls, Liberace made his film debut in *South Sea Sinner* (1949), starring Shelley Winters and Macdonald Carey. In 1952, he starred on television in *The Liberace Show*, which quickly became an international success. During his concert appearances in the mid-1950s, Liberace started to wear the colorful and flamboyant outfits that soon became his trademark. By the 1970s, he was spending more than $100,000 per year on his jewel-encrusted, fur-covered costumes and jewelry.

Though best known as a concert performer and for his hundreds of television appearances, Liberace also appeared in several more films, including *Sincerely Yours* (1955), *When the Boys Meet the Girls* (1965), and *The Loved One* (1965)—a filmed version of Evelyn Waugh's scathingly funny novel about the funeral industry in southern California, which was not-so-loosely based on Forest Lawn–Glendale.

The side of his sarcophagus is decorated with a facsimile of Liberace's elaborate signature, complete with a candelabra-topped piano and the phrase "Sheltered Love." (Since Liberace's theme song was "I'll Be Seeing You," this phrase must have some other meaning.)

The sarcophagus also contains the remains of Liberace's brother, George Liberace (1911–1983), and their mother, Frances Liberace (1891–1980).

Liberace was born Wladziu Valentino Liberace on May 16, 1919, in West Allis, Wisconsin. He died February 4, 1987, in Palm Springs, California.

On the opposite side of the walkway, tucked away in the northeast corner of the courtyard, is a small doorway leading to the Columbarium of Radiant Dawn. As you walk through the doorway into the columbarium, on the right side about ten feet from the doorway and six feet up from the floor, you'll find a plaque marking the remains of comedian **Lucille Ball (1911–1989)**. Though best known as the ditzy redheaded star of the 1950s sitcom *I Love Lucy*, Ball was also a pioneering television producer and studio executive.

From an early age, Ball dreamed of being a performer. She took music lessons and dropped out of high school to take acting classes—though she was sent home when her teachers told her she was "too shy." Ball finally landed a spot in the Ziegfeld Follies road show, and as a chorus girl in a few Broadway musicals. She came to Hollywood and made her film debut as a chorus girl in *Roman Scandals* (1933), starring Eddie Cantor. She played small roles as unnamed telephone operators, college girls, fashion models, and store clerks in dozens of films for the next several years, including *Three Little Pigskins* (1934), starring the Three Stooges; *Top Hat* (1935) and *Follow the Fleet* (1936), both starring Fred Astaire and Ginger Rogers; *The Three Musketeers* (1935); *The Whole Town's Talking* (1935); and *Room Service* (1938), starring the Marx Brothers.

One of Ball's first big films, which showcased her acting ability and her natural talent for comedy, was *Stage Door* (1937), an ensemble drama about a boarding house full of aspiring actresses, also starring Katharine Hepburn, Ginger Rogers, Ann Miller, and Eve Arden. While starring in *Too Many Girls* (1940), Ball met Desi Arnaz, a Cuban bandleader and rhumba singer who had a role in the film as a football player. They were married seven months later but spent most of the first ten years of their marriage apart—Arnaz was traveling with his band, and Ball was appearing in films including *The Big Street* (1942), *Du Barry Was a Lady* (1943), *Lured* (1947), *Sorrowful Jones* (1949), *Fancy Pants* (1950), and *The Fuller Brush Girl* (1950). To remedy the situation, Ball and Arnaz came up with the idea of costarring in a television series about a scatterbrained woman and her Cuban bandleader husband. Although CBS wanted Ball, they were strongly opposed to the idea of Arnaz playing her husband, fearing that the audience wouldn't be able to understand him because of his thick accent. So Ball and Arnaz created the Desilu company to produce the series and took a stage version of the show on the road to gauge public opinion. Based on the rave reviews, CBS agreed to take both performers, and *I Love Lucy* debuted in 1951.

During its six-year, 153-episode run, *I Love Lucy* became one of the most popular television series in history, with some of the most memorable slapstick scenes ever filmed—Ball trying to do a commercial for a vitamin drink and getting tipsy from the high alcohol content, Ball adding too much yeast to a recipe and getting trapped in her kitchen by a monster loaf of bread, and Ball working in a candy factory and trying to keep up when the conveyer belt goes faster and faster.

Ball and Arnaz were divorced in 1960, and Ball took over Desilu—she was the first woman in Hollywood to run a studio. Ball returned to television in *The Lucy Show* from 1962 to 1968, and *Here's Lucy* from 1968 to 1974. She had an ill-fated fourth series, *Life With Lucy*, which lasted only one season in 1986. Ball appeared in several more films in the 1960s, the most popular being *Yours, Mine and Ours* (1968), which costarred Henry Fonda. Her last film was *Mame* (1974).

Ball married nightclub comedian Gary Morton in 1961. The plaque over her grave also contains the name "Morton." Buried next to Ball is her mother, Desiree E. Ball (1892–1977).

Ball was born Lucille Desiree Ball on August 6, 1911, in Celoron, New York. She died April 26, 1989, in Los Angeles.

Three spaces to the left and one space up from Ball is the plaque marking the remains of actor **Strother Martin (1919–1980)**, best known for his supporting roles in a series of Westerns in the 1960s, and as the chain gang boss in *Cool Hand Luke* (1967) who tells Paul Newman, "What we've got here is a failure to communicate."

As a teenager, Martin was an excellent swimmer and the National Junior Springboard Diving Champion. After attending college on a diving scholarship and serving in the U.S. Navy during World War II, Martin came to Hollywood as a swimming instructor for celebrities, including Marion Davies and the children of Charlie Chaplin. He worked as a swimming extra in several films, making his debut as a springboard diver in *The Damned Don't Cry* (1950), starring Joan Crawford. Martin also worked on several films for directors Sam Peckinpah and John Ford and developed the weasely character he often described as "prairie scum," in films including *The Black Whip* (1956), *Cowboy* (1958), *The Wild and the Innocent* (1959), *The Horse Soldiers* (1959), *The Man Who Shot Liberty Valance* (1962), *McLintock!* (1963), *Showdown* (1963), *Invitation to a Gunfighter* (1964), *Shenandoah* (1965), *The Sons of Katie Elder* (1965), *Nevada Smith* (1966), *Butch Cassidy and the Sundance Kid* (1969), *The Wild Bunch* (1969), *True Grit* (1969), *The Ballad of Cable Hogue* (1970), *Hannie Caulder* (1971), *Red Sky at Morning* (1971), *Rooster Cogburn* (1975), and *The Great Scout and Cathouse Thursday* (1976).

Martin is buried with his wife, Helen Martin (1909–1997).

Martin was born Strother Martin Jr. on March 26, 1919, in Kokomo, Indiana. He died August 1, 1980, in Thousand Oaks, California.

On the opposite wall of the columbarium, beneath a statue of a woman holding a baby, is a plaque marking the remains of animator **Walter Lantz (1900–1994)**, best known as the creator of cartoon character Woody

Woodpecker, and his wife, Gracie Lantz (1903–1992), who provided Woody's voice and distinctive laugh for twenty-five years.

As a teenager, Lantz enrolled in an art school correspondence course, and he joined the animation staff of the International Film Service studios in New York City when he was sixteen. Lantz then moved to Hollywood, where he worked briefly for director Frank Capra and as a gag writer for director Mack Sennett. In 1928, Lantz was hired by Universal studio head Carl Laemmle to oversee the studio's animation department. Lantz arrived just as a young cartoonist named Walt Disney was leaving, taking with him his idea for an animated mouse, which Universal had rejected. But Disney left behind another popular character called Oswald Rabbit, which Lantz inherited. Lantz also worked as writer, animator, and director on cartoons starring Dinky Doodle, Pete the Pup, the Katzenjammer Kids, and Andy Panda.

Lantz came up with his most famous creation while on his honeymoon in 1940. According to the legend, Lantz was inspired by a woodpecker hammering incessantly on the roof of his honeymoon cottage. Lantz's wife, Gracie Stafford Lantz, suggested that Lantz create a cartoon character based on the annoying bird. Lantz took her advice, and Woody Woodpecker made his film debut in *Knock Knock* (1940), an Andy Panda cartoon, with Mel Blanc providing Woody's voice. After Blanc left the studio to work for Warner Bros., writer Ben "Bugs" Hardaway supplied Woody's voice, but Blanc's distinctive woodpecker laugh was still used in the cartoons. When "The Woody Woodpecker Song" was released in 1948, featuring Blanc's laugh, he sued Lantz for half a million dollars, claiming that his voice had been used without his permission. Although a judge ruled that Blanc had failed to copyright his contribution, Lantz paid Blanc an out-of-court settlement.

In 1950, Lantz needed a new voice for Woody, and was listening to audition tapes. Although his wife said she could provide the voice, Lantz turned her down because Woody was a male woodpecker. So Gracie Lantz secretly prepared her own anonymous tape, and slipped it in with the other audition tapes. Not knowing it was his wife's voice, Lantz picked her tape and Gracie, an actress who appeared in several films in the late 1930s and early 1940s, supplied Woody's voice and distinctive laugh until Lantz stopped making new Woody Woodpecker cartoons in 1975. Gracie Lantz initially declined screen credit for her contribution, thinking children would be disappointed if they found out that Woody's voice was supplied by a woman.

Woody appeared in hundreds of cartoon shorts through the 1940s and 1950s. In 1957, *The Woody Woodpecker Show* debuted on television, hosted by Walter Lantz, who demonstrated tips and techniques of animation between the cartoons. Woody Woodpecker remains popular around the world, primarily because the cartoons rely heavily on physical humor and sight gags with little dialogue, and so don't need to be translated for non-English-speaking audiences.

From 1932 to 1956, Lantz was nominated ten times for an Academy Award for Best Cartoon Short Subject, but he never won. In 1979, he was given a special Academy Award, "for bringing joy and laughter to every part of the world through his unique animated motion pictures."

The Lantzes' plaque identifies them as "voice and creator of Woody Woodpecker."

Lantz was born Walter Lanza on April 27, 1900, in New Rochelle, New York. He died March 22, 1994, in Burbank, California.

Go back out into the courtyard and through the archway next to Liberace's sarcophagus. In the middle of the archway, on the right side, is a short corridor called the Sanctuary of Light. On the right side of the corridor, in the fourth space from the end, second space up from the floor, you'll find the crypt of coin-flipping, tough-guy actor **George Raft (1895–1980).**

Raft's early life and career seem to mirror the stories told in the gangster films that became his specialty. He was born in the tough Hell's Kitchen neighborhood of New York City, left home at thirteen, found work as a prizefighter, and counted mobsters and racketeers among his closest friends. But, rather than follow his pals into a life of crime, Raft became a dancer, performing in nightclubs and eventually on Broadway.

Raft came to Hollywood in 1928 and was initially touted as the next Valentino. He made his screen debut in a small role as a dancer in *Gold Diggers of Broadway* (1929) and appeared in small roles as a dancer or gangster in several films before his first big role as Guino Rinaldo, the coin-tossing henchman of Paul Muni's Tony Camonte in *Scarface* (1932). Raft spent the rest of his career playing gangsters and convicts in films including *Each Dawn I Die* (1939), *Invisible Stripes* (1939), *They Drive by Night* (1940), *Background to Danger* (1943), *Johnny Angel* (1945), *Nocturne* (1946), *Intrigue* (1947), and *A Dangerous Profession* (1949). When Raft wasn't appearing in crime dramas, he was spoofing his image in comedies including *Some Like It Hot* (1959), *The Ladies' Man* (1961), *The Patsy* (1964), and *Casino Royale* (1967). Raft's success and believability in these films may have been partially due to his continuing association with real-life mobsters, including Bugsy Siegel, and his ownership of casinos in London and Havana.

Raft is also known by the roles he turned down. He passed on the role of "Mad Dog" Earle in *High Sierra* (1941) because the character dies onscreen, and he also turned down the role of Sam Spade in *The Maltese Falcon* (1941) because he thought it was going to be a low-quality film. Both roles went to Humphrey Bogart, and both films are now considered classics.

Raft was born George Ranft on September 27, 1895, in New York City. He died November 24, 1980, in Los Angeles.

Directly to the left of Raft's crypt is the crypt of comedian **Freddie Prinze (1954–1977)**.

Prinze, a talented comedian, seems to have become the poster boy for the phrase "too much, too soon." After an incredibly successful early career as a stand-up comedian—with his first appearance on Johnny Carson's *Tonight Show* when he was only nineteen—Prinze got his own television series, *Chico and the Man*, which debuted in the fall of 1974 and was an immediate hit. At the end of the 1974–75 television season, *Chico and the Man* was the number three show on the air, according to the Nielsen ratings.

But fame came at a high price for Prinze. He became heavily dependent on drugs and obsessed with death, often carrying a handgun and pointing it at his head. In January 1977, despondent over a pending divorce, a restraining order keeping him away from his wife and new son, and his inability to kick an addiction to cocaine and prescription drugs, Prinze shot himself in the head in his Los Angeles apartment. He was twenty-two.

Prinze is the father of popular film actor Freddie Prinze Jr., who was only ten months old when his father died.

Prinze was born Freddie James Prinze on June 22, 1954, in New York City. He died January 29, 1977, in Los Angeles.

Go back and continue through the archway, toward the statue of Christ. As soon as you pass through the archway, turn left and you'll see yet another large white sarcophagus with a statue of a woman on top. This one contains the remains of producer **Albert Broccoli (1909–1996)**, better known as "Cubby," and best known for the James Bond films. (Broccoli received his nickname when he was a chubby youngster.)

After working as a scientist for several years, Broccoli entered the film business in 1938 as an assistant director at 20th Century-Fox studios. In the early 1950s, he formed Warwick Pictures in England and produced primarily action and war films, including *The Red Beret* (1953) and *Hell Below Zero* (1954), both starring Alan Ladd, and *The Cockleshell Heroes* (1955). Broccoli produced the first James Bond film, *Dr. No* (1962), and sixteen subsequent films in the Bond series, including *From Russia With Love* (1963), *Goldfinger* (1964), *Diamonds Are Forever* (1971), *The Spy Who Loved Me* (1977), *For Your Eyes Only* (1981), *Octopussy* (1983), and *License to Kill* (1989). Broccoli's daughter, Barbara Broccoli, and stepson, Michael Wilson, continue to produce the films in the Bond series.

Broccoli received the Irving G. Thalberg Memorial Award at the 1982 Academy Award ceremonies. The award is presented annually to a producer "who has been responsible for a consistently high quality of motion picture production."

Broccoli was born Albert Romolo Broccoli on April 5, 1909, in New York City. He died June 27, 1996, in Beverly Hills, California.

Continue past Broccoli's sarcophagus to the northern wall of the courtyard. On that wall, in the fourth column from the left, third space up from the ground, you'll find the crypt of comedian **Morey Amsterdam (1908–1996)**, best known as comedy writer Buddy Sorrell on *The Dick Van Dyke Show* in the early 1960s.

Amsterdam was the son of a concert violinist who wanted his son to follow in his professional footsteps as a musician. And he did—sort of. Amsterdam was trained as a concert cellist, and he performed a musical act in Chicago nightclubs with his brother, who played the piano. But gradually, Amsterdam began to add more and more jokes until the act became more comedy than music. When he was sixteen, Amsterdam was performing in a speakeasy owned by Al Capone. After witnessing a gun battle in the club, Amsterdam decided to seek his fortune in the somewhat safer atmosphere of southern California.

In addition to performing on three different radio shows in the late 1940s, Amsterdam wrote jokes for Fanny Brice, Milton Berle, Fred Allen, Jimmy Durante, and Will Rogers. He also wrote novelty songs, including "Why, Oh Why Did I Ever Leave Wyoming?" One of the radio shows was transformed into a television show in 1948, and the same year Amsterdam also hosted a variety show called *The Morey Amsterdam Show,* which ran for two years. Amsterdam also hosted *Broadway Open House,* another variety show, which debuted in 1950. Amsterdam was a regular guest panelist on several television quiz and variety shows throughout the 1950s, and was known as the "Human Joke Machine." Given any topic, Amsterdam could immediately produce a string of jokes.

In a perfect example of art imitating life, Amsterdam, a quick-witted, wise-cracking comedy writer, was given the role of Buddy Sorrell, a quick-witted, wisecracking comedy writer, on *The Dick Van Dyke Show,* which debuted in 1961 and ran for five years and is usually at or near the top of any list of the all-time best sitcoms. Amsterdam wrote much of his dialogue for the show, and also occasionally played the cello. After the show ended in 1966, Amsterdam continued to perform in nightclubs and in guest appearances on television. In his final appearance a few months before he died, Amsterdam and his former *Dick Van Dyke* costar, Rose Marie, appeared together on an episode of *Caroline in the City* in 1996.

The marker on Amsterdam's crypt contains this epitaph: "Loving husband and father, he gave the world 74 years of comedy and entertainment."

Amsterdam was born December 14, 1908, in Chicago, Illinois. He died October 27, 1996, in Beverly Hills, California.

Retrace your steps back to the Liberace sarcophagus. Walk past it and down a short set of stairs at the southern end of the courtyard. In the southeast corner of the next courtyard, you'll see a small doorway leading to the Columbarium of Valor. As you enter the columbarium, on the west wall, in the second column from the right about ten feet up from the floor, in space G-64660, you'll find a plaque marking the remains of actor **McLean Stevenson (1927–1996),** best known for his role as Lt. Col. Henry Blake on the television series *M*A*S*H,* from 1972 to 1975.

Stevenson started his show business career in his thirties, as a comedian and writer for the Smothers Brothers. After appearing as a performer on *The Smothers Brothers Comedy Hour,* Stevenson made guest appearances on several sitcoms before taking the role on *M*A*S*H* in 1972 as the bumbling but lovable commanding officer of the medical unit. When Stevenson tired of his supporting role, he left the series in 1975. He subsequently appeared in several made-for-television movies and starred in a string of short-lived sitcoms, including *The McLean Stevenson Show, In the Beginning,* and *Hello, Larry.*

Stevenson was also a regular guest on Johnny Carson's *Tonight Show* and several game shows.

Stevenson's first name came from McLean County, Illinois, where he was born and raised. He was the grandson of Adlai Stevenson, who served as vice president under President Grover Cleveland from 1893 to 1897, and the cousin of Illinois governor Adlai Stevenson, who was twice the unsuccessful Democratic nominee for president (1952 and 1956).

Interestingly, Roger Bowen, who played Lieutenant Colonel Blake in Robert Altman's film version of *M*A*S*H* (1970), died the day after Stevenson died.

> *Stevenson was born November 14, 1927 (some sources say 1929), in Normal, Illinois. He died February 15, 1996, in Los Angeles.*

Head back out the Courts of Remembrance the same way you came in, past the Bette Davis sarcophagus. Just across the road is the small Remembrance Section. In roughly the center of the section, in Plot 1041, you'll find the grave of comedian and television pioneer **Ernie Kovacs (1919–1962)**. Kovacs is often called the first true comedy genius of television—even though none of his many television series lasted very long on the air.

After a career as a radio broadcaster and newspaper columnist, Kovacs starred in several television series in the early 1950s, beginning with *It's Time for Ernie*, in May 1951, and followed by *Kovacs on the Corner, Ernie in Kovacsland, Kovacs Unlimited,* and *The Ernie Kovacs Show.*

Kovacs was one of the first performers to really use the full visual potential of television, making it almost a costar in his act. Unlike many of the other television series of the early 1950s, Kovacs's shows weren't just recycled radio programs or old vaudeville acts. Kovacs used television and simple special effects to create visual humor that could never be done on radio and had never before been attempted on television. For example, Kovacs tilted both a table and the camera at the same angle, so the table appeared to be level. When he sat down and tried to pour milk into a glass on the table, the milk appeared to defy gravity and flowed out of the pitcher at an angle. In Kovacs's world, figures in paintings moved, office furniture moved in time to music, and women gradually disappeared as they got undressed. Kovacs also broke the "fourth wall," which traditionally separates the entertainer from the audience; he often spoke to his camera crew, the studio audience, and even the audience watching at home—"I'd like to thank you all for inviting me into your living rooms this evening. It's just a shame you didn't straighten up a little." In early 1957, Kovacs presented the first half-hour, prime-time television show done entirely in pantomime. For Kovacs, television was a brand-new toy to play with.

Kovacs also created memorable characters, including poet Percy Dovetonsils, magician Natzoh Hepplewhite, Professor Bernie Cosnowski, the silent Eugene, Mr. Question Man, and the Nairobi Trio—three men in trench coats and ape masks who played music. Kovacs's humor is difficult to describe; you really have to see it to appreciate it.

Kovacs appeared in only a handful of films, usually in supporting roles, including *Operation Mad Ball* (1957), *Bell, Book and Candle* (1958), *It Happened to Jane* (1959), *Our Man in Havana* (1960), *Strangers When We Meet* (1960), *Wake Me When It's Over* (1960), *North to Alaska* (1960), *Five Golden Hours* (1961), and *Sail a Crooked Ship* (1962).

On January 12, 1962, Kovacs was putting the finishing touches on a new film in which he was costarring with comedian Buster Keaton. Kovacs left work at about 11 P.M. to attend a party at the home of director Billy Wilder in the Brentwood area of Los Angeles, in honor of Milton and Ruth Berle's newly adopted son. Kovacs drove to the party in his white Rolls-Royce, while his wife, singer Edie Adams, drove from home in their new Corvair station wagon. At about 1:30 A.M., Kovacs and Adams left the party to head home to their seventeen-room mansion on Bowmont Drive in Los Angeles, with Adams driving the Rolls and Kovacs following her, behind the wheel of the tiny Corvair.

About five minutes later, Kovacs was headed south on Beverly Glen Boulevard. As he turned left onto Santa Monica Boulevard, he lost control of the car on the rain-slicked street and skidded sideways into a steel utility pole at an estimated fifty miles per hour. The impact crushed the driver's door, and Kovacs suffered a fractured skull and broken ribs, which ruptured his aorta. He died quickly, ten days before his forty-third birthday. His body was partially thrown from the passenger-side door of the wreckage, and an unlit cigar was found on the pavement near Kovacs's hand, leading to speculation that he had lost control of the car as he tried to light the cigar.

Kovacs's grave marker features a facsimile of his signature, but his handwriting is nearly illegible, so the marker also includes his tiny printed name, in parentheses, beneath the signature. The epitaph includes a quote from Kovacs—"Nothing in moderation"—and the phrase "We all loved him."

Kovacs is buried next to his daughter, Mia Susan Kovacs (1959–1982), who also died in a car crash. Her grave marker includes the inscription "Daddy's girl—We all loved her, too."

Kovacs was born January 23, 1919, in Trenton, New Jersey.
He died January 13, 1962, in Los Angeles.

Continue across the Remembrance Section, cross another road, and you'll be in the Gentleness Section. In the center of that section is a statue of a seated young woman and a small boy praying. About 115 feet to the right of that statue and 100 feet from the road, in Plot 833, you'll find the grave of animator **Fred Bean "Tex" Avery (1908–1980),** known for his wild, slapstick cartoons produced at MGM and Warner Bros. studios in the 1930s and 1940s.

Avery was born in Texas, a descendant of Judge Roy Bean and Daniel Boone. He started drawing comic strips while in high school and even studied at the Chicago Art Institute. Avery moved to southern California after he graduated from high school, and got a job working as an animator at the Walter Lantz Studios in 1929. Six years later, he went to Warner Bros. studios, where he worked with Chuck Jones and Bob Clampett. Avery supervised the Looney Toons and Merrie Melodies series, and he is credited with creating Daffy Duck and Porky Pig as well as coming up with Bugs Bunny's trademark comment, "What's up, doc?"

Avery went to work at MGM studios in 1941, where he supervised all cartoon production. Avery was given relative freedom at MGM, and he took advantage of it. His cartoons had a wild, fast-paced, anything-can-happen style, including characters speaking directly to the audience (and the audience, seen in silhouette at the bottom of the screen, responding). While Avery's cartoons at Warner Bros. and MGM never approached Disney's work in terms of technical polish, he was unmatched in wild physical humor and piling gag upon gag. While Disney may have tried to tell a story or attempt to educate his audience, Avery's goal was just to be funny, with fast pacing, violent humor, and sexy characters.

In 1954, Avery went back to work for Walter Lantz and created the Chilly Willy character, before working on television commercials.

Avery's impact on cartoons and feature films continues. Jessica Rabbit in *Who Framed Roger Rabbit* (1988) is certainly based on Avery's characters, and Jim Carrey's performance in *The Mask* (1994) is almost a live-action version of an Avery cartoon.

Avery was born Frederick Bean Avery on February 26, 1908, in Taylor, Texas. He died August 26, 1980, in Burbank, California.

Drive over to the southwest side of the cemetery, to the small Revelation Section. Beginning at the intersection between the Revelation, Enduring Faith, and Murmuring Trees Sections, walk about a hundred feet up the hill into the Revelation Section, toward a tall pine tree. Just behind the tree, in Plot 3540, you'll find the graves of **Ozzie Nelson (1906–1975)** and **Harriet Hilliard Nelson (1909–1994),** the parents on one of the longest-running family sitcoms in television history.

Ozzie Nelson started his career, after graduating from college with a law degree, as the leader of a popular dance band. In 1935, he married the band's singer, Harriet Hilliard, and they were regular performers on radio, including Red Skelton's show, through the 1930s and early 1940s. (Harriet Hilliard was born Peggy Lou Snyder, but took her mother's maiden name when she began performing.) Though it was initially a musical act, more and more comedy was added to the Nelsons' performances. Their success on radio resulted in the creation of their own show in 1944, *The Adventures of Ozzie and Harriet,* which ran for eight years on radio and fourteen more on television, from 1952 to 1966. The series also featured the Nelsons' two sons, Ricky and David. (In the early years of the radio show, the Nelsons' children were played by two young actors, but in 1949, Ricky and David joined the cast as themselves.) Ozzie Nelson also produced the series, wrote and directed most of the episodes, and wrote the theme music.

Before starting his career as America's favorite father, Ozzie Nelson also appeared in several films, including *Sweetheart of the Campus* (1941), *The Big Street* (1942), and *Honeymoon Lodge* (1943), typically in minor roles as a bandleader or saxophone player. Harriet Nelson, meanwhile, had a slightly longer and larger film career, with roles in musicals and dramas, including *Follow the Fleet* (1936), starring Fred Astaire and Ginger Rogers; *The Life of the Party* (1937); *Cocoanut Grove* (1938); *Confessions of Boston Blackie* (1941); *Canal Zone* (1942); *The Falcon Strikes Back* (1943); *Hi, Buddy* (1943); and *Take It Big* (1944).

The radio and television series basically mirrored the Nelsons' lives as the boys grew up and got married, with Ricky's and David's real wives playing their wives on the show. The four Nelsons also appeared in *Here Come the Nelsons* (1952), which helped launch the television series.

Ozzie and Harriet Nelson returned to television in 1973 with a series titled *Ozzie's Girls*. The new series featured the Nelsons still living in the same house, but renting out the boys' rooms to college girls. *Ozzie's Girls* was canceled after one season.

Not only did Ozzie and Harriet Nelson play "characters" named Ozzie and Harriet Nelson on their two television series, but the house used in the exterior shots in the series was the house they actually lived in, at 1822 Camino Palmero Street, near North Fuller Avenue, about a block north of Hollywood Boulevard. The New England–style house, which is currently surrounded by a thick hedge and an iron gate, is reportedly haunted by Ozzie Nelson's ghost.

Buried next to Harriet Nelson is her mother, Hazel D. Hilliard (1888–1971).

> *Ozzie Nelson was born Oswald George Nelson on March 20, 1906 (some sources say 1907), in Jersey City, New Jersey. He died June 3, 1975, in Los Angeles.*
>
> *Harriet Nelson was born Peggy Lou Snyder on July 18, 1909 (some sources say 1914), in Des Moines, Iowa. She died October 2, 1994, in Laguna Beach, California.*

Two rows up from the Nelsons is the grave of their son, Eric Hilliard Nelson, better known as actor and singer **Ricky Nelson (1940–1985).**

Ricky Nelson literally grew up on television, joining the cast of *The Adventures of Ozzie and Harriet* radio show when he was nine years old and continuing through the fourteen-year run of the television series, from 1952 to 1966. Ricky Nelson, who became a successful musician in later life, can credit his musical career to an episode of *Ozzie and Harriet*.

Ozzie Nelson often used real-live events and family situations as the basis for the television series. When the real Ricky developed an interest in music as a teenager after a girlfriend developed a crush on Elvis Presley, Ozzie used that as inspiration for an episode of the series. In 1957, Ricky recorded the Fats Domino hit "I'm Walkin'," and Ozzie Nelson wrote a script in which the television Ricky becomes interested in music and records a song. The episode aired the same time as the record's release, and the record sold one million copies in a week. For the next six years, Ricky Nelson was a fixture on the pop charts, with songs including "Poor Little Fool," "Hello, Mary Lou," "Travelin' Man," "Teenage Idol," and "Fools Rush In"—all of which benefited from weekly exposure on the television series. Although Ricky Nelson certainly had an impact on popular music, the impact made by his parents may have been more important and far-reaching. By supporting and promoting Ricky's career every week on their television series in the late 1950s and early 1960s, Ozzie and Harriet were sending a message to parents that maybe rock-and-roll music wasn't such a serious threat to the morals of the country after all.

As a screen actor, Ricky Nelson had a short-lived career, appearing in several films, including *Rio Bravo* (1959), *The Wackiest Ship in the Army* (1960), and *Love and Kisses* (1965)—which was written and directed by Ozzie Nelson. As a musician, he was much more successful. He recorded thirty-three Top 40 hits during a seven-year period. Ricky eventually dropped the "y" from his name and, as Rick Nelson, he became one of the first "country-rock" musicians. With his Stone Canyon Band, Nelson's "Garden Party," released in 1972 and one of his biggest hits, was his pointed assertion that he wanted to be considered a contemporary musician, not a nostalgia act.

Nelson was a hard-working, dedicated musician who performed as many as two hundred concerts per year. He was touring with his band when he died in a plane crash in Texas on New Year's Eve, 1985, at the age of forty-five. Shortly after his death, Nelson was inducted into the Rock and Roll Hall of Fame. His twin sons, Matthew and Gunnar Nelson, are following in his musical footsteps.

Ricky Nelson was born Eric Hilliard Nelson on May 8, 1940, in Teaneck, New Jersey. He died December 31, 1985, in DeKalb, Texas.

A few hundred feet northwest of the Nelsons and about a hundred feet from the road, in the Hillside Section, Plot 4972, you'll find the grave of the ultimate Western sidekick, **George "Gabby" Hayes (1885–1969).**

Hayes started his career as a vaudeville and stage actor and made enough money to retire in his early forties. When he lost his savings in the 1929 stock market crash, he was forced to return to work in films. After appearing in dozens of Westerns as either a clean-shaven bad guy or a whiskered old-timer, Hayes made his reputation in the 1930s as Hopalong Cassidy's sidekick, Windy Halliday. Later, Hayes was teamed with Roy Rogers from 1939 to 1947, and he also played supporting roles to such Western stars as John Wayne and Randolph Scott. In a rare non-Western film, Hayes played a small role in *Mr. Deeds Goes to Town* (1936), starring Gary Cooper and Jean Arthur.

After his final film appearance in 1950, Hayes hosted *The Gabby Hayes*

Show on television from 1950 to 1956, which included his stories of the old West and presentations of his films.

Offscreen, Hayes was an elegant and dapper gentleman, the complete opposite of his film image. Hays is buried with his wife, Olive E. Hayes. Their simple grave markers include only their names, no birth or death dates.

Hayes was born George Francis Hayes on May 7, 1885, in Wellsville, New York. He died February 9, 1969, in Burbank, California.

Cross the road into the Enduring Faith Section. At the northeast edge of that section, about ten feet from the road, in Plot 387, you'll find the grave of the "Sarong Girl" and costar of the Bob Hope–Bing Crosby *Road* films, **Dorothy Lamour (1914–1996).**

Lamour worked as an elevator operator and band singer before she was named Miss New Orleans 1931 and headed for Hollywood, where she made her debut as a chorus girl in *Footlight Parade* (1933). She slipped into her sarong for the first time to play the title role in *The Jungle Princess* (1936), as sort of a female version of Tarzan, costarring with Ray Milland. Lamour played similar characters in *The Hurricane* (1937), *Her Jungle Love* (1938), *Typhoon* (1940), *Moon Over Burma* (1940), and *Beyond the Blue Horizon* (1942).

But Lamour, with her sultry looks and long dark hair, is best known for her appearances in the *Road* films, with Hope and Crosby. The lightly scripted films were a popular and entertaining combination of adventure, slapstick, ad-libs, inside jokes, and cameos by top Hollywood stars, from Humphrey Bogart to Dean Martin and Jerry Lewis. Lamour typically played the seductive tropical princess, and Hope and Crosby would vie for her affection while they battled whatever obstacles they might encounter. Lamour appeared in *Road to Singapore* (1940), *Road to Zanzibar* (1941), *Road to Morocco* (1942), *Road to Utopia* (1946), *Road to Rio* (1947), *Road to Bali* (1952), and *Road to Hong Kong* (1962). In the final film, in the ultimate twist, Joan Collins played the female lead, and Lamour appeared in a small role as herself.

Lamour also costarred with Hope in the comedies *Caught in the Draft* (1941), *They Got Me Covered* (1943), and *My Favorite Brunette* (1947). She appeared in dramatic roles in *Spawn of the North* (1938), *A Medal for Johnny* (1943), *Johnny Apollo* (1945), and *Donovan's Reef* (1963).

By the early 1950s, Lamour's film career was in decline and she began performing in nightclubs and onstage, where she toured in *Hello, Dolly!*

Lamour was married to bandleader Herbie Kaye from 1935 to 1939, then married William Ross Howard III in 1943. Her grave marker identifies her as Dorothy Lamour Howard, and Howard (1907–1978) is buried next to her.

Lamour was born Mary Leta Dorothy Slaton on December 10, 1914, in New Orleans, Louisiana. She died September 22, 1996, in Los Angeles.

Drive toward the main entrance of the cemetery and turn left at the four-way stop. On the right side, in the Sheltering Hills Section, about 130 feet past the intersection and 25 feet from the road, in Plot 125, you'll find the grave of the business-minded brother in the Disney partnership, Walt's older brother, **Roy O. Disney (1893–1971).**

In 1923, Roy and Walt Disney and animator Ub Iwerks came to Hollywood and formed a production company to produce a series combining live action with animation, called *Alice in Cartoonland.* Five years later, the animators came up with the idea for a new cartoon character they called Mickey Mouse.

While Walt Disney and Iwerks were sharing the writing and directing duties on dozens of new comedy shorts over the next few years, Roy Disney was running the business end of the operation. Roy Disney's previous financial experience came from a few years of working as a bank teller. Although the two brothers often argued about the studio operations, Walt Disney credited his brother with keeping the studio in business during the early lean years. At the studio, Roy Disney's skill at financial planning matched his brother's talent as a writer and animator. Walt was the dreamer, and Roy was responsible for finding the money to pay for the dreams, negotiating deals and loans, and managing the company's worldwide empire.

Roy Disney was also responsible for putting together the financial backing for the creation of Disneyland in Anaheim, California, which opened in 1955, and he also supervised the planning and completion of Walt Disney World in Florida after his brother's death in 1966.

Roy Disney's grave identifies him as, "A great and humble man. He left the world a better place." He's buried with his wife, Edna Francis Disney (1890–1984).

Disney was born June 24, 1893, in Chicago, Illinois. He died December 20, 1971, in Burbank, California.

Walk about 225 feet toward the main entrance, toward a statue of a woman holding a small baby. About 30 feet in front of that statue, in Plot 1948, you'll find the grave of one of the screen's most popular singing cowboys, **Gene Autry (1907–1998).**

Autry was working as a railroad laborer and telegrapher when Will Rogers heard him sing in the telegraph office and encouraged him to go into show business. In 1928, with his $5 mail-order guitar, Autry began singing on local radio stations as "Oklahoma's Yodeling Cowboy." Three years later, he had his own radio show. Autry's 1931 recording of "That Silver-Haired Daddy of Mine"—which he cowrote—was the first record ever certified gold for having sold more than one million copies.

Autry made his film debut as a square-dance-caller and singer in *In Old Santa Fe* (1934), a Western starring Ken Maynard. The following year, Autry starred in his own thirteen-part Western serial, titled *Phantom Empire*, and he had his first feature-film starring role in *Tumbling Tumbleweeds* (1935). Two years later, Autry was voted the top Western star by the theater exhibitors of America, and he remains the only Western performer who has ever appeared on the list of top ten box-office attractions.

Autry, wearing his white hat with his guitar on his shoulder and riding his faithful steed, Champion, starred in dozens of Westerns throughout the 1930s and 1940s. Autry was one of the most popular screen cowboys, and his films, which were typically made for about $50,000 each, usually grossed ten times that amount. Autry also hosted a network radio show, and his recordings, many of which he wrote, sold in the millions, including "Back in the Saddle Again" (which became his theme song), "You're the Only Star in My Blue Heaven," "Sing Me a Song of the Saddle," "Be Honest With Me," "Old November Moon," "Blue Montana Skies," "Under Fiesta Stars," "Lonely River," "I Hang My Head and Cry," "Silver Spurs," "Dixie Cannonball," "You Are My Sunshine," and "Home on the Range." Autry also cowrote "Here Comes Santa Claus" and "Rudolph the Red-Nosed Reindeer," which became the first record to be certified platinum and remains one of the best-selling recordings of all time, with more than thirty million copies sold.

In 1950, Autry conquered another medium when he made his television debut with *The Gene Autry Show*. For the next five years, he produced and starred in ninety-one half-hour episodes of the series, as well as producing other Western television series. In the early 1960s, Autry purchased the California Angels baseball team and, in 1988, he opened the Gene Autry Museum of Western Heritage in Los Angeles.

Autry was a shrewd businessman and real-estate investor. He owned the Gene Autry Hotel in Palm Springs, California, as well as television station KTLA in Los Angeles. For many years, he was ranked on the *Forbes* magazine list of the four hundred richest Americans. Autry is the only celebrity to have five different stars on the Hollywood Walk of Fame, honoring his achievements in each of the five areas of recognition—film, television, radio, recording, and live theater (in recognition of his performances at rodeos).

Autry's large grave marker identifies him as "America's favorite cowboy" and "A believer in our Western heritage" and lists his many accomplishments and occupations, including movie star, singer, composer, baseball fan and owner, media entrepreneur, and philanthropist.

Autry is buried next to his first wife, Ina Mae Spivey Autry (1911–1980). They were married from 1932 until her death.

Autry was born Orvon Gene Autry on September 29, 1907 (some sources say 1908 or 1911), in Tioga, Texas. He died October 2, 1998, in Studio City, California.

About three hundred feet past Autry's grave, in the same row as the statue, in Plot 1999, you'll find the grave of actor, producer, and director **Jack Webb (1920–1982)**, best known as Sergeant Joe Friday on the radio and television series *Dragnet*.

Webb started his career in radio, first as a disc jockey, then as the host of a comedy show in San Francisco, then as *Pat Novak, Private Eye*, a precursor to his later success with realistic crime dramas. He made his screen debut in a small, uncredited role in *Hollow Triumph* (1938), starring Paul Henreid and Joan Bennett, and had a larger role in *Sunset Boulevard* (1940). After appearing in several military dramas, Webb developed his idea for *Dragnet*, a realistic look at the workings of the Los Angeles Police Department, which debuted on radio in 1949. *Dragnet* came to television in 1951, and ran for eight more years, with most of the episodes directed by Webb.

During that time, Webb also appeared in several feature films, including *Pete Kelly's Blues* (1955) and *The D.I.* (1957), both of which he also directed. Webb revived the *Dragnet* television series from 1967 to 1970, and he also produced the popular television series *Adam-12*, from 1968 to 1975, and *Emergency*, from 1972 to 1977.

Due primarily to his performances on *Dragnet*, Webb was known for his deadpan, emotionless acting style. And, like his signature phrase from that series, Webb's simple, unadorned grave marker contains "Just the facts, ma'am"—his name, date of birth, and date of death.

Webb was born John Randolph Webb on April 2, 1920, in Santa Monica, California. He died December 23, 1982, in West Hollywood, California.

3

Hollywood Forever Cemetery

~

6000 Santa Monica Boulevard
Los Angeles, California 90038

~ HISTORY

In the Hollywood glamour days of the 1920s and 1930s, Hollywood Forever Cemetery—then known as Hollywood Memorial Park—was the premier burial spot for celebrities, studio executives, and members of Hollywood high society. Everyone who was anyone was buried in Hollywood Memorial Park, often with great fanfare and spectacle, with hundreds of fans and mourners there for the final sendoff.

The cemetery was founded in 1899 by developers I. N. Van Nuys and Isaac Lankershim. It originally covered one hundred acres. Nearly forty acres along the south side of the property were sold to Paramount Pictures studios in 1920.

Within this cemetery, visitors can find the final resting places of screen legends Rudolph Valentino, Douglas Fairbanks Sr., Janet Gaynor, Peter Lorre, Nelson Eddy, and Tyrone Power; directors Cecil B. De Mille, William Desmond Taylor, and John Huston; and Columbia Pictures founder Harry Cohn. Charlie Chaplin's first wife is buried here, as well as his mother, his ex–mother-in-law, and his namesake son.

The cemetery is also the final home to many prominent figures in the growth and development of Los Angeles and Hollywood, including Harvey and Daeida Wilcox, the true founders of Hollywood; Al and Charles Christie and David Horsley, who ran the first film studio in Hollywood; William A. Clark Jr., philanthropist and founder of the Los Angeles Philharmonic; Col. Griffith J. Griffith, who donated the land that became Griffith Park; Gen. Harrison Gray Otis, founder of the *Los Angeles Times*; Harry Chandler, publisher of the *Los Angeles Times*; and Hollywood developer Charles Toberman.

As Forest Lawn Memorial Park in nearby Glendale grew in size and popularity in the late 1930s and 1940s, Hollywood Memorial Park slipped into decline. By the early 1990s, Hollywood Memorial Park took on the Norma Desmond role as an aging and forgotten legend, a faded shadow of its former glory. The cemetery grounds were battered by normal wear and tear and the feet of thousands of visitors. The mausoleums suffered damage from a 1994 earthquake, and needed repairs were not done. The roads through the cemetery were riddled with potholes, weeds sprouted among the tombstones, windows in the rust-stained mausoleums were cracked or broken, and dead leaves swirled through the musty-smelling hallways. The huge reflecting pool in front of the Fairbanks memorial was murky and choked with weeds, and graffiti was scrawled on De Mille's crypt.

The main entrance to Hollywood Forever Cemetery, formerly known as Hollywood Memorial Park.

At this point, the story of Hollywood Forever becomes a story of drama and intrigue, hidden pasts, and secret finances. And a thrilling last-minute rescue—a true Hollywood ending.

From 1939 until state inspectors showed up in 1995 to check the cemetery's financial operations, the cemetery was run by Jules A. Roth. On the surface, Roth appeared to be a cemetery manager sent over from Central Casting—smooth, neatly dressed, and debonair, with a small, well-trimmed mustache. But Roth had kept his shady past well hidden. He had been convicted of grand theft and securities fraud in 1932, and served five years in San Quentin. While running Hollywood Memorial Park, Roth lived well, spent lavishly, and traveled frequently—often on his own luxury yacht. He reportedly purchased expensive paintings and sculpture, supposedly for display at the cemetery, but actually displayed at his elegant home in the Hollywood Hills. Still, Roth wanted to make more money from the cemetery. He considered drilling for oil under the property; he made $9 million by selling off two strips of the cemetery's land along Santa Monica Boulevard, where developers immediately put up gaudy strip malls.

Families with relatives in the cemetery were complaining about the condition of the property. Some remains, including those of legendary Hollywood makeup artist Max Factor, were removed from the cemetery and buried elsewhere.

When the state inspectors arrived, they discovered that Roth had illegally mixed money from Hollywood Memorial Park with another cemetery and mortuary he operated. Money that should have been spent on cemetery upkeep and repairs was apparently being diverted to other uses, though the full extent of the mishandling of funds may never be known, since the statute of limitations prevented state auditors from looking back more than a few years. When Roth died in early 1998, inspectors were still going over the books. (Roth is buried in the Cathedral Mausoleum at Hollywood Forever, next to his parents and his wife. His crypt marker identifies him as "General Manager and President Emeritus—Hollywood Cemetery.")

The Hollywood Cemetery Association, the official owner of the property, filed for bankruptcy in 1997, with only $1.8 million in the cemetery maintenance fund, a $2.3 million debt, and needed repairs estimated at $7 million to $10 million. A few months later, the cemetery was put on the auction block, but the high bid was only $275,000, far below the bank-required minimum. If a new owner hadn't been found, the cemetery might have been closed permanently. But in April 1998, Tyler Cassity, the twenty-eight-year-old son of a St. Louis mortuary chain owner, came to the rescue, purchasing the cemetery for $375,000 and re-naming it "Hollywood Forever." He immediately launched an extensive and expensive renovation.

Within a few months, the roads inside the sixty-two-acre cemetery were patched, mausoleums were repaired and cleaned, graffiti was removed, weeds were cut, and new signs were installed. In many areas where settling ground had left grave markers uneven and sloping, the markers were dug up and straightened.

Cassity is also reportedly making efforts to attract additional permanent celebrity residents to Hollywood Forever, as well as tourists to visit the property, which has become one of the friendliest cemeteries for celebrity-seekers. The cemetery offers daily tours of the grounds, and the flower shop near the main entrance has been converted into a gift shop, where brochures and maps of the grounds are available as well as celebrity memorabilia, including photographs, books, film posters, coffee mugs, and T-shirts. The gift shop walls are decorated with photos, posters, and other memorabilia, including framed copies of celebrity death certificates.

For many years, a retired Hollywood studio employee planted tall, narrow cypress trees at the graves of many of the celebrities buried here, making the locations even easier to find.

∼ DIRECTIONS

Located on Santa Monica Boulevard between Gower Street and Van Ness Avenue, Hollywood Forever is about a mile southwest of the famous intersection of Hollywood and Vine and is directly north of the Paramount studios.

∼ HOURS

The cemetery grounds are open from 7 A.M. to 7 P.M. every day of the week.

∼

The Tour

Since Hollywood Forever contains so many celebrities, it's easier to divide your visit into several smaller tours—the Grounds, the Cathedral Mausoleum, the Columbarium and the Abbey of the Psalms, and the Beth Olam cemetery and mausoleums.

Tour 1: The Grounds

After coming in the main entrance off Santa Monica Boulevard, continue heading south, past the administration building and flower shop and a small fountain. Follow the white arrows painted on the road. When the arrows turn toward the right, toward the Abbey of the Psalms mausoleum, keep going straight for another 150 feet. On the left side, next to the road, you'll find the grave of **Mel Blanc (1908–1989),** the man of a thousand cartoon voices. His grave marker includes one of his popular phrases—Porky Pig's "That's All Folks."

Blanc started as a musician with NBC Radio and later played the violin, tuba, and bass with various bands. He joined the cartoon department at Warner Bros. studios in 1937 as a voice specialist, and supplied the voices of dozens of cartoon characters in nearly one thousand films and cartoon shorts, including Bugs Bunny, Daffy Duck, Elmer Fudd, Tweety Pie, Sylvester, Yosemite Sam, Foghorn Leghorn, Pepe Le Pew, Marvin the Martian, the Tasmanian Devil, and Speedy Gonzales, as well as most of the supporting players and many of the sound effects.

In the 1940s, Blanc joined the cast of *The Jack Benny Show* on radio, initially supplying the sound of Benny's Maxwell automobile. When the Benny show moved to television in 1950, Blanc continued to supply the sound effects and also played supporting roles in the series. In 1960, Blanc joined the cast of *The Flintstones*, the first full-length animated television program in prime time, providing the voices for neighbor Barney Rubble and the Flintstones' dog, Dino. He also provided the voice of George Jetson's boss, Cosmo Spacely, in the animated series, *The Jetsons*.

The marker over the grave of Mel Blanc, famous for his cartoon voices, includes an appropriate farewell—"That's all folks."

Blanc continued working up until his death, and even beyond. Archival recordings of his voice were used in the live-action film *The Flintstones in Viva Rock Vegas* (2000). Blanc's son, Noel Blanc, provided many of the cartoon voices created by his father after Blanc's death.

As you stand in front of Blanc's grave, turn to your left and take in a good view of the famous "Hollywood" sign atop Mount Lee.

Blanc was born Melvin Jerome Blanc on June 30, 1908 (some sources say 1892), in San Francisco, California. He died July 10, 1989, in Los Angeles.

Turn around and head north, back toward the main entrance. Turn right at the first intersection. About a hundred feet past the intersection on the left side, about ten feet from the road and in front of three tall, narrow evergreen trees, you'll find the grave of one of the stars of the *Our Gang* comedy series, **Carl "Alfalfa" Switzer (1927–1959).**

Switzer first appeared in the *Our Gang* comedies in 1935, when he was only seven years old, and appeared in nearly seventy-five of the comedy shorts over the next five years. Switzer was the tall, skinny, freckle-faced kid with the uncontrollable cowlick and equally uncontrollable singing voice. One of Alfalfa's most memorable *Our Gang* performances was his spectacularly off-key rendition of "I'm in the Mood for Love" in *The Pitch Singer* (1936).

After his *Our Gang* days ended in 1940, Switzer appeared in small, often uncredited parts in nearly fifty films, including *My Favorite Blonde* (1942), *The Human Comedy* (1943), *Going My Way* (1944), *It's a Wonderful Life* (1946), *A Letter to Three Wives* (1946), *State of the Union* (1948), *Pat and Mike* (1952), and *The Defiant Ones* (1958). Switzer even played a slave in Cecil B. De Mille's *The Ten Commandments* (1956).

When the *Our Gang* shorts were broadcast on television, beginning in the 1950s as *The Little Rascals*, Switzer and the rest of the performers gained a new generation of fans, but they didn't enjoy any financial benefits. Their contracts didn't include any consideration of residuals for the rebroadcast of their films on television.

The dog on Carl "Alfalfa" Switzer's grave marker probably symbolizes his love of hunting, not his Our Gang costar, Petey.

Switzer had several run-ins with the law during the 1950s. He was once arrested for cutting down trees in Sequoia National Forest, and in 1958 he was shot by an unknown assailant in front of a bar in the San Fernando Valley.

Between acting jobs, Switzer worked as a bar-tender and part-time hunting guide, where his customers included Roy Rogers and Henry Fonda, who attempted to help Switzer by finding small parts for him in films. Before one of his hunting expeditions, Switzer borrowed a hunting dog from a friend, Moses "Bud" Stiltz. The dog ran away, and Switzer offered a $35 reward for its return. A few days later, a man found the dog and brought it to the bar where Switzer worked to claim the reward, which Switzer paid him, along with giving him $15 worth of free drinks. Several days later, after a night of drinking, Switzer decided that Stiltz owed him the $50 he had spent to get the dog back, so he went to Stiltz's home in Mission Hills to retrieve the money.

Stiltz and Switzer got into a heated argument. Stiltz claimed Switzer hit him on the head with a large clock and pulled a knife on him. Stiltz grabbed a gun and shot Switzer in the stomach. He died on the way to the hospital, at the age of thirty-one. A coroner's inquest ruled that the shooting was justifiable homicide. Even in death, Switzer had unfortunate timing. He had the bad luck of dying the same day as legendary director Cecil B. De Mille, and the primary news coverage the next day concerned De Mille's passing.

There is some question about the significance of the dog on Switzer's grave stone. Though many *Our Gang* fans insist it's supposed to be Petey, the dog who appeared in the comedies, it is more likely a hunting dog, to signify Switzer's longtime interest in hunting.

Switzer was born August 7, 1927 (some sources say 1928), in Paris, Illinois. He died January 21, 1959, in Mission Hills, California.

Continue heading east and turn left at the next intersection. You'll see a small lake on your right. About 250 feet from the intersection and about 15 feet from the road, next to a tall cypress tree, you'll find the grave of **Adolph Menjou (1890–1963),** who appeared in nearly 150 films and personified the image of dapper elegance, both onscreen and off.

After graduating with an engineering degree from Cornell University, Menjou traveled to New York, where he worked in a series of jobs before trying his hand at acting in 1915. As a young actor, Menjou reported for work to appear in *Nearly a King* (1916), starring John Barrymore, but Barrymore became upset when he saw Menjou. "Who is that fellow?" Barrymore asked the director. "I don't like his face. He looks too much like me. He'll confuse the plot." To remedy the situation, Menjou grew a mustache, which he kept neatly trimmed and waxed, and which contributed to his dapper, debonair image.

After serving for three years in World War I, reaching the rank of captain in the Ambulance Corps, Menjou returned to his acting career. He appeared in a supporting role in *The Shiek* (1921), starring Rudolph Valentino, and was King Louis XIII in *The Three Musketeers* (1921), starring Douglas Fairbanks. Menjou's big break came with his starring role in *A Woman of Paris* (1923), written and directed by Charlie Chaplin. After that, he was typically cast as a suave man-of-the-world in sophisticated comedies and dramas, first as a leading man, then in supporting roles. Menjou appeared in *Morocco* (1930), *A Farewell to Arms* (1932), *Little Miss Marker* (1934), *Stage Door* (1937), *A Star Is Born* (1937), *Golden Boy* (1939), *Roxie Hart* (1942), *State of the Union* (1948), and *Paths of Glory* (1957), among many other films. Menjou was nominated for an Academy Award as Best Actor for his performance in *The Front Page* (1931). He also hosted *Your Favorite Story*, an anthology series that ran on television from 1953 to 1954.

Menjou was regularly included on "best dressed" lists in the 1930s and 1940s, and men across the country cultivated the "Menjou mustache." A well-known political conservative in Hollywood, Menjou was one of the founders of the Motion Picture Alliance for the Preservation of American Ideals in 1944. In 1947, he was a "friendly witness" at the hearings of the House Un-American Activities Committee.

Menjou was born Adolphe Jean Menjou on February 18, 1890, in Pittsburgh, Pennsylvania. He died October 29, 1963, in Beverly Hills, California.

About fifty feet directly north of Menjou's grave, with the grave marker surrounded by roses and other flowering plants, you'll find the grave of **John Huston (1906–1987)**—actor, writer, producer, and director. He was nominated fourteen times for the Academy Award—eight times for writing, five times for directing, and once for acting—and won twice.

Huston was born into a show business family, but it took him several attempts to get into the business himself. And once he did, he was responsible for writing and/or directing some of the most popular and best-known American films of all time. Huston, the son of actor Walter Huston, made his first stage appearance at the age of three, and spent most of his childhood traveling with his parents on the vaudeville circuit. He made his Broadway debut at nineteen but quickly became bored with acting and moved to Mexico, where he became an officer in the cavalry. He returned to acting and appeared in bit parts in three films directed by William Wyler, a friend of his father—*The Shakedown* (1929), *Hell's Heroes* (1930), and *The Storm* (1930). But Huston again left Hollywood and worked for several years as a journalist for newspapers and magazines. He returned to the film business and was hired as a scriptwriter, contributing to several films starring his father, including *A House Divided* (1931) and *Law and Order* (1932). He left again, living for several years in Europe.

In 1938, Huston returned to Hollywood again. He worked on scripts for several films for Warner Bros. and the Goldwyn Company, including *Jezebel* (1938), *The Amazing Dr. Clitterhouse* (1938), *Wuthering Heights* (1939), and *High Sierra* (1941), as well as two films that won Academy Award nominations for Huston for Best Screenplay—*Dr. Erlich's Magic Bullet* (1940) and *Sergeant York* (1941). In 1941, Huston was given a chance to direct his first film—*The Maltese Falcon*, starring Humphrey Bogart and Mary Astor, from his own script, which was based on the novel by Dashiell Hammett. The film, which many critics still consider to be the best detective film ever made, received an Academy Award nomination for Best Picture, and Huston was again nominated for Best Screenplay.

But Huston left Hollywood once more. This time, he enlisted in the Signal Corps and directed three World War II documentaries. He was promoted to major and was awarded the Legion of Merit for his courageous work under battle conditions in Europe and in the Pacific. Finally, in 1945, Huston returned to Hollywood for good. He continued writing, directing, and sometimes performing both duties on a lengthy series of successful films. In 1948, he won his only two Academy Awards, for writing and directing *The Treasure of the Sierra Madre*, for which his father won the Academy Award as well, for Best Supporting Actor. Huston also received double nominations for writing and directing *The Asphalt Jungle* (1950) and *The African Queen* (1951). He also wrote and directed *Let There Be Light* (1946), *Key Largo* (1948), *We Were Strangers* (1949), *The Red Badge of Courage* (1951), *Beat the Devil* (1953), *Moby Dick* (1956), *The List of Adrian Messenger* (1963), and *The Night of the Iguana* (1964). During this period, Huston won Academy Award nominations for directing *Moulin Rouge* (1952), which he also wrote, and for writing *Heaven Knows, Mr. Allison* (1967), which he also directed.

Huston also directed *The Roots of Heaven* (1958), *The Unforgiven* (1960), and *The Misfits* (1961). By the early 1960s, Huston was beginning to return to the screen as an actor. For his first major role, in *The Cardinal* (1963), he was nominated for an Academy Award as Best Supporting Actor. By the early 1970s, after acting performances in films such as *Candy* (1968), *De Sade* (1969), *Myra Breckinridge* (1970), and *Battle for the Planet of the Apes* (1973), Huston's star appeared to be fading, and he moved to Mexico. But he bounced back with a strong performance in *Chinatown* (1974), and he won another Academy Award nomination for writing *The Man Who Would Be King* (1975), which he also directed.

Huston played small roles in several films, including a few made for television, through the late 1970s and early 1980s. In 1983, he was given the Lifetime Achievement Award from the American Film Institute, but two years later he proved that his career wasn't over yet. He won his final Academy Award nomination for directing *Prizzi's Honor* (1985), which also served to pass the torch to the next generation of Hustons—his daughter, Angelica, won the Academy Award for Best Supporting Actress for her performance in the film, making Huston the only person to direct both a parent and a child to Oscar-winning performances.

In 1998, the American Film Institute released its list of "100 Greatest American Movies," in commemoration of the first hundred years of American cinema. Three films written and directed by John Huston appeared in the top thirty on that list—*The African Queen, The Maltese Falcon,* and *The Treasure of the Sierra Madre,* as well as *Chinatown,* which featured Huston as an actor.

Huston is buried next to his mother, Rhea Huston (1882–1938). Their grave marker is made of pink marble, imported from Ireland.

Huston was born August 5, 1906, in Nevada, Missouri. He died August 28, 1987, in Middletown, Rhode Island.

About 120 feet north of Huston's grave and about 40 feet from the road, you'll find a small white stone bench. Next to the bench, you'll find the grave of **Harold Rosson (1895–1988),** pioneering cinematographer and former husband of Jean Harlow.

Rosson, the brother of directors Arthur Rosson and Richard Rosson and actress Helene Rosson, started his career as an actor with Vitagraph studios in 1908. He moved to Hollywood in 1913 and started working behind the scenes, first as a cameraman. He worked as a cinematographer on nearly 150 films, mostly at MGM studios, including *The Docks of New York* (1928), *Tarzan the Ape Man* (1932), *The Scarlet Pimpernel* (1934), *Treasure Island* (1934), *As You Like It* (1936), *Captains Courageous* (1937), *A Yank at Oxford*

(1938), *Edison, the Man* (1940), *Men of Boys Town* (1941), *Duel in the Sun* (1946), *Command Decision* (1948), *On the Town* (1949), *The Stratton Story* (1949), *The Red Badge of Courage* (1951), *Singin' in the Rain* (1952), *The Enemy Below* (1957), *No Time for Sergeants* (1958), and *El Dorado* (1967).

Rosson worked with Harlow on five films—*Red Dust* (1932), *Red-Headed Woman* (1932), *Bombshell* (1933), *Hold Your Man* (1933), and *The Girl From Missouri* (1934). Rosson and Harlow were married in 1933, but divorced two years later when Harlow accused Rosson of "mental cruelty" for reading in bed.

In 1937, Rosson was given a special Academy Award for his pioneering Technicolor work on *The Garden of Allah* (1936). He was nominated for an Academy Award for Best Cinematography five times, for *The Wizard of Oz* (1939), *Boom Town* (1940), *Thirty Seconds Over Tokyo* (1944), *The Asphalt Jungle* (1950), and *The Bad Seed* (1956).

Rosson's brothers are buried near him.

Rosson was born April 6, 1895, in New York City,
He died September 6, 1988, in Palm Beach, Florida.

Continue heading north from Rosson's grave and cross the road. In front of you, along the northern wall of the cemetery grounds, you'll see an abandoned pump house. A few feet to the left of the pump house, in front of a brown urn filled with flowers, you'll find the grave of **Florence Lawrence (1890–1938)**, who appeared in nearly three hundred films and is credited with being the first movie star.

Lawrence began her performing career at age three, working in her parents' traveling tent show. In 1906, Lawrence began appearing in films, first for the Edison Company, then for the Biograph Company in New York City. From 1908 to 1910, she appeared in more than one hundred short films directed by D. W. Griffith. She also appeared as Juliet in the first filmed version of *Romeo and Juliet* (1909).

Like other studios, Biograph did not identify its actors by name, for fear that they would become too popular as individuals and start to ask for more money. But Biograph did promote Lawrence as the first "Biograph Girl." In 1910, Carl Laemmle, founder of Universal Pictures, lured Lawrence to come to work for his Independent Motion Picture Co. and promoted her as the "IMP Girl." (After Lawrence left Biograph, the title of "Biograph Girl" went to Mary Pickford.) To gain publicity for his new star, Laemmle first circulated a story

Florence Lawrence, the "First Movie Star," was forgotten by Hollywood and took her own life in 1938.

that Lawrence had been killed in a traffic accident. He then said the story was a hoax, and that she would be appearing in the next IMP production, *The Broken Oath* (1910). Laemmle was also the first filmmaker to identify his star by name. And so, Florence Lawrence became the first movie star.

Lawrence appeared in more than one hundred films over the next five years. In 1915, she was severely burned in a fire at the studio, reportedly while trying to rescue another performer. She disappeared from the screen for several years, returning to play supporting roles in the late 1920s and early 1930s, including a small part in *Secrets* (1933), ironically starring Mary Pickford, her successor as the "Biograph Girl," and small parts in *The Old-Fashioned Way* (1934) and *The Man on the Flying Trapeze* (1935), both starring W. C. Fields. Her last screen appearance was a bit part in *One Rainy Afternoon* (1936). Lawrence committed suicide by taking poison in her Beverly Hills home in 1938.

For many years, Lawrence's grave was unmarked. Recently, a memorial marker was added, paid for by actor Roddy McDowall, who had a large collection of film memorabilia and served on the National Film Preservation Board. Lawrence's grave marker identifies her as "The Biograph Girl" and "The First Movie Star." Lawrence's mother, Charlotte Bridgwood (1861–1929), who was known professionally as Lotta Lawrence, is buried in the Columbarium behind the chapel at Hollywood Forever.

Lawrence was born Florence Bridgwood on January 2, 1890 (some sources say 1880 or 1886), in Hamilton, Ontario, Canada. She died December 28, 1938, in Beverly Hills, California.

Cross back over the road, toward the lake. About ten feet from the road, you'll see two large, white mausoleum crypts with the name "De Mille" etched on the front. One of these crypts contains the remains of legendary director **Cecil B. De Mille (1881–1959).**

De Mille's parents were both playwrights. After his father died, his mother supported the family by running a school for girls and a theatrical company, which De Mille helped operate for twelve years, often appearing in the productions himself. In 1913, De Mille joined with Jesse Lasky and Samuel Goldfish (later Goldwyn) to form the Jesse L. Lasky Feature Play Company in Los Angeles. De Mille urged the group to consider switching from the short, two-reel films that were popular at the time to a full-length, six-reel feature. The company's first production was *The Squaw Man* (1914), a feature-length Western, shot in a rented horse barn and on the hills around Hollywood. *The Squaw Man,* written and directed by De Mille and Oscar Apfel—De Mille even appeared in the film as an extra—was an enormous financial and critical success and helped transform Los Angeles into a film center. (*The Squaw Man* was also the only film to be made three times by the same director. De Mille made another silent version of the film in 1918, and a sound version in 1931.) In 1916, the Jesse L. Lasky Feature Play Company company merged with Adolph Zukor's Famous Players to form the Famous Players–Lasky Corporation. Over the years, with additional mergers and corporate realignments, that corporation became Paramount Pictures, and De Mille was the creative force at the studio for decades.

De Mille directed nearly one hundred films, often also working as writer, editor, producer, and sometimes even as actor. The vast majority of his work was on silent films made before 1930. More than anything else, De Mille was

Legendary director Cecil B. De Mille is buried next to his wife at Hollywood Forever.

known for his massive biblical and historical epics, including *The Ten Commandments* (1923 and 1956), *The King of Kings* (1927), *The Sign of the Cross* (1932), *Cleopatra* (1934), and *Samson and Delilah* (1949). De Mille also directed *The Plainsman* (1936), *Union Pacific* (1939), and *Unconquered* (1947).

De Mille, one of the thirty-six founders of the Academy of Motion Picture Arts and Sciences, was nominated for an Academy Award as Best Director only once, for *The Greatest Show on Earth* (1952). He did not win, although he did take home an Academy Award for his role as producer when the film won the Best Picture award. He also won the Academy Award for Best Picture for *The Ten Commandments* (1956). In 1950, De Mille was awarded an honorary Academy Award, "for thirty-seven years of brilliant showmanship," and he won the Irving G. Thalberg Memorial Award in 1953.

As an actor, De Mille appeared as himself in several films, including *Star Spangled Rhythm* (1942), *Variety Girl* (1947), *Sunset Boulevard* (1950), and *The Buster Keaton Story* (1957). He also supplied the voice of God in *The Ten Commandments* (1956).

De Mille is buried next to his wife of fifty-six years, Constance Adams De Mille (1874–1960).

De Mille was born Cecil Blount De Mille on August 12, 1881, in Ashfield, Massachusetts. He died January 21, 1959, in Los Angeles.

About thirty-five feet behind the De Mille crypts, in front of two tall cypress trees, you'll find the graves of actress **Janet Gaynor (1906–1984),** who won the first Academy Award as Best Actress then retired from the screen at the height of her career, and her second husband, costume designer **Adrian (1903–1959).**

After working as a secretary, theater usher, and shoestore clerk in Los Angeles, Gaynor decided to try her hand at acting shortly after she graduated from high school. She made her debut in small, uncredited roles in short comedies and Westerns in 1924, working steadily for two years before she landed a major role in *The Johnstown Flood* (1926). In the same year, Gaynor also appeared in *The Shamrock Handicap, The Blue Eagle, The Midnight Kiss,* and *The Return of Peter Grimm.*

Gaynor won the first Academy Award for Best Actress for her work in three films—*Sunrise* (1927), *Seventh Heaven* (1927), and *Street Angel* (1928). When talking pictures became popular, Gaynor was one of the few performers who made a successful transition. From the late 1920s to the mid-1930s, Gaynor was one of Hollywood's top box-office attractions. The sweet and wholesome Gaynor was teamed with actor Charles Farrell in twelve films during this period, and they were known as "America's Favorite Lovebirds."

Gaynor was again nominated for the Academy Award as Best Actress for her performance in *A Star Is Born* (1937). Gaynor appeared in two films in 1938—*Three Loves Has Nancy,* with Robert Montgomery; and *The Young at Heart,* with Douglas Fairbanks Jr. The following year, at the height of her career, Gaynor married costume designer Adrian and announced her retirement from films. Though she made several television and radio appearances during the 1940s and 1950s, her only screen appearance was a small role in the comedy *Bernardine* (1957).

In 1983, Gaynor was injured in an auto accident that left her with eleven broken ribs, a broken pelvis and collarbone, and various internal injuries. She never fully recovered from her injuries, and she died the following year.

Adrian, who sometimes worked under the name of Gilbert Adrian, graduated from the New York School of Applied and Fine Arts and was then hired by Irving Berlin to work on *George White's Scandals* on Broadway. When Adrian moved to Los Angeles, he traveled in the private railroad car of Rudolph Valentino and his wife, designer Natacha Rambova, working on the designs for Valentino's upcoming films, *The Eagle* (1925) and *Cobra* (1925). Adrian was hired as a production designer by Cecil B. De Mille, then as the chief costume designer at MGM studios. Adrian, who became one of Hollywood's best-known costume designers, was known for creating the glamorous looks for some of MGM's biggest stars, including Greta Garbo, Jean Harlow, Norma Shearer, Greer Garson, Marion Davies, and Joan Crawford.

Adrian was the costume designer on more than two hundred films, from lavish period musicals, to modern drama, to gritty crime stories, including *Mata Hari* (1931), *Rasputin and the Empress* (1932), *Grand Hotel* (1932), *Dinner at Eight* (1933), *Bombshell* (1933), *The Merry Widow* (1934), *The Barretts of Wimpole Street* (1934), *Naughty Marietta* (1935), *Anna Karenina* (1935), *Romeo and Juliet* (1936), *The Great Ziegfeld* (1936), *Camille* (1937), *Marie Antoinette* (1938), *The Wizard of Oz* (1939), *Ninotchka* (1939), *The Philadelphia Story* (1940), *Pride and Prejudice* (1940), *Boom Town* (1940), *Dr. Jekyll and Mr. Hyde* (1941), *Ziegfeld Girl* (1941), *Woman of the Year* (1942), and *Rope* (1948).

After Adrian died in 1959, Gaynor married producer Paul Gregory. Her grave marker identifies her as Janet Gaynor Gregory. For many years, Adrian's grave was unmarked. Recently, however, a stone was added to match Gaynor's marker.

Gaynor was born Laura Gainor on October 6, 1906, in Philadelphia, Pennsylvania. She died September 14, 1984, in Palm Springs, California.

Adrian was born Adrian Adolph Greenberg on March 3, 1903, in Naugatuck, Connecticut. He died September 13, 1959, in Los Angeles.

About twenty feet past Gaynor and Adrian, just before you reach the lake, you'll find a marker for actress and "blonde bombshell" **Jayne Mansfield (1933–1967)**, next to a small rose garden. This marker is a cenotaph, a memorial placed in honor of a person who is buried elsewhere, so that mourners and fans can have a place to pay their respects. Mansfield is actually buried in Fairview Cemetery, in Plainfield, Pennsylvania, beneath a large, white, heart-shaped marker.

The inscription on her cenotaph—"We live to love you more each day"— is the same as the inscription on her grave marker. The cenotaph also includes a small photograph, and a fairly large error. Mansfield was born in 1933, not 1938. (Her grave marker in Pennsylvania has the right date.)

Mansfield was born Vera Jane Palmer on April 19, 1933 (some sources say 1932) in Bryn Mawr, Pennsylvania. She died June 29, 1967, near New Orleans, Louisiana.

Walk along the edge of the lake about one hundred feet, toward the Cathedral Mausoleum. About ten feet from the shore, in front of another tall cypress tree, you'll find the grave of **Virginia Rappe (1895–1921)**, an actress remembered more for her death than her life.

Rappe's career began as a model. When producer Mack Sennett saw her picture on the sheet music for "Let Me Call You Sweetheart," he offered her a job with his Keystone Film Company, and she appeared in small roles in several films. Rappe had also attracted the attention of former Keystone comedian Roscoe "Fatty" Arbuckle, who invited her to a party at the St. Francis Hotel in San Francisco in 1921 to celebrate the signing of his new three-year, $3 million contract with Paramount Pictures. The festivities lasted for several days in a suite of three rooms on the twelfth floor of the hotel. At one point, Arbuckle grabbed Rappe, escorted her into a bedroom, and closed the door.

What happened behind that door will never be known for sure, but when the door opened again, Rappe was writhing on the bed, crying out in pain. Within a few days, she would be dead—the coroner determined that her death was caused by a ruptured bladder, which led to peritonitis—and Arbuckle would be charged with her murder. After three trials, Arbuckle would be found not guilty of all charges, with the jury even going so far as to apologize to him, but his career as a performer would be over.

The sensationalistic press made the most of the trial. There were reports that Arbuckle, who weighed nearly three hundred pounds, caused the injury to Rappe when he was on top of her during a forced sexual encounter. Other stories claimed he had raped her with a foreign object, perhaps a champagne bottle. Most of these stories included the most lurid, graphic detail possible.

Arbuckle first went on trial in November 1921. The prosecution claimed that when Arbuckle brought Rappe into the bedroom, he said, "I've been waiting for this for a long time," and witnesses reported hearing Rappe's screams from behind the locked door. Arbuckle's version of the story was that shortly after they entered the bedroom, Rappe became ill and vomited several times. He led her to the bed, then returned to the party. When he went back to check on her, he discovered her moaning in pain and barely coherent.

The sensational trial was front-page news for weeks. In the press, Rappe was presented as an innocent, naive starlet, and Arbuckle was assumed to be guilty. The press didn't mention that Rappe's bladder may have been damaged in a recent abortion, or that in the weeks prior to the party she had exhibited symptoms of a bladder infection, and the contractions of her abdominal muscles while she vomited might have caused her diseased bladder to rupture. In the press, and to the public, Arbuckle had become a symbol of Hollywood's immorality. Across the country, theaters stopped showing his films.

At the first trial, however, when Arbuckle took the witness stand in his own defense, the jury was unable to reach a verdict, though they voted 10 to 2 for acquittal. At the second trial, Arbuckle did not take the stand, and the jury might have seen this as his admission of guilt. Again, they could not reach a decision, but this time they voted 10 to 2 for conviction. At the third trial, which began in March 1922, Arbuckle again took the witness stand. At the end of the trial, the jury deliberated only a few minutes before finding Arbuckle not guilty of all charges. In fact, the jury wrote a note of apology to Arbuckle: "Acquittal is not enough for Roscoe Arbuckle. We feel that a great injustice has been done him. We feel also that it was our only plain duty to give him this exoneration. There was not the slightest proof adduced to connect him in any way with the commission of a crime. . . . The happening at the hotel was an unfortunate affair for which Arbuckle, so the evidence shows, was in no way responsible. We wish him success and hope that the American people will take the judgment of 14 men and women who have sat listening for 31 days to the evidence that Roscoe Arbuckle is entirely innocent and free from all blame."

Unfortunately, the public and the Hollywood establishment thought otherwise. Paramount canceled Arbuckle's contract and, in April 1922, less than a week after Arbuckle was cleared of all charges, the newly formed Hays Office banned Arbuckle from making any films. Though the ban was lifted a few months later, Arbuckle's career never recovered from the incident. For years, Arbuckle could not find a job in Hollywood. He eventually began working as a director of comedy shorts, using the name William B. Goodrich, based on Buster Keaton's suggestion that he use the name Will B. Good. Arbuckle died in 1933.

Before her death, Rappe appeared in small roles in four films—*Paradise Garden* (1917), *The Foolish Virgin* (1917), *A Twilight Baby* (1920), and *An Adventuress* (1922), which starred Rudolph Valentino and was released after her death. During Arbuckle's trials, theaters across the country began to show these films, in an attempt to take advantage of the sensational circumstances surrounding her death. Eventually, a national association of theater owners voted to ban the showing of her films in an effort to stop the exploitation.

Rappe's grave is one of two locations at Hollywood Forever said to be haunted. (The other is the area around actor Clifton Webb's crypt in the Abbey of the Psalms mausoleum.) Some visitors to Hollywood Forever have reported what sounds like a woman sobbing or crying out in pain near Rappe's grave.

Rappe was born Virginia Rapp in 1895 (some sources say 1896) in New York City. She died September 9, 1921, in San Francisco, California.

Next to Rappe's grave, you'll find the grave of actor, writer, and director **Henry "Pathe" Lehrman (1886–1946),** who was Rappe's fiancé at the time of her death and became her most vocal defender. Lehrman visited Rappe's grave at least once a week until he died.

According to legend, former trolley car conductor Lehrman approached director D. W. Griffith in 1909 and told him he was from the French-based Pathe studios and was looking for work as an actor and writer. Griffith hired him to work on two-reel comedies, and by the time he found out that Lehrman's résumé was fake he was impressed enough by Lehrman's work that he promoted him to director. (The story also gave Lehrman a nickname that stayed with him for the rest of his life.)

Virginia Rappe, the actress at the center of the "Fatty" Arbuckle scandal, is buried next to Henry Lehrman, her fiancé.

In 1912, Lehrman left Griffith and went to work at Mack Sennett's Keystone Film Company, directing, writing, and appearing in many films in the Keystone Kops series. While with Sennett in 1914, Lehrman directed Charlie Chaplin's first four films—*Mabel's Strange Predicament, Between Showers, Making a Living,* and *Kid Auto Races at Venice,* the first film featuring Chaplin's "Little Tramp" character. Lehrman also worked for a while at his own studio—Lehrman Knock-Out, or L-KO Pictures—and then moved to the Fox studios.

After 1930, Lehrman worked primarily as a writer on films including *Moulin Rouge* (1934), *Bulldog Drummond Strikes Back* (1934), and *Show Them No Mercy!* (1935).

Lehrman was born April 21, 1886, in Vienna, Austria.
He died November 7, 1946, in Los Angeles.

From the graves of Rappe and Lehrman, continue walking toward the Cathedral Mausoleum. After walking about a hundred feet, you'll find a small family mausoleum next to the lake, with the name "Douras" over the door. Though their names don't appear anywhere on the outside of the mausoleum, inside are two celebrities you'd never expect to find in the same room, let alone sharing a mausoleum—actress **Marion Davies (1897–1961),** best known as the not-so-secret mistress of publisher William Randolph Hearst, and actor **Arthur Lake (1905–1987),** best known as the goofy, bumbling Dagwood in the *Blondie* film series of the 1940s.

Marion Davies' large private mausoleum is next to the marble bench marking the grave of Tyrone Power.

The story of how they ended up together revolves around one of the most enduring mysteries in Hollywood, a mystery that may never be solved.

The first mystery—the name on the mausoleum—is easily solved. Marion Davies was born Marion Douras, and she never legally changed her name. She started her career as a model and dancer in New York, making her stage debut in a Broadway chorus line at the age of sixteen. She was dancing on Broadway in the Ziegfeld Follies in 1916 when she caught the attention of newspaper publisher William Randolph Hearst, who took a personal and professional interest in her. At the time, Davies was twenty and Hearst was fifty-four.

With his considerable fortune and the power of his newspaper chain, Hearst was determined to make Davies into a movie star. Hearst even purchased a film production company, Cosmopolitan Pictures, to promote Davies' career.

Davies made her screen debut in *Runaway, Romney* (1917), which she also wrote. She starred in several dramas, but she was at her best in comedies, beginning with *Getting Mary Married* (1919). Hearst, however, preferred to see his young protégée and paramour in elaborate and expensive costume dramas and period romances, including *Cecilia of the Pink Roses* (1918), *When Knighthood Was in Flower* (1922), and *Bride's Play* (1922). Though the films were heavily promoted in the Hearst newspapers, most lost money, primarily because Hearst insisted on sparing no expense in the production. For one film, which included a dramatic entrance by Davies down a long staircase, Hearst insisted that the roof of a sound stage at the Warner Bros. studios be raised to accommodate the set. (Visitors to the Warner Bros. studios can still see that sound stage, slightly taller than all the others. Recently, some of the shipboard scenes in *The Perfect Storm* [2000] were filmed there.) Hearst reportedly lost $7 million on the Cosmopolitan production company from 1919 to 1923, when the films were distributed by Paramount.

In 1925, Davies and Cosmopolitan moved to MGM studios, where she performed in some of her best and most successful films—mostly comedies—including *Tillie the Toiler* (1927); *The Patsy* (1928); *Show People* (1928); *Marianne* (1929); *Not So Dumb* (1930); *The Bachelor Father* (1931); *Peg o' My Heart* (1933); *Going Hollywood* (1933), costarring with Bing Crosby; *Page Miss Glory* (1935); and *Cain and Mabel* (1936), costarring with Clark Gable. But the advent of sound films had a severe impact on Davies' career. She spoke with a slight stutter, and although she was able to overcome this impediment in her films, she retired after appearing in *Ever Since Eve* (1937).

In Orson Welles's fictionalized version of Hearst's life, *Citizen Kane* (1941), the publisher promotes the career of his girlfriend, an untalented opera singer, which has resulted in many people assuming that Davies must have been untalented and would not have succeeded without Hearst. In fact, Davies was a talented actress, and probably would have been successful without Hearst's intervention in her career. And if she had focused on comedies from the start, she might have been even more successful. Welles himself attempted to correct that erroneous assumption when he said, "Marion Davies was one of the most delightfully accomplished comediennes in the whole history of the screen."

Davies and Hearst remained a couple after her retirement from films, and they were well known in social circles for throwing elaborate parties at the several homes they shared in California, including Hearst's San Simeon estate, his mansion in Beverly Hills, and his Santa Monica beach house. They were often described as the "most famous unmarried couple in America." Hearst and Davies certainly would have married, but Hearst's wife would not grant him a divorce. Hearst died in Davies' Beverly Hills home in August 1951. Two months later, the fifty-four-year-old Davies married for the first time, eloping to Las Vegas with longtime friend Horace G. Brown Jr., a former actor and retired military sea captain who bore an amazing resemblance to Hearst.

After her retirement from films, Davies was a successful businesswoman and philanthropist. She founded the Marion Davies Children's Clinic and donated $2 million for the construction of the children's wing at the UCLA Medical Center.

Now for the mystery: Though the relationship between Davies and Hearst wasn't much of a secret, the fact that they had a child together was. When Davies gave birth to their daughter in the early 1920s in Paris, France, she gave the child to her older sister, Rose Van Cleve, to raise. The girl was brought up as Patricia Van Cleve. She spent much of her childhood at Hearst's San Simeon estate, traveled extensively with Davies and Hearst, and was well taken care of by her "Aunt Marion." Although there were whispered rumors around Hollywood for decades—Patricia Van Cleve seemed to have Hearst's distinctive nose and long face—they were never publicly discussed.

Later, Patricia Van Cleve married actor Arthur Lake (which explains how he ended up in the mausoleum), but she never told their two children—Arthur Jr. and Marion—about her real mother. Finally, just hours before she died in 1993, she told her son the whole story.

When Davies told Hearst that she was pregnant with his child, he put her on a steamship to Europe. She gave birth to a baby girl at a small hospital near Paris sometime between 1920 and 1923; Van Cleve said she was never sure of the exact date. When Davies and the baby returned, it was decided to give her to Davies' sister, Rose, and her husband, George Van Cleve. The Van Cleves' own infant child had recently died, and the dead baby's birth certificate was altered to make it appear that Patricia was their child. Although Patricia lived with the Van Cleves, Hearst and Davies paid for her upbringing and her education—and George Van Cleve, a former Arrow shirt model, became head of Hearst's Cosmopolitan Pictures. Hearst even selected Lake, a friend of Hearst's sons, to be Patricia's husband, and the couple were married at San Simeon in 1937.

Patricia did a little modeling and acting. In 1940, she was named one of thirteen "Baby Stars" selected by the Motion Picture Publicists Association, no doubt with some pressure from Hearst, and in 1950 she appeared on the cover of the *Sunday Mirror* magazine—a Hearst publication.

"She lived her life on a satin pillow," Arthur Lake Jr. said after his mother's death. "They took away her name, but they gave her everything else." When Davies died in 1961, Patricia was at her bedside.

Still, despite Patricia's story, there is no absolute proof of her claims. Although there is certainly a great deal of circumstantial evidence supporting her, some still contend that her story isn't true. They point to the fact that Davies appeared in at least two films released every year from 1918 to 1925, which would cover the possible years of Patricia's birth. Of course, the films could have been completed well before their release, which would have given Davies enough time to keep her pregnancy secret.

Though there are no names on the mausoleum to identify the occupants, several members of Davies' family are buried inside, including her mother, Rose Reilly Douras (1862–1928), and her father, Bernard J. Douras (1853–1935), as well as Arthur Lake and Patricia Van Cleve Lake. In front of the mausoleum are three markers identifying the graves of Davies' cousin, Maitland Rice Lederer (1896–1934), and two of her sister Rose's ex-husbands, George Barnes Van Cleve (1880–1949) and Louis Adlon (1908–1947). The Douras family mausoleum was initially built in 1928 as a temporary location, following the death of Davies' mother. The family intended to build a larger family mausoleum at Calvary Cemetery (see Chapter 9), but those plans were never completed.

Davies was born Marion Cecilia Douras on January 3, 1897, in Brooklyn, New York. She died September 22, 1961, in Los Angeles.

Arthur Lake was born into a show business family. His mother was an actress, and his father and uncle were circus acrobats known as "The Flying Silverlakes." Lake and his sister, Florence, traveled and performed with them from a young age. His first film role, at the age of twelve, was a small part in *Jack and the Beanstalk* (1917). He appeared in juvenile roles in nearly forty films from the early 1920s to the late 1930s—an assortment of dramas, comedies, mysteries, romances, and musicals including several silent comedies starring Reginald Denny; *Indiscreet* (1931), starring Gloria Swanson; *Girl o' My Dreams* (1933), starring Lon Chaney Jr. and Mary Carlisle; *True Confession* (1937), starring Carole Lombard and Fred MacMurray; and *Topper* (1937), starring Constance Bennett and Cary Grant.

In 1938, the year after he married Patricia Van Cleve, Lake was cast as Dagwood Bumstead in *Blondie*, the first filmed installment of the popular comic strip, with Penny Singleton in the title role. Lake campaigned hard for the role, and he benefited from his relationship with publisher William Randolph Hearst, whose newspapers ran the *Blondie* comic strip. "I had a couple of people rooting for me named Marion Davies and William Randolph Hearst," Lake later recalled. The first *Blondie* film, which cost only $85,000 to produce, brought in revenue of $9 million. Over the next twelve years, Lake and Singleton appeared in a total of twenty-eight films in the *Blondie* series, making it the one of the longest-running series in film history. Typically, the plots would include the bumbling and befuddled Dagwood getting into some sort of trouble, usually with his boss, Mr. Dithers, and Blondie would come to his rescue. The popular series helped Columbia Pictures survive through lean budget years. Once the series started, however, Lake was so typecast in the role that he only appeared in small roles in a handful of other films. Lake and Singleton also performed for seven years on the *Blondie* radio series.

In 1957, Lake attempted to revive Dagwood in a *Blondie* television series, with Pamela Britton as Blondie, but the series lasted only one season.

Lake was born Arthur Silverlake on April 17, 1905, in Corbin, Kentucky. He died January 9, 1987, in Rancho Mirage, California.

Just behind and to the left of the Douras mausoleum is a small marker over the grave of English music hall performer **Hannah Chaplin (1866–1928)**, the mother of comedian and filmmaker Charlie Chaplin, who often cited his mother's influence and inspiration on his acting and comedy techniques.

Charlie's parents were both singers, though his father was the more successful and more popular of the two. When Charlie was two years old, his father abandoned his family, and his mother's health, both mental and physical, began to deteriorate. Within a few years, she was institutionalized in the Cane Hill Asylum in England. For most of Charlie's childhood, she was in and out of the asylum, and Charlie and his brother, Sydney, would be placed in various charitable institutions and orphanages or sent to live with friends. When Hannah Chaplin lost her voice and her performing career ended, she supported her family by working as a seamstress.

When he was old enough, Charlie escaped by becoming a music hall performer himself. Meanwhile, his mother's health continued to decline. She was crippled by severe headaches and was unable to work. She also battled alcoholism and was diagnosed with syphilis and acute psychosis, which included disorientation, agitation, confusion, and delusional thinking. Throughout his mother's life, however, Charlie was a loyal, supportive, and loving son. After he achieved fame in Hollywood, he brought his mother to the United States in 1921, and her mental condition was blamed on the psychological trauma she suffered when she witnessed air raids in London during World War I.

Several biographers and film historians have noted that many of the female characters in Charlie's films—simple, well-intentioned, but physically or emotionally flawed women—were based on his mother.

Hannah Chaplin has been portrayed twice in films—by model and actress

Twiggy Lawson in *Young Charlie Chaplin* (1989), and by her granddaughter (Charlie's daughter) Geraldine Chaplin in *Chaplin* (1992).

Hannah Chaplin was born Hannah Harriet Pedlingham Hill on August 6, 1866 (some sources say 1865), in London, England. She died August 28, 1928, in Glendale, California.

On the opposite side of the Douras mausoleum, just a few feet from the lake, is a white granite bench with a three-foot-high white granite book propped up against one end. On the spine of the book are the masks of tragedy and comedy. The bench marks the grave of actor **Tyrone Power (1914–1958),** the third of four actors in the Tyrone Power line and one of the great romantic swashbuckling stars of the screen from the early 1930s until his sudden death in 1958.

Power was the son of classical stage and screen actor Tyrone Power Sr. (1869–1931) and the great-grandson of popular Irish stage actor and comedian Tyrone Power (1797–1841). His mother, Helen Emma Reaume Power, was a Shakespearean actress and a respected drama coach. And Power's son, Tyrone Power IV, born two months after Power's death, is currently building his acting career.

Power appeared in several high school plays, and after graduation in 1931, he toured the country with his father's Shakespearean acting troupe. When his father appeared in a production of *Hamlet* in New York, Power joined him onstage, playing a small role as a page. In late 1931, Power's father was to play the lead role in *The Miracle Man,* and Power was also promised a small role in the film, so father and son headed to Hollywood. But, when Power's father

A closer view of Tyrone Power's grave marker.

died before the film was completed, his son's role in the film was eliminated. Power remained in Hollywood, and appeared in small roles in *Tom Brown of Culver* (1932) and *Flirtation Walk* (1934), starring Dick Powell and Ruby Keeler. When larger roles didn't seem to materialize, he returned to New York to work on the stage.

In 1936, a talent scout for 20th Century-Fox studios saw Power, filmed a screen test with him, and sent it to studio chief Darryl Zanuck, who was impressed enough to bring Power back to Hollywood. Power had one line in *Girls' Dormitory* (1936) and a larger role in *Ladies in Love* (1936), starring Janet Gaynor, Loretta Young, and Constance Bennett. This was also the last film in which Power was billed as "Tyrone Power Jr." Based on the positive audience response to the young actor, Zanuck gave Power the starring role in *Lloyds of London* (1936), a part originally intended for Don Ameche.

The studio took full advantage of Power's growing reputation as a romantic leading man. In 1937, he was paired with Loretta Young in three films, *Love Is News, Café Metropole,* and *Second Honeymoon,* and with skating star Sonja Henie in *Thin Ice.* He also starred in *In Old Chicago* (1937) and *Alexander's Ragtime Band* (1938), and both films were nominated for the Academy Award as Best Picture. Power's star was rising quickly, though he seemed to be getting more attention for his dashing good looks than for his acting ability.

Power had become a major box-office attraction, and Zanuck wanted to keep him busy. Power appeared in eight films in 1939 and 1940, mostly costume dramas or light comedies, including *Jesse James* (1939), costarring with Henry Fonda; *Rose of Washington Square* (1939), costarring with Alice Faye and Al Jolson; *Second Fiddle* (1939), costarring with Sonja Henie; *The Rains Came* (1940), costarring with Myrna Loy; *Daytime Wife* (1940), costarring with Linda Darnell; and *The Mark of Zorro* (1940)—Power's first major swashbuckling role. After the huge success of *Zorro,* Power starred as a bullfighter torn between destiny and love in *Blood and Sand* (1941), costarring with Linda Darnell and rising star Rita Hayworth.

After such a long and busy schedule, Power took some time off and returned to the East Coast, where he appeared in several stage productions. Power returned to Hollywood and starred in the adventure epics *Son of Fury* (1942) and *The Black Swan* (1942) before leaving again for some real-life adventure—he enlisted in the U.S. Marine Corps, and quickly rose to the rank of first lieutenant. Power, who had been a licensed pilot since 1937, attended flight school and was assigned to a transport squadron carrying supplies in the South Pacific. By the time Power returned to Hollywood, he had been away from films for nearly four years. Zanuck wanted to bring Power back with a bang, so he cast him in the lead in *The Razor's Edge* (1946), a dark melodrama about the search for the meaning of life. The film was nominated for an Academy Award as Best Picture, and critics praised Power's deep and passionate performance. His next film, *Nightmare Alley* (1947), costarring Joan Blondell and Coleen Gray, was even darker. Power played a carnival barker who becomes a successful, if deceitful, mind reader, then falls to the depths of carnival humiliation. Though Power delivered stellar performances in his first two postwar films, neither was popular with his fans, so Power returned to costumed, swashbuckling epics with *Captain From Castile* (1947), *Prince of Foxes* (1949), and *The Black Rose* (1950). In between, Power starred in light comedies, including *The Luck of the Irish* (1948) and *That Wonderful Urge* (1948).

In 1950, Power again returned to his stage roots, playing the lead for six months in a production of *Mister Roberts* in London, England. When Power returned to Hollywood this time, he discovered that the type of roles he had played in recent years, both as an adventure hero and a romantic leading man, were going to younger actors. Instead, Power appeared in several smaller films, including *Rawhide* (1951), *Diplomatic Courier* (1952), *Pony Soldier* (1952), and *The Mississippi Gambler* (1953). After taking more time off to appear in stage plays, Power starred in *The Long Gray Line* (1955), the story of a legendary coach at West Point. The film was a huge success and helped to revive Power's career as an actor, instead of just a movie star and matinee idol.

Power next appeared in the title role in *The Eddy Duchin Story* (1956), another box-office hit, and followed with powerful performances in *The Sun Also Rises* (1957) and *Witness for the Prosecution* (1957). The following year, Power began work on *Soloman and Sheba*, a biblical epic he was also co-producing. The forty-four-year-old actor was filming a dueling scene with George Sanders on location in Madrid, Spain, when he complained of chest pains and went to his dressing room. The production company nurse was called, and she recommended that Power, who had suffered a heart attack, be taken to a hospital. Power was driven to the hospital in costar Gina Lollobrigida's Mercedes, and was pronounced dead shortly after his arrival. Power's close friend, actor Yul Brenner, replaced him in the film.

Prior to his funeral, Power's third wife, Deborah Anne, requested that the actor's second wife, Linda Christian, and his two children stay away from the services. An estimated three thousand fans showed up at the Chapel of the

Psalms at the cemetery, while Power's widow knelt beside her husband's casket and held his hand throughout the services. Meanwhile, Christian and her two children, Romina Power, eight, and Taryn Power, six, attended a memorial Mass about a mile away. Three hours after the funeral services at the cemetery were completed, Christian and her children were finally allowed to visit the cemetery to place a white wreath on Power's grave.

Two months after Power's death, Deborah Anne gave birth to Power's third child, Tyrone Power IV, an actor who currently performs under the name Tyrone Power Jr.

Power was born Tyrone Edmund Power III on May 5, 1914 (some sources say 1913), in Cincinnati, Ohio.
He died November 15, 1958, in Madrid, Spain.

From Power's grave, walk toward the main entrance of the Cathedral Mausoleum. About twenty-five feet before you reach the road, turn left, walk about fifteen feet, and you'll find the grave of singer and actor **Nelson Eddy (1901–1967),** best known for his pairing with Jeanette MacDonald in a series of eight musicals in the 1930s and early 1940s.

The son and grandson of musicians, Eddy started singing as a boy soprano in church choirs. After moving to Philadelphia as a teenager, he worked in an assortment of jobs before winning a competition in 1922 to join the Philadelphia Civic Opera. He also performed with the New York Metropolitan Opera and performed in the late 1920s and early 1930s on radio and in concerts around the country. While performing at a concert in 1933—at which he performed eighteen encores—Eddy was spotted by an assistant to MGM studio chief Louis B. Mayer and signed to a contract. Eddy's screen debut was a small role in *Broadway to Hollywood* (1933). After small roles in two more MGM musicals, Eddy was paired with Jeanette MacDonald in *Naughty Marietta* (1935), the story of a French princess who escapes an arranged marriage and finds true love with a dashing sea captain. The film was a tremendous box-office success and was nominated for an Academy Award as Best Picture. And, of course, that meant more Eddy-MacDonald pairings, beginning with *Rose-Marie* (1936)—perhaps their best-known film together, certainly their most remembered and most-often parodied, featuring Eddy in the uniform of a Canadian Mountie, singing "Indian Love Call" with MacDonald. Eddy and MacDonald, now billed as "America's Singing Sweethearts," continued with *Maytime* (1937), *Sweethearts* (1938), *The Girl of the Golden West*

(1938), *New Moon* (1940), *Bitter Sweet* (1940), and their final film together, *I Married an Angel* (1942).

Eddy appeared in several other films during this time, including *Rosalie* (1937), with Eleanor Powell, and *Let Freedom Ring* (1939), with Virginia Bruce, but they were not nearly as successful.

After his blockbuster films with MacDonald, Eddy's career slipped. He appeared in only a handful of films after that, including *The Phantom of the Opera* (1943), *Knickerbocker Holiday* (1944), and *Northwest Outpost* (1947), before retiring from films and returning to the concert circuit. Eddy suffered a stroke while appearing onstage, and died soon after.

Eddy is buried between his mother, Isabel K. Eddy (1879–1957), and his wife, Ann Denitz Eddy (1894–1987).

> *Eddy was born Nelson Ackerman Eddy on June 29, 1901, in Providence, Rhode Island. He died March 6, 1967, in Miami Beach, Florida.*

From Eddy's grave, walk west about fifty feet and you'll find two large white mausoleum crypts (similar to the De Mille crypts), with the name "Cohn" etched on the front. One of these crypts contains the remains of **Harry Cohn (1891–1958),** founder and longtime head of Columbia Pictures.

Harry Cohn started his entertainment career as a performer in a musical

The grave of Harry Cohn, the founder of Columbia Pictures, in front of the Cathedral Mausoleum at Hollywood Forever.

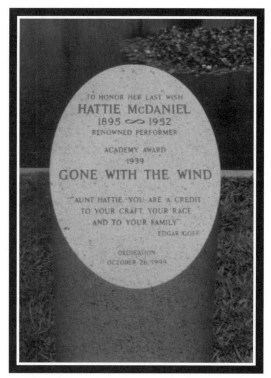

TO HONOR HER LAST WISH
HATTIE McDANIEL
1895 ∽ 1952
RENOWNED PERFORMER

ACADEMY AWARD
1939
GONE WITH THE WIND

"AUNT HATTIE, YOU ARE A CREDIT
TO YOUR CRAFT, YOUR RACE
AND TO YOUR FAMILY"
EDGAR GOFF

DEDICATION
OCTOBER 26, 1999

Hattie McDaniel wanted to be buried at Hollywood Forever, but the cemetery had a "whites only" policy when she died in 1952.

act in vaudeville with Harry Ruby. Cohn's brother, Jack, was working as a film editor for Carl Laemmle's Universal Pictures, and in 1918, Laemmle hired Harry to be his secretary at the new Universal studio complex north of Los Angeles. After a few years of working for Universal, the Cohn brothers and a friend, Joe Brandt, launched their own business—CBC Film Sales Co.

Harry Cohn was responsible for all phases of production of the films that were distributed by CBC Film Sales Co. He set up shop in an area of Hollywood near Gower Street and Sunset Boulevard known as "Poverty Row," where low-budget production companies used rented space, castoff sets, castoff stories, and castoff actors from the big studios. In 1924, in an effort to appear more respectable, CBC Film Sales changed its name to Columbia Pictures, with Brandt as president, Harry Cohn as vice president in charge of production in Los Angeles, and Jack Cohn as vice president in charge of sales in New York City.

Columbia was still a small-time operation in 1927 when Cohn hired Frank Capra, a writer and director of two-reel comedies for Mack Sennett. Over the next ten years, Capra became a star director, helping Columbia to become a major studio. Capra produced hit after hit for Columbia, including *Platinum Blonde* (1931), *Lady for a Day* (1933), *It Happened One Night* (1934), *Mr. Deeds Goes to Town* (1936), *Lost Horizon* (1937), *You Can't Take It With You* (1938), and *Mr. Smith Goes to Washington* (1939).

Though his days on "Poverty Row" were over, Cohn continued to supervise every detail at the studio, reviewing all expenses and doing whatever he could to cut costs. He was notoriously ruthless, would hire and fire employees on the slightest whim, and was often said to be the most feared and hated man in Hollywood.

When Capra left Columbia in 1940, his spot as the biggest star at the studio was filled by a young, raven-haired Mexican dancer named Margarita Carmen Cansino. Under Cohn's guidance, her hair was lightened and her name changed to Rita Hayworth, and she was Hollywood's reigning love goddess and pinup queen through the 1940s.

Cohn is buried next to his wife, Joan Perry Cohn (1911–1996). In between them, in a small urn, are the remains of their daughter, Jobella, who died shortly after birth in 1943.

Throughout their decades together at Columbia, Harry Cohn and his brother, Jack, often argued, and they occasionally stopped speaking to each other for long periods. Jack Cohn (1889–1956) is buried beneath a small, simple grave marker in front of Cohn's crypt. Jack's wife, Jeanette Cohn (1891–1969), and their sons, producers Ralph Cohn (1914–1959) and Robert Cohn (1920–1996), are buried nearby.

Cohn was born July 23, 1891, in New York City.
He died February 27, 1958, in Phoenix, Arizona.

About a hundred feet directly west of Cohn, at the southern edge of the lake, you'll find a memorial to Academy Award–winning actress **Hattie McDaniel (1895–1952)**. When McDaniel died, her last request was to be buried in Hollywood Memorial Park, but the cemetery had a "whites only" policy at that time, so McDaniel was buried in Rosedale Cemetery in Los Angeles where, ironically, she broke the color barrier.

McDaniel appeared in nearly one hundred films, and she won the

A recently installed memorial to Hattie McDaniel at Hollywood Forever offers a view of the famous Hollywood sign.

Academy Award for Best Supporting Actress for her performance as Mammy in *Gone With the Wind* (1939)—she was the first black performer to win an Oscar. She also starred in her own radio and television series. When Tyler Cassity took over ownership of Hollywood Forever, he offered to move McDaniel's remains to honor her final request, but her family decided to leave her where she is. So Cassity put up the four-foot-tall gray-and-pink-granite memorial in October 1999, and invited the public to the dedication ceremonies on the forty-seventh anniversary of McDaniel's death.

The memorial includes a quote from Edgar Goff, McDaniel's grand-nephew and her last living relative: "Aunt Hattie, you are a credit to your craft, your race, and to your family."

Looking across the lake from McDaniel's memorial is another good location at Hollywood Forever to see the "Hollywood" sign on Mount Lee.

Hattie McDaniel was born June 10, 1865, in Wichita, Kansas.
She died October 24, 1952, in Los Angeles.

South of the McDaniel memorial, just across the road, is the spectacular memorial to the ultimate swashbuckling actor, **Douglas Fairbanks Sr. (1883–1939).** At the end of a 120-foot-long reflecting pool, Fairbanks's sarcophagus rests on a white granite platform in front of a large white wall, highlighted by his profile in brass.

Fairbanks began appearing in amateur theater in Denver, Colorado, at the age of twelve, and he continued on the stage while attending the Colorado School of Mines. After moving to New York City, he made his debut on Broadway in 1902, in a play titled *Her Lord and Master.* Five years later, just as he was building his career as a leading man onstage, he married an industrialist's daughter and left the theater to work in his father-in-law's soap company. Luckily—for film fans at least—the soap company went bankrupt and Fairbanks returned to the theater the following year.

By 1910, Fairbanks was a star on Broadway, thanks to the same qualities that would eventually make him a star in Hollywood—boundless enthusiasm, moral courage, a mischievous attitude, and fearless physical agility, all topped by a twinkling eye and a roguish grin. He made his film debut in *The Lamb* (1915), and a year later he was popular and successful enough to establish his own production company, Douglas Fairbanks Pictures.

In 1919, Fairbanks was on a World War I Liberty Bond tour with comedian Charlie Chaplin when he met and fell in love with "America's

Sweetheart," actress Mary Pickford. They were married the following year and moved into "Pickfair," their mansion in Beverly Hills. Pickfair quickly became the social center of Hollywood, and Fairbanks and Pickford became the closest thing to royalty the country had ever seen. Also in 1919, Fairbanks, Chaplin, Pickford, and director D. W. Griffith formed United Artists, a film production and distribution company.

After starring primarily in comedies up to that point, Fairbanks began to specialize in action and adventure films throughout the 1920s, beginning with *The Mark of Zorro* (1920), and followed by *The Three Musketeers* (1921), *Robin Hood* (1922), *The Thief of Bagdad* (1924), *Don Q, Son of Zorro* (1925), *The Black Pirate* (1926), *The Gaucho*

The massive memorial to Douglas Fairbanks Sr. at Hollywood Forever cemetery includes a 120-foot-long reflecting pool.

(1927), and *The Iron Mask* (1929). As a trained stage actor, Fairbanks had no problems making the transition to talking pictures, but his advancing age and choice of projects began to hurt his career. In one of his first talkies, Fairbanks and Pickford appeared in *The Taming of the Shrew* (1929)—the only film in which they costarred—but it was a box-office failure. Fairbanks next appeared in *Reaching for the Moon* (1930), a musical comedy featuring a young Bing Crosby in one of his first film roles, then attempted to revive his swashbuckling ways in *The Private Life of Don Juan* (1934). The film, in which Fairbanks played an aging Don Juan, living off his legend and reputation, was a cruel twist on reality, and it was Fairbanks's last film. In 1936, he divorced Pickford and married a former chorus girl, Lady Sylvia Ashley, then announced his retirement from acting.

After Fairbanks died in 1939, his body was stored in a temporary vault at Forest Lawn–Glendale while his memorial was being built. The memorial site, known as "Fairbanks Garden," includes his marble sarcophagus, surrounded on three sides by tall marble columns and featuring a brass profile relief of the actor surrounded by olive branches. The memorial cost an estimated $40,000—at the time, it was the most expensive memorial monument ever built in southern California. The dedication of the Fairbanks Garden was held on May 25, 1941, as Charlie Chaplin delivered a eulogy in front of a crowd of 1,500 mourners, including Fred Astaire, Norma Shearer, Randolph Scott, and Darryl Zanuck.

Chaplin called Fairbanks "an eternal boy. . . . His was a happy life. His rewards were great, his joys many. Now he pillows his head upon his arms, sighs deeply, and sleeps."

Fairbanks's wife at the time of his death, Lady Sylvia Ashley, designed his massive memorial. She was later married briefly to Clark Gable, then to a Russian prince named Djordjadze. She died in 1977 and is also buried at Hollywood Forever. Her grave is about fifty feet east of Cecil B. De Mille's crypt, and about ten feet from the road. Her grave marker identifies her as Princess Sylvia Djordjadze.

Fairbanks's crypt contains the quote "Good night, sweet prince," from

The Cathedral Mausoleum at Hollywood Forever contains the "temporary" crypt of Rudolph Valentino.

Shakespeare's *Hamlet*. The same quote is etched on Tyrone Power's grave marker and John Barrymore's original crypt at Calvary Cemetery. (For more on Barrymore, see Chapter 9.)

Fairbanks was one of the thirty-six founders of the Academy of Motion Picture Arts and Sciences, and he served as the organization's first president. In 1940, two months after his death, he was recognized with a special Academy Award, for "the unique and outstanding contribution of Douglas Fairbanks, first president of the Academy, to the international development of the motion picture."

> *Fairbanks was born Douglas Elton Ulman on May 23, 1883, in Denver, Colorado. He died December 12, 1939, in Santa Monica, California.*

Tour 2: The Cathedral Mausoleum

Directly west of the Fairbanks grave, located at the southwest corner of the cemetery property, is the large Cathedral Mausoleum. As you enter the mausoleum, the main corridor is flanked by thirteen larger-than-life-size Carrara marble statues—the Twelve Apostles, plus St. Paul. The statues, which were carved in Italy, were originally brought to the cemetery to be part of the two-thousand-seat Court of the Apostles amphitheater, to be built immediately behind the Cathedral Mausoleum for special events and community ceremonies.

Walk down the main corridor of the mausoleum and turn down the second corridor on the right. On the right side of that corridor, in the sixth column in from the main corridor, the second space up from the bottom, you'll find the crypt of director **William Desmond Taylor (1877–1922)**, buried behind a marker with his real name, William Deane-Tanner.

In the early silent era of films, Taylor was a popular and successful director, and he served as president of the Screen Directors Guild. He was an elegant, worldy gentleman, a well-dressed intellectual who enjoyed discussing fine art and fine books.

Taylor arrived in Hollywood in 1912, working first as an actor, then as a director. The well-educated Taylor, with his knowledge of art and literature, quickly became the leading director of the Famous Players–Lasky Corporation. Taylor was equally successful directing action and adventure films, drama and romance, and comedy. He directed Mary Pickford in three films—*How Could You, Jean?* (1918), *Johanna Enlists* (1918), and *Captain Kidd Jr.* (1919).

On the morning of February 2, 1922, Taylor was found dead in his apartment, shot once in the back with a .38-caliber bullet. Police eliminated robbery as a motive, as Taylor was still wearing a large diamond ring and a large amount of cash was found in the apartment. There were no signs of forced entry, so Taylor must've known his killer.

Taylor had two visitors the night he died—comedian Mabel Normand and Mary Miles Minter, a young actress Taylor had directed in several films. Though Normand was questioned by police, she was never considered a serious suspect in the shooting. But the police investigation did reveal Normand's $2,000-per-month cocaine habit, helping to tarnish her career. Minter, who was only seventeen at the time of Taylor's death, told police that she and the director were engaged, and that they were waiting until she turned eighteen to get married. Love letters from Minter were found in Taylor's apartment. The news that Minter, the embodiment of virginal innocence on the screen, was having an affair with a man more than twice her age destroyed her image and ended her film career.

A more serious suspect was Minter's mother, Charlotte Shelby, an ambitious and greedy stage mother. The police investigation revealed that Taylor was also romantically involved with Shelby. As for possible motives for murder, Shelby may have discovered Taylor's involvement with her daughter, or she may have simply feared that Taylor would marry her daughter and take away her primary source of income. After the shooting, Shelby reportedly left on a European vacation that lasted three years.

And police also discovered that the well-respected director was not the man he appeared to be. Taylor was, in fact, William Deane-Tanner from New York City. In his previous life, he had been a well-known art connoisseur who managed an antique shop. In 1908, after seven years of marriage, he had disappeared, leaving a wife and daughter behind. He had surfaced in Hollywood in 1912, with a new identity and a fictional past as an actor and director.

Taylor's murder, which took place while Roscoe "Fatty" Arbuckle was on trial for the murder of actress Virginia Rappe, further enhanced Hollywood's reputation as a sin-soaked Sodom spinning out of control. In response, the studios formed a new regulatory agency, officially known as the Motion Picture Producers and Distributors of America, Inc., but informally called the

Hays Office, which set up a strict code of conduct for the film industry.

The Taylor murder has never been solved and remains a popular topic of discussion and speculation among Hollywood historians and mystery fans.

Taylor's crypt identifies him as "Beloved father of Ethel D. Deane-Tanner"—the daughter he left behind in New York.

Taylor was born William Cunningham Deane-Tanner
on April 26, 1877 (some sources say 1872), in Carlow, Ireland.
He died February 1, 1922, in Los Angeles.

About forty feet past Taylor's crypt, on the left side of the corridor, a few inches above the floor, you'll find the small niche containing the cremated remains of actor **Peter Lorre (1904–1964).**

Lorre worked as a stage actor in Austria and Germany for many years before he was cast as the psychopathic child killer in *M* (1931), made in Germany and directed by Fritz Lang. When the Nazis came to power in Germany, Lorre worked in Paris and London before coming to Hollywood and appearing in Hitchcock's *The Man Who Knew Too Much* (1934). After appearing in *Crime and Punishment* (1935) and *Secret Agent* (1936), Lorre played the title role of an Asian detective in a series of *Mr. Moto* films.

Among Lorre's most memorable roles are the evil, weasely Joel Cairo in *The Maltese Falcon* (1941) and the evil, weasely Ugarte in *Casablanca* (1942). Throughout the 1940s and early 1950s, Lorre often appeared in dark, mysterious, menacing roles in a series of film-noir dramas and crime films, including *Strange Cargo* (1940), *Island of Doomed Men* (1940), *The Face Behind the Mask* (1941), *Background to Danger* (1943), *Passage to Marseille* (1944), *The Mask of Dimitrios* (1944), *Hotel Berlin* (1945), *The Chase* (1946), *Black Angel* (1946), *The Beast With Five Fingers* (1946), *Beat the Devil* (1953), and *20,000 Leagues Under the Sea* (1954).

Lorre also had a flair for comedy, which he exhibited in *Arsenic and Old Lace* (1944) and *My Favorite Brunette* (1947). In later years, Lorre often lampooned his own image, in films such as *Muscle Beach Party* (1964). His last film was *The Patsy* (1964), starring Jerry Lewis.

Lorre is buried next to his third wife, Anne Marie Lorre (1922–1971).

Lorre was born Laszlo Lowenstein on June 26, 1904, in
Rosenberg, Hungary. He died March 23, 1964, in Los Angeles.

Go back into the main corridor. In the southeast corner, between the statues of St. Peter and St. James Minor, is a wall of niches containing cremation urns. About three feet from the right edge of the wall and five feet up from the floor, in the center of a row of bronze urns shaped like books, you'll find the name of **Eleanor Powell (1912–1982),** the tap-dancing star of MGM musicals in the 1930s and early 1940s.

Powell began dancing at eleven and appeared on Broadway at seventeen, where she was billed as "The World's Greatest Tap Dancer." She made her film debut as a background dancer in *Queen High* (1930), then returned to dance in *George White's Scandals* (1935), *Broadway Melody of 1936* (1935), *Rosalie* (1937), *Honolulu* (1939), *Lady Be Good* (1941), *Ship Ahoy* (1942), and *I Dood It* (1943). Though primarily a solo performer, Powell danced memorably with Fred Astaire in *Broadway Melody of 1940.* Most of Powell's films featured somewhat limited stories, with the plot just an excuse to link the dance numbers.

Aside from a cameo appearance in *Duchess of Idaho* (1950), Powell retired from the screen after her marriage to actor Glenn Ford in 1944. After their divorce in 1959, she revived her career with a nightclub and stage act. She then turned her interests to church and charity work and became an ordained minister in the Unity Church.

Powell's urn contains the inscription "Forever Beloved."

Powell was born Eleanor Torrey Powell on November 21, 1912, in Springfield, Massachusetts. She died February 11, 1982, in Beverly Hills, California.

Next to that wall of niches, between the statues of St. James Minor and St. John, is another corridor. Walk down that corridor about fifty feet, then turn right. At the far end of that hallway on the right side, in the second space up from the floor, you'll find the crypt of **Barbara La Marr (1896–1926),** "The Girl Who Was Too Beautiful," one of the first big stars of Hollywood, and one of its first victims.

La Marr's parents moved to a small town in California when she was a teenager, but she quickly left home to explore the opportunities available to an attractive girl in the big city of Los Angeles. She was arrested for dancing in a burlesque show when she was fourteen, and a judge said she was "too beautiful to be alone in a big city, alone and unprotected," a comment that led to her eventual screen nickname. She began her film career as a writer in 1920 for the Fox Film Corporation, but studio executives recognized the appeal of this beautiful, energetic woman, and put her in front of the cameras. Her screen debut was in *Harriet and the Piper* (1920). She had small parts in *The Nut* (1921) and *The Three Musketeers* (1921), both starring Douglas Fairbanks, and quickly graduated to starring roles in *Arabian Love, Domestic Relations, Trifling Woman,* and *The Prisoner of Zenda,* all released in 1922.

La Marr was also keeping busy outside the studio. She was already on her fifth marriage, was a familiar face on the Hollywood party scene, and had developed a strong relationship with alcohol and drugs. La Marr claimed that she slept only two hours per night—"I have better things to do," she said.

Onscreen, La Marr was equally adept at comedy, drama, or romance. The raven-haired beauty appeared in nine films in 1923, including *St. Elmo,* with John Gilbert, and *The Eternal City,* with Lionel Barrymore. But her wild off-screen life was beginning to wear her down, and she appeared in only four films in 1924, and two in 1925. Her last film was *The Girl From Montmartre* (1926), costarring with Lewis Stone.

Her body weakened by drugs and her wild life, La Marr was diagnosed with tuberculosis and died in early 1926—a few months before her thirtieth birthday. An estimated forty thousand mourners attended her funeral.

Though La Marr is perhaps not as well remembered as some of her silent-screen contemporaries, like Mary Pickford, Clara Bow, Mabel Normand, Thelma Todd, or Gloria Swanson, she is certainly not forgotten. Her crypt is often decorated with flowers, photographs, notes from fans, and even lip prints. And when, years after La Marr's death, MGM studio chief Louis Mayer, who was one of her greatest fans, needed a new name for a young starlett named Hedwig Kiesler, he decided to name her in honor of La Marr—and gave her the name Hedy Lamarr.

La Marr's crypt contains the inscription "With God in the joy and beauty of youth."

La Marr was born Reatha Dale Watson on July 28, 1896
(some sources say 1900), in Yakima, Washington.
She died January 30, 1926, in Altadena, California.

Walk back out into the corridor and turn right, then turn right again. At the far end of this hallway, on the left side, in the third space up from the floor, you'll find the crypt of legendary actor **Rudolph Valentino (1895–1926).** More than seventy years after his sudden death, fans and admirers still bring flowers almost every day to place on Valentino's crypt, which identifies him as "Rodolfo Guglielmi Valentino."

Born in Italy, Valentino arrived in the United States in 1913, intending to seek his fortune in the land of opportunity. Instead, he lived in shabby immigrant neighborhoods in New York City, worked a series of odd jobs, and was arrested several times on suspicion of petty theft and blackmail. Eventually, Valentino found success as a dancer in nightclubs around Broadway, then he joined the cast of *The Merry Monarch,* a musical review on a national tour. But the show folded in Utah, and Valentino continued west on his own, first to San Francisco, then to Los Angeles, in 1917.

For the next few years, Valentino played small parts in a series of small films, making his screen debut in an uncredited role as a dancer in *Alimony*

Any time you visit the crypt of silent-film star Rudolph Valentino, you'll probably find fresh flowers left by fans.

(1917), for which he was paid five dollars per day. Gradually, he was given larger roles, usually playing villains, in films including *Eyes of Youth* (1919), *Big Little Person* (1919), *Stolen Moments* (1920), and *Passion's Playground* (1920).

Valentino's big break came in 1921, when scriptwriter June Mathis and director Rex Ingram were preparing a production of *The Four Horsemen of the Apocalypse* for Metro Pictures Corp. Ingram and Mathis, who was also chief of Metro's script department, both wanted Valentino to play the lead in the film—a grim, antiwar story of cousins who end up fighting on opposite sides in World War I. Due in no small part to Valentino's performance in a dramatic and romantic tango scene, the film was a huge success, and Valentino became an instant star. With his dark, smoldering good looks and dancer's grace, coupled with his exotic background, Valentino became the symbol of fantasy and passion for women across the country.

Valentino followed with equally passionate roles in costume romances including *The Shiek* (1921), *Blood and Sand* (1922), *The Young Rajah* (1922), and *Monsieur Beaucaire* (1924). Valentino-mania was reaching a peak, with women fainting in the aisles in theaters whenever his films were shown. In response, the *Chicago Tribune* took issue with Valentino and his legions of imitators as the new image of masculinity in 1926, asking, "When will we be rid of all these effeminate youths, pomaded, powdered, bejeweled and bedizened, in the image of Rudy—that painted pansy?" With his manhood publicly questioned, Valentino challenged the writer to a boxing match. When the writer did not respond, Valentino claimed victory and vindication.

After completing work on *The Son of the Shiek* (1926), Valentino went on a nationwide tour to promote the film. While in New York City on August 15, 1926, he complained of stomach pain and was taken to Polyclinic Hospital. Exploratory surgery revealed an acute perforated gastric ulcer. Although the perforation was repaired, Valentino contracted a post-surgical infection and died. He was thirty-one. Almost immediately, rumors begin to surface that Valentino has been poisoned or shot by a jilted lover, or a jealous husband. At his funeral services in New York City, an estimated crowd of one hundred thousand gathered outside the funeral home. When his body was brought back to Hollywood, thousands of fans stood in railroad stations across the country just to see the train as it sped past. In Los Angeles, an estimated eighty thousand mourners crowded in and around the cemetery grounds when Valentino's casket was carried into the Cathedral Mausoleum. A small airplane flew overhead, showering the funeral procession with thousands of rose petals.

Actress Pola Negri, who said that she and Valentino had been engaged, attended Valentino's funeral services in Los Angeles, flinging herself on his coffin and repeatedly fainting—though most witnesses said she did it as a stunt for the press.

The original plan was that Valentino's stay in the mausoleum would be only temporary, until a more suitable memorial could be built somewhere on the cemetery grounds. The memorial, designed by architect Matlock Price, was to include several life-size statues of Valentino in his most-celebrated screen roles. Valentino's friend June Mathis and her husband, cinematographer Silvano Balboni, owned two crypts in the mausoleum, and they agreed to let one of them be used for Valentino's body. Less than a year after Valentino's death, Mathis died of a heart attack at the age of thirty-five and was also buried in the Cathedral Mausoleum, next to Valentino.

A few years later, when all plans for a new Valentino memorial had fallen through, Mathis's widower, Silvano Balboni, sold Valentino's "temporary" crypt to the Valentino family, and the crypt became Valentino's permanent home.

One of the greatest and most enduring Hollywood legends concerns the mysterious "Lady in Black" who visits Valentino's crypt each year on the anniversary of his death. The visits began on the first anniversary when the woman, clad in black from head to toe, including a heavy black veil, entered the mausoleum, left roses at Valentino's crypt, and departed without saying a word. But who was the "Lady in Black"? And what was her relationship with Valentino?

According to the most popular and enduring version of the legend, Valentino was friends with a woman whose daughter, Ditra Flame, was seriously ill in a hospital. Valentino went to visit the girl and brought her a single red rose. "You're not going to die at all," Valentino told her. "You are going to outlive me by many years. But one thing for sure—if I die before you do, you please come and stay by me because I don't want to be alone, either. You come and talk to me."

Shortly after Valentino's visit, little Ditra got better. When Valentino died a few years later, she remembered his request and brought a bouquet of red roses to his crypt every year on the anniversary of his death, but she never spoke about it, and never told anyone her story. The press noticed her visits, and widely publicized the story of the mysterious "Lady in Black."

In the early 1940s, a former Ziegfeld showgirl named Marian Watson, who performed as Marian Brenda, began visiting Valentino's crypt and claimed that she was the original "Lady in Black." According to various reports, Valentino either proposed to her the night before he was hospitalized in 1926, or she secretly married him in 1925 and gave birth to at least one of his children. Other women began to come forward and claim that they were the original "Lady in Black," and told various stories about their relationships with Valentino.

Perhaps in response to all the "Lady in Black" pretenders, Ditra Flame finally took off her black veil and told her story in 1947. She continued to visit Valentino's crypt until 1954, when she became one of many "Ladies in Black," and the annual memorial service had became a gaudy and sensational spectacle. She resumed her annual visits in 1977, but wearing street clothing instead of the traditional mourning outfit. Flame died in 1984, and her gravestone, in San Jacinto, California, identifies her as the "Lady in Black."

The second generally recognized "Lady in Black" was Estrellita del Regil, a former Spanish actress who began visiting Valentino's crypt in the early

1970s as a tribute to her late mother, who she felt was Valentino's unrequited love. She continued her visits until 1993, when illness prevented her from making her annual pilgrimage.

Taking the role as the third "Lady in Black" was Vicki Callahan, who did not originally intend to carry on the tradition. She was simply a great fan of the silent star and wanted to pay her respects. But when she was shown, dressed in black, on a television news broadcast in 1995 placing roses at Valentino's crypt, and was identified as the "third Lady in Black," Callahan accepted the job, and continues to make her annual visits.

Valentino was born Rodolfo Alfonzo Raffaele Pierre Philibert Gugliemi di Valentina on May 6, 1895, in Castellaneta, Italy. He died August 23, 1926, in New York City.

Across the hallway from Valentino's crypt, you'll find the crypt of actor **Peter Finch (1916–1977),** one of only two performers to have received the Academy Award for Best Actor posthumously.

Finch spent his childhood in France, India, and Australia. He worked in vaudeville as a comedian's stooge, then returned to Australia, where he made his film debut in a comedy, *Dad and Dave Come to Town* (1938). Finch became a leading actor in Australia before returning to London to work onstage and in films, including *The Heart of the Matter* (1954), *Elephant Walk* (1954), *A Town Like Alice* (1956), *Windom's Way* (1958), *The Nun's Story* (1959), *Kidnapped* (1960), *The Trials of Oscar Wilde* (1960), *The Pumpkin Eater* (1964), and *Far From the Madding Crowd* (1967).

Finch was twice nominated for the Academy Award for Best Actor. In addition to his win for *Network* (1976), which was awarded several months after Finch's death, he was also nominated for *Sunday Bloody Sunday* (1971). Finch also received seven nominations as Best Actor from the British Academy of Film and Television Arts, winning the award five times.

Finch's crypt includes the inscription "Distinguished actor, loving husband and father."

Finch was born Frederick George Peter Ingle-Finch on September 28, 1916, in London, England. He died January 14, 1977, in Los Angeles.

Tour 3: Columbarium and the Abbey of the Psalms

Just west of the main entrance to the cemetery is a small chapel, and behind the chapel is a two-story columbarium, with urns of various sizes and shapes containing cremated remains. You can enter the columbarium through the chapel, but if a funeral service is in progress, you might have to use a side door.

The columbarium, which opened in the 1920s, is a little-known and seldom-visited location at Hollywood Forever, which is unfortunate because it's such an interesting place—a two-story, sepia-tinted space, sort of a combination indoor garden and rotunda, complete with a small fountain in the center of the first floor. The walls are lined with niches containing brass urns, and there are small benches and plants scattered around.

Once inside, head up the stairs. Although the first floor is pretty crowded, the niche spaces on the second floor are fairly empty. Immediately at the top of the stairs, in a niche on your left, you'll see a somewhat eerie white bust of a woman, her head completely wrapped in a veil. This niche contains the remains of **Charlotte Bridgwood (1861–1929)**. Beneath the bust is a plaque that identifies Bridgwood as "mother of Florence Lawrence, the first movie star." Bridgwood was a stage actress known professionally as Lotta Lawrence.

Along the back wall of the columbarium, about three feet up from the floor, you'll find a bronze urn in the shape of a book. The urn contains the remains of **Ben Lyon (1901–1979)**, best remembered as the star of and one of the daring aerial cameramen on Howard Hughes's *Hell's Angels* (1930).

In addition to appearing in films since 1918, Lyon was an experienced pilot when he took the role in Hughes's first attempt at directing, and he shot many of the dramatic and breathtaking dogfight scenes over London. Due primarily to those scenes, the film was nominated for an Academy Award for Best Cinematography.

After appearing in a few more films during the early 1930s, including *Lady With a Past* (1932) and *I Cover the Waterfront* (1933), Lyon and his wife, actress Bebe Daniels, moved to England, where they became popular performers in film, onstage, on radio, and entertaining U.S. troops. Lyon also served as a combat pilot in the British Royal Air Force during World War II. In 1977, Lyon was awarded the Order of the British Empire by Queen Elizabeth II for his work during World War II.

After the war, Lyon worked as a casting director for 20th Century-Fox studios. In the summer of 1946, he was browsing at a newsstand and noticed the same model on four different magazine covers. He tracked her down, arranged for a screen test, and showed the test to studio executive Darryl Zanuck. He also suggested that the model change her name from Norma Jeane Baker to Marilyn Monroe.

Lyon was born February 6, 1901, in Atlanta, Georgia.
He died March 22, 1979, on a cruise ship sailing
near Honolulu, Hawaii.

Next to Lyon's urn is a small bronze vault containing the remains of Lyon's wife, actress **Bebe Daniels (1901–1971),** who made her film debut as Dorothy in a silent version of *The Wonderful World of Oz* (1910), appeared in more than two hundred films during her career, and later found fame as a radio and television star in England.

As a child, Daniels appeared in more than 100 two-reel comedy shorts starring Harold Lloyd, mostly in his *Lonesome Luke* series. Cecil B. De Mille then directed Daniels in three films—*Male and Female* (1919), *Why Change Your Wife?* (1920), and *The Affairs of Anatol* (1921). Daniels costarred with Douglas Fairbanks in *Reaching for the Moon* (1930), with Rudolph Valentino in *Monsieur Beaucaire* (1924), with William Powell in *Dangerous Money* (1924), with Warner Baxter in *42nd Street* (1933), and with John Barrymore in *Counselor at Law* (1933). Daniels typically played in comedies, but she was equally effective in romances and dramas. And, in *Rio Rita* (1929), she proved she could sing, too.

After she married actor Ben Lyon in 1930, the couple traveled across the country, performing in several plays, and ended up in London, England, in 1936 for a three-week engagement. But the play was so successful, the run was extended, and Lyon and Daniels decided to move to London. They appeared onstage and in films in England, were also hosts of a popular program called *Life With the Lyons,* first on radio, then on television.

Daniels's urn lists her name as "Bebe Virginia Daniels Lyon."

Daniels was born Phyllis Virginia Daniels on January 14, 1901, in
Dallas, Texas. She died March 16, 1971, in London, England.

In the northeast corner of the room, you'll find the niche containing the remains of writer **Jesse L. Lasky Jr. (1910–1988),** the son of Hollywood studio pioneer Jesse Lasky Sr.

Lasky Jr. wrote novels, biographies, plays, poetry, and nearly fifty screen-plays, including several for his father's partner, director Cecil B. De Mille. Lasky wrote the scripts for *Sabotage* (1936), *Secret Agent* (1936), *Union Pacific* (1939), *Reap the Wild Wind* (1942), *Unconquered* (1947), *Samson and Delilah* (1949), and *The Ten Commandments* (1956). In the late 1950s, he moved to Europe and divided the rest of his life between residences in England and Spain, occasionally returning to Hollywood.

Lasky's remains are in a wooden box with a bronze plaque on the top. The niche also contains a copy of his autobiography, *Whatever Happened to Hollywood?*

Lasky was born Jesse Louis Lasky Jr. on September 19, 1910
(some sources say 1908), in New York City.
He died April 11, 1988, in London, England.

Now, go back down the stairs, and exit the first-floor room through the door on the west side. The corridor will lead you to a short, narrow hallway with white-and-green tile walls. Along both sides of the hallway are niches for cremation urns. About fifteen feet down the hall, on the right side, five feet up from the floor, you'll find an urn with the name "Flugrath," which contains the remains of silent-film actress **Viola Dana (1897–1987).**

Dana, the sister of actresses Edna Flugrath and Shirley Mason, appeared in more than one hundred films, making her debut in *A Christmas Carol* (1910). As a teenager, she was playing lead roles in comedies and dramas pro-duced by the Edison Company. In 1915, she married director John H. Collins, but he died three years later.

Dana moved to Metro Pictures Corp. and was one of the studio's busiest performers through the silent era, appearing in comedies, dramas, even Westerns. The petite Dana—she was only four-foot-eleven—retired when talking pictures became popular. Her last screen appearance was in *The Show of Shows* (1929) for Warner Bros., which was basically a filmed ver-sion of a vaudeville show, starring dozens of performers from the Warner studio.

Dana was born Virginia Flugrath on June 28, 1897 (the
inscription on her urn is incorrect), in Brooklyn, New York.
She died July 3, 1987, in Woodland Hills, California.

Farther down the hallway, on the right side, about ten feet from the exit and five feet up from the floor, you'll find a small plaque marking the crypt of **Elmo Lincoln (1889–1952).** The plaque identifies Lincoln as "The First Tarzan."

A former police officer, Lincoln appeared in several early silent films directed by D. W. Griffith, including *Judith of Bethulia* (1914), *The Birth of a Nation* (1915), *Intolerance* (1916), and *The Fall of Babylon* (1919). Lincoln also played the magic genie in *Aladdin and the Wonderful Lamp* (1917). Lincoln was not the first choice to play the lead in *Tarzan of the Apes* (1918), but he got the part when World War I broke out a few days after production started, and the actor originally cast in the role walked off the set to enlist. The film was a box-office success, one of the first films to earn more than $1 million.

Lincoln donned the loincloth for two more films—*The Romance of Tarzan* (1918) and *The Adventures of Tarzan* (1921). Lincoln symbolically passed the torch to perhaps the best-known Tarzan, Johnny Weissmuller, when he appeared in a small role in *Tarzan's New York Adventure* (1942). Lincoln also had a small role in *Tarzan's Magic Fountain* (1949), with Lex Barker playing the ape-man.

Lincoln also had small roles in *Union Pacific* (1939), *The Hunchback of Notre Dame* (1939), and *A Double Life* (1947).

Lincoln was born Otto Elmo Linkenhelt on February 6, 1889, in Rochester, Indiana. He died June 27, 1952, in Los Angeles.

After leaving the columbarium and chapel area, walk across the lawn to the Abbey of the Psalms, a large mausoleum along the western edge of the cemetery grounds. Enter through the gate at the northeast corner of the building, the entrance closest to the chapel. You'll see the words "Sanctuary of Faith" written on the floor at the entrance. About thirty-five feet down the hall, on the left, in the second space up from the floor, you'll find the crypt of actress **Joan Hackett (1934–1983),** with one of the most amusing epitaphs you'll ever see: "Go Away—I'm Asleep."

Hackett was a former fashion model who studied acting under Lee Strasberg and appeared on the television series *Young Dr. Malone* and *The Defenders* before she starred on Broadway in *Call Me By My Rightful Name* in 1961. Hackett was an accomplished dramatic and comedic actress, and appeared in more than thirty films during her short career, including *The Group* (1966), *Will Penny* (1968), *Support Your Local Sheriff!* (1969), *The Last*

Joan Hackett's crypt contains a humorous warning.

of *Sheila* (1973), *The Terminal Man* (1974), *One Trick Pony* (1980), and *The Escape Artist* (1982). She was nominated for an Academy Award for Best Supporting Actress for her performance in *Only When I Laugh* (1981).

Hackett also appeared regularly on various television series, including *Bonanza, Dr. Kildare, Gunsmoke, Combat!, Dan August, The Twilight Zone, The Love Boat, Trapper John, M.D.,* and *Taxi.* And the explanation of her epitaph is fairly simple—Hackett commonly hung a sign with the same warning on her dressing room door.

Joan Hackett was born May 1, 1934, in New York City. She died October 8, 1983, in Encino, California.

Continue down the corridor and turn right at the second hallway, which leads to the "Sanctuary of Trust" corridor. As soon as you enter that corridor, directly in front of you in the space just above the floor, you'll see the crypt of **Charles Chaplin Jr. (1925–1968),** son of comedian Charlie Chaplin.

Chaplin's parents, Charlie and actress Lita Grey, were married in 1924, when he was thirty-five and she was sixteen. They had two sons—Charles Jr., born in 1925, and Sydney, born in 1926—and were divorced in 1927.

Though Charlie Chaplin had unhappy memories of his first marriage, to actress Mildred Harris, his memories of his second marriage, to Grey, were apparently even worse. He doesn't even mention her name in his autobiography, and he sums up their entire relationship in one paragraph: "During the filming of 'The Gold Rush' (1925) I married for the second time. Because we have two grown sons of whom I am very fond, I will not go into any details.

For two years we were married and tried to make a go of it, but it was hopeless and ended in a great deal of bitterness."

Chaplin Jr. appeared in several films, beginning with a small role as a clown in *Limelight* (1952), which starred his father. He also appeared in *Fangs of the Wild* (1954), *The Court Martial of Billy Mitchell* (1955), *The Beat Generation* (1959), and *The Big Operator* (1959). In several films, Chaplin Jr. appeared with other relatively unsuccessful children of popular film stars, including *High School Confidential* (1958) and *Night of the Quarter Moon* (1959), both with John Barrymore Jr., and *Girls Town* (1959), with Harold Lloyd Jr.

Chaplin Jr. is buried next to his maternal grandmother, Lillian Grey (1888–1985).

Charles Spencer Chaplin Jr. was born June 28, 1925, in Beverly Hills, California. He died March 20, 1968, in Los Angeles.

From Chaplin Jr.'s crypt, turn left and walk toward the main entrance of the mausoleum. When you reach the main entrance, turn right and walk about forty feet and down a few stairs, to a central rotunda area. Turn right, and walk down a corridor labeled "Sanctuary of Memories." About one hundred feet down that corridor, on the left side, about five feet up from the floor, you'll find the crypt of **Iron Eyes Cody (1904–1999),** an American Indian actor who appeared in more than one hundred films but is best known for standing beside a littered highway and shedding a tear in the "Keep America Beautiful" television advertisements in the 1970s.

Cody's career began when a film crew came to his family's farm in the Oklahoma territory to shoot *Back to God's Country* (1919), and Cody got a job as an extra. His family then moved to Los Angeles, where Cody's father, Thomas Longplume Cody, worked as a technical adviser on Westerns. Cody appeared in dozens of Westerns from the late 1920s through the 1940s, usually in small, often uncredited roles. By the late 1940s, Cody was appearing in larger roles in films, including *The Paleface* (1948), with Bob Hope and Jane Russell, and *Sitting Bull* (1954), in which he portrayed Chief Crazy Horse. Cody also often worked as a technical adviser on films, on issues related to American Indian culture and history.

Throughout the 1950s and early 1960s, Cody appeared in nearly every television Western series, including *Bonanza, Gunsmoke, The Virginian,*

Rawhide, The Adventures of Rin Tin Tin, The Adventures of Wild Bill Hickok, and *Maverick.*

In 1996, a newspaper in Louisiana reported that Cody was not really an American Indian born in the Oklahoma territory, as he claimed, but was actually of Italian heritage, and was born in a small town in southern Louisiana. Cody denied the report.

Cody is buried next to his wife, who is simply identified as "Mrs. Iron Eyes Cody (1907–1978)." Her name was Bertha "Birdie" Parker Cody.

Depending on which source you believe, Cody was either born Oscar Cody in 1904 on a farm in the Oklahoma territory, or Oscar DeCorti on April 3, 1907, in Gueydan, Louisiana. Either way, he died January 4, 1999, in Los Angeles.

Head back toward the main entrance of the mausoleum. Just after you walk up the stairs, turn right. On the wall on the right side, in the second space up from the floor, you'll find the crypt of former circus performer, dancer with the Folies-Bergere in Paris, and silent-screen star **Renee Adoree (1898–1933).** Adoree's crypt is usually decorated with her photograph.

Adoree came to the United States in 1920, and made her film debut in *The Strongest* (1920). After appearing in supporting roles in several films, she achieved stardom after appearing in *The Big Parade* (1925), with John Gilbert. Adoree appeared in nine more films with Gilbert, including *Show People* (1928), *La Boheme* (1926), *The Cossacks* (1928), *His Glorious Night* (1929), and *Redemption* (1930). Adoree's last film was *Call of the Flesh* (1930), starring Ramon Novarro. She died of tuberculosis a week after her thirty-fifth birthday.

Adoree was born Jeanne de la Fonte on September 30, 1898, in Lille, France. She died October 5, 1933, in Tujunga, California.

Continue down the corridor, the "Sanctuary of Refuge," heading south. About fifty feet down, on the left side, in the very top row, you'll find the crypt of the first of Charlie Chaplin's four wives, actress **Mildred Harris (1901–1944).** The twenty-eight-year-old Chaplin met the sixteen-year-old Harris at a party given by producer Samuel Goldwyn in early 1918. Harris actively pursued Chaplin, and a few months later told him that she was pregnant. They were quickly married on October 23, 1918. But her pregnancy scare turned out to be false alarm. The following year, she did become pregnant and gave birth to their first child, Norman Spencer Chaplin, who was born severely deformed in July 1919 and died three days after his birth (see Chapter 14).

During their marriage, Harris attempted to transform Chaplin into the traditional, domesticated husband, but Chaplin was neither prepared nor inclined to take on that role. Harris began to give press interviews to discuss her unhappy marriage and Chaplin's failures as a husband. Although the public enjoyed reading these reports, the intensely private Chaplin did not, and they served to further separate the couple. Chaplin and Harris were divorced in November 1920.

The general feeling at the time of their marriage was that Harris was a mediocre actress with a talent for climbing professional and social ladders, and she made every attempt to capitalize on Chaplin's fame. Shortly after their marriage, she began to perform as "Mildred Harris Chaplin," which her husband strongly opposed. She also attempted, unsuccessfully, to have Chaplin intervene in her contract negotiations with MGM studios. And when their child was born, she listed his name as "Charles Spencer Chaplin Jr.," which her husband also opposed. On the death certificate, the name was changed to "Norman Spencer Chaplin." Immediately following their divorce, Harris started a romance with the Prince of Wales. She married two more times and died of pneumonia at the age of forty-two.

Chaplin was not too kind to Harris in his autobiography, which was published in 1964. Of their marriage, Chaplin said he was not in love with Harris and, "I felt I had been caught in the mesh of a foolish circumstance which had been wanton and unnecessary—a union that had no vital basis." He described Harris as, "no mental heavyweight. . . . She had no sense of reality. . . . She was in a continual state of dazzlement.

"Although I had grown fond of Mildred, we were irreconcilably mismatched," Chaplin wrote. "Her character was not mean, but exasperatingly feline. I could never reach her mind. It was cluttered with pink-ribboned foolishness. She seemed in a dither, always looking for other horizons." Chaplin also blamed his marriage for having a negative effect on his career. "Without question marriage was having an effect on my creative faculties," he wrote.

As an actress, Harris appeared in more than a hundred films beginning in 1912, including a small part as a harem girl in D. W. Griffith's *Intolerance* (1916). But her career began to slide after her divorce from Chaplin and she quickly went from starring to supporting roles in films including *The Power of the Press* (1928), *No, No, Nanette* (1930), *Night Nurse* (1931), *Reap the Wild Wind* (1942), and *Hail the Conquering Hero* (1944).

Harris was born November 29, 1901, in Cheyenne, Wyoming.
She died July 20, 1944, in Los Angeles.

Continue another fifty feet down the "Sanctuary of Refuge" corridor. On the right side, in the second space up from the floor, you'll find the crypt of director **Victor Fleming (1889–1949),** who began working under the guidance of D. W. Griffith and later directed such classics as *Bombshell* (1933), *Treasure Island* (1934), *Captains Courageous* (1937), *The Wizard of Oz* (1939), and *Gone With the Wind* (1939), for which he won the Academy Award as Best Director.

Fleming worked as an automobile mechanic and photographer before he entered the film business in 1910 as an assistant cameraman. As an assistant to Griffith, Fleming worked on several films starring Douglas Fairbanks, including *When the Clouds Roll By* (1919), which was Fleming's directorial debut. Throughout the 1920s and 1930s at MGM studios, Fleming gained a reputation as a dependable and capable craftsman who could get the best performances from his actors, but he was not known as a great or even a particularly creative director. That type of workman-like reputation was encouraged and rewarded at the studio that discouraged individuality among its directors, and where the slogan was, "The only star at MGM is Leo the Lion." The MGM management style at the time even included interchangeability of directors. If a particular director was unavailable for retakes or additional scenes for his film, another equally capable director would be used. For this reason, even though Fleming was given the Academy Award for *Gone With the Wind,* so many other people were involved with this massive project that it's difficult to determine exactly what impact he had on the production, or the final product.

But, nevertheless, Fleming's body of work includes many stellar productions among his nearly fifty films, including *Red Dust* (1932), *The Good Earth* (1937), *Test Pilot* (1938), and *A Guy Named Joe* (1943).

Fleming was born February 23, 1889 (some sources
say 1883), in Pasadena, California. He died
January 6, 1949, in Flagstaff, Arizona.

Just past Fleming's crypt, turn left and go through a short hallway into the "Sanctuary of Light." Turn right, and walk about fifty feet. On the right side, just above the floor, you'll see the crypt of popular character actor **Vito Scotti (1918–1996).** You might not recognize his name, but you'd certainly recognize his face. Or at least a few of them.

Scotti was short with wavy black hair, a neatly groomed mustache, dark twinkling eyes, and a smiling, energetic disposition. He appeared in supporting roles in more than sixty films and an equal number of television appearances. Though he usually played Italian characters, he also played Japanese, Mexican, Spanish, Italian, Russian, Arab, Gypsy, and American Indian roles —just about any ethnicity.

Scotti's parents were both musicians, and he trained with improvisational comedy groups in New York City. After serving in World War II, he made his film debut in *Cry of the City* (1948), starring Victor Mature and Richard Conte. Scotti played an assortment of hotel clerks, doormen, cooks, and other assorted character roles for the next forty years, including the train engineer in *Von Ryan's Express* (1965), Senor Sanchez in *Cactus Flower* (1969), Nazorine the pastry shop owner in *The Godfather* (1972), and the restaurant manager in *Get Shorty* (1995), his last film role.

But Scotti is probably best remembered for his work in television. Among his more memorable roles were artist Vito Giotto in *The Dick Van Dyke Show,* Police Captain Gaspar Formento in *The Flying Nun,* and Dr. Markovich in *The Monkees.* As the sign of a truly successful character actor, Scotti often played different roles on different episodes of the same series, including three different characters in *The Addams Family,* four characters in *Gunsmoke,* four characters in *The Rifleman,* and five characters in *Columbo.* And Scotti was the most frequent guest on *Gilligan's Island,* appearing in four episodes of the series. Scotti also appeared in episodes of *The Andy Griffith Show, Bewitched, The Bionic Woman, Bonanza, Charles in Charge, CHiPs, The Golden Girls, Happy Days, Hogan's Heroes, Mad About You, The Man From U.N.C.L.E., My Favorite Martian, Perry Mason, Rawhide, The Virginian,* and *Who's the Boss?*

Scotti was born January 26, 1918, in San Francisco, California.
He died June 5, 1996, in Woodland Hills, California.

Now walk back toward the short hallway you just came through. About ten feet past that hallway, on the left side, in the very top row, you'll see the crypt of **Darla Hood (1931–1979),** child star in the *Our Gang* comedy shorts of the 1930s and early 1940s. Hood joined the *Our Gang* troupe in 1935, when she was four years old, and appeared in more than 150 installments of the series, often playing the object of Alfalfa's affections. Hood was the tiny, chubby-cheeked, dark-haired cutie who always appeared much more intelligent and sophisticated than her scruffy *Our Gang* playmates.

During her *Our Gang* tenure, Hood appeared in a few other films, including *The Bohemian Girl* (1936), starring Laurel and Hardy, and *Neighborhood House* (1936), starring Charley Chase. After leaving the *Our Gang* kids in 1941, Hood appeared in small roles in two films—*Born to Sing* (1942) and *Happy Land* (1943)—then announced her retirement at the age of fourteen. She came out of retirement in 1950 to appear on television on *The Ken Murray Show,* and also appeared in small parts in *Calypso Heat Wave* (1957) and *The Bat* (1959). In the 1960s and 1970s, Hood sang the jingles for television commercials, and she was the voice of the mermaid in the Chicken of the Sea ads.

Hood was born Darla Jean Hood on November 8, 1931, in Leedey, Oklahoma. She died June 13, 1979, in Los Angeles.

Continue about twenty feet past Hood's crypt. On the right, in the second space up from the floor, you'll see the crypt of film studio poineer **Jesse L. Lasky Sr. (1880–1958).**

After working as a reporter in California, a gold prospector in Alaska, and a bandleader in Hawaii, Lasky returned to California to form a musical act with his sister, Blanche. He later worked as a vaudeville promoter and, in 1913, he teamed up with his brother-in-law, Samuel Goldfish (later Samuel Goldwyn), and a friend, Cecil B. De Mille, to form the Jesse L. Lasky Feature Play Company. The company's first production was *The Squaw Man* (1914), a full-scale, feature-length Western, shot in a rented horse barn and on the hills around Hollywood. Some scenes were reportedly filmed in an area that's now the Forest Lawn–Hollywood Hills cemetery. *The Squaw Man,* written and directed by De Mille and Oscar Apfel, was an enormous success and helped transform Los Angeles into a film center.

In 1916, the Jesse L. Lasky Feature Play Company company merged with Adolph Zukor's Famous Players to form the Famous Players–Lasky Corporation, with Jesse Lasky as vice president in charge of production. Over the years, with additional mergers and corporate realignments, that corporation became Paramount Pictures.

In 1932, Lasky left Paramount and worked as an independent producer for several years.

Lasky was also one of the thirty-six founders of the Academy of Motion Picture Arts and Sciences, and his productions were nominated three times for the Academy Award for Best Picture—*The Way of All Flesh* (1927), *The White Parade* (1934), and *Sergeant York* (1941).

The plaque on his crypt reads: "Beloved son of California who, in 1913, headed the company that produced the first feature-length motion picture made in Hollywood."

Lasky is the father of screenwriter Jesse Lasky Jr. (1908–1988).

Lasky was born Jesse Louis Lasky on September 13, 1880, in San Francisco, California. He died January 13, 1958, in Beverly Hills, California.

Just to the right of Lasky's crypt is another short hallway, leading to the "Sanctuary of Peace." Turn right in that corridor, and walk about twenty feet. On the left, in the second space up from the floor, you'll find the reportedly haunted crypt of actor **Clifton Webb (1889–1966).**

Webb was trained as an actor and dancer at a very young age, and he was an experienced performer by the time he reached his teens. He quit school at thirteen to study music and painting, and at seventeen he sang with the Boston Opera Company. Later, he danced at nightclubs and dancehalls in New York City at the same time as another young dancer who would later find success in films, Rudolph Valentino. Webb then began appearing in musical comedies and dramas on both the Broadway stage and in London.

In the early 1920s, Webb came to Los Angeles and made his film debut with a small role in *Polly With a Past* (1924). After appearing in a handful of films, Webb went back to Broadway in 1930. He returned to Hollywood as the elegantly creepy society columnist Waldo Lydecker in *Laura* (1944), for which he was nominated for the Academy Award as Best Supporting Actor. He was also nominated for his supporting role in *The Razor's Edge* (1946) and for his leading role in *Sitting Pretty* (1948).

Webb specialized in playing fastidious, acerbic, and somewhat prissy characters, and is perhaps best known for playing Mr. Belvedere, the baby-sitter and housekeeper in *Sitting Pretty* and its two sequels, *Mr. Belvedere Goes to College* (1949) and *Mr. Belvedere Rings the Bell* (1951). Webb also appeared in *Cheaper by the Dozen* (1950), *Stars and Stripes Forever* (1952), *Titanic*

(1953), *Mister Scoutmaster* (1953), *Three Coins in the Fountain* (1954), *The Man Who Never Was* (1956), and *The Remarkable Mr. Pennypacker* (1959).

Despite his image as a pedantic fussbudget, Webb was a well-known figure on the Hollywood party circuit, usually escorting his mother, Mabelle, to parties and dances until she died in 1960. Visitors to the mausoleum have reported seeing a ghostly figure of a well-dressed man near Webb's crypt, and his home on Rexford Drive in Beverly Hills was reportedly haunted from the time of Webb's death until it was torn down. Before his death, Webb told friends that he loved the home, and he would never leave it, even after his death.

Webb is buried next to his mother. Her crypt marker says simply, "My beloved Mabelle, 1869–1960."

Webb was born Webb Parmalee Hollenbeck on November 11, 1889, in Indianapolis, Indiana. He died October 13, 1966, in Beverly Hills, California.

From Webb's crypt, turn left and head back toward the main entrance of the mausoleum. About seventy-five feet down the corridor, turn right into a short corridor labeled "Shrine of Eternal Love." On the right is a small alcove with the name "Talmadge" over the entrance. Inside are the crypts of the three Talmadge sisters, all silent-screen actresses. The crypt also includes their parents, Frederick J. Talmadge (1869–1925) and Margaret L. Talmadge (1870–1933), the stereotypical stage mother who drove her three daughters to succeed.

Norma Talmadge (1897–1957) was the oldest and most successful of the three sisters. She began modeling at an early age and attracted the attention of producers at Vitagraph studios in New York City. She made her screen debut in *The Household Pest* (1910). With her mother's prodding, Norma appeared in dozens of short films over the next few years and became one of Vitagraph's busiest and most popular stars. In 1915, Norma and her mother went to Hollywood, where Norma appeared in several films, but she returned to New York City when her contract ran out. She married producer Joseph Schenck in 1917, and he took charge of her career, setting up the Norma Talmadge Film Corporation.

With Schenck's guidance, Norma developed her screen specialty—the tearful, long-suffering heroine. Throughout the 1920s, Norma was one of the top stars of the silent screen. But when talking pictures became popular, Norma's career slipped. Her last film was *Du Barry, Woman of Passion* (1930). Norma married George Jessel in 1934 and hoped to revive her career by appearing on his radio show. But the show was canceled, and she divorced Jessel in 1939.

She is buried next to her fourth husband, Dr. Carvel M. James (1902–1980).

The middle sister, **Natalie Talmadge (1900–1969)**, appeared in several films but is best known as the wife of comedian Buster Keaton. She appeared in supporting roles in several comedies starring Keaton and Roscoe "Fatty" Arbuckle, and also in supporting roles in several films starring her sisters, Norma and Constance.

Natalie married Keaton in 1921, and her last film appearance was in his *Our Hospitality* (1923). She divorced Keaton in 1932 and focused on raising their two children. She spent her final years as a recluse in an apartment in Santa Monica, California.

Although the youngest sister, **Constance Talmadge (1903–1973)**, was also a successful silent-film actress, she was never in competition with her older sister, Norma. While Norma specialized in weepy melodramas, Constance was a talented comedian. She made her film debut in 1914 and worked steadily thereafter. Her breakthrough performance was in D. W. Griffith's *Intolerance* (1916), which helped establish her as a star. She appeared in a long series of successful silent comedies through the 1920s. Her last film was *Venus* (1929); she never made a talking picture.

Constance is buried next to her fourth husband, Walter M. Giblin (1901–1964).

Norma Talmadge was born May 26, 1897 (some sources say 1893 or 1895), in Jersey City, New Jersey.
She died December 24, 1957, in Las Vega, Nevada.

Natalie Talmadge was born in 1900 (some sources say 1895, 1897, or 1899), in Brooklyn, New York.
She died June 19, 1969, in Santa Monica, California.

Constance Talmadge was born April 19, 1903 (some sources say 1897 or 1898), in Brooklyn, New York.
She died November 23, 1973, in Los Angeles.

Tour 4: Beth Olam Cemetery

In the southwest corner of Hollywood Forever is Beth Olam Cemetery, which was founded in 1899 as a separate Jewish section of Hollywood Memorial

Park. Beth Olam Cemetery was the second Jewish cemetery in Los Angeles and the oldest still in its original location. The cemetery includes two mausoleums—one along the southern wall of the property and a newer three-level structure at the south end of the Abbey of the Psalms mausoleum.

Beth Olam has a separate entrance on Gower Street, south of Santa Monica Boulevard. Just inside the entrance is a new garden area, featuring an eternal flame in honor of the six million Jews who died in the Holocaust in World War II, and a plaque dedicated to the memory of Anne Frank. The garden area was dedicated on June 4, 2000. Although Beth Olam is technically a separate cemetery, it is part of Hollywood Forever, and easily accessible from the grounds of the main cemetery.

After coming out the main entrance of the Abbey of the Psalms mausoleum, turn right and walk about 125 feet. When you see the "P-P" marker near the curb on the left side of the road, turn left and walk about 150 feet. There, in front of yet another cypress tree, you'll find the grave of actor **Paul Muni (1895–1967),** who was nominated six times for the Academy Award for Best Actor during his thirty-year film career.

Muni started his acting career in Yiddish theaters in New York City, often appearing onstage with his parents. He made his English-language debut on Broadway in 1926 and three years later went to Hollywood. Muni made his film debut in *The Valiant* (1929), and was nominated for an Academy Award as Best Actor—one of only five actors to receive that honor for their first screen appearance. Muni was unhappy with his next film, *Seven Faces* (1929), in which he played seven different roles, and he returned to Broadway. A few years later, Muni came back to Hollywood, playing the title roles in *Scarface* (1932) and *I Am a Fugitive From a Chain Gang* (1932), for which he received another Academy Award nomination as Best Actor. Muni was also nominated for *Black Fury* (1935), and he played a Chinese farmer in *The Good Earth* (1937).

Muni also played the title roles in three successful biographies—*The Story of Louis Pasteur* (1936), *The Life of Emile Zola* (1937), and *Juarez* (1939). For his portrayal of Pasteur, Muni received his fourth Academy Award nomination and his only victory. He was also nominated for his portrayal of Emile Zola. Throughout his career, and particularly when he was playing biographical roles, Muni was known as a meticulous and conscientious actor who took great care to make sure his portrayals were authentic.

Beginning in the early 1940s, Muni went back and forth between film work and Broadway performances. His last film appearance was in *The Last Angry*

Man (1959), which brought him his last Academy Award nomination as Best Actor. His retirement from films was the result of failing eyesight.

Muni is buried with his wife of forty-six years, Bella Muni (1898–1971).

Muni was born Meshilem Meier Weisenfreund on September 22, 1895 (some sources say 1896 or 1897), in Lemberg, Austria-Hungary (now part of the Ukraine). He died August 25, 1967, in Santa Barbara, California.

Along the south side of the Abbey of the Psalms mausoleum is the New Beth Olam Mausoleum, with a separate entrance on the south side of the building. The three Ritz brothers, popular nightclub and film comedians in the 1930s and 1940s, are all in this mausoleum, but in separate locations.

After you enter the mausoleum, turn left in the main hallway, then turn right down the first corridor, labeled "T-4." About twenty feet down that corridor on the right side, in the first space up from the floor, you'll find the crypt of **Al Ritz (1901–1965).**

Go back out into the main hallway, down to the next corridor, labeled "T-5." About 125 feet down that corridor on the left side, in the fifth space up from the floor, you'll find the crypt of **Jimmy Ritz (1904–1985).**

At the start of the T-5 corridor is a stairway leading up to the second level of the mausoleum. Take those stairs up, then turn left and walk about fifty feet down the corridor, and you'll see a small doorway on your left, leading to another stairway. Take those stairs up to the third level of the mausoleum. At the top of the stairs, turn left and walk about forty feet. On the right side, in the top row, you'll find the crypt of **Harry Ritz (1907–1986).**

The Ritz brothers started their careers separately in nightclubs and onstage, offering an assortment of music, dance, and comedy. The first to enter show business was Al Ritz. He won a ballroom dance contest, which inspired his two younger brothers to become performers. They changed their name from Joachim after seeing the name Ritz on either a laundry truck or a cracker truck—the origin of the name depended on which brother was telling the story—and began appearing onstage and in nightclubs as a precision dance act in 1925.

By 1929, they had added slapstick comedy to their act and were performing on Broadway and headlining at the biggest vaudeville houses across the country. Studio executive Darryl F. Zanuck reportedly saw their act at a nightclub in Los Angeles and signed them to a film contract. The Ritzes made their film debut in

Hotel Anchovy (1934). Through the rest of the 1930s, the Ritz brothers supplied musical-comedy relief in a series of films, including *Sing, Baby, Sing* (1936), *One in a Million* (1936), *On the Avenue* (1937), *You Can't Have Everything* (1937), and *Life Begins in College* (1937). Most fans and critics point to *Kentucky Moonshine* (1938) and *The Gorilla* (1939) as their best performances.

By the early 1940s, the Ritz brothers were given starring roles in comedies, including *Argentine Nights* (1940), *Behind the Eight Ball* (1942), *Never a Dull Moment* (1943), and *Hi'ya, Chum* (1943), but these films weren't too popular with their fans, and the brothers announced their retirement from films in 1943. Their act, which combined singing, dancing, and comedy at a frenzied pace, seemed more suited to nightclubs and stage performances, and they were a popular act in Las Vegas for many years.

The Ritzes made several successful television appearances in the late 1950s and early 1960s, and they were planning a comeback in films when Al Ritz died in 1965, after suffering a heart attack following a performance in New Orleans.

Al Ritz was born Alfred Joachim on August 27, 1901 in Newark, New Jersey. He died December 22, 1965, in New Orleans, Louisiana.

Jimmy Ritz was born Samuel Joachim on October 5, 1904 (some sources say 1903), in Newark, New Jersey. He died November 17, 1985, in Los Angeles.

Harry Ritz was born Harry Joachim on May 22, 1906, in Newark, New Jersey. He died March 29, 1986, in San Diego, California .

Go back to the main entrance of the mausoleum. This time, turn right down the corridor labeled "T-1." About twenty feet down the corridor, on the left, you'll find a small alcove containing cremated remains. On the right, in the second column from the back of the alcove about three feet up from the floor, you'll find the plaque of musician **Nelson Riddle (1921–1985).**

Riddle was the composer and musical director on more than one hundred films and television series. He was nominated for the Academy Award for Best Score five times, for *Li'l Abner* (1959), *Can-Can* (1960), *Robin and the Seven Hoods* (1964), *Paint Your Wagon* (1969), and *The Great Gatsby* (1974), for which he won his only Oscar.

Riddle often worked on films starring Frank Sinatra, including *Guys and Dolls* (1955), *High Society* (1956), *Johnny Concho* (1956), *The Joker Is Wild* (1957), *All the Way* (1957), *Pal Joey* (1957), *A Hole in the Head* (1959), *Can-Can* (1960), *Ocean's Eleven* (1960), *Four for Texas* (1963), *Come Blow Your Horn* (1963), *Paris, When It Sizzles* (1964), *Robin and the Seven Hoods* (1964), and *Marriage on the Rocks* (1965). Later, Riddle did the musical arrangements for Sinatra's albums and concerts.

Riddle also won three Grammy Awards, for his "Cross Country Suite" composition in 1958, and for the musical arrangements for two albums by Linda Ronstadt—*What's New* (1983) and *Lush Life* (1985).

Riddle was born June 1, 1921, in Oradell, New Jersey.
He died October 6, 1985, in Los Angeles.

Go to the main entrance of the original Beth Olam Mausoleum, a vine-covered building along the south wall of the cemetery. From the main hallway, turn right down the second corridor, labeled "M-2." About 125 feet down that corridor on the left, in the third space up from the floor, you'll find the crypt of gangster **Benjamin Siegel (1906–1947),** better known as "Bugsy." Though technically not an entertainer, Siegel had a noticeable impact on Hollywood in the late 1930s and 1940s, and helped transform Las Vegas from a sandy stop on the highway into an international entertainment center.

Siegel even had movie-star looks. Always well dressed, just a shade under six-feet tall with thick black hair and deep blue eyes, Siegel might have had a career on the screen. In fact, there were reports that Siegel had arranged for a screen test for himself at one of the major studios. But Siegel was a cold-blooded, heartless sociopath who saw other people only as a way for him to achieve his goals. And if he could reach those goals faster by having one of those people brutally murdered, Siegel could easily give the order or pull the trigger himself and not lose a minute's sleep over it.

Siegel spent his last years in Hollywood, rubbing elbows with his show business friends, turning himself into a celebrity, and living the high-profile lifestyle that ultimately led to his violent death. Though popularly known as "Bugsy," Siegel hated the nickname. He had earned it because of his tendency to overreact, explode, or "go bugs" whenever he was angered or frustrated; calling him "Bugsy" to his face was a good way to see him "go bugs."

Siegel started his life of crime at an early age with small-time extortion, demanding money from street vendors in Brooklyn, New York, and setting fire to their wares if they didn't pay. Siegel met fellow gangsters-to-be Meyer Lansky and Lucky Luciano, and the trio became involved in just about every criminal activity in the New York City area, from gambling to murder. And Siegel was gaining a reputation as a hot-tempered guy who would shoot first and never bother to ask questions later. Siegel was even known to kill childhood friends if they got in his way.

When the heat from the police made things uncomfortable for Siegel on the East Coast, he moved west. Siegel, his wife, and their two daughters rented a thirty-five-room mansion in the upscale Holmby Hills area near Los Angeles in 1936, and Siegel started to hang around with an old friend he had grown up with, actor George Raft. Siegel lived a well-publicized life in Hollywood, moving from party to party and from starlet to starlet, including Jean Harlow.

Benjamin "Bugsy" Siegel, buried in the Beth Olam Mausoleum next to Hollywood Forever, is remembered by "the family."

Siegel's first "business" project was to control the extras' union, then lean on actors and producers to pay up, or the extras needed for their next film wouldn't show up. In his first year in Hollywood, Siegel collected an estimated $400,000.

Next, Siegel moved to Las Vegas. Despite the legend, he wasn't the first person to set up a gambling operation in the state. He simply bought a controlling interest in a newly built hotel and came up with a plan to offer top-level entertainment and accommodations, along with the gambling. Siegel called his hotel-casino the Flamingo, and he convinced his Hollywood pals and mob chiefs from across the country to invest in his desert dream. Since gambling was legal in Nevada, Siegel told his mob pals, the Flamingo would be a legitimate front for money laundering and other activities, as well as an endless legal revenue source. Siegel was convinced that a first-class, top-level resort would attract top-level gamblers from across the country.

When the $1 million Flamingo project turned into a $6 million project, and the operation hadn't produced a penny of profit for the investors a year after it opened, the mob bosses became concerned. At a mob meeting in Havana, Cuba, Lansky, Siegel's old friend from Brooklyn, reported that Siegel had been skimming money from the Flamingo and stashing it in Swiss bank accounts. The mob's response was quick and clear—Siegel had to be eliminated.

Siegel did everything he could to make the Flamingo a success. He hired top entertainment, including George Jessel, Jimmy Durante, and Xavier Cugat's orchestra. He even convinced a few of his Hollywood pals to show up, including Clark Gable, Lana Turner, and Joan Crawford. But overall, in its first few months, the Flamingo was a flop. Siegel may have been a victim of Flamingo contractors and employees who were stealing from him, and Lansky convinced his mob pals to delay the hit on Siegel. The Flamingo started to turn a small profit in early 1947, and Lansky was quick to point out that Siegel might have been right about Las Vegas after all.

But on June 20, 1947, Siegel was alone in the home of his current girl-friend, Virginia Hill, off Sunset Boulevard in Beverly Hills. He had just returned from a haircut and manicure and was reading a newspaper and sitting in a front room, when a volley of bullets crashed through the window behind him. The first shot hit the forty-one-year-old Siegel in the head, the others tore into his body. The man who built a career on violence and intimidation was dead, killed by an unknown assailant. Although Siegel was a nationally known figure and his death was front-page news across the country, only five people—all relatives—attended his funeral. Lansky was still in Havana, Hill was in Europe, and none of Siegel's Hollywood pals managed to show up for the services.

Siegel's murder has never been solved, although there are several theories. One is that Lansky was unable to delay the mob hit on Siegel any longer. Another is that other Flamingo investors wanted the high-profile Siegel out of the picture, since he was bringing attention from both the mob and the police. Another is that the mob simply thought that Siegel's high-profile lifestyle with celebrities was drawing too much attention to him and his criminal activities.

The Flamingo flourished after Siegel's death, as have the stories of his role in the growth of Las Vegas. Although Siegel never became a movie star himself, he has been portrayed many times in films, including by Harvey Keitel in *The Virginia Hill Story* (1974), Joe Penny in *Gangster Wars* (1981), Marc

Figueroa in *The Revenge of Al Capone* (1989), Richard Grieco in *Mobsters* (1991), Armand Assante in *The Marrying Man* (1991), Warren Beatty in *Bugsy* (1991), and Eric Roberts in *Lansky* (1999).

The plaque on Siegel's crypt states, "In loving memory from the family." But which family?

Siegel was born Benjamin Siegelbaum on February 28, 1906
(some sources say 1902 or 1905), in Brooklyn, New York.
He died June 20, 1947, in Beverly Hills, California.

Pierce Brothers Westwood Village Memorial Park

~

1218 Glendon Avenue
Los Angeles, California 90024

~ HISTORY

Pierce Brothers Westwood Village Memorial Park, a tiny cemetery tucked away in a residential area just off busy Wilshire Boulevard, probably has more well-known names per acre than any other cemetery in the world. In fact, if you visit the cemetery at any time, you're likely to see more tourists and sightseers than actual mourners.

When Westwood cemetery was founded in 1904, it was a much larger cemetery located in a rural area on the outskirts of Los Angeles. After selling off some land in 1927, the cemetery remained fairly quiet, peaceful, and unnoticed until 1962, when Marilyn Monroe was buried there. Since then, she has been joined by dozens of well-known figures from the world of entertainment. Although tiny Westwood can never replace either of the Forest Lawn cemeteries or Hollywood Forever in terms of history or the sheer number of celebrities buried there, it has certainly become the current burial place of choice among the Hollywood elite.

Today, the star-studded and well-maintained cemetery is surrounded by high-rise office buildings and quiet residential streets, and it is within earshot of the busy traffic on Wilshire Boulevard. It features a single circular road that allows visitors to drive directly into the park. The road circles a grassy oval lawn where most of the stars are buried. In the southwest corner of the property are the cemetery offices. Next to the offices is a small chapel, built in 1962. The northern and eastern borders of the park are lined by walls of outdoor crypts.

In 1997, the Garden of Serenity opened at Westwood in the southeast corner of the property. The area features a small sunken garden with bubbling fountains and a scattering garden, surrounded by niches for cremated remains, as well as a handful of semiprivate gravesites and a private, gated area in the rear. Except for the crypts and grave markers, Westwood could easily be mistaken for a park of an office courtyard. In fact, it's a popular spot for people who work in the nearby office buildings to come and stroll, read, or just relax in a peaceful setting during their lunch hours.

Westwood is also a friendly location for celebrity-hunters. Visitors who stop in the main office can pick up a list of some of the celebrities buried there, but the list does not include any specific locations or a map of the grounds. Westwood employees, however, will happily provide any necessary assistance and point out the location of a particular celebrity's final resting place.

∼ DIRECTIONS

Even though it's less than a block south of busy Wilshire Boulevard near the UCLA campus, the entrance to Westwood cemetery can be particularly hard to find. The tiny cemetery is roughly bordered by Wilshire on the north, Glendon Avenue on the west, Wellworth Avenue on the south, and Malcolm Avenue on the east. There's only one entrance to the cemetery, and it can't be seen directly from any of those streets. Take the San Diego Freeway (405) to the Wilshire Boulevard exit, a little less than a mile north of Santa Monica Boulevard. Take Wilshire Boulevard east about a half-mile to Glendon Avenue. (Glendon is the first stoplight past Westwood Boulevard.) Turn right on Glendon, then a quick left into the first driveway. At the end of the driveway, just before the theater parking lot, turn right into the cemetery. If you're coming from the east, Glendon Avenue is about two miles west of the intersection of Wilshire and Santa Monica Boulevard.

∼ HOURS

The cemetery grounds and the on-site office are both open every day from 8 A.M. to 5 P.M.

∼

The Tour

With a total area of less than three acres, Westwood is small enough to tour easily on foot. A small drive circles the property, so pick a spot to park and walk over to the main entrance. The tour starts at the entrance and goes clockwise around the outer edge of the cemetery property, then covers the larger central lawn area.

About sixty feet east of the entrance, along the northern edge of the property, is a gray marble, Egyptian-style private mausoleum, with "The Armand Hammer Family" printed above the door in gold letters. This mausoleum, not surprisingly, contains the remains of **Armand Hammer (1898–1990),** art collector, philanthropist, and founder and CEO of Occidental Petroleum.

Hammer was also the founder of the Armand Hammer Museum of Art, which is located a few hundred feet away, at the corner of Wilshire and Westwood Boulevards. The museum is located in the Occidental Petroleum Cultural Center, in a wing that was added to the oil company's headquarters to house the museum. The University of California at Los Angeles assumed management of the museum in 1994, and it's now referred to as the UCLA Hammer Museum.

The museum opened on November 28, 1990; Hammer died less than two weeks later.

Tiny Westwood Memorial Park is tucked away behind the tall office buildings on Wilshire Boulevard.

About ten feet in front and ten feet to the right of the door to the Hammer mausoleum is the grave of **Eva Gabor (1921–1995),** the youngest of the three Gabor sisters, who is best known for her role as the high-society socialite turned farm wife on *Green Acres* in the late 1960s.

A former café singer and ice skater from Hungary, Gabor was the first member of her family to arrive in the United States. She made her film debut in a supporting role in *Pacific Blackout* (1941), starring Robert Preston, and also appeared in *Forced Landing* (1941), *Star-Spangled Rhythm* (1942), *A Royal Scandal* (1945), *The Wife of Monte Cristo* (1946), *Song of Surrender* (1949), *Love Island* (1952), *The Mad Magician* (1954), *The Last Time I Saw Paris* (1954), *Artists and Models* (1955), *My Man Godfrey* (1957), and *Gigi* (1958). With her heavy Hungarian accent, which she never lost even after more than fifty years in the United States, Gabor typically played aristocratic women and countesses of eastern European descent.

In 1965, Gabor starred with Eddie Albert in the television sitcom *Green Acres*, the story of a New York City attorney and his socialite wife who buy a farm and live among the eccentric local characters in the mythical town of Hooterville. While Albert's buttoned-up lawyer never really fits in among the locals, Gabor's Lisa Douglas—despite singing "New York is where I'd rather stay" in the show's theme song—always seems to be more comfortable in her new surroundings, with her own style of bizarre eccentricities.

After *Green Acres* was canceled in 1971, Gabor regularly appeared on television talk shows and game shows throughout the 1970s. She also contributed her voice to several animated films, including *The Aristocats* (1970) and *The Rescuers* (1977). Gabor and Albert also returned to Hooterville to star in a made-for-television film, *Return to Green Acres* (1990).

Gabor's grave marker includes the inscription "Our Darling Eva—We love you, You are in our hearts forever."

Gabor was born February 11, 1921, in Budapest, Hungary.
She died July 4, 1995, in Los Angeles.

Two spaces to the right of Gabor is the grave of **John Cassavetes (1929–1989),** independent filmmaker and Academy Award–nominated actor, writer, and director.

Cassavetes started his career as an actor known for his intensity in television dramas in the early 1950s, including *The Philco Television Playhouse, The United States Steel Hour,* and *Alfred Hitchcock Presents*. In the 1960s, he brought that same hard-edged intensity to guest appearances on television series, including *The Fugitive, The Virginian, Combat!, Voyage to the Bottom of the Sea,* and *Rawhide.*

Cassavetes made his film debut in *Taxi* (1953), and he also appeared in *Crime in the Streets* (1956), *Edge of the City* (1957), and *Affair in Havana* (1957). In 1959, Cassavetes starred in the television detective series *Johnny Staccato* and used his earnings to finance his first film, *Shadows* (1961), the controversial story of an interracial relationship, which Cassavetes wrote, directed, and edited. The film is still considered one of the first and most important independent American films. As a director, Cassavetes was an innovative, experimental filmmaker who focused on gritty realism and often used an improvisational approach with his actors.

Cassavetes continued to act in the 1960s, appearing in *The Killers* (1964), *The Dirty Dozen* (1967)—for which he received an Academy Award nomination as Best Supporting Actor—*Devil's Angels* (1967), and *Rosemary's Baby* (1968). Cassavetes also continued to use his income from acting jobs to finance his films. He produced, wrote, and directed *Faces* (1968), which won Cassavetes his second Academy Award nomination, this time for Best Original Screenplay. For *A Woman Under the Influence* (1974), Cassavetes received an Academy Award nomination for Best Director. The film starred Peter Falk as a husband struggling to deal with the increasing mental instability of his wife, played by Gena Rowlands—Cassavetes' wife, who was nominated for an Academy Award as Best Actress for her performance.

Cassavetes also wrote and directed *Gloria* (1980), the story of an ex–mob mistress, played by Rowlands, who protects a young boy after his parents are killed. The film earned Rowlands her second Academy Award nomination as Best Actress.

Cassavetes and Rowlands are the parents of actor and director Nick Cassavetes.

Between the graves of Eva Gabor and Cassavetes is Cassavetes' mother-in-law, Lady Rowlands (1904–1999), an actress who appeared in several of his films.

Cassavetes was born December 9, 1929, in New York City.
He died February 3, 1989, in Los Angeles.

Continue heading east, toward the large garden mausoleum area along the northeast corner of the property. About twenty feet before you reach the mausoleum, along the northern edge of the cemetery property, you'll find the grave of super-agent **Irving "Swifty" Lazar (1907–1993)**, known for his bald head, huge goggle-shaped eyeglasses, and his post–Academy Award parties held at the swankiest restaurants in Hollywood. Lazar earned his nickname after accepting and completing a dare from client Humphrey Bogart—to make five movie deals for the actor in one day.

After Lazar graduated from Brooklyn Law School in 1930, he worked in a law office and began representing show business clients. His logic was simple—an agent's commission was 10 percent, compared to an attorney's 1 percent. Lazar spent the next ten years traveling the country, booking bands and nightclub acts. After enlisting in the U.S. Army in 1942, Lazar wrote a memo to his commanding general, telling him that he could bring composers Rodgers and Hammerstein, writers George S. Kaufman and Moss Hart, and actors Clark Gable and Jimmy Stewart to write and perform in a military show—even though Lazar had never met any of them. Hart was so impressed by Lazar's bravado that he invited him to Hollywood and introduced him to many of his celebrity friends. Lazar started his career as primarily a literary agent, representing Hart and authors Truman Capote, Arthur Schlesinger, Vladimir Nabokov, and Noel Coward, and composers Cole Porter and George and Ira Gershwin. In his later years, Lazar stopped representing actors, he said, because their constant need for comfort and reassurance made them too time-consuming as clients.

For more than thirty years, Lazar's party after the Academy Award ceremonies was the most sought-after ticket in Hollywood—sometimes even more prestigious than going to the actual award ceremony. In the years before his death, Lazar hosted his party at Wolfgang Puck's trendy Spago eatery. The formal festivities usually attracted most of the Oscar winners, as well as other well-known names from the entertainment industry, from Elizabeth Taylor and Jimmy Stewart to Michael Jackson and Madonna.

Lazar is buried with his wife, Mary (1932–1993).

Lazar was born Irving Paul Lazar on March 28, 1907, in New York City. He died December 30, 1993, in Beverly Hills, California.

About ten feet past Lazar's grave, just before you reach the garden mausoleum, you'll see a large red and gold marker covering the grave of singer and songwriter **Mel Torme (1925–1999),** considered one of the finest male jazz singers and popularly known as the "Velvet Fog," due to his smooth, mellow high baritone voice—even though he reportedly hated that nickname.

Torme started singing professionally at the age of three, was a popular child actor on the radio, and played drums in several bands while still a teenager. In the 1940s, Torme formed his own group, The Mel-Tones, one of the first jazz-influenced vocal groups. The group had a major hit with "What Is This Thing Called Love," featuring jazz clarinetist Artie Shaw. As a solo artist, Torme had a number one hit in 1949 with "Careless Love."

With the increasing popularity of rock-and-roll music in the late 1950s and 1960s, Torme's popularity slipped. Although he continued to perform and record during this time, he also pursued other interests, including writing. Torme wrote several books, including biographies of Judy Garland and Buddy Rich, a novel titled *Wynner,* and his autobiography, *It Wasn't All Velvet.* Torme also wrote more than three hundred songs. The best known is probably "The Christmas Song (Chestnuts Roasting on an Open Fire)," which was recorded by Torme, Nat "King" Cole, Bing Crosby, and many others, and has become one of the most popular songs of all time.

With the renewed interest in jazz in the 1970s and 1980s, Torme was discovered by a new generation of fans. On the popular 1980s television comedy series *Night Court,* the judge, played by Harry Anderson, was a big fan of Torme, and kept a framed photograph of the silken-voiced singer in his chambers. Not only did Torme enjoy the reference, but he made several guest appearances on the series. In 1982 and 1983, Torme won Grammy Awards for Best Male Jazz Vocalist for the albums *An Evening with George Shearing and Mel Torme* and *Top Drawer.*

Torme appeared in several films, usually in supporting roles in musicals and comedies, including *Higher and Higher* (1944), *Ghost Catchers* (1944), *Junior Miss* (1945), *Good News* (1947), *Words and Music* (1948), *Girls Town* (1959), *The Patsy* (1964), and *Land of No Return*

The grave of singer-songwriter Mel Torme includes a huge red and gold memorial marker.

(1975). Torme also provided one of the funniest moments in the animated film *Daffy Duck's Quackbusters* (1988), in which he provides Daffy's singing voice.

Torme's grave marker includes this inscription: "Music, the greatest good that mortals know, and all of heaven we have below. . . . So many gifts so lovingly shared."

Torme was born Melvin Howard Torme on September 13, 1925, in Chicago, Illinois. He died June 5, 1999, in Los Angeles.

A few feet past Torme's grave is the western wall of the garden mausoleum. In the lower right corner of the wall, you'll find the crypt of **Heather O'Rourke (1975–1988),** best known for her performances as the terrified young girl who is sucked into a spectral dimension by evil spirits in *Poltergeist* (1982) and its two sequels.

O'Rourke began her acting career at the age of five, appearing in episodes of *Fantasy Island, Webster,* and *CHiPs* in the early 1980s. In 1982, she had a semi-regular role on the popular television sitcom *Happy Days.*

Fans often leave flowers, stuffed animals, and other toys at the crypt of Heather O'Rourke.

O'Rourke was eating lunch in the commissary at MGM studios with her mother and sister when writer and director Steven Spielberg, who was looking for a child to star in *Poltergeist*, saw her and asked if she would do a screen test for the film. O'Rourke, as Carol Anne Freeling, the youngest daughter in a family that finds their home haunted by unfriendly spirits, had the most memorable line in the first *Poltergeist* film—"They're heeeeere!"—and in the second, *Poltergeist II* (1986)—"They're baaaaack!" O'Rourke was the only actor from the first two films to appear in the next sequel, *Poltergeist III* (1988), in which the evil spirits follow her when she visits her aunt and uncle.

A few months after she finished work on *Poltergeist III*, O'Rourke complained of abdominal pains, and was taken to a hospital in San Diego, California, where she died on the operating table. O'Rourke had been suffering from intestinal stenosis, a congenital obstruction of the digestive tract. The blockage, which had been previously undetected, caused an infection that resulted in her death, just a few weeks after her twelfth birthday. *Poltergeist III* was released after O'Rourke's death and was dedicated to her memory. A few months after O'Rourke's death, her mother filed a wrongful-death lawsuit against the hospital where O'Rourke had been treated, charging that the girl's condition had been improperly diagnosed and that the intestinal obstruction could have been eliminated with a simple surgical procedure.

The marker on O'Rourke's crypt identifies her as "Carol Anne—*Poltergeist I, II, III.*" Despite her film roles, O'Rourke said her proudest accomplishment was being elected president of her fifth-grade class.

O'Rourke was born December 27, 1975, in San Diego, California.
She died February 1, 1988, in San Diego, California.

Two spaces above O'Rourke's crypt, in the third space up from the floor, is a crypt that was occupied for three and a half years by the remains of actor **Peter Lawford (1923–1984)**—until he was evicted because the mortuary bills weren't paid, and his ashes were scattered in the Pacific Ocean.

After the death of the former Kennedy in-law and Sinatra Rat Packer, his fourth wife, Patricia Seaton Lawford, arranged to have his remains buried at Westwood. After the funeral services, Patricia Lawford received a bill for $10,000, but she said she could not pay it, since Lawford's estate contained more debt than assets. Lawford's children refused to help with the payment, she said, and even the Kennedy family wouldn't help with the bill. Nothing more was done until May 1988 when the Westwood Mortuary, under new ownership, attempted to collect on the unpaid bill.

Patricia Lawford admits in her biography of her late husband that "everyone has their own version of what happened," when she said she was "faced with the choice of either paying the bills or removing Peter's remains." Even though she said the mortuary was willing to reduce the amount owed, and even with donations from Lawford's fans, she was still unable to make the payment and decided to remove Lawford's remains.

Since the cost of disinterment would be about $2,500, Patricia Lawford made a deal with the *National Enquirer* tabloid for them to pay the expenses in exchange for exclusive coverage of the event. In May 1988, she removed the urn containing Lawford's ashes and, accompanied by the *Enquirer* reporter and photographer, took a boat out into the Pacific Ocean and scattered Lawford's remains.

James Spada, author of *Peter Lawford: The Man Who Kept the Secrets,* tells a slightly different version of the story. Spada claims that Patricia Lawford received a $50,000 payment from Lawford's Screen Actors Guild pension, and could have paid the funeral expenses from that money. Instead, Spada suggests that the event was a publicity stunt to help promote her upcoming book.

After Lawford's remains were moved out, the crypt remained empty until 2001, when the remains of **Jack Lemmon (1925–2001)** were entombed there. Lemmon was the "everyman" actor who excelled in both comedic and dramatic roles, and won Academy Awards in both areas. His career included everything from belly-laugh comedy to gut-wrenching tragedy, from Shakespeare to *The Simpsons*. In nearly one hundred films, Lemmon typically played slightly flawed but deeply likeable characters struggling not to exceed, but just to survive.

The Harvard-educated son of a Boston doughnut company executive, Lemmon began his acting career in college. After serving in the navy during World War II, Lemmon worked as a beer-hall piano player in New York City and appeared in radio productions, television dramas, and off-Broadway plays before making his film debut in *It Should Happen to You* (1954), costarring Judy Holliday. The following year, Lemmon costarred with Henry Fonda, William Powell, and James Cagney in *Mister Roberts* (1955), the filmed version of the successful Broadway play. Lemmon's performance as Ensign Frank Pulver, the scheming laundry and morale officer on board a World War II supply ship, earned him an Academy Award as Best Supporting Actor.

After appearing in several more comedies over the next few years, including *You Can't Run Away From It* (1956), *Operation Mad Ball* (1957), and *Bell, Book and Candle* (1958), Lemmon costarred with Tony Curtis and Marilyn Monroe in *Some Like It Hot* (1959), which is generally considered one of the best American comedic films ever made. (The film probably wouldn't have become a comedy classic, however, if the producers had gotten their wish of Frank Sinatra to play Lemmon's role.) Lemmon and Curtis play Chicago musicians who witness a mob murder and hide out in drag as members of an all-female band, with Monroe as the ukulele-playing band singer. While Curtis pursues Monroe, Lemmon is pursued by a wealthy eccentric, played by Joe E. Brown. The film was nominated for six Academy Awards, including a nomination for Lemmon as Best Actor, but it took home only one statuette, for Best Costume Design. *Some Like It Hot* was also Lemmon's first film with director Billy Wilder.

Lemmon and Wilder next teamed in *The Apartment* (1960), costarring Shirley MacLaine and Fred MacMurray. Lemmon played a mid-level executive who tries to climb the corporate ladder by loaning out his apartment for his bosses' afternoon trysts. A stellar mix of comedy and tragedy, *The Apartment* won Academy Awards for Best Picture, Best Director, and Best Screenplay, and Lemmon was again nominated for Best Actor.

Lemmon earned his fourth Academy Award nomination for *The Days of Wine and Roses* (1962), in which he played a public relations executive who sinks to the depths of alcoholism then tries to pull both himself and his wife, played by Lee Remick, back up to sobriety. Several times during the film, just before taking a drink, Lemmon would say, "It's magic time." In fact, Lemmon used that phrase throughout his career, just before stepping in front of the cameras.

Lemmon returned to comedy with *Irma La Douce* (1963), *Under the Yum Yum Tree* (1963), *Good Neighbor Sam* (1964), *How to Murder Your Wife* (1965),

The Great Race (1965), and *The Fortune Cookie* (1966), which was also directed by Billy Wilder and is notable as Lemmon's first film with longtime costar and offscreen friend Walter Matthau. Two years later, Lemmon and Matthau costarred in their most famous collaboration, *The Odd Couple* (1968), written by Neil Simon, with Lemmon as the persnickety Felix Unger and Matthau as the slovenly Oscar Madison, two recently divorced men forced to share an apartment.

Lemmon and Matthau costarred in seven more films—*The Front Page* (1974), *Buddy Buddy* (1981), *Grumpy Old Men* (1993), *Grumpier Old Men* (1995), *The Grass Harp* (1996), *Out to Sea* (1997), and *The Odd Couple II* (1998). Lemmon also directed Matthau in *Kotch* (1971)—a performance that netted Matthau an Academy Award nomination as Best Actor. (Lemmon and Matthau also both appeared in *JFK* [1991], though in smaller roles, not as costars.)

Lemmon finally won his Academy Award for Best Actor for his performance in *Save the Tiger* (1973), as a bitter, corrupt businessman. Lemmon was the first actor to win Academy Awards as both Best Actor and Best Supporting Actor. (Since then, four other actors have taken home both awards—Gene Hackman, Jack Nicholson, Robert DeNiro, and Kevin Spacey.)

Lemmon played primarily dramatic roles in the 1980s and 1990s, including Academy Award–nominated performances in *The China Syndrome* (1979), *Tribute* (1980), and *Missing* (1982), giving him a total of eight Oscar nominations in his career. Lemmon also starred in *That's Life* (1986), *Dad* (1989), *Glengarry Glen Ross* (1992), and *Short Cuts* (1993). He guest-starred on an episode of the animated television series *The Simpsons* in 1997, and he won his only Emmy Award for his performance in the television film *Tuesdays With Morrie* (1999).

In 1988, Lemmon received the Life Achievement Award from the American Film Institute. Ten years later, the AFI released its list of the 100 Greatest American Movies, in commemoration of the first hundred years of American cinema, and *Some Like It Hot* was ranked number fourteen. Two years later, the AFI released its list of the hundred funniest American movies, with three films starring Lemmon in the top twenty—*Some Like It Hot* was ranked number one, *The Odd Couple* was number seventeen, and *The Apartment* was number twenty.

Lemmon died a few days before the first anniversary of Matthau's death.

Lemmon was born John Uhler Lemmon III on February 8, 1925, in Boston, Massachusetts. He died June 27, 2001, in Los Angeles.

One space to the left and one space down from Lemmon's crypt, in the center column, second space up from the floor, you'll find the crypt of author **Truman Capote (1924–1984),** a powerful and flamboyant writer whose talent ranged from the sparkling *Breakfast at Tiffany's* to the chilling *In Cold Blood.* Both novels were made into successful films.

Capote was born the son of a lawyer and a former Miss Alabama. After his parents divorced, his mother re-married and the family moved to New York City, where the seventeen-year-old Capote landed a clerical job at the *New Yorker* magazine. During his two years at the *New Yorker,* Capote had several short stories published in other magazines. Capote published his first novel, *Other Voices, Other Rooms,* in 1948. The autobiographical story of a sexually confused teenage boy coming to terms with his maturity and his place in the world brought Capote critical acclaim. His second novel, *The Grass Harp,* was turned into an unsuccessful Broadway play.

Capote's *In Cold Blood,* published in 1965 and based on the true story of the brutal murder of a Kansas farm family by two drifters, pioneered a new literary form—the "nonfiction novel." In addition to writing numerous short stories and nonfiction essays for various magazines in the 1960s and 1970s, Capote also published *The Muses Are Heard* in 1956, *Music for Chameleons* in 1980—his last published book—and other short novels and collections of short stories.

Capote's career in Hollywood started when he cowrote *Beat the Devil* (1953) with director John Huston, adapting the novel by James Helvick. He also wrote the script for *The Innocents* (1961), based on the Henry James novel *The Turn of the Screw.* Capote's novels first came to the screen with *Breakfast at Tiffany's* (1961) followed by *In Cold Blood* (1967). Since his death, several of his short stories have been adapted into made-for-television movies, and in 1996 a film version of *The Grass Harp* was released to critical acclaim.

In the 1970s, Capote seemed to focus less on writing and more on being a celebrity. He was a popular figure on the high-society party scene and a regular guest on television talk shows. He also underwent treatment for alcoholism and drug abuse. Capote spent the last years of his life working on *Answered Prayers,* which he described as his "masterwork." After chapters of the unfinished novel were published in *Esquire* magazine, and many of Capote's friends recognized the thinly veiled, viciously drawn descriptions of themselves, the author became a social outcast—and to the quintessential social butterfly, that was perhaps the cruelest fate. The novel was never finished, though there have been some rumors that Capote did complete the book and it's hidden away in a safe-deposit box.

Capote died at the home of his close friend Joanne Carson, the ex-wife of talk-show host Johnny Carson. His crypt contains only half of his cremated remains. The other half was given to Joanne Carson.

Capote was born Truman Streckfus Persons on September 30, 1924, in New Orleans, Louisiana. He died August 25, 1984, in Los Angeles.

The section of the garden mausoleum along the northern edge of the cemetery property contains three small alcoves. The third alcove is called the Sanctuary of Tranquility. As you enter that alcove, on the wall on the right, in the second space in from the entrance and the first space up from the ground, you'll find the crypt of **Buddy Rich (1917–1987),** often described—even by himself—as "The World's Greatest Drummer."

Rich was drumming nearly his entire life. Born the son of vaudeville entertainers, Rich started playing drums onstage at the age of eighteen months, billed as "Traps, the Drum Wonder," sitting behind a bass drum that was taller than he was. The self-taught drum prodigy was playing on Broadway at the age of four, as "Infant Traps," and was the highest-paid child performer in show business. Rich continued performing throughout his childhood, and he started playing with established bands in his late teens. He performed with Bunny Berigan, Artie Shaw, and Tommy Dorsey. In the mid-1940s, Rich formed his own band, but with little success.

As a drummer, Rich was unmatched for speed, endurance, and power, and he could also play with a light, sensitive touch. Rich performed and recorded with some of the biggest names in jazz during the 1950s, including Charlie Parker, Art Tatum, Lionel Hampton, Les Brown, Dizzy Gillespie, and Harry James. Finally, in 1966, Rich again formed his own band and toured and recorded with them for the last twenty years of his life. Rich was also a frequent guest on *The Tonight Show Starring Johnny Carson,* often playing drum duets with the host, an amateur drummer.

Frank Sinatra, who sang with Dorsey's band while Rich played drums in the 1940s, gave the eulogy at Rich's funeral.

Rich's crypt marker describes him as "One of a Kind," and there is often at least one drumstick left by fans in the flower vases on his crypt.

Rich was born Bernard Rich on September 30, 1917, in Brooklyn, New York. He died April 2, 1987, in Los Angeles.

The back wall of the Sanctuary of Tranquility alcove contains niches for cremated remains. On that wall, in the sixth column from the left and the fourth space up from the ground, you'll find the niche containing the remains of writer, producer, and director **Nunnally Johnson (1897–1977).**

Johnson started his writing career as a newspaper reporter and magazine writer. One of his short stories, published in the *Saturday Evening Post,* became the basis for *Rough House Rosie* (1927), a comedy starring Clara Bow. Johnson came to Hollywood in 1932 and immediately started work as a screenwriter. After a short stint at Paramount studios, Johnson went to work for 20th Century Pictures, where he wrote *The House of Rothschild* (1934), *Bulldog Drummond Strikes Back* (1934), *Thanks a Million* (1935), *The Prisoner of Shark Island* (1936), and *Jesse James* (1939). Johnson also served as associate producer on many of his films, beginning in the late 1930s.

Johnson received his first Academy Award nomination for Best Screenplay for *The Grapes of Wrath* (1940), adapting John Steinbeck's novel about Oklahoma farmers in the 1930s escaping the dust bowl and migrating to California. Johnson, in his role as associate producer, also shared the Best Picture nomination with producer Darryl F. Zanuck. Johnson also received Best Screenplay nominations for *The Pied Piper* (1942) and *Holy Matrimony* (1943). He wrote *Tobacco Road* (1941), *Roxie Hart* (1942), *The Woman in the Window* (1944), *The Keys to the Kingdom* (1944), *The Southerner* (1945), *The Gunfighter* (1950), and *Mr. Hobbs Takes a Vacation* (1962), as well as *Something's Got to Give* (1962)—the film Marilyn Monroe was working on when she died.

Johnson tried his hand at directing in the 1950s, usually working with his own scripts, including *Night People* (1954), *Black Widow* (1954), *How to Be Very, Very Popular* (1956), *The Man in the Gray Flannel Suit* (1956), *The Three Faces of Eve* (1957), and *The Man Who Understood Women* (1959). Johnson wrote the screenplay for *The World of Henry Orient* (1964), based on the novel written by his daughter, Nora. His last screen credit was for *The Dirty Dozen* (1967).

Johnson was born December 5, 1897, in Columbus, Georgia.
He died March 25, 1977, in Los Angeles.

Walk out of the alcove and continue heading east. Just around the corner, along the northern wall, in the second space from the left and second space up from the ground, you'll find the crypt of **Marilyn Monroe (1926–1962),** perhaps the most famous blonde in history, who became the ultimate symbol of Hollywood glamour, sex appeal and, ultimately, tragedy.

(Incidentally, it's almost impossible *not* to find Monroe's crypt. If there aren't several people standing in front of it, as there usually are, just look for the fresh flowers, cards, letters, and other mementos left by her fans.)

The details of Monroe's short, extremely public life are well known. She was born to a mentally unstable mother and absentee father, raised in foster homes, and seemed to spend her life searching for affection and attention. She married for the first time a few weeks after her sixteenth birthday and was divorced three years later. She began to take acting classes and worked as a model—in 1947 she was named Miss California Artichoke Queen—and she made her film debut in a small role in *The Shocking Miss Pilgrim* (1947), starring Betty Grable. She also had a small role in *Love Happy* (1950), starring the Marx Brothers. Larger roles in *The Asphalt Jungle* (1950) and *All About Eve* (1950) resulted in a long-term contract at 20th Century studios and starring roles in *Niagara* (1953), *How to Marry a Millionaire* (1953), and *Gentlemen Prefer Blondes* (1953), which launched her as a sex symbol.

In December 1953, one of Monroe's early modeling assignments, a nude calendar shot in which she was stretched out on a red velvet sheet, appeared in the first issue of *Playboy* magazine, which also featured a photo of Monroe on the cover. *Playboy* publisher Hugh Hefner paid $500 for the rights to use the photo, and Monroe was identified as the magazine's first "Sweetheart."

Decades after her death, fans still leave flowers, photos, and other mementos in front of Marilyn Monroe's crypt.

Later, the term was changed to "Playmate of the Month." Rather than damage her career, however, the publicity from the photo seemed to make Monroe an even bigger and more popular star. Monroe explained that she took the modeling assignment in 1949 for the $50 because her car had recently been repossessed, and the public seemed to sympathize.

In January 1954, Monroe married Joe DiMaggio, the recently retired baseball superstar of the New York Yankees. But DiMaggio, a traditional family man, wanted Monroe to give up her acting career and become a traditional housewife, which she was reluctant to do. When DiMaggio watched his wife filming a scene for *The Seven-Year Itch* (1955), with hundreds of men on the street watching her stand over a subway grate to see her skirt blown up over her waist, that was all he could stand. DiMaggio and Monroe were divorced in October 1954, only nine months after their wedding.

Monroe continued to study acting, working with Lee Strasberg, and hoping to get film roles beyond her sex symbol image. She married playwright Arthur Miller in 1956, divorced him in 1961, and exhibited her improving acting talents in *Bus Stop* (1956), *The Prince and the Showgirl* (1957), *Some Like It Hot* (1959), *Let's Make Love* (1960), and *The Misfits* (1961). She died in 1962 while filming *Something's Got to Give* (1962), and the unfinished film was never released.

As an actress, Monroe's specialty seemed to be innocent sexuality, with a high level of vulnerability and natural humor. In most of her films, she plays characters who don't realize how beautiful they are. Offscreen, Monroe developed a reputation as a difficult and undependable actress who was fighting a losing battle against alcohol and drug abuse. She would often show up late on the set, if she showed up at all. She constantly frustrated more serious actors, including Sir Laurence Olivier, her costar in *The Prince and the Showgirl*, and Clark Gable, her costar in *The Misfits*, who was quoted after the filming as saying, "Working with Marilyn Monroe in *The Misfits* nearly gave me a heart attack. I have never been happier when a film ended." In fact, Gable did suffer a fatal heart attack shortly after the film was completed.

In the early 1960s, Monroe was romantically linked to President John Kennedy and, later, to his brother, Attorney General Robert Kennedy, among others. In May 1962, she made one of her most sensational public appearances when she sang a breathy, seductive version of "Happy Birthday" to President Kennedy at a celebration at Madison Square Garden in New York City, wearing a nearly transparent, $12,000 dress that she was literally sewn into. (In 1999, the dress was sold at auction for nearly $1.3 million.)

DiMaggio and Monroe remained friends after their divorce, and spoke to each other often. In fact, after Monroe's divorce from playwright Arthur Miller in 1961, DiMaggio and Monroe had begun seeing each other again, and several biographers have reported that the couple was planning to re-marry.

On August 6, 1962, Monroe was found dead in the home she had recently purchased for $75,000 on Fifth Helena Drive in the Brentwood section of Los Angeles—the first home she ever owned. She was found lying nude on her bed, clutching a telephone receiver in her hand. The initial report was that she had died of an overdose of sleeping pills. She was thirty-six years old.

Monroe had called her psychiatrist the evening before and told him that she was having trouble getting to sleep, and the psychiatrist suggested that she go for a drive. An estimated fifteen medicine bottles, some with prescription labels, were found on the nightstand near Monroe's bed, including an empty bottle that had contained Nembutal capsules—a powerful barbiturate. (Due to the high risks of addiction and the dangers of overdose, Nembutal is now rarely prescribed for insomnia.) The prescription for fifty Nembutal capsules had been written two or three days before Monroe's death, with a suggested dosage of one capsule per night.

In the years since Monroe's death, several theories have been suggested as to the real cause of her death—she was killed by organized crime, either as an act of revenge against the Kennedys, or on orders from the Kennedys because she had kept a detailed diary of her affairs with them; she was killed by Communists, either as revenge against, or on orders from, the Kennedys; she was killed by her housekeeper, who administered her medication and who had recently been fired by Monroe. Proponents of each of these theories are unable to prove beyond any doubt that they are correct, but what they *do* prove is that, decades after her death, the public is still interested in Monroe, still willing to buy books on the subject, and still willing to believe that the ultimate sex goddess would not kill herself. Even so, the official cause of Monroe's death is listed as an accidental suicide.

Monroe's funeral services were held three days after her death at Westwood Memorial Park—the second funeral held in the new chapel. DiMaggio took control of the funeral arrangements, and only thirty-one close friends and relatives were invited to the services. More than fifty Los Angeles police officers were at the cemetery to keep the uninvited out, assisted by forty security guards hired by 20th Century-Fox studios. Bleachers were set up outside the north wall of the cemetery to accommodate the press, and hundreds of fans stood quietly outside the cemetery gates. DiMaggio had invited Carl

Marilyn Monroe's simple crypt at Westwood Memorial Park.

Sandburg to speak at the services, but the poet was ill and could not attend. Monroe's former acting coach, Lee Strasberg, delivered the eulogy. None of Marilyn's costars or friends from the entertainment industry were invited, even though many flew to Los Angles to attend the services. At the time, DiMaggio said, "We could not in conscience ask one personality to attend without perhaps offending many, many others." But privately, DiMaggio blamed the film and entertainment community for Monroe's death.

Monroe was buried in an $800 coffin, wearing a simple green dress with a green scarf tied around her neck. In her hands was a tiny bouquet of baby pink roses, placed there by DiMaggio. After the services, just before the coffin was closed, DiMaggio leaned over, kissed Monroe on the lips, and whispered, "I love you, I love you." That evening, after the funeral services were completed and Monroe's body was placed in the crypt, DiMaggio returned to the cemetery alone for a final, private farewell. For the next twenty years, until 1983, DiMaggio arranged to have six red roses sent to Monroe's crypt, three times a week. And when DiMaggio died in March 1999, his last words were reported to be, "I'll finally get to see Marilyn."

Even though Monroe appeared in only thirty films during her career, including the early bit parts, her star still shines brightly. At the end of the twentieth century, various magazines came out with their lists of the top film stars, the sexiest women, and the most popular people of the century, and Monroe's name was always near the top of those lists. She may also be the most imitated actress in history, with everyone from Jayne Mansfield to Madonna trying to copy her look. And it's impossible to walk down Hollywood Boulevard and not see Monroe's image on T-shirts, posters, and other products in nearly every store window.

But if Monroe was the embodiment of Hollywood glamour and style, why was she buried in what was then a particularly unfashionable and relatively unknown little cemetery on the edge of town? Monroe often visited the cemetery, where her former guardian, Grace McKee Goddard (1895–1953), and her surrogate mother, Ana Atchinson Lower (1880–1948), were buried. Monroe lived with Lower from the age of twelve until her first marriage in 1942, just after she turned sixteen. After Lower's death, Monroe used to spend many hours at the cemetery, sitting on a bench near her grave. (Both Goddard and Lower are buried within a few feet of each other, in the large urn garden in the southwest corner of the central lawn area—the opposite corner from Monroe's crypt. Their grave markers are directly west of the large tree near the curb in the urn garden.) In fact, on one occasion, Monroe saw cemetery workers digging a grave, and she asked them if she could climb down into the open hole. "I went down and lay on the ground and looked up at the sky from there," she later recalled. "The ground is cold under your back, but it's quite a view."

When Monroe's childhood friend and foster sister, Eleanor "Bebe" Goddard, died recently, she was cremated and her ashes were scattered in the garden of roses in front of the Westwood Chapel. Her small bronze plaque, on the east side of the garden, doesn't include her birth or death dates, but it identifies her as "Norma-Jeane's foster sister."

You may notice that there's an empty space to the left of Monroe's crypt. If you're making any pre-need plans and thinking about spending eternity resting next to the ultimate sex symbol, you should know that Hugh Hefner, founder and publisher of *Playboy* magazine, has already purchased the spot, reportedly paying $85,000 for the pleasure of spending eternity next to his first "Sweetheart." The last remaining crypt on the same wall as Monroe was recently priced at $125,000.

Even decades after her death, Monroe is still Westwood's most popular resident, attracting an estimated 350 visitors every day. In fact, cemetery employees complain about the difficulty they have trying to remove the lipstick marks left by adoring fans on her marble crypt.

A few feet in front of Monroe's crypt is a white stone bench, which was paid for and installed in 1992, on the thirtieth anniversary of her death, by two Monroe fan clubs—All About Marilyn and Marilyn Remembered. Every year on the anniversary of her death, the Marilyn Remembered fan club hosts a memorial service at Westwood, usually attracting hundreds of friends, fans, and impersonators and dozens of floral arrangements in front of her crypt.

Monroe has been portrayed more than two dozen times in various theatrical and made-for-television films, including by Catherine Hicks in *Marilyn: The Untold Story* (1980), Heather Thomas in *Hoover vs. The Kennedys* (1987), Susan Griffiths in *Marilyn and Me* (1991), Stephanie Anderson in *Calendar*

Girl (1993), Melody Anderson in *Marilyn and Bobby: Her Final Affair* (1993), Ashley Judd and Mira Sorvino in *Norma Jean and Marilyn* (1996), and Barbara Niven in *The Rat Pack* (1998).

While Monroe was on a flight over the Arizona desert a few years before her death, the plane's engine faltered briefly. Monroe and her seatmate, a reporter for a London newspaper, discussed what would have happened if the plane had crashed, and she was asked what she wanted to appear on her epitaph. "I'll settle for this," she joked, "Here lies Marilyn Monroe—38-23-36."

Monroe was born Norma Jeane Mortensen, later changed to Baker, on June 1, 1926, in Los Angeles. She died August 5, 1962, in Los Angeles.

About thirty feet to the east of Monroe's crypt, in the corner of the cemetery property, is the Room of Prayer, a small, locked columbarium. Inside is a niche containing the cremated remains of actor **Caroll O'Connor (1924–2001).**

Along the eastern edge of the property are three more garden mausoleum alcoves. The first is called the Sanctuary of Peace. As you enter the alcove, on the wall on the right, in the second and third spaces from the right, and the first spaces up from the ground, you'll find the crypts of actress Elizabeth Taylor's parents, Francis S. Taylor (1897–1968) and Sara S. Taylor (1895–1994). On the same wall, in the third and fourth spaces from the right, in the fourth row up from the floor, you'll find the crypts of Gaetano "Guy" Crocetti (1894–1967) and Angela Barra Crocetti (1897–1966). They are the

Singer and actor Dean Martin's crypt includes the title of his theme song.

parents of actor and singer **Dean Martin (1917–1995),** who is buried in the next alcove, the Sanctuary of Love. As you enter that alcove, on the wall on the left, in the fourth space from the left and third space up from the ground, you'll find Martin's crypt, which is usually decorated with flowers, ribbons, and an American flag.

After dropping out of high school, Martin worked in a steel mill, as an unsuccessful amateur boxer, and a dealer in illegal gambling houses in his native Steubenville, Ohio. He discovered that singing was less dangerous and more lucrative, and he began performing in nightclubs around the country. While appearing in Atlantic City in 1946, Martin met a young comedian named Jerry Lewis, and they joined to form an act that became an immediate sensation, featuring the romantic crooning of the laid-back Martin coupled with the manic comedy of the uninhibited Lewis. Martin and Lewis made their film debut in *My Friend Irma* (1949), and also appeared together in *My Friend Irma Goes West* (1950), *At War With the Army* (1950), *That's My Boy* (1951), *Sailor Beware* (1951), *Jumping Jacks* (1952), *The Caddy* (1953), *The Stooge* (1953), *Money From Home* (1953), *Scared Stiff* (1953), *Three-Ring Circus* (1954), *Living It Up* (1954), *Artists and Models* (1955), *You're Never Too Young* (1955), *Pardners* (1956), and *Hollywood or Bust* (1956). Martin and Lewis became the most popular comedy team and the highest-paid entertainers in the country. From 1951 to 1956, they were always among the top ten box-office attractions.

When the pair broke up in 1956, fans were certain that Lewis would continue to be successful on his own, but they weren't so sure about Martin. While Lewis was certainly one of a kind, did the entertainment world really need another handsome, wavy-haired crooner? Martin's first film without Lewis was *Ten Thousand Bedrooms* (1957), a breezy romantic comedy in which he cultivated his image as a sophisticated swinger. Costarring in his next film with Marlon Brando and Montgomery Clift in *The Young Lions* (1958), Martin proved he was a talented actor who could handle more dramatic roles. Martin costarred with future Rat Pack partner Frank Sinatra in *Some Came Running* (1958), and with John Wayne in the Western *Rio Bravo* (1959). *Ocean's Eleven* (1960) brought the entire Rat Pack together—Sinatra, Martin, Sammy Davis Jr., Joey Bishop, and Peter Lawford—for a film featuring a group of old army pals getting together to rob the casinos in Las Vegas. The Pack also appeared together in *Sergeants 3* (1962). Martin and Sinatra costarred in *Four for Texas* (1963), *Robin and the Seven Hoods* (1964), and *Marriage on the Rocks* (1965).

Martin starred in a series of successful Westerns and sophisticated romantic comedies in the 1960s, including *Bells Are Ringing* (1960), *Who's Been Sleeping in My Bed?* (1963), *Kiss Me, Stupid* (1964), *The Sons of Katie Elder* (1965), *Texas Across the River* (1966), *Rough Night in Jericho* (1967), *Bandolero!* (1968), and *Five Card Stud* (1968). He also starred as sexy secret agent Matt Helm in *The Silencers* (1966), *Murderer's Row* (1966), *The Ambushers* (1967), and *The Wrecking Crew* (1969).

On the small screen, Martin starred in *The Dean Martin Show*, a weekly music and variety series, beginning in 1965. The show typically featured the sleepy-eyed Martin in his tuxedo, with a cigarette and a glass of booze (though, more likely, it was apple juice), laughing and ad-libbing his way though a series of songs and skits with his celebrity guests. The popular show continued through 1974.

When Martin's son, Dino, an actor and member of the Air National Guard, died in a plane crash in 1987, Martin retired from public life, returning briefly for a national concert tour with Sinatra and Davis.

Martin's crypt marker includes the title of his signature song, "Everybody Loves Somebody Sometime." Unfortunately, several fans have placed lit cigarettes on top of Martin's bronze crypt marker, and there are a few burn marks on the marble.

Martin was born Dino Paul Crocetti on June 7, 1917, in Steubenville, Ohio. He died December 25, 1995, in Los Angeles.

On the opposite wall in the Sanctuary of Love, in the lower left corner, you'll find the crypt of **Oscar Levant (1906–1972)**—pianist, composer, actor, humorist, and well-known hypochondriac.

Levant quit school at fifteen to study music, intending to become a concert pianist. A minor role in a Broadway musical, *Burlesque*, resulted in a role in the film version of the play, *The Dance of Life* (1929). Levant remained in Hollywood, writing film scores and songs, and occasionally appearing in supporting roles onscreen, including *Rhythm on the River* (1940), *Rhapsody in Blue* (1945), *Humoresque* (1946), *The Barkleys of Broadway* (1949), *An American in Paris* (1951), and *The Band Wagon* (1953). Levant typically played himself, or a character based on himself, with witty and sardonic commentary on the events going on around him.

Levant gained fame as a sarcastically witty and knowledgeable panelist on the *Information Please* radio program from 1938 to 1943—until he was forced to leave the program after getting into a fistfight with the show's creator and producer. Levant later appeared frequently on television, often as a guest on talk shows, where he would discuss his views of social issues and his own various psychological problems and neuroses. Levant also hosted a local radio show in Los Angeles. When he urged his audience not to buy his sponsor's product, he predicted that he'd be fired for making the comments. He was right. As Levant's behavior became more erratic, only late-night talk-show host Jack Paar would risk having Levant as a guest. When Paar left television in 1965, so did Levant. For much of his life, Levant was a frequent visitor to various rest homes and mental institutions, and he became dependent on pain-killers and other prescription drugs. He was a virtual recluse during the last decade of his life. Levant wrote three autobiographical books—*The Memoirs of an Amnesiac, The Unimportance of Being Oscar,* and *A Smattering of Ignorance.*

Levant is also credited with originating Hollywood's nickname of "Tinseltown" when he said, "Peel away the phony tinsel from this town, and you know what you'll find? Real tinsel!"

*Levant was born December 27, 1906, in Pittsburgh,
Pennsylvania. He died August 14, 1972,
in Beverly Hills, California.*

Directly across the road from the Sanctuary of Love, right next to the curb, you'll find the grave of Levant's wife, dancer and actress **June Gale Levant (1918–1996).** She appeared in supporting roles in two dozen films between 1934 and 1940, including *Melody in Spring* (1934), *Rainbow's End* (1935), *One in a Million* (1936), *The Riding Avenger* (1936), *Thin Ice* (1937), *Four Men and a Prayer* (1938), *My Lucky Star* (1938), *Charlie Chan at Treasure Island* (1939), and *City of Chance* (1940). She retired from the screen when she married Levant in 1939.

Head back to the new Garden of Serenity area in the southeast corner of the cemetery property. At the northern edge of the garden area, alongside the road, are seven private gravesites, separated by small marble benches and low hedges. In one of these gravesites—currently unmarked, but reportedly the third space from the left—are the remains of **George C. Scott (1927–1999),** an intense and powerful actor in nearly one hundred films, best known for his performance in *Patton* (1970), and for being the first actor to turn down an Academy Award.

After serving in the U.S. Marine Corps during World War II, Scott began his acting career in local productions before moving to Broadway. He made his film debut in *The Hanging Tree* (1959), a Western starring Gary Cooper. For his performance as the prosecuting attorney in *Anatomy of a Murder* (1959), starring Jimmy Stewart and Lee Remick, Scott won an Academy Award nomination as Best Supporting Actor, and received another nomination for his performance as a sleazy pool hall gambler in *The Hustler* (1961), starring Paul Newman and Jackie Gleason.

During the early 1960s, Scott continued to appear on Broadway and in films, and he delivered a rare comic performance as the hawkish General Buck Turgidson in *Dr. Strangelove* (1964). Scott starred in *The Yellow Rolls-Royce* (1964), *The Bible* (1966), and *The Flim-Flam Man* (1967), before his powerful performance as the eccentrically brilliant General George Patton in *Patton* (1970). When Scott received an Academy Award nomination as Best Actor, he denounced the award ceremony as a "meat parade" and said he would not accept the award if he won. He did not attend the ceremonies, and when his name was announced as the winner, there was no one to accept the prize. (Two years later, Marlon Brando also refused to accept the Academy Award for Best Actor when he won for *The Godfather* (1972), but Brando sent an actress posing as a Native American in his place to make a brief speech on Brando's behalf, protesting the treatment of Native Americans in films and on television.)

Despite Scott's previous comments, he was nominated again for his performance in *The Hospital* (1971), but didn't win. Scott also starred in *They Might Be Giants* (1971), *The New Centurions* (1972), *Oklahoma Crude* (1973), *The Day of the Dolphin* (1973), *Bank Shot* (1974), *The Hindenberg* (1975), *Islands in the Stream* (1977), *Movie Movie* (1978), *Hardcore* (1979), and *Taps* (1981). In the 1980s and 1990s, he appeared in a series of made-for-television films, including *A Christmas Carol* (1984), *The Last Days of Patton* (1986), *The Ryan White Story* (1989), *Titanic* (1996), *12 Angry Men* (1997), and *Inherit the Wind* (1999).

Scott also directed himself in two films—*Rage* (1972) and *The Savage Is Loose* (1974), the latter costarring his wife, Trish Van Devere.

Scott was born George Campbell Scott on October 18, 1927 (some sources say 1926), in Wise, Virginia. He died September 22, 1999, in Westlake Village, California.

Directly to the right of Scott's unmarked grave, in the fourth space from the left, is the grave of **Walter Matthau (1920–2000),** the bloodhound-faced actor who was equally adept at thoughtful, dramatic roles and in comedy roles as the sloppy, scheming, or just plain cranky curmudgeons he seemed born to play. Next to Matthau's grave is a small marble bench with the inscription "We only part to meet again; we will with thee go forever."

The son of Russian Jewish immigrants in New York City, Matthau started working at the age of eleven, selling refreshments in a Yiddish theater, and soon started performing on the stage. After serving in the U.S. Army Air Corps during World War II, Matthau returned to New York and enrolled in acting school, and got his first role on Broadway in 1948 as an understudy in *Anne of a Thousand Days,* starring Rex Harrison. As proof that Matthau was "born old," his part in the play was that of an eighty-three-year-old English bishop. Matthau was only twenty-eight at the time.

Matthau also appeared regularly on television in dramatic anthology series, usually playing villains. He made his film debut in *The Kentuckian* (1955), starring Burt Lancaster. After dramatic supporting roles in *Slaughter on Tenth Avenue* (1957), *A Face in the Crowd* (1957), *King Creole* (1958)—starring Elvis Presley—*Lonely Are the Brave* (1962), *Charade* (1963), *Ensign Pulver* (1964), and *Fail-Safe* (1964), Matthau achieved stardom and won a Tony Award on Broadway in *The Odd Couple* as slovenly sportswriter Oscar Madison in a role written especially for him by Neil Simon. When Hollywood finally noticed his comedic talents, Matthau costarred with Jack Lemmon as a crooked personal-injury lawyer in *The Fortune Cookie* (1966) and won the Academy Award as Best Supporting Actor. Matthau and Lemmon costarred again in the film version of *The Odd Couple* (1968), *The Front Page* (1974), *Buddy Buddy* (1981), *Grumpy Old Men* (1993), *Grumpier Old Men* (1995), *Out to Sea* (1997), and *The Odd Couple II* (1998). Lemmon directed Matthau in a dramatic role in *Kotch* (1971), the story of an elderly man who refuses to be put out to pasture by his children, which earned Matthau an Academy Award nomination as Best Actor.

Matthau continued to star in comedies, including *Hello, Dolly* (1969), *Cactus Flower* (1969), and *Plaza Suite* (1971), as well as dramatic roles in *Charley Varrick* (1973), *The Laughing Policeman* (1973), and *The Taking of Pelham One Two Three* (1974). Matthau costarred with George Burns in Neil Simon's *The Sunshine Boys* (1975), as a pair of cantankerous old ex-vaudeville stars who reunite for a television special. The roles were originally to have been played by Red Skelton and Jack Benny, but when Skelton dropped out and Benny died just before production was scheduled to begin, Matthau and Burns got the parts. For their performances, Burns won the Academy Award for Best Supporting Actor in his comeback role, and Matthau received an Academy Award nomination as Best Actor.

Matthau's last screen appearance was in *Hanging Up* (2000), in which he portrayed the dying father of Diane Keaton, Meg Ryan, and Lisa Kudrow.

Matthau died July 1, 2000, in Santa Monica, California, after suffering a heart attack at his home. He was buried the next day, in a plain pine coffin, with only about fifty family members and close friends attending his services, according to his request.

One of Matthau's most enduring jokes concerns his real name, which is usually listed as "Walter Matuschanskayasky," even in official biographies. Throughout his life, Matthau seemed to enjoy making up names, and he must've enjoyed giving out this tongue twister during interviews. When he filled out his Social Security forms in 1937, he listed his middle name as "Foghorn," and he often said that his wife's real name was Carol Wellington-Smythe Marcus, which he later admitted he made up because it sounded more "aristocratic."

After Matthau's death, his son, actor and director Charles Matthau, admitted that his father made up the longer version of his "real" name for his appearance in *Earthquake* (1974). Originally, Matthau agreed to appear in the film when he thought his role would be much larger. When he ended up playing a cameo appearance as a drunk in the film, he used the name "Walter Matuschanskayasky" in the credits, and later told interviewers that was his real name. In fact, his real name was Walter Matthow.

Matthau was born Walter Matthow on October 1, 1920, in New York City. He died July 1, 2000, in Santa Monica, California.

Walk around to the front of the Garden of Serenity area, and down into the center area. The wall surrounding the center area contains mostly empty niches for cremated remains. Along the northern wall, in the top row, fifth space from the right, you'll find the niche containing the remains of **Brian Keith (1921–1997)**, who appeared in more than one hundred films and is best known as Uncle Bill in the late 1960s television comedy *Family Affair*.

The son of actor Robert Keith and actress Helen Shipman, Keith made his film debut at the age of three as a cherub in *Pied Piper Malone* (1924). He also appeared with his father in *The Other Kind of Love* (1924). After serving in World War II, Keith appeared in several Broadway plays, and made his adult film debut in *Arrowhead* (1953). Keith appeared in dozens of war films and Westerns during the 1950s and 1960s, including *The Bamboo Prison* (1954), *The Violent Men* (1955), *Desert Hell* (1958), *Ten Who Dared* (1960), *The Hallelujah Trail* (1965), and *Nevada Smith* (1966).

In 1966, Keith starred as Bill Davis, a bachelor trying to raise three children with the help of his butler, Mr. French, in *Family Affair*. After the series was canceled in 1971, Keith starred on television in *The Brian Keith Show* from 1972 to 1974, *Archer* in 1975, *Hardcastle and McCormick* from 1983 to 1986, *Heartland* in 1989, and *Walter and Emily* in 1991. On the big screen, Keith also appeared in *The Wind and the Lion* (1975), *Hooper* (1978), and *Sharky's Machine* (1987). His last film was *Follow Your Heart* (1998).

Keith's daughter, Daisy Keith (1969–1997), an actress who worked with her father on the *Heartland* television series, killed herself in May 1997. A month later, Keith, who was suffering from lung cancer and emphysema, shot himself to death at his home in Malibu, California. They are buried together.

Keith was born Robert Keith Richey Jr. on November 14, 1921, in Bayonne, New Jersey. He died June 24, 1997, in Malibu, California.

Walk back to the southwest corner of the Garden of Serenity, up four stairs, and to the gate on the opposite site of the private area in the rear. About ten feet past the gate, just to the right of the sidewalk, you'll see the niche containing the remains of comedian and singer **Fanny Brice (1891–1951)**, the original "Funny Girl."

Brice, the daughter of a New York City saloon owner, entered an amateur talent contest at the age of thirteen and won the $10 first prize for singing "When You Know You're Not Forgotten by the Girl You Can't Forget." Brice then joined a traveling road show and performed in burlesque houses in New York City before signing a contract with Florenz Ziegfeld to sing in his Ziegfeld Follies for $75 per week. Brice made her debut in the Follies in 1910 and appeared in all but two installments of the popular entertainment show through the mid-1930s. In addition to her wildly energetic and comedic song presentations, Brice could also perform sentimental ballads, including "My Man," which she first sang at the Follies in 1921 and which became her musical trademark.

Brice made her film debut in *My Man* (1928), one of the first "talkies," although much of the film has been lost. She also appeared in *Be Yourself!*

(1930), *The Man from Blankley's* (1930), *Crime Without Passion* (1934), *The Great Ziegfeld* (1936), *Everybody Sing* (1938), and *Ziegfeld Follies* (1946).

Brice was more active on Broadway, however. In addition to the Follies shows, she starred in *The Honeymoon Express, Nobody Home, Why Worry?, Midnight Frolic, Fanny, Sweet and Low,* and *Crazy Quilt,* where she introduced her Baby Snooks character in 1931. Brice brought Baby Snooks, the lisping, mischievous brat, to her weekly radio show in 1936, and also performed as the character onstage and in her nightclub act. Brice continued her Baby Snooks radio show until just before her death.

Brice was married to barber Frank White from 1911 to 1913, to gambler and con man Jules "Nick" Arnstein from 1919 to 1927, and to composer and producer Billy Rose from 1929 to 1939.

In 1964, *Funny Girl,* a Broadway musical based on Brice's life and produced by her son-in-law, Ray Stark, premiered on Broadway, with Barbra Streisand in the title role. Streisand also starred in the film version of *Funny Girl* (1968), for which she won the Academy Award as Best Actress, and the sequel, *Funny Lady* (1975).

Brice was originally buried at Home of Peace Memorial Park (see Chapter 10), but her remains were moved to Westwood in May 1999 after the new Garden of Serenity was opened.

In front of Brice's niche is a large sarcophagus containing the remains of her daughter, Frances Brice Stark (1919–1992). On the other side of the wall from Brice's niche are the remains of her mother, Rose (1867–1941), and brother, Lew (1893–1966), a dancer who occasionally performed with his sister in vaudeville.

Brice was born Fanny Borach on October 29, 1891, in New York City. She died May 29, 1951, in Los Angeles.

On the right side of the stairs is a raised flower bed used for the scattering of ashes. In the center of the wall around the flowers is a marker for **Audree Neva Wilson (1917–1997),** identifying her as "The Original Surfer Girl." Wilson was the mother of Carl, Brian, and Dennis Wilson, three of the founding members of the Beach Boys. (Carl, who died in 1998, is buried on the central lawn area at Westwood.)

On the right side of the flower bed, in front of the Westwood Chapel, is a large open area containing no graves or other markers. Elizabeth Taylor has reportedly reserved this space, whenever she needs it, for a private mausoleum.

Actress Dominique Dunne is the second young star of Poltergeist to be buried at Westwood Memorial Park.

When the mausoleum is built, the remains of Taylor's parents will be moved here from their current location in the nearby Sanctuary of Peace alcove.

From the main entrance to the Garden of Serenity area, cross the road and walk into the central lawn area. About one hundred feet to the left (west), and fifteen feet in from the curb, you'll find the grave of actress **Dominique Dunne (1959–1982)**, who appeared in *Poltergeist* (1982) and was killed by an angry ex-boyfriend a few months after the film's release.

After graduating from high school in southern California, Dunne studied acting at the University of Colorado. She left school after a year and returned to Hollywood to pursue her career. She landed her first role in the made-for-television film *Diary of a Teenage Hitchhiker* (1979), and appeared in several more made-for-television films, including *Valentine Magic on Love Island* (1980), *The Haunting of Harrington House* (1980), *The Day the Loving Stopped* (1981), and *The Shadow Riders* (1982). Dunne also appeared on several television series in the early 1980s, including *CHiPs, Hill Street Blues, Fame, St. Elsewhere,* and *Lou Grant.* She made her big-screen debut in *Poltergeist* (1982), playing Dana Freeling, the oldest daughter in a family that finds their home haunted by unfriendly spirits.

In late 1982, Dunne had been living with her boyfriend, John David Sweeney, a chef at the trendy Ma Maison restaurant in Beverly Hills, in a home in West Hollywood. He moved out, and then attempted to move back on October 30, 1982. Dunne did not want him to return, and they got into an argument in the driveway of the home; Sweeney choked her. Dunne never regained consciousness, and she died five days later, just a few weeks before her twenty-third birthday. Sweeney was convicted of voluntary manslaughter, and sentenced to six and a half years in prison. Dunne's life and death were the subject of a documentary, *Dominique Dunne: An American Tragedy* (1998).

Dunne was the daughter of novelist Dominick Dunne, and the sister of actor Griffin Dunne.

> *Dunne was born November 23, 1959, in Santa Monica, California.*
> *She died November 4, 1982, in Los Angeles.*

Continue heading west to the far southwest corner of the central lawn area, and you'll find a large urn garden containing hundreds of small, square, bronze plaques identifying buried cremated remains. In the top row, the thirteenth space in from the right, you'll find the plaque identifying the grave of **Sebastian Cabot (1918–1977)**, best remembered for his role as Mr. French, the burly, bearded butler on *Family Affair*, with Brian Keith.

After dropping out of school at fourteen, Cabot held a variety of jobs, including chauffeur for British actor Frank Pettingell. At Pettingell's urging, Cabot tried his hand at acting and became a popular performer on the British radio, stage, and screen before coming to the United States in the 1950s and appearing in supporting roles in *Ivanhoe* (1952), *The Captain's Paradise* (1953), *Romeo and Juliet* (1954), *Kismet* (1955), *Johnny Tremain* (1957), *Terror in a Texas Town* (1958), *The Time Machine* (1960), and *The Family Jewels* (1965).

Cabot provided voices for many animated characters from the Disney studios, in films including *The Sword in the Stone* (1963) and *The Jungle Book* (1967). He was also the narrator for *Winnie the Pooh and the Honey Tree* (1966), *Winnie the Pooh and the Blustery Day* (1968), and *The Many Adventures of Winnie the Pooh* (1977).

Cabot appeared in his first television series in 1960, costarring in *Checkmate* as a criminologist working for a San Francisco–based detective agency. The series lasted until 1962. From 1966 to 1971, Cabot costarred in *Family Affair* as Mr. French, the very proper butler assisting a bachelor trying to raise three children in New York City.

> *Cabot was born July 6, 1918, in London, England. He died*
> *August 23, 1977, in Victoria, British Columbia, Canada.*

In the first row above the urn garden, about twenty-five feet west of Cabot's grave and about fifteen feet from the curb along the western edge of the central lawn area, partially hidden by a large collection of plants and flowers, you'll find the grave of **Jim Backus (1913–1989),** best known as haughty millionaire Thurston Howell III on the television series *Gilligan's Island* in the mid-1960s, and for providing the voice of the comically nearsighted cartoon character Mr. Magoo.

Backus was a graduate of the American Academy of Dramatic Arts in 1933 and was a veteran of stage, vaudeville, and radio by the time he made his film debut in the drama *Easy Living* (1949), starring Victor Mature, Lucille Ball, and Lizabeth Scott. The same year, Backus first provided the voice of Mr. Magoo in the animated short *Ragtime Bear*—the first installment in nearly a hundred Mr. Magoo cartoons. On the big screen, Backus appeared in supporting roles in comedies, including *Father Was a Fullback* (1949), *One Last Fling* (1949), *Ma and Pa Kettle Go to Town* (1950), and *Pat and Mike* (1952), and dramas, including *Iron Man* (1951), *M* (1951), and *Deadline, USA* (1952). In 1952, Backus starred in his first television series, *I Married Joan*, featuring the adventures of a city judge and his scatterbrained wife, played by Joan Davis. The series lasted three years. Backus also continued his film career, notably playing James Dean's father in *Rebel Without a Cause* (1955), and also appearing in *The Opposite Sex* (1956), *Man of a Thousand Faces* (1957), *Ask Any Girl* (1959), *The Wheeler Dealers* (1963), and *It's a Mad Mad Mad Mad World* (1963). In his comedy roles, Backus specialized in playing the oblivious upper-crust dandy.

In 1964, Backus returned to television as Thurston Howell III, a millionaire stranded on a deserted island with six other castaways after their ship sinks in a storm, in *Gilligan's Island*. The series is often cited as an example of one of the more mindless programs ever televised, although it remains popular in syndication more than thirty years after it was canceled in 1967. (Originally, the Western series *Gunsmoke* was scheduled to be canceled, but William Paley, then president of the CBS network and a big *Gunsmoke* fan, decided to cancel *Gilligan's Island* instead.) Backus also starred in several made-for-television movies based on the series, including *Rescue from Gilligan's Island* (1978), *The Castaways on Gilligan's Island* (1979), and *The Harlem Globetrotters on Gilligan's Island* (1981). Backus also provided the voice for Mr. Howell in the animated film, *Gilligan's Planet* (1982)

After *Gilligan*, Backus played Mr. Dithers in *Blondie* in 1968, a one-season television series based on the popular *Blondie* films of the 1940s. Backus continued to appear in made-for-television films and make guest appearances on various series through the late 1970s.

Backus was born James Gilmore Backus on February 25, 1913, in Cleveland, Ohio. He died July 3, 1989, in Los Angeles.

About fifty feet directly north of Backus, you'll find a small, black marble marker over the grave of **Lew Ayres (1908–1996),** who achieved quick fame in Hollywood and is best known for his role as Dr. Kildare in a series of films in the late 1930s and early 1940s.

The boyishly handsome Ayres was a dance band musician when he was spotted by Hollywood talent scouts while playing in the Cocoanut Grove nightclub in 1928. He quickly made his film debut in a bit part in *The Sophomore* (1929), then costarred with Greta Garbo in *The Kiss* (1929). Ayres next played a patriotic German soldier in *All Quiet on the Western Front* (1930), and the film's antiwar message had a profound impact on Ayres and would affect his later career. Ayres next starred in a series of minor films in the 1930s, including *The Spirit of Notre Dame* (1931), *Iron Man* (1931), *State Fair* (1933), *Don't Bet on Love* (1933)—costarring with his future wife, Ginger Rogers—*Silk Hat Kid* (1935), *The Lottery Lover* (1935), *The Last Train From Madrid* (1937), and *Holiday* (1938), in which he played Katharine Hepburn's spoiled younger brother.

Ayres played the title role in *Young Dr. Kildare* (1938), costarring with Lionel Barrymore and Laraine Day. The film launched a long and profitable series of films, including *Calling Dr. Kildare* (1939), *The Secret of Dr. Kildare* (1939), *Dr. Kildare's Strange Case* (1940), *Dr. Kildare's Crisis* (1940), *Dr. Kildare Goes Home* (1940), *The People vs. Dr. Kildare* (1941), *Dr. Kildare's Wedding Day* (1941), and *Dr. Kildare's Victory* (1941).

In 1941, the deeply religious Ayres was drafted to serve in World War II but, because of his strong antiwar beliefs, he declared himself a conscientious objector and refused to fight in combat. During those patriotic times, the film-going public was stunned, Ayres was dropped by the studio, and many exhibitors refused to show his films. The popular *Dr. Kildare* series continued without Ayres, however, focusing on Barrymore's crusty character, beginning with *Calling Dr. Gillespie* (1942). Ayres later volunteered for non-combat medical service, and he served with the U.S. Army as a medical orderly and chaplain's assistant, distinguishing himself under fire on the frontlines in the South Pacific.

After the war, Ayres returned to Hollywood and attempted to resurrect his career. He regained public acceptance with his roles in *The Dark Mirror* (1946), *The Unfaithful* (1947), and *Johnny Belinda* (1948), for which he received an Academy Award nomination as Best Actor. Ayres was offered the title role in a television series based on Dr. Kildare, but the network refused to honor his request that the series not be sponsored by any cigarette manufacturers. Ayres appeared in a few films after that, including *Donovan's Brain* (1953), *Advice and Consent* (1962), *The Carpetbaggers* (1964), and *Damien: Omen II* (1978). He also appeared in many made-for-television films in the 1970s and 1980s.

Ayres's interest in religion resulted in his producing, directing, and narrating two documentaries—*Altars of the East* (1955) and *Altars of the World* (1976), both based on his own research and writing.

Ayres was born Lewis Frederick Ayres III on December 28, 1908, in Minneapolis, Minnesota. He died December 30, 1996, in Los Angeles.

Directly to the right (east) of Ayres's grave is the unmarked grave of **Frank Zappa (1940–1993),** an outrageous, eclectic, and wildly original musician known for his bizarre mixture of 1950s pop, rhythm and blues, experimental jazz, and even classical music.

Zappa taught himself to play guitar and drums and performed in various bands as a teenager. In 1964, he joined a group called the Soul Giants, which later became the Mothers of Invention. Their debut album, *Freak Out!*, released in 1966, contained a mixture of protest songs, social commentary, and experimental jazz. Later albums included *Absolutely Free* in 1967, *We're Only in It for the Money* in 1968, *Uncle Meat* in 1968, and *Burnt Weeny Sandwich* in 1969. Zappa quickly became a counterculture favorite, even though he spoke out against drug use, preferring to limit his chemical vices to cigarettes and coffee.

Zappa wrote and directed *200 Motels* (1971), a zany, free-form film based on his experiences on the road. With the Mothers of Invention and also as a solo performer, Zappa continued to record albums throughout the 1970s, including *Weasels Ripped My Flesh* in 1970, *The Grand Wazoo* in 1972, *Overnite Sensation* in 1973, *Apostrophe* in 1974, *One Size Fits All* in 1975, *Zoot Allures* in 1976, and *Sheik Yerbouti* in 1979, which became Zappa's best-selling album. In all, Zappa recorded more than forty albums.

Though Zappa was generally ignored by most mainstream radio stations, he did have a few hits during his career, including "Don't Eat the Yellow Snow" in 1974, "Dancin' Fool" in 1979, and "Valley Girl" in 1982, featuring his daughter, Moon Unit, as a typically airheaded San Fernando Valley teenager. In 1985, Zappa testified before a congressional committee on the growing controversy over song lyrics and censorship—then released a recording titled "Porn Wars," setting the legislators' comments to music. He won his only Grammy Award in 1988 for Best Rock Instrumental for his *Jazz From Hell* album.

Zappa was even unique in choosing names for his four children—Moon Unit, Dweezil, Ahmet Rodan, and Diva Muffin.

Zappa died of cancer on December 4, 1993, a few weeks before his fifty-third birthday. He was buried before dawn the next morning, in a private ceremony at Westwood. In 1995, Zappa was posthumously inducted into the Rock and Roll Hall of Fame.

Zappa was born Frank Vincent Zappa on December 21, 1940, in Baltimore, Maryland. He died December 4, 1993, in Los Angeles.

About fifty feet to the right (east) of Zappa's grave, in the same row, is the grave of writer and director **Frank Tuttle (1892–1963)**, best known for directing the film-noir classic *This Gun for Hire* (1942), starring Alan Ladd and Veronica Lake.

Tuttle started his career writing and directing comedies, dramas, mysteries and romances in the early 1920s. Beginning in the 1930s, he focused more on directing, switching back and forth between musicals and film-noir dramas. His work includes *Kid Boots* (1926), *The Big Broadcast* (1932), *This Is the Night* (1932), *Roman Scandals* (1933), *Here Is My Heart* (1934), *Waikiki Wedding* (1937), *Charlie McCarthy, Detective* (1939), *Paris Honeymoon* (1939), and two more films starring Alan Ladd—*Lucky Jordan* (1942) and *Hell on Frisco Bay* (1955).

Tuttle's career suffered in the 1950s when he appeared as a friendly witness before the House Un-American Activities Committee, admitted his past membership in the Communist Party, and named many of his colleagues. Tuttle was one of four prominent directors who became informers for the HUAC committee—the others were Edward Dmytryk, Robert Rossen, and Elia Kazan. After that, Tuttle was shunned by many in the entertainment community, and he retired in the late 1950s.

Tuttle was born Frank Wright Tuttle on August 6, 1892, in New York City. He died January 6, 1963, in Los Angeles.

Immediately to the right of Tuttle's grave is the unmarked grave of singer **Roy Orbison (1936–1988),** known for his dark sunglasses and his clear, powerful voice on songs including "Only the Lonely," "Crying," and "Oh, Pretty Woman."

Orbison formed his first band, the Wink Westerners, while he was still in high school. With Orbison playing guitar and singing, the band played throughout western Texas and developed a loyal following. The band even appeared regularly on weekly television shows in Odessa and Midland in the early 1950s.

After Orbison graduated from high school, the Wink Westerners disbanded. While he was in college, Orbison recorded his first song, "Ooby Dooby," which was written by a couple of his classmates. Orbison decided to pursue a career as a rock 'n' roll star, and follow in the footsteps of Elvis Presley. Though Orbison didn't have the moves or the looks of Presley, he did have a powerful voice with remarkable, near-operatic range, which he used best on the haunting ballads that later made him famous. Orbison signed a contract with Sun Records, and "Ooby Dooby" became a hit in 1956. Orbison decided he wanted to focus on songwriting instead of performing, and he wrote several hits for other performers. When both the Everly Brothers and Elvis Presley decided against recording Orbison's "Only the Lonely," the songwriter decided to record it himself in 1960, and it became an international hit, topping the charts in the United Kingdom and nearly reaching the top spot in the United States. Over the next five years, Orbison enjoyed unprecedented success in Britain and America, with stylish and melancholy ballads including "Blue Angel," "Running Scared," "Crying," "Dream Baby," "Working for the Man," "In Dreams," "Blue Bayou," "It's Over," and "Oh, Pretty Woman," which topped the charts in the United States for three weeks in 1964.

Orbison often performed in the United Kingdom, and became close friends with a young group of four musicians known as the Beatles, often appearing with them in concert. Ironically, when the Beatles and similar groups became popular in the mid-1960s, Orbison's fame started to fade. He also endured personal tragedy when his wife was killed in a motorcycle accident in 1966 and their two sons were killed in a fire at their home in 1968.

Orbison attempted to revive his career by starring in *The Fastest Guitar Alive* (1967), a disappointing tale of Civil War espionage. Orbison's career was at a low point for much of the 1970s, but he bounced back in 1980, winning his first Grammy Award for his duet with Emmylou Harris, "That Lovin' You Feelin' Again." In the late 1970s and 1980s, new artists were recording

Orbison's songs, including Linda Ronstadt's version of "Blue Bayou" and Don McLean's version of "Crying."

In the late 1980s, Orbison was discovered by a new generation of fans. In 1987, he was inducted into the Rock and Roll Hall of Fame, and the following year, he joined with musicians Bob Dylan, Tom Petty, George Harrison, and Jeff Lynne to form the Traveling Wilburys. Less than a month after the group released its first album, Orbison suffered a heart attack and died at the age of fifty-two. At the time of his death, the first album by the Traveling Wilburys was number eight on the *Billboard* pop charts—the first time Orbison had an album in the top ten in nearly twenty-five years. In 1990, the Traveling Wilburys won the Grammy Award for Best Album of the year. Orbison's last album, *Mystery Girl,* released after his death in 1989, became the biggest-selling record of his career, with two top-ten hits—"You Got It" and "I Drove All Night."

In 1999, Orbison's recordings of "Only the Lonely" and "Oh, Pretty Woman" were both selected for the Grammy Hall of Fame, which was established "to honor early recordings of lasting, qualitative or historical significance."

Orbison was buried at Westwood in a black coffin, appropriately enough. Family members had originally planned to place a large, black granite marker over his grave, but for some reason, more than ten years after his death, the space is still unmarked.

Orbison was born April 23, 1936, in Vernon, Texas.
He died December 6, 1988, in Hendersonville, Tennessee.

In the same row, about fifty feet to the right (east), is the grave of composer **Sammy Cahn (1913–1993),** who was nominated a record-setting twenty-six times for the Academy Award for Best Song, winning the award four times.

Cahn, a classic Tin Pan Alley lyricist, wrote his first song—"Like Niagara Falls, I'm Falling for You"—when he was sixteen. His first song for a film was the title song in *52nd Street* (1937), and he received his first Academy Award nomination for "It Seems I've Heard That Song Before," from *Youth on Parade* (1942). Cahn won the award for "Three Coins in the Fountain," from the 1954 film of the same name; "All the Way," from *The Joker Is Wild* (1957); "High Hopes," from *A Hole in the Head* (1959); and "Call Me Irresponsible," from *Papa's Delicate Condition* (1963). He was nominated for "The Second Time Around," from *High Time* (1960); "My Kind of Town," from *Robin and the Seven Hoods* (1964); and "Thoroughly Modern Millie," from the 1967 film of the same name, among many other nominations. Cahn was a favorite composer of Frank Sinatra's; Sinatra recorded more than eighty of his songs.

Cahn's grave marker includes the inscription "Sleep With a Smile."

Cahn was born Samuel Cohen on June 18, 1913, in New York City. He died January 15, 1993, in Los Angeles.

About twelve feet to the right (east) of Cahn's grave is the grave of actress **Donna Reed (1921–1986).** Although she won an Academy Award as Best Supporting Actress for playing a prostitute in *From Here to Eternity* (1953), Reed is probably best remembered for her performance as Mary Bailey in the holiday classic *It's a Wonderful Life* (1946), and for her wholesome, long-running family sitcom in the late 1950s and 1960s.

After winning a beauty contest in her Iowa hometown, Reed headed for Hollywood and was elected Campus Queen at Los Angeles City College. MGM studios noticed and quickly took advantage of her wholesome good looks. Reed made her film debut in *Babes on Broadway* (1941), starring Mickey Rooney and Judy Garland. Reed was a busy actress in the early 1940s, appearing in *The Get-Away* (1941), *Shadow of the Thin Man* (1941), *The Bugle Sounds* (1941), *Calling Dr. Gillespie* (1942), *The Courtship of Andy Hardy* (1942), *Apache Trail* (1942), *The Human Comedy* (1943), *Thousands Cheer* (1943), *They Were Expendable* (1945), and *The Picture of Dorian Gray* (1945), among many others.

She costarred with Jimmy Stewart in Frank Capra's *It's a Wonderful Life,* as the loving and supportive wife of a man who gets to see what the world would have been like if he had never been born. After a few more films as the supportive, wholesome wife or girlfriend, Reed went to the other extreme in *From Here to Eternity,* playing the role of the prostitute Alma—although her profession is never specifically identified in the film because of the censorship restrictions in Hollywood in the early 1950s. In addition to Reed's Oscar, the film won Academy Awards for Best Picture, Best Supporting Actor (Frank Sinatra, in his "comeback"), Best Director (Fred Zinnemann), and Best Screenplay (Daniel Taradash). Burt Lancaster and Montgomery Clift were both nominated for Best Actor, and Deborah Kerr was nominated for Best Actress.

Despite her Oscar, Reed appeared in only a few films in the mid-1950s, including *The Benny Goodman Story* (1955), *The Far Horizons* (1955)—in which she plays the Native American guide Sacajawea—and *Ransom!* (1956). In 1958, Reed came to television with *The Donna Reed Show,* the quintessentially wholesome family sitcom. Reed was nominated for the Emmy Award as Best Actress in a Series four times, from 1959 to 1962. After the series was canceled in 1966, Reed disappeared from television and film for many years. She returned in 1984, taking the role of ranch matriarch Ellie Ewing Farlow after Barbara Bel Geddes left the series. When Bel Geddes returned the following year and Reed was fired, she sued the producers and accepted a $1 million settlement. Reed died several months after the lawsuit was settled.

Although Reed often played the perfect wife and mother in films and on television, she was married three times and divorced twice. The name on her grave marker identifies her as Donna Reed Asmus, with a space available for her third husband, U.S. Army Col. Grover W. Asmus.

Reed was born Donna Belle Mullenger on January 27, 1921, in Denison, Iowa. She died January 14, 1986, in Beverly Hills, California.

In the same row, another seventy-five feet to the right (east), is a small marker identifying the grave of **Lloyd Nolan (1902–1985),** a popular character actor who appeared in more than one hundred films, usually in supporting roles, and is best remembered for his role as the eternally cranky Dr. Chegley in the television series *Julia,* from 1968 to 1971.

After acting onstage starting in 1927, Nolan made his screen debut in *G Men* (1935), starring James Cagney. Nolan appeared in dozens of low-budget action and detective films during the 1930s and 1940s, typically playing a wisecracking reporter or detective, including *Atlantic Adventure* (1935), *One-Way Ticket* (1935), *Lady of Secrets* (1936), *Counterfeit* (1936), *King of Gamblers* (1937), *Tip-Off Girls* (1938), *Dangerous to Know* (1938), *King of Alcatraz* (1938), *Johnny Apollo* (1940), *Dressed to Kill* (1941), *Guadalcanal Diary* (1943), *A Tree Grows in Brooklyn* (1945), and *Lady in the Lake* (1946).

Nolan won the New York Drama Critics Award in 1954 for his portrayal of the mentally unbalanced Captain Queeg in the Broadway production of *The Caine Mutiny Court-Martial,* and he also won an Emmy Award in 1955 for playing the same role on television in a live production of the play on the *Ford Star Jubilee* series. (Humphrey Bogart played the role in the big-screen production of *The Caine Mutiny* [1954].)

In 1968, Nolan appeared in the television series *Julia* starring Diahann Carroll. Nolan also appeared in *Ice Station Zebra* (1968), *Airport* (1970), and

Earthquake (1974). His final film role was in *Hannah and Her Sisters* (1986), as Hannah's father. The film was released after Nolan's death.

> *Nolan was born Lloyd Benedict Nolan on August 11, 1902, in San Francisco, California. He died September 27, 1985, in Los Angeles.*

In the same row, about thirty feet to the right (east), and about fifteen feet before you reach a tall tree, you'll find the grave of actress **Eve Arden (1908–1990),** the quick-witted and wisecracking comedian best known as the title character in the *Our Miss Brooks* series, first on radio in the late 1940s, then television in the 1950s. In dozens of films in the 1940s, Arden typically played the single and sarcastic best friend of the leading lady.

Arden started performing onstage at the age of sixteen, and she made her film debut (under her real name, Eunice Quedens) in *Song of Love* (1929). She also appeared in a bit part in *Dancing Lady* (1933), starring Clark Gable and Joan Crawford. Arden then went to New York City, where she made her Broadway debut in the Zeigfeld Follies in 1934, costarring with Fanny Brice.

Arden returned to Hollywood to costar in *Stage Door* (1937), the story of several would-be actresses sharing a boarding house. Arden, perfecting her character as the fast-talking, wisecracking, cynical softie, more than held her own in the film, which also starred Katharine Hepburn, Ginger Rogers, Lucille Ball, Ann Miller, and Gail Patrick. She followed that with appearances in *Having Wonderful Time* (1938), *Cocoanut Grove* (1938), and *At the Circus* (1939), costarring the Marx Brothers. In her role as circus acrobat Peerless Pauline, Arden was perhaps the only female costar who could match Groucho quip for quip. Arden followed that with dramatic roles in *The Forgotten Woman* (1939) and *Women in the Wind* (1939), before returning to comedy in *Eternally Yours* (1939), *Comrade X* (1940), *That Uncertain Feeling* (1941), *Whistling in the Dark* (1941), and *Cover Girl* (1944).

Arden's dramatic performance in *Mildred Pierce* (1945), starring Joan Crawford, earned her an Academy Award nomination for Best Supporting Actress. Beginning in 1948, Arden starred on radio as Connie Brooks, a wise-cracking high school English teacher in the comedy series *Our Miss Brooks*. In 1952, the series moved to television, and Arden was nominated five times for Emmy Awards as Best Actress in a Series and Best Comedienne, winning in 1954. Arden also starred in a film based on the series, *Our Miss Brooks* (1956). Arden appeared in two more television sitcoms—*The Eve Arden Show*, which ran for one season in 1957, and *The Mothers-in-Law,* costarring Kaye Ballard, from 1967 to 1969.

Arden returned to the classroom in 1978, portraying the principal of Rydell High School in *Grease,* the film version of the long-running Broadway musical, and in the less-successful sequel, *Grease 2* (1982). She published her autobiography, *Three Phases of Eve,* in 1985.

Arden's grave marker includes the inscription "Wife, mother, actress, author—The world will remember," and identifies her as Eve Arden West. She is buried next to her husband, actor Brooks West (1916–1984).

> *Arden was born Eunice Quedens on April 30, 1907 (some sources say 1908 or 1912), in Mill Valley, California. She died November 12, 1990, in Los Angeles.*

Walk around to the other side of the tree, all the way to the edge of the lawn. Directly across the road from the Sanctuary of Love alcove, you'll find a

small urn garden, with about twenty small, bronze markers. On the far left side, in the middle, you'll find the simple marker identifying the grave of **Burt Lancaster (1913–1994),** the powerful, two-fisted actor with the thousand-watt smile, best known for his tough-guy roles and nominated four times for the Academy Award as Best Actor.

A high school athlete, Lancaster enrolled in college on a basketball scholarship but dropped out to join an acrobatic act, performing a high-bar routine with traveling circuses, in nightclubs, and on

A simple marker adorns the grave of actor Burt Lancaster.

vaudeville. Lancaster was drafted in 1942, and with his experience as a performer, he was assigned to a new division created to bring entertainment to the troops in Europe, usually in the form of a traveling vaudeville-type show. Lancaster often served as master of ceremonies for the shows, and he also performed his old circus act.

When he returned from the service in 1945, he was still in his army uniform, riding in an elevator in New York City headed for a job interview, when he was spotted by a talent scout and signed for a role in the Broadway play *A*

taph "Hers was a gift of love, a miracle of life for all the world to see and hear forever."

Riperton was born Minnie Julia Riperton on November 8, 1947, in Chicago, Illinois. She died July 12, 1979, in Los Angeles.

Ten feet directly to the left (west) of Riperton's grave is the grave of another popular singer-songwriter, **Carl Wilson (1946–1998),** one of the founding members and lead guitarist of the quintessential southern California surf band, the Beach Boys.

Wilson learned to play the guitar as a teenager and, with older brothers Brian and Dennis, cousin Mike Love, and friend Al Jardine, formed the Beach Boys in 1961. The group decided to write songs to capitalize on the current surfing craze, even though none of the group members were avid surfers. The Beach Boys made their first public appearance on New Year's Eve 1961 in Long Beach, California, though at the time, they could play only three songs.

The Beach Boys first album, *Surfin' Safari,* was released in 1962, two months before Carl Wilson's sixteenth birthday.

The group expanded their repertoire with songs including "I Get Around," "Good Vibrations," "Surfin' USA," "Surfin' Safari," "Surfer Girl," "Little Deuce Coupe," "Fun, Fun, Fun," "In My Room," "409," "Little Old Lady from Pasadena," "Help Me, Rhonda," "God Only Knows," "Wouldn't It Be Nice?" and "Be True to Your School"—simple songs celebrating simple times, with Carl Wilson often supplying the lead vocals.

After the surfing craze faded, the Beach Boys continued to perform throughout the 1970s, though in later years they were typically a nostalgia act, performing their old songs. Carl Wilson left the group and released a solo album in 1981, but he rejoined the group after Dennis Wilson died in a swimming accident in 1983, and he continued to tour with them until shortly before his death.

The Beach Boys had a comeback hit in the summer of 1988, when their song "Kokomo," from the soundtrack of the film *Cocktail* (1988), was the number one song in the country. The song also gave the band the record of the longest time span between number one hits—it had been twenty-four years since "I Get Around" topped the charts in 1964.

The Beach Boys were inducted into the Rock and Roll Hall of Fame on January 20, 1988. A little more than a year later, Wilson died of lung cancer at the age of fifty-one. After his death, Wilson's sons, Jonah and Justyn, set up the Carl Wilson Foundation, under the auspices of the American Cancer Society, to help raise awareness and money for the fight against cancer, and to assist cancer victims. The foundation sponsors an annual Carl Wilson Walk Against Cancer.

Wilson's grave marker includes two hearts on either side of his name, plus the inscription "The Heart and Voice of an Angel—The World Is a Far Lesser Place Without You."

Wilson was born Carl Dean Wilson on December 21, 1946, in Hawthorne, California. He died February 6, 1998, in Los Angeles.

From Wilson's grave, walk about sixty feet to the left (west), in the same row, and you'll find the grave of **Dorothy Stratten (1960–1980)**, model, actress, and *Playboy* magazine's 1980 Playmate of the Year.

Stratten was working at a fast-food restaurant in Canada in 1978 when her boyfriend, Paul Snider, submitted her picture to *Playboy* magazine. Stratten and Snider were married in June 1979, and she first appeared in *Playboy* in August 1979. In April 1980, Stratten was named *Playboy*'s Playmate of the Year.

The *Playboy* publicity helped Stratten launch a film career, and she made her debut in bit parts in *Skatetown, U.S.A.* (1979) and *Americathon* (1979), then starred in *Galaxina* (1980), a science-fiction comedy. She also starred in *They All Laughed* (1981), written and directed by Peter Bogdanovich. Stratten and Bogdanovich fell in love during the filming, and she and Snider separated in May 1980.

On the afternoon of August 14, 1980, Stratten went to visit Snider at the home they once shared on Clarkson Road in west Los Angeles. Snider killed the twenty-year-old Stratten with a single blast to her face from a twelve-gauge shotgun, then turned the gun on himself. *They All Laughed* was released after her death, and in 1988 Bogdanovich married Stratten's younger sister, Louise. At the time of their marriage, Bogdanovich was forty-nine and Louise was twenty. In 2001, Louise filed for divorce.

Stratten's story was told in the films *Death of a Centerfold: The Dorothy Stratten Story* (1981), starring Jamie Lee Curtis and Bruce Weitz, and *Star 80* (1983), starring Mariel Hemingway and Eric Roberts.

Stratten's grave marker includes a lengthy passage from Ernest Hemingway's *A Farewell to Arms*: "If people bring so much courage to this world the world has to kill them to break them, so of course it kills them. . . . It kills the very good and the very gentle and the very brave impartially. If you are none of these you can be sure that it will kill you too but there will be no special hurry. . . . We love you, D.R." ("D.R." was Bogdanovich's nickname for Stratten, from the initials of her first and middle names.)

Stratten was born Dorothy Ruth Hoogstraten on February 28, 1960, in Vancouver, British Columbia, Canada. She died August 14, 1980, in Los Angeles.

On the northern side of the lawn area, just about in the middle and about twenty feet south of the curb, is a large tree, with a small wooden bench on the south side of the tree. As you walk toward the tree, somewhere in the center of the lawn area is the unmarked grave of **Bob Crane (1928–1978),** best known for his role in the long-running television comedy *Hogan's Heroes* in the 1960s, and for his mysterious death in his Arizona apartment.

Crane was a successful and popular radio disc jockey in Los Angeles when he decided to try acting. His first role was a small part in *Return to Peyton Place* (1961). He also appeared in *Man-Trap* (1961), before joining the cast of *The Donna Reed Show* on television in 1963. Crane starred in *Hogan's Heroes* beginning in 1965, playing the leader of a group of prisoners of war in a German prison camp during World War II. For his performance in the series— which was loosely based on the film *Stalag 17* (1953)—Crane was twice nominated for an Emmy Award as Best Lead Actor in a Comedy Series. Though popular, the series was also mildly controversial, as many people, particularly veterans, didn't think a World War II prison camp was the proper setting for a comedy. (And it was also ironic that the two main German army officers were played by Werner Klemperer and John Banner, who were both Jewish.)

After *Hogan's Heroes* was canceled in 1971, Crane appeared in two films produced by Disney studios—*Superdad* (1974) and *Gus* (1976)—as well as a short-lived television series, *The Bob Crane Show,* in 1975.

In the late 1970s, Crane began appearing in dinner theater plays around the country. While appearing in *Beginner's Luck* in 1978 in Scottsdale, Arizona, Crane was found brutally murdered in his apartment. The crime has never been solved.

Crane was originally buried in Oakwood Memorial Park (see Chapter 8). His remains were moved to Westwood in 1999.

Crane was born July 13, 1928, in Waterbury, Connecticut. He died June 29, 1978, in Scottsdale, Arizona.

About ten feet in front of the bench is the grave of **Natalie Wood (1938–1981)**, who was one of the few successful child actors who achieved success as a teenage star and a leading lady. However, Wood is often remembered primarily for her tragic and mysterious death.

Wood made her film debut at the age of five, as an extra in *Happy Land* (1943). The film's director, Irving Pichel, remembered Wood several years later when he needed a girl to costar with Orson Welles and Claudette Colbert in *Tomorrow Is Forever* (1946), and signed Wood for the part. Wood next appeared in *The Ghost and Mrs. Muir* (1947) and *Miracle on 34th Street* (1947), the holiday classic in which she plays the skeptical child who doesn't believe in Santa Claus.

Wood literally grew up onscreen, appearing in *Father Was a Fullback* (1949), *Scudda Hoo! Scudda Hey* (1948)—one of Marilyn Monroe's first films—*Never a Dull Moment* (1950), *The Star* (1952), and *The Silver Chalice* (1954). By the mid-1950s, Wood had graduated to more substantial roles, including *Rebel Without a Cause* (1955), costarring James Dean and Sal Mineo, which earned her an Academy Award nomination as Best Supporting Actress. Wood also starred as John Wayne's niece in *The Searchers* (1956).

Unlike many young actors, Wood made a smooth transition into adult roles as a dark-eyed beauty, costarring with more-established (and sometimes much older) actors including Frank Sinatra, Tony Curtis, Gene Kelly, Warren Beatty, and her future husband, Robert Wagner, in films including *Marjorie Morningstar* (1958), *Kings Go Forth* (1958), *Cash McCall* (1959), *All the Fine Young Cannibals* (1960), and *Splendor in the Grass* (1961), which earned her a second Academy Award nomination, this time as Best Actress. Wood also starred in two successful musicals—although she didn't do her own singing—as stripper Gypsy Rose Lee in *Gypsy* (1961) and as the tragic lover Maria in *West Side Story* (1961).

Wood received her third Academy Award nomination, as Best Actress, for her performance in *Love With the Proper Stranger* (1963), with Steve McQueen. She also starred in *Sex and the Single Girl* (1964), *Inside Daisy Clover* (1965), *The Great Race* (1965), *This Property Is Condemned* (1966), and *Bob & Carol & Ted & Alice* (1969). Wood appeared in only a few films in the 1970s, including made-for-television versions of *Cat on a Hot Tin Roof* (1976) and *From Here to Eternity* (1979).

Wood and Wagner were married for the first time in 1957, and they divorced in 1962. After a brief marriage to producer Richard Gregson from

1969 to 1971, she and Wagner re-married in 1972, aboard Wagner's fifty-five-foot yacht, the *Splendour*.

In 1981, Wood was working with costar Christopher Walken on a science-fiction thriller titled *Brainstorm*. In late November, Wood, Wagner, and Walken went out to spend a few days over the long Thanksgiving weekend on the *Splendour* in the Pacific Ocean near Santa Catalina Island. During one of the nights at sea, Wood apparently tried to leave the yacht and get into an eleven-foot rubber dinghy, but she fell into the water and drowned. Ironically, she had a well-known lifelong fear of dark water. Her body was found floating in the water the next morning, clad in her flannel nightgown, knee-high wool socks and a down jacket. She was forty-three.

An investigation into her death revealed that Wagner and Walken had quarreled on the yacht shortly before Wood attempted to leave in the dinghy, and she may have been trying to get away from them. When she slipped and fell into the cold water, the weight of her water-soaked jacket would have made it difficult for her to climb into the dinghy. Her death was ruled an accidental drowning.

Brainstorm was completed using a stand-in for Wood, and it was released to poor reviews in 1983.

Wood's grave identifies her as Natalie Wood Wagner, and includes the inscription "Beloved daughter, sister, wife, mother and friend—More than love." Her grave is usually surrounded by potted plants and flowers, and covered with coins.

Wood was born Natasha Nikolaevna Gurdin on July 20, 1938, in San Francisco, California. She died November 29, 1981, in the waters off Santa Catalina Island, California.

About fifteen feet to the right (east) of Wood's grave and one row down, you'll find the grave of **Richard Conte (1914–1975),** best known for his film roles as a world-weary soldier, crusty gangster, or cynical convict.

Conte was working as a singing waiter at a resort in Connecticut in 1935 when he was discovered by director Elia Kazan, who offered him a scholarship to New York's Neighborhood Playhouse. Conte came to Hollywood and made his film debut with a bit part in *Heaven With a Barbed Wire Fence* (1939) before returning to New York to work on Broadway. Conte next appeared in several war dramas, including *Guadalcanal Diary* (1943), *The Purple Heart* (1944), *A Walk in the Sun* (1945), *A Bell for Adano* (1945), and

Captain Eddie (1945), and then a series of gritty, film-noir crime dramas, including *Somewhere in the Night* (1946), *13 Rue Madeline* (1946), *Cry of the City* (1948), *Call Northside 777* (1948), *House of Strangers* (1948), *Whirlpool* (1949), *The Sleeping City* (1950), *The Blue Gardenia* (1953), *New York Confidential* (1955), *I'll Cry Tomorrow* (1955), *The Big Combo* (1955), and *The Big Tip Off* (1955).

In the late 1950s and early 1960s, Conte moved to more-sinister roles in *Ocean's Eleven* (1960), *Circus World* (1964), *The Greatest Story Ever Told* (1965), *Assault on a Queen* (1966), and *Lady in Cement* (1968). One of Conte's more memorable roles was as the treacherous Don Emilio Barzini in *The Godfather* (1972)—his last film in Hollywood. Conte then moved to Italy, where he appeared in a series of Italian-made crime and action films.

Conte's grave marker, which features an image of a pyramid on each corner, identifies him as "actor, writer, painter, composer, poet—A man of many talents and graces, loved by a thousand unknown faces." The marker also includes a cryptic listing of Conte's birth and death dates: "1910–1975–?"

Conte was born Nicholas Peter Conte on March 24, 1910, in Jersey City, New Jersey. He died April 15, 1975, in Los Angeles.

Above Conte's grave is another urn garden, with about eighty small markers. On the far right edge of the urn garden, in the fourth space from the top, you'll find the grave of actor **Richard Basehart (1914–1984)**, best known for his role in the television series *Voyage to the Bottom of the Sea* in the 1960s.

After several years as a reporter and radio announcer, Basehart took up acting and made his Broadway debut in 1943. Two years later, he won the New York Drama Critics Award for his starring role in *The Hasty Heart* and was lured to Hollywood. Basehart made his film debut in *Repeat Performance* (1947), and earned critical praise for his starring role in *He Walked By Night* (1948). Basehart also appeared in *The House on Telegraph Hill* (1951), *Fourteen Hours* (1951), *Decision Before Dawn* (1951), *Titanic* (1953), *La Strada* (1954), *Moby Dick* (1956), *The Brothers Karamazov* (1958), and the title role in *Hitler* (1962).

From 1964 to 1968, Basehart starred as Admiral Nelson in the television series *Voyage to the Bottom of the Sea*, which chronicled the adventures of a nuclear-powered submarine conducting deep-sea research. Although the most memorable episodes of the series concerned the sub's encounters with giant squids and other creatures, many of the plots were commentaries on current issues, including nuclear proliferation and pollution. The series was based on a film of the same name, released in 1961 and produced, directed, and written by Irwin Allen, starring Walter Pidgeon as Admiral Nelson.

After the series was canceled, Basehart appeared primarily in made-for-television films, with a few exceptions, including *Rage* (1972), *The Island of Dr. Moreau* (1977), and

Darryl J. Zanuck, the founder of 20th Century Pictures, has a grave marker that tells his life story in great detail.

Being There (1979). He also provided the narration for dozens of documentaries. The day after he narrated the closing ceremonies of the 1984 Olympic Games in Los Angeles, Basehart suffered a stroke from which he never recovered.

Basehart's marker includes only the date of his birth, and the inscription "His like shall never come again—Diana." Basehart and Diana Lotery were married in 1962.

Basehart was born August 31, 1914, in Zanesville, Ohio.
He died September 17, 1984, in Los Angeles.

Head back to Wood's grave. On the opposite side, about forty feet to the left (west), in the same row, you'll find the grave of **Darryl F. Zanuck (1902–1979),** founder of 20th Century Pictures and the last of Hollywood's big studio bosses.

Zanuck had his first taste of Hollywood at the age of eight when he played an Indian boy in a silent Western filmed near his hometown of Wahoo, Nebraska. At fourteen, Zanuck lied about his age, joined the Nebraska National Guard, and saw action in France during World War I. When some of his letters home were published in *Stars and Stripes,* Zanuck decided to become a writer, and he published several short stories in various magazines.

Zanuck submitted writing samples to several studios, and he was hired by Warner Bros. in 1923 as a staff screenwriter. Zanuck was sent to work writing for the most popular star at the studio—a German shepherd dog named Rin-Tin-Tin. Zanuck was named studio manager in 1928, and head of production a year later. As studio head Jack Warner's chief assistant, Zanuck helped guide Warner Bros. into the sound era, and he also helped establish the studio as the home of gritty gangster films in the early 1930s.

Zanuck left Warner Bros. in 1933 to form his own studio, 20th Century Pictures, in partnership with Joseph Scheck. The studio merged with Fox Film Corporation in 1935 to form 20th Century-Fox studios, with Zanuck as chief of production. Zanuck continued to write scripts under his own name, as well as the pseudonyms Gregory Rogers, Melvin Crossman, and Mark Canfield. In fact, Zanuck received his first Academy Award nomination for Best Original Screenplay for *G Men* (1935), as Gregory Rogers.

Zanuck was known as a "hands-on" boss during his lengthy tenure at 20th Century-Fox, often rewriting scripts and assisting with the directing and editing. While Zanuck was there, the studio won the Academy Award for Best Picture three times, for *How Green Was My Valley* (1941), *Gentleman's Agreement* (1947), and *All About Eve* (1950), and received nominations for *In Old Chicago* (1937), *Alexander's Ragtime Band* (1938), *The Grapes of Wrath* (1940), *Wilson* (1944), *The Razor's Edge* (1946), and *Twelve O'Clock High* (1949).

In 1956, Zanuck left the studio to become an independent producer, working in France, and he received another Academy Award nomination for Best Picture for *The Longest Day* (1962). The same year, 20th Century-Fox found itself in deep financial trouble, due primarily to the astronomical production costs of *Cleopatra* (1963), starring Elizabeth Taylor and Richard Burton, and the studio's board of directors asked Zanuck to return. He was elected president of the studio, and appointed his son, Richard Zanuck, as vice president in charge of production. After firing his son a few years later, Zanuck resigned in 1971.

Zanuck won the Irving G. Thalberg Memorial Award, which is presented by the Academy of Motion Picture Arts and Sciences, "for consistently high quality of production," in 1938, 1945, and 1951.

Zanuck's large grave marker includes the logo for 20th Century-Fox studios, as well as a lengthy and detailed review of his life, focusing on his record in two world wars—he also served as a lieutenant colonel in a documentary film unit of the U.S. Signal Corps during World War II. His marker identifies Zanuck as, "A man who used his imaginative, creative genius to deliver inspiration through his celebrated motion pictures. He imparted a lifetime message of decency, love, patriotism, justice, equality and hope throughout the nation and the world."

Zanuck is buried with his wife, Virginia Fox Zanuck (1906–1982), an actress who appeared in a handful of silent films during the early 1920s, most of them comedy shorts starring Buster Keaton, including *Neighbors* (1920), *The Playhouse* (1921), *Cops* (1922), *The Electric House* (1922), and *The Love Nest* (1923). She retired from films when she married Zanuck in 1924.

Zanuck was born Darryl Francis Zanuck on September 5, 1902, in Wahoo, Nebraska. He died December 22, 1979, in Palm Springs, California.

About twenty-five feet to the left (west) of Zanuck's grave is another urn garden, with about 150 markers. On the far right side of the urn garden, next to a small stone bench, is the marker identifying the grave of **Cornel Wilde (1915–1989),** the handsome, romantic, swashbuckling actor who gave up potential careers as a surgeon or an athlete to focus his attention on acting, and is best known for his roles in *A Song to Remember* (1945) and *The Naked Prey* (1966).

Wilde spent much of his childhood in Europe, and he was fluent in six languages. When he returned to the United States, he planned to become a surgeon. He had even been awarded a scholarship to medical school in 1935. He was also a member of the U.S. Olympic fencing team, but he quit the team just before the 1936 Olympics in Berlin, Germany, to devote his energies to his blossoming theater career.

Wilde appeared in stage productions in New York City and elsewhere, including the role of Tybalt in the 1940 Broadway production of *Romeo and Juliet,* starring Laurence Olivier and Vivien Leigh. The rehearsals for the play were held in Los Angeles, and while he was on the West Coast, Wilde was signed to a contract with Warner Bros. He made his film debut in a small role in *The Lady With Red Hair* (1940), and quickly graduated to supporting roles in *High Sierra* (1941), *Knockout* (1941), *The Perfect Snob* (1941), and *Wintertime* (1943). Despite his handsome looks and powerful physique, Wilde was cast as the sickly composer Frederic Chopin in *A Song to Remember*

(1945), and for that role he earned an Academy Award nomination as Best Actor.

Wilde spent much of the late 1940s and 1950s starring in romances, costume dramas and even a few comedies and musicals, including *Leave Her to Heaven* (1945), *Centennial Summer* (1946), *The Bandit of Sherwood Forest* (1946), *It Had to Be You* (1947), *Forever Amber* (1947), *Road House* (1948), *Two Flags West* (1950), *The Greatest Show on Earth* (1952), and *The Big Combo* (1955). In the mid-1950s, Wilde formed his own production company, Theodora Productions, so he could direct his own films. He produced, directed, and starred in several films in the late 1950s and 1960s, including *Storm Fear* (1956), *Lancelot and Guinevere* (1963), and the critically acclaimed *The Naked Prey* (1966).

Wilde was born Cornelius Louis Wilde on October 13, 1915, in New York City. He died October 16, 1989, in Los Angeles.

5

Holy Cross Cemetery

~

5835 West Slauson Avenue
Culver City, California 90230

~ HISTORY

Holy Cross Cemetery, founded in 1939 and covering two hundred acres, is the largest of the eleven Catholic cemeteries in the Los Angeles Archdiocese. Only one hundred acres are currently in use, but there is expansion in progress on the northwest side of the cemetery property.

The cemetery is located on a hillside near the San Diego Freeway (405), a few miles from the Los Angeles International Airport. On a clear day, the property offers spectacular views of downtown Los Angeles and the Century City area to the north, and the airport control tower to the south. In the late afternoon, you can even see the sun glistening off the Pacific Ocean, about five miles away.

The property is divided into about thirty separate sections, some featuring large statues, including Michelangelo's *Pieta,* as well as statues of St. Patrick, St. Francis, and the Holy Family. Behind the altar in the mausoleum chapel is a 1,300-square-foot mural called *The Resurrection,* painted by Isabel Piczek, which took more than two years to complete. The mural is a brightly colored, impressionistic version of the resurrection of Jesus Christ, complete with figures and symbols representing various religious themes and characters.

The Hungarian-born Piczek had her first professional art exhibit when she was eleven years old. Five years later, she won a competition to decorate the Dining Room of the Jesuits at the Biblical Institute in Rome, where she painted a 390-square-foot mural. Since then, Piczek has created murals, mosaics, and stained-glass windows for nearly five hundred churches across the United States and in six other countries. In addition, Piczek is an internationally respected scientist and scholar who has been conducting research on the authenticity of the Shroud of Turin, thought by many to be Christ's burial cloth.

Since Holy Cross is such a big cemetery, with dozens of different sections and winding roads through the property, it's best to stop in the office and get a cemetery map. The office is just to the left when you enter the cemetery gates on Slauson Avenue. On the map, each section is designated by a separate letter, which corresponds to the letters printed on the curbs around the section. In addition, the curb markings also include a name for the section, and all the section names are listed on the back of the map.

Luckily, Holy Cross also has an easy to find and easy to follow system of plot markers throughout the property. The small, circular, concrete markers identify the plot numbers and, in some sections, also identify the tier numbers. If you're looking for "Tier 56, Lot Number 47," for example, look for a marker with "T56, 47" on it.

∼ DIRECTIONS

From downtown Los Angeles, head west to the San Diego Freeway (405). Take the San Diego Freeway south. A little more than three miles south of the Santa Monica Freeway (10), exit at Slauson Avenue and head east. The cemetery gates are on the north side of Slauson Avenue, a little less than a mile from the freeway.

∼ HOURS

The grounds are open every day from 7 A.M. to 6 P.M. The mausoleum is open from 8 A.M. to 5 P.M. Monday through Saturday, and 11 A.M. to 5 P.M. on Sunday.

∼

The Tour

Just past the cemetery administrative offices, on the left side of the road, is a small grotto area dedicated to Our Lady of Lourdes, complete with an altar. On the right side of the altar, in an area surrounded by a small, stone wall in front of a statue of a kneeling angel, is the grave of actress **Rita Hayworth (1918–1987).**

Hayworth was the daughter of Spanish dancer Eduardo Cansino and Volga Haworth, who met and married while both were performing in the Ziegfeld Follies. Hayworth made her first screen appearance when she was eight years old, dancing with her parents in two short musicals titled *Anna*

Case with the Dancing Cancinos and *La Fiesta*, both released in 1926. Hayworth became her father's dance partner when she was fourteen, performing at clubs in the Los Angeles area. Eduard Cansino owned a dancing school in Los Angeles, but the school was suffering during the depression, and he hoped that a film producer would see him perform and sign him to a contract. Winfield Sheehan, the head of production at Fox studios, saw their act, but he only wanted Hayworth, not her father. Her first name, Margarita, was shortened to Rita, and she appeared in a small role as a dancer on a gambling ship in *Dante's Inferno* (1935), starring Spencer Tracy and Claire Trevor.

Hayworth appeared as "Rita Cansino" in small roles in several more films for Fox, including *Under the Pampas Moon* (1935), *Charlie Chan in Egypt* (1935), *Paddy O'Day* (1935), and *Human Cargo* (1936), usually playing a Spanish dancer. But when

Actress Rita Hayworth was buried in front of a statue of a kneeling angel at Holy Cross Cemetery.

Fox merged with 20th Century studios, Sheehan was replaced as head of production by Darryl Zanuck, and Hayworth was dropped by the studio.

Hayworth was hired by Columbia studios for a small role in *Meet Nero Wolfe* (1936), and she also appeared in several Westerns for smaller studios. In 1937, the eighteen-year-old Hayworth married forty-year-old Edward Judson, a car salesman who dedicated himself to promoting Hayworth's career. First, he brought her back to Columbia, where studio boss Harry Cohn suggested changing her last name from Cansino to Hayworth, a revised spelling of her mother's maiden name. Judson agreed, realizing that the new name might help Hayworth expand behind her previous string of roles as Spanish dancers. The studio also suggested lightening Hayworth's hair from its natural black to an auburn color. Judson hired a press agent to make sure

Hayworth's name appeared in gossip and society columns, and he brought her to high-profile nightclubs and movie premieres.

After appearing in several supporting roles in the late 1930s, Hayworth started to attract attention with larger roles in films such as *Only Angels Have Wings* (1939), starring Cary Grant and Jean Arthur; *Blood and Sand* (1941), starring Tyrone Power and Linda Darnell; and *The Strawberry Blonde* (1941), starring James Cagney and Olivia de Havilland. Hayworth returned to her dancing roots when she costarred with Fred Astaire in *You'll Never Get Rich* (1941) and *You Were Never Lovelier* (1942), and with Gene Kelly in *Cover Girl* (1944). Hayworth had become a star, and her performance in the title role in *Gilda* (1946) made her a superstar. Hayworth plays a nightclub singer (although her singing in the film was dubbed) involved in a love triangle set in a gambling casino in Argentina. Hayworth smolders through her performance, doing a pseudo-striptease on stage while removing just one elbow-length glove.

Hayworth had a reputation for falling in love with her costars. After she costarred with Victor Mature in *My Gal Sal* (1942), Hayworth and Judson separated, and she announced that she was engaged to Mature. Instead, four months after her divorce from Judson, she married director-actor Orson Welles. She followed her success in *Gilda* by costarring with Welles in *The Lady From Shangai* (1948), but Welles decided to change Hayworth's look, cutting her hair and dying it blonde. This wasn't the Hayworth audiences wanted to see, and although the film showed flashes of Welles's creativity and brilliance, it was a failure at the box office. Six months after the film was released, Hayworth and Welles were divorced.

Before her divorce from Welles was final, Hayworth traveled to Europe, where she met and fell in love with Prince Aly Khan, the playboy son of Prince Aga Khan III, the spiritual leader of millions of Moslems. Hayworth and Khan were married in 1949, and they had a daughter, Princess Yasmin Aga Khan. Hayworth continued to appear in a handful of films, including *An Affair in Trinidad* (1952), and she divided her time between the United States and Europe. In early 1953, Hayworth and Khan were divorced, and she returned to films, with starring roles in *Salome* (1953), *Miss Sadie Thompson* (1953), and *Pal Joey* (1957), costarring with Frank Sinatra and the woman who would replace her as the queen of Columbia studios, Kim Novak. Hayworth also married again, to singer Dick Haymes in 1953, but they divorced two years later.

Hayworth played a supporting role in *Separate Tables* (1958) and married the film's co-producer, James Hill. They were divorced three years later. By the early 1960s, film roles were few and far between for Hayworth, who was also beginning to show signs of Alzheimer's disease. Her final screen appearance was in *The Wrath of God* (1972), a Western starring Robert Mitchum.

Hayworth attempted to revive her career in early 1972 with stage performances, but she was unable to remember her lines. In her final years, increasingly suffering from the effects of Alzheimer's disease, Hayworth was cared for by her daughter, Princess Yasmin Khan. Since before her mother's death in 1987, Princess Yasmin Khan has been an internationally known spokeswoman and active fundraiser to increase awareness and finance research to find a cure for Alzheimer's disease.

Hayworth's grave marker includes the inscription "To yesterday's companionship and tomorrow's reunion."

Hayworth was born Margarita Carmen Cansino on October 17, 1918, in Brooklyn, New York. She died May 14, 1987, in New York City.

Directly in front of the grotto altar, in the third row, is the grave of crooner and Academy Award–winning actor **Bing Crosby (1904–1977).**

Crosby started his career as a singer and drummer in a small combo while studying law at Gonzaga University in Spokane, Washington. Crosby and his band, the Rhythm Boys, appeared in several films in the early 1930s. His first starring role was in *The Big Broadcast* (1932). Crosby also appeared in several two-reel musical comedies produced by Mack Sennett, and audiences loved his natural, easygoing style, as both an actor and a singer.

Crosby appeared in a series of musicals in the 1930s, including *Blue of the Night* (1933), *College Humor* (1933), *Going Hollywood* (1933), *She Loves Me Not* (1934), *Here Is My Heart* (1934), *Rhythm on the Range* (1936), *Anything Goes* (1936), *Waikiki Wedding* (1937), *Sing, You Sinners* (1938), and *Dr. Rhythm* (1938). Crosby teamed with offscreen pal Bob Hope in *Road to Singapore* (1940), the first in a series of seven *Road* pictures—lightly scripted mixes of adventure, slapstick, ad-libs, inside jokes, and cameos by top Hollywood stars, from Humphrey Bogart to Dean Martin and Jerry Lewis. The other films in the series were *Road to Zanzibar* (1941), *Road to Morocco* (1942), *Road to Utopia* (1946), *Road to Rio* (1947), *Road to Bali* (1952), and *Road to Hong Kong* (1962).

Crosby costarred with Fred Astaire in *Holiday Inn* (1942), and Crosby's version of Irving Berlin's "White Christmas" quickly became the biggest-

This simple marker identifies the grave of singer and actor Bing Crosby.

selling recording of all time. For his dramatic performance as Father O'Malley in *Going My Way* (1944), Crosby won the Academy Award as Best Actor, and he was nominated for the same award in the sequel, *The Bells of St. Mary's* (1945). Crosby received his third nomination for his performance in *The Country Girl* (1954).

Crosby returned to musicals with *White Christmas* (1954), *High Society* (1956), and *Robin and the Seven Hoods* (1964). His final film role was a dramatic performance in a remake of *Stagecoach* (1966). Crosby appeared regularly on television in the 1960s and 1970s, performing on variety shows and hosting an annual Christmas program that usually featured members of his family.

Crosby died in 1977, just after finishing a round of golf in Madrid, Spain.

Despite his laid-back image, Crosby was a savvy businessman. When he died, Crosby was reportedly one of the wealthiest entertainers in Hollywood, with an estate estimated at up to $400 million. Although Crosby mentions his seven children in his will, he does not include any money or other items for any of them. Crosby did, however, set up a trust fund, which received all the rest of the money from his estate, and it can be assumed that Crosby provided for his children to receive money from the trust fund. However, unlike his will, the details of the administration of the trust fund are not a matter of public record, so we can't know for sure. There have been reports that the trust includes a provision that none of his children will receive any money from the trust until they reach the age of sixty-five.

Crosby included the following statement in his will: "Except as otherwise provided in this will and the trust . . . I have intentionally and with full knowledge omitted to provide for my heirs, and I have specifically failed to provide for any child of mine whether mentioned in this will or in said trust or otherwise."

In his will, Crosby also provided detailed funeral instructions, with a request that "my funeral services be conducted in a Catholic church; that they be completely private with attendance limited to my wife and the above-mentioned children; that a low Mass be said and that no memorial service of any kind be held. I further direct that, insofar as possible, services be held without any publicity, other than that which my family permits after my burial, which shall be in a Catholic cemetery."

After his death, several of his sons painted a picture of Crosby as a cold and distant father, who severely punished his children. Son Gary Crosby wrote a controversial tell-all biography, titled *Going My Own Way*, in 1983. Two other sons, Lindsay and Dennis, committed suicide.

Next to Crosby is the grave of his first wife, an actress and singer who performed under the name of Dixie Lee but is buried under her real name, Wilma W. Crosby (1911–1952). They were married in 1930 and had four sons, Gary, Philip, Dennis, and Lindsay. Crosby married his second wife, actress Kathryn Grant, in 1957, and they had three children, Harry, Nathaniel, and Mary Frances.

Next to Wilma Crosby are Bing Crosby's parents, Harry Lowe Crosby (1870–1950) and Catherine H. Crosby (1872–1964).

Crosby purchased four plots at the cemetery when his father died in 1950. At the time, he planned that the spaces would be used by his father, his mother, himself, and his wife, Dixie. By the time Crosby died in 1977, the other three spots were already filled, and he was married to Kathryn. And there were no other plots available nearby. So where would Kathryn be buried?

Crosby anticipated that problem when he wrote out his funeral instructions. Instead of being buried at the customary depth of six feet, Crosby was buried nine feet deep, so that, if Kathryn wishes, she can be buried in his plot, on top of him, and his grave marker can be replaced with one containing both of their names.

Crosby was born Harry Lillis Crosby on May 2, 1904
(some sources say 1901 or 1903), in Tacoma, Washington.
He died October 14, 1977, in Madrid, Spain.

Six spaces to the right of Bing Crosby is the grave of **Bela Lugosi (1882–1956)**, best known for his performances as Dracula, and for his many horror film roles.

Lugosi was a classically trained actor in his native Hungary, appearing onstage and in films as a romantic leading man from 1901 to 1919. Lugosi was also politically active and helped to organize an actors' union. When the

Hungarian monarchy was dissolved and the Communists took power in 1919, Lugosi fled to Germany, where he continued to act onstage and in films. Two years later, Lugosi came to the United States, where he first played the role of Count Dracula for a year on Broadway in 1927, and for two years on the road. Lugosi's Dracula was a high-powered, magnetic mix of smoldering sexuality and terror, and critics compared him to Rudolph Valentino. But when Universal Studios decided to make a film version of Dracula, Lugosi wasn't their first choice for the role. Lon Chaney was first offered the part, but he died in 1930 before filming began. Several other actors were considered for the role, including John Carradine and Paul Muni, before Lugosi finally signed the contract. For this career-defining role of a lifetime, Lugosi was paid $500 per week for seven weeks, with no considerations for future royalties. When *Dracula* was released in 1931, it was an instant hit, and Lugosi was Hollywood's new King of Horror. (Perhaps due to his feelings that he was shortchanged in his Dracula contract, Lugosi helped organize the Screen Actors Guild in 1933.)

Lugosi turned down the role of the monster in *Frankenstein* (1931) but continued with a series of horror film roles, including *Murders in the Rue Morgue* (1932), *White Zombie* (1932), *The Death Kiss* (1932), *Chandu the Magician* (1932), *The Island of Lost Souls* (1933), *Night of Terror* (1933), *The Black Cat* (1934), *Mark of the Vampire* (1935), *The Raven* (1935), *Son of Frankenstein* (1939), *The Gorilla* (1939), *The Phantom Creeps* (1939), *Black Friday* (1940), *The Devil Bat* (1940), *The Wolf Man* (1941), *The Ghost of Frankenstein* (1942), and *Frankenstein Meets the Wolf Man* (1943), in which he finally played the role of the monster.

By the early 1940s, the public's interest in horror films began to fade, and so did Lugosi's career. He was forced to take roles in low-budget, low-quality films that typically took advantage of Lugosi's reputation more than his limited acting ability, including *Spooks Run Wild* (1941), *Ghosts on the Loose* (1942), *The Corpse Vanishes* (1942), *Zombies on Broadway* (1945),

Bela Lugosi was buried in his Dracula cape at Holy Cross Cemetery.

Scared to Death (1947), *Bela Lugosi Meets a Brooklyn Gorilla* (1952), *Mother Riley Meets the Vampire* (1952), and *Bride of the Monster* (1956).

In 1955, Lugosi checked himself into a drug-treatment center, admitting to a twenty-year addiction to morphine and other narcotics. When he was released following treatment, he teamed up with producer Ed Wood to appear in *Plan 9 From Outer Space* (1958), generally considered by most critics to be the worst film ever made. Lugosi died during production, and his scenes were completed by a stand-in—reportedly Wood's dentist—holding a cape over his face.

Lugosi was buried wrapped in his Dracula cape, as he had requested. At his funeral service, a couple of other actors well known for playing spooky characters in films, Peter Lorre and Vincent Price, approached his open coffin. When they saw Lugosi in his cape, Lorre reportedly asked Price, "Do you think we should drive a stake through his heart, just in case?"

Martin Landau played Lugosi in *Ed Wood* (1994), for which he won an Academy Award as Best Supporting Actor.

Lugosi was born Bela Ferenc Dezso Blasko on October 20, 1882, in Lugos, Austria-Hungary (now Lugoj, Romania). He died August 16, 1956, in Los Angeles.

Three rows behind Lugosi (away from the grotto altar and toward the cemetery offices), is the grave of **Jack Haley (1898–1979),** best known as the Tin Woodsman in *The Wizard of Oz* (1939).

Haley was a comedian, singer, and dancer in vaudeville who made his screen debut in *Broadway Madness* (1927). Through the 1930s, Haley appeared in a series of light comedies and musicals, typically playing the slow-witted, soft-voiced, amiable friend of the lead, including *Follow Thru* (1930), *Sitting Pretty* (1933), *Here Comes the Groom* (1934), *The Girl Friend* (1935), *Poor Little Rich Girl* (1936), *Mister Cinderella* (1936), *Wake Up and Live* (1937), *Alexander's Ragtime Band* (1938), and *Rebecca of Sunnybrook Farm* (1938).

Haley wasn't the first choice to play the Tin Woodsman in *Oz*, however. Buddy Ebsen, best known as Jed Clampett in *The Beverly Hillbillies* television series of the 1960s, was originally cast in the role, but had to withdraw after he developed a serious allergic reaction to the chemicals used in the Woodsman's silver makeup.

After *Oz*, Haley returned to his second-banana roles in *Moon Over Miami*

(1941), *Higher and Higher* (1944), *Take It Big* (1944), and *Scared Stiff* (1945). After a long absence from the screen, Haley returned for a small role in *Norwood* (1970), directed by his son, Jack Haley Jr.

Haley was born John Joseph Haley on August 10, 1898
(some sources say 1899), in Boston, Massachusetts.
He died June 6, 1979, in Los Angeles.

Walk up toward the grotto altar and follow the paved walkway on the left of the altar. About twenty-five feet to the left of the path, in Section 152, you'll find the grave of **Sharon Tate Polanski (1943–1969)**, the wife of director Roman Polanski, who was murdered by the followers of Charles Manson.

The daughter of a military man, Tate traveled around the world as a child. She graduated from high school in Italy—where she was voted Homecoming Queen—and appeared as an extra in several Italian films before coming to Hollywood in the early 1960s. Her first big break came when she was cast as a bank secretary in *The Beverly Hillbillies,* and appeared in fifteen episodes of the television comedy from 1963 to 1965. Tate was originally cast in the role of Billie Jo Bradley in the television series *Petticoat Junction,* but she was dropped after it was discovered that she had posed nude in *Playboy* magazine.

Actress Sharon Tate Polanski is buried with her mother, sister, and unborn son at Holy Cross Cemetery.

After uncredited bit parts in several films, including *The Wheeler Dealers* (1963), *The Americanization of Emily* (1964), and *The Sandpiper* (1965), Tate appeared in *The Fearless Vampire Killers* (1967), written and directed by Polanski. Tate had her biggest screen role later that year in the filmed version of Jacqueline Susann's best-selling trashy novel, *Valley of the Dolls* (1967), and she was nominated for a Golden Globe award as Most Promising Female Newcomer. Tate and Polanski were married in early 1968, and Tate next appeared in *The Wrecking Crew* (1969), a spy spoof starring Dean Martin and Elke Sommer.

On August 9, 1969, Tate, who was eight months pregnant, and several houseguests were brutally murdered in her Los Angeles home by followers of Charles Manson. Tate was stabbed sixteen times, and a nylon cord was tied around her neck. After the murder, Tate's mother, Doris Tate, became an outspoken advocate for the rights of crime victims and helped pass a law to give victims and the relatives of victims the right to speak at trials and parole hearings. The Doris Tate Crime Victims Bureau is named in her honor. After Doris Tate's death in 1992, her daughter, Patricia Tate, continued her work until her death in 2000.

Tate is buried with her unborn baby, Paul Richard Polanski, who was killed at the same time; her mother, Doris Gwendolyn Tate (1924–1992); and her sister, Patricia Gay Tate (1957–2000).

> *Tate was born January 24, 1943, in Dallas, Texas.*
> *She died August 9, 1969, in Los Angeles.*

Walk west past Polanski's grave, toward the small stone wall at the edge of the cemetery property. Two rows away from the wall, in Section 186, you'll find the grave of suave, debonair Parisian matinee idol **Charles Boyer (1899–1978).**

Boyer studied philosophy at the Sorbonne in Paris before switching to acting. He made his film debut in France in 1920 and came to Hollywood in 1929, developing an image as the personification of elegance, charm, and romance. He costarred with some of the top actresses in Hollywood during the 1930s and 1940s, such as *The Garden of Allah* (1936), with Marlene Dietrich; *Conquest* (1937), with Greta Garbo; *History Is Made at Night* (1937), with Jean Arthur; *Algiers* (1938), with Hedy Lamarr; *Love Affair* (1939) and *When Tomorrow Comes* (1939), both with Irene Dunne; *All This and Heaven, Too* (1940), with Bette Davis; *Hold Back the Dawn* (1941), with Olivia de

Havilland; *Gaslight* (1944), with Ingrid Bergman; and *Confidential Agent* (1945), with Lauren Bacall.

Boyer was nominated four times for an Academy Award as Best Actor, for his performances in *Conquest, Algiers, Gaslight,* and *Fanny* (1961), and he received an honorary award from the academy in 1943, "for his progressive cultural achievement in establishing the French Research Foundation in Los Angeles as a source of reference."

Boyer married actress Pat Paterson in 1934. Two days after she died in 1978, Boyer took a fatal overdose of barbiturates. Their only child also committed suicide in 1965.

Boyer is buried with his wife, Patricia Paterson Boyer (1910–1978), and their son, Michael Charles Boyer (1943–1965).

Boyer was born August 28, 1899 (some sources say 1897), in Figeac, France. He died August 26, 1978, in Phoenix, Arizona.

Past Boyer's grave, in the row directly next to the stone wall, in Section 195, you'll find the grave of actress **Zasu Pitts (1900–1963)**. The main name on the marker is Woodall, which was Pitts's married name.

Pitts received her unique name as a family compromise. Both of her mother's sisters, Eliza and Susan, wanted her to be named after them, so her mother came up with the name by taking the last two letters of Eliza and the first two letters of Susan.

Pitts appeared in more than two hundred films in her long career, first as a young heroine in silent films and later as a daffy character actress in supporting roles through the 1950s. Pitts was discovered by Mary Pickford and appeared in several Pickford films, including *Rebecca of Sunnybrook Farm* (1917), *The Little Princess* (1917), and *How Could You, Gene?* (1918). The highlights of Pitts's silent films were her dramatic roles in *Greed* (1924), and *The Wedding March* (1928), but she was primarily a comic actress in sound films, due primarily to her squeaky, plaintive voice and nervous speech patterns. Pitts was originally cast as the distraught mother in *All Quiet on the Western Front* (1930), but when preview audiences laughed at her attempt at a dramatic performance, she was replaced in the film by Beryl Mercer. (In fact, Pitts is said to have been the inspiration for the cartoon character Olive Oyl in the Popeye series.)

Pitts costarred with Thelma Todd in a series of comedy shorts in the early 1930s, and also played supporting roles in films including *Destry Rides Again*

(1932), *Back Street* (1932), *Broken Lullaby* (1932), *Professional Sweetheart* (1933), *Dames* (1934), *Ruggles of Red Gap* (1935), *It All Came True* (1940), *No, No, Nanette* (1940), *Life With Father* (1947), *Francis* (1950), and *It's a Mad Mad Mad Mad World* (1963), her last film.

Pitts married her second husband, John E. Woodall, in 1933.

Pitts was born January 3, 1900 (some sources say 1898), in Parsons, Kansas. She died June 7, 1963, in Los Angeles.

Walk around behind the grotto altar. On the opposite site of the altar, about six feet behind the small, stone wall near Hayworth's grave, is the grave of comedian **Jimmy Durante (1893–1980)**.

The "Schnozzola," so named because of his prominent, bulbous nose, Durante started his career playing the piano and singing in New York City nightclubs. He moved to Broadway, appearing in the Ziegfeld production of *Show Girl* in 1919, and then went to Hollywood, making his film debut in *Roadhouse Nights* (1930). Durante was then teamed with Buster Keaton, who was nearing the end of his career, in several unsuccessful comedies, including *The Passionate Plumber* (1932), *Speak Easily* (1932), and *What! No Beer?* (1933). Durante was more successful on his own, providing musical and comedic relief in supporting roles in *The Phantom President* (1932), *Palooka* (1934), *Strictly Dynamite* (1934), *Little Miss Broadway* (1938), *Melody Ranch* (1940), *The Man Who Came to Dinner* (1942), *Music for Millions* (1944), *It Happened in Brooklyn* (1947), and *On an Island With You* (1948).

Durante was a popular performer on musical and comedy variety shows on television in the 1950s and 1960s, and he won an Emmy Award as Best Comedian in 1953. His final film appearance was in *It's a Mad Mad Mad Mad World* (1963), and he also provided the narration for the animated Christmas film *Frosty the Snowman* (1969).

Durante's career was revived posthumously when his recordings of "As Time Goes By" and "Make Someone Happy" were included on the popular soundtrack of *Sleepless in Seattle* (1993).

Durante was born James Francis Durante on February 10, 1893, in New York City. He died January 29, 1980, in Santa Monica, California.

Across the walkway near Durante's grave is a statue of Michelangelo's *Pieta*. About twenty-five feet directly behind the statue, in Tier 56, Lot 62, you'll find the grave of the quintessential Irish actor, **Pat O'Brien (1899–1983)**.

O'Brien decided to pursue an acting career instead of entering the seminary to study for the priesthood, but he made up for it by wearing a clerical collar in dozens of films. As often as he played the quintessential Irish cop, O'Brien could also effectively play the other side of the law, as a charming con man. O'Brien's first major role was as cynical, hard-boiled reporter Hildy Johnson in *The Front Page* (1931). In the mid-1930s, he began working at Warner Bros. and was a steady, dependable performer in dozens of films over the next thirty years, often costarring with James Cagney or boyhood friend Spencer Tracy.

O'Brien and Cagney costarred in *Here Comes the Navy* (1934), *The Irish in Us* (1935), *Ceiling Zero* (1935), *Devil Dogs of the Air* (1935), *A Dream Comes True* (1935), *Boy Meets Girl* (1938), *The Fighting 69th* (1940), and *Torrid Zone* (1940). In perhaps their best film together, *Angels With Dirty Faces* (1938), O'Brien and Cagney play boyhood friends who are both heading for a life of crime. The police catch Cagney, and he becomes a career criminal, but O'Brien escapes and grows up to become a priest who later seeks a final favor from Cagney on death row.

In *Knute Rockne, All American* (1940), perhaps the film for which he is best remembered, O'Brien played the legendary Notre Dame football coach who delivers an impassioned locker room speech, urging his players to "win one for the Gipper" (played by Ronald Reagan). For the rest of his life, O'Brien willingly repeated the famous pep talk at dinners and various public functions

O'Brien also delivered memorable performances in *China Clipper* (1936), *The Great O'Malley* (1937), *Escape to Glory* (1940), *Flight Lieutenant* (1942), *Broadway* (1942), *The Navy Comes Through* (1942), *His Butler's Sister* (1943), *Man Alive* (1945), *Fighting Father Dunne* (1948), *The Boy With Green Hair* (1948), *The Fireball* (1950), *The People Against O'Hara* (1951), *Okinawa* (1952), *The Last Hurrah* (1958), and *Some Like It Hot* (1959).

O'Brien's final film appearance was in the historical drama *Ragtime* (1981), costarring one more time with his old friend Cagney.

O'Brien was born William Joseph Patrick O'Brien on November 11, 1899, in Milwaukee, Wisconsin. He died October 15, 1983, in Santa Monica, California.

In the same row as O'Brien's grave, about fifty feet to the left, in Tier 56, Lot 47, you'll find the grave of actor **Jackie Coogan (1914–1984),** who first gained fame starring with Charlie Chaplin in *The Kid* (1921) and was later known as Uncle Fester on the television series *The Addams Family* in the 1960s.

Chaplin first saw the four-year-old Coogan performing in a dance act with his father at the Orpheum Theater in Los Angeles in 1918. Chaplin described Coogan as "charming" with "an engaging personality," but he didn't think much more about him until a few weeks later when he read that Roscoe "Fatty" Arbuckle, another popular silent-film comedian, had signed Coogan to a film contract. Chaplin then realized that Coogan would be perfect in his films, especially as a young partner for Chaplin's "Little Tramp" character, but it was too late. Coogan had already been signed by Arbuckle. "What an idiot I was not to have thought of it before," Chaplin recalled in his autobiography.

While Chaplin was still upset about missing the opportunity, he was told that Arbuckle had actually signed Coogan's father, Jack Coogan Sr., not the little boy. Chaplin called Coogan Sr., and asked if his son was available for a film. He was, and Chaplin immediately started to work on *The Kid,* his first feature-length film. In the film, Coogan plays a child abandoned by his mother, played by Edna Purviance. Chaplin finds the boy and takes care of him, but the mother decides she wants him back, so the authorities take him away. Chaplin steals the boy back, but loses him again. Chaplin remembered Coogan as a natural performer. "There were a few basic rules to learn in pantomime and Jackie soon mastered them," he wrote. "He could apply emotion to the action and action to the emotion, and could repeat it time and time again without losing the effect of spontaneity. . . . Jackie Coogan was sensational." (Ironically, Coogan Sr.'s contract with Arbuckle didn't work out, and his only film appearance was a small role as a pickpocket in *The Kid.*)

Despite Chaplin's concerns about mixing drama with comedy, *The Kid* opened to rave reviews and is now considered a silent classic. And Coogan worked steadily after that, appearing in *Peck's Bad Boy* (1921), *Oliver Twist* (1922), *Daddy* (1923), *A Boy of Flanders* (1924), *Little Robinson Crusoe* (1924), *Tom Sawyer* (1930), and *Huckleberry Finn* (1931). By the early 1930s, Coogan had become the youngest self-made millionaire in history, but his career as a child star was over.

When Coogan's father died in a car crash in 1935, his mother married his business manager. That same year, Coogan turned twenty-one and was supposed to receive the estimated $4 million he had made during his career.

When his mother and stepfather refused to give him the money, Coogan sued them in 1938 and discovered that they had spent most of his money, with only about $200,000 left. Under California law at the time, Coogan had no rights to the money he had earned, and he was awarded slightly more than $100,000 by the courts in 1939. Because of the public outcry over the situation, California passed the the "Child Actors Bill," better known as the Coogan Act, to set up a trust fund to protect the earnings of young actors. Today, the vast majority of earnings of child performers are required to be placed in protected bank accounts, known as Coogan Accounts.

In 1937, Coogan married actress Betty Grable, but their marriage lasted only three years. After serving in the army during World War II, Coogan returned to Hollywood and attempted to revive his career. Though Coogan appeared in a few films, including *Kilroy Was Here* (1947), *French Leave* (1948), *Outlaw Women* (1952), *The Joker Is Wild* (1957), *High School Confidential* (1958), and *Sex Kittens Go to College* (1960), he eventually found success on television. After starring in *McKeever and the Colonel* from 1962 to 1963, Coogan took the role of the bizarre Uncle Fester in *The Addams Family* in 1964, playing a bald-headed character who liked to blow things up and could illuminate electric light bulbs by putting them in his mouth. The series lasted for two years.

> Coogan was born John Leslie Coogan Jr. on October 26, 1914, in
> Los Angeles. He died March 1, 1984, in Santa Monica, California.

Walk southwest from Coogan's grave, down the hill toward the edge of the cemetery property. About two hundred feet away, in Tier 29, Lot 58, you'll find the grave of actress **Audrey Meadows (1926–1996)**, best known as Jackie Gleason's long-suffering wife, Alice Kramden, on the television series *The Honeymooners* in the 1950s.

Meadows followed her older sister, Jayne, into acting, first working on Broadway, then on television as a regular performer on *The Bob and Ray Show* in the early 1950s. She joined the cast of *The Jackie Gleason Show* in 1952, replacing Pert Kelton in the role of Alice Kramden. When the series ended in 1959, Meadows appeared in several films, including *That Touch of Mink* (1962), *Take Her, She's Mine* (1963), and *Rosie!* (1968). Meadows was also a regular guest panelist on several quiz shows during the 1950s and 1960s.

Meadows was nominated four times for an Emmy Award as Best

Supporting Actress in a Comedy Series, from 1954 to 1957. She won the award in 1955.

Meadows married her second husband, Robert Six, CEO of American Airlines, in 1961. He died in 1986. Her grave marker identifies her as Audrey Meadows Six.

Meadows was born Audrey Cotter on February 8, 1926 (some sources say 1924), in Wuchang, China. She died February 3, 1996, in Los Angeles.

Go back to the front of the grotto area, and follow the road past the *Pieta*. On your right will be Section D, Sacred Heart, and on your left will be Section F, Holy Rosary. A few hundred feet down the road, another road will branch off to the right. Just past that road, on your left, will be Section L, Immaculate Heart. Stay toward the right, next to Section D. About seventy-five feet past the intersection, you'll see a log-shaped trash can on your right. Walk about one hundred feet south of that trash can, toward a tall, four-pronged eucalyptus tree. About fifteen feet west of that tree, in Lot 193, you'll find the grave of actor **Edgar Kennedy (1890–1948)**, the comic master of the "slow burn" in nearly three hundred films.

Kennedy started his career as a vaudeville comedian, and began his film career working for Mack Sennett in Keystone comedies in 1914, often playing supporting roles to Charlie Chaplin, Mabel Normand, and Roscoe "Fatty" Arbuckle. In 1928, Kennedy moved to the Hal Roach studios, and regularly appeared in comedies starring Stan Laurel and Oliver Hardy, some of which Kennedy also directed. During this period, Kennedy perfected his "slow burn"—a delayed but explosive reaction to a frustrating situation. Kennedy also appeared in several shorts in Roach's *Our Gang* series. In 1931, Kennedy launched his own series of comedy shorts, called *The Average Man*, in which he played a henpecked husband, harassed by his in-laws and unable to cope with the pressures of everyday life. The *Average Man* series lasted for seventeen years, and Kennedy appeared in more than a hundred episodes.

Kennedy also played supporting roles in *Duck Soup* (1933), starring the Marx Brothers; *Tillie and Gus* (1934), starring W. C. Fields; *Twentieth Century* (1934), starring John Barrymore and Carole Lombard; *San Francisco* (1936), starring Clark Gable, Jeanette MacDonald, and Spencer Tracy; *A Star Is Born* (1937), starring Janet Gaynor and Fredric March; *Heaven Only Knows* (1947), starring Robert Cummings; and *Unfaithfully Yours* (1948), starring Rex

Harrison and Linda Darnell. His last role was playing Doris Day's uncle in *My Dream Is Yours* (1949).

Kennedy was born April 26, 1890, in Monterey, California.
He died November 9, 1948, in Woodland Hills, California.

Turn left at the next intersection and look for Section M, Precious Blood. In the center of that section is a large crucifix that marks the grave of actress **Rosalind Russell (1908–1976)**, the tough-talking, wisecracking queen of screwball comedy.

Russell started her career as a dramatic actress, playing upper-class ladies in *Evelyn Prentice* (1934), *The President Vanishes* (1934), *Craig's Wife* (1936), and *Night Must Fall* (1937). Her first major comedic role was in *Four's a Crowd*

(1938), costarring Errol Flynn and Oliva de Havilland, and she followed that with similar performances in *The Women* (1939) and *His Girl Friday* (1940), in which she costarred with Cary Grant and perfected the role of the smart, well-tailored career woman who was more than a match for any man.

Russell also starred in *No Time for Comedy* (1940), *Design for Scandal* (1941), *Roughly Speaking* (1945), *Picnic* (1955), *A Majority of One* (1961), *Five-Finger Exercise* (1962), and *The Trouble With Angels* (1966). Russell was nominated four times for an Academy Award as Best Actress, for her performances in *My Sister Eileen* (1942), *Sister Kenny* (1946), *Mourning Becomes Electra* (1947), and *Auntie Mame* (1958), but never won. She won the Jean Hersholt Humanitarian Award in 1973.

A huge crucifix marks the grave of actress Rosalind Russell.

In 1962, Russell took over the role of Mama Rose from Ethel Merman in the Broadway musical *Gypsy*.

Russell married producer Frederick Brisson in 1941. Her grave marker identifies her as Rosalind Russell Brisson, and lists only the date of her death. Brisson (1913–1984) is buried nearby.

Russell was born June 4, 1908 (some sources say 1912), in Waterbury, Connecticut. She died November 28, 1976, in Beverly Hills, California.

Four rows behind the crucifix and about fifteen feet to the right, in Lot 764, you'll find the grave of **Diane Carol Sherbloom (1942–1961)**, the 1961 national champion ice dancer who was killed in a plane crash along with the rest of the U.S. Figure Skating Team on the way to the World Championship competition in Europe.

Sherbloom and her partner, Larry Pierce, won the national ice dancing championship on January 25, 1961, in Colorado Springs, Colorado. After competing in the North American Championships in early February in Philadelphia, all eighteen members of the U.S. Figure Skating Team, along with their parents, coaches, judges, and skating association officials, were scheduled to fly to Prague, Czechoslovakia, for the World Championship competition, which was scheduled to begin on February 22.

The team plane flew from Philadelphia to New York City, then departed for Brussels, Belgium, on February 14, on the way to Prague. Early the next morning, the Sabena Airlines 707 crashed on approach to the Brussels Airport, killing all seventy-two passengers and crew, as well as one person on the ground. The crash was blamed on a malfunctioning stabilizer-adjusting mechanism. Sherbloom was eighteen years old.

Sherbloom was born September 21, 1942, in Los Angeles. She died February 15, 1961, in Brussels, Belgium.

About one hundred feet directly to the right of Russell's crucifix, in Lot 542, you'll find the grave of actress **Gia Scala (1935–1972)**.

Scala was born in England and raised in Rome. She came to Hollywood in 1955 and made her film debut in a small role in *All That Heaven Allows* (1955), starring Rock Hudson and Jane Wyman. She appeared in roles of increasing size in films throughout the late 1950s and early 1960s, including *Never Say*

Goodbye (1956), *The Price of Fear* (1956), *Don't Go Near the Water* (1957), *The Garment Jungle* (1957), *Tip on a Dead Jockey* (1957), *The Big Boodle* (1957), *The Tunnel of Love* (1958), *The Angry Hills* (1959), and *The Guns of Navarone* (1961), starring Gregory Peck, Anthony Quinn, and David Niven.

After Scala's mother died in 1957, Scala attempted suicide several times, including once when she threw herself off the Waterloo Bridge into the Thames River in England in 1959, but was rescued by a passing cabdriver.

Scala made guest appearances on several television series in the 1960s, including *Alfred Hitchcock Presents*, *Voyage to the Bottom of the Sea*, *Twelve O'Clock High*, and *It Takes a Thief*. Scala returned to Europe in the mid-1960s and appeared in films produced in Italy, Spain, and England.

In July 1971, back in Los Angeles, Scala was seriously injured when the sports car she was driving overturned on a winding road in the Hollywood Hills. In April 1972, she was found dead in her home. Although the initial reports showed that her death was caused by a drug overdose, the autopsy revealed that Scala was also suffering from severe coronary arteriosclerosis, which may have been a contributing factor in her death. She was thirty-seven.

Scala is buried next to her mother, Eileen Sullivan Scoglio (1917–1957).

Scala was born Giovanna Scoglio on March 3, 1935
(some sources say 1934), in Liverpool, England.
She died April 30, 1972, in Los Angeles.

On the same side of the crucifix, about 50 feet in front and 250 feet to the right, and about 10 feet from the road separating Section M from Section C, Our Lady of Grace, in Lot 232, you'll find the grave of *The Girl on the Red Velvet Swing*, **Evelyn Nesbit (1884–1967)**—model, actress, and the central figure in the first "Crime of the Century."

Nesbit made her first public appearance at the age of five, singing in church at a memorial service. When she was thirteen, she began her career as a model, and quickly became one of the most popular and recognizable people in New York City. While modeling in 1901 for Charles Dana Gibson, famous for his "Gibson Girl" paintings, the sixteen-year-old Nesbit met renowned—and married—architect Stanford White, fifty, and they carried on a brief love affair. Nesbit was later involved with actor John Barrymore before she met and married the wealthy but mentally unbalanced Harry Thaw in 1905. Though Nesbit was strongly opposed to the marriage, her mother insisted that Thaw would be able to provide the family with financial security.

Thaw was consumed by a jealous rage against White for taking his wife's virginity. On June 25, 1906, Thaw approached White in the rooftop cabaret theater at New York City's Madison Square Garden—which White designed—and shot him three times at point-blank range. Thaw's three-month trial for murder transfixed the nation in a way unequaled until O. J. Simpson was the focus of the next "Crime of the Century" nearly a hundred years later. During the trial, it became public that White often sought the company of young girls and entertained them in his private apartment in the Madison Square Garden tower, which featured the famous red velvet swing. Nesbit testified that White enjoyed watching her swing nude.

In many ways, White and his wild life were actually on trial. A New York newspaper described the case as, "not a mere murder. The flash of that pistol lighted up depths of degradation, an abyss of moral turpitude that the people must think of because it reveals some of the hidden features of powerful, reckless, openly flaunted wealth. . . . It is a case that for intense interest and deep disgrace has not been equaled in the history of this country."

To save her husband, Nesbit testified that White had gotten her drunk on champagne and forced himself on her while she was unconscious. After an initial hung jury, Thaw was found not guilty by reason of insanity. Thaw spent eight years in an asylum for the criminally insane and, upon his release in 1916, he immediately filed for divorce from Nesbit.

While Thaw was incarcerated, Nesbit returned to the stage and attempted to find work as a dancer in vaudeville. She made her film debut in *Threads of Destiny* (1914) and starred in a series of semi-autobiographical dramas, including *Redemption* (1917), *The Woman Who Gave* (1918), *I Want to Forget* (1918), *Her Mistake* (1918), *Woman, Woman!* (1919), *Thou Shalt Not* (1919), *A Fallen Idol* (1919), *My Little Sister* (1919), and *The Hidden Woman* (1922). Nesbit also gave birth to a son she said was Thaw's, but Thaw denied that he was the father. Russell Thaw, born in 1910, appeared in several of his mother's films.

Nesbit turned to drugs and twice attempted suicide. She spent her final years in California, teaching sculpture. In an interview shortly before her death in 1967, she described White as "the most wonderful man I ever knew," and added, "Stanny White was killed, but my fate was worse. I lived." Harry Thaw also attempted suicide in 1917, but he spent many more years living in mental hospitals. He died in Miami Beach, Florida, in 1947.

Nesbit was portrayed onscreen by Joan Collins in *The Girl in the Red Velvet Swing* (1955), and by Elizabeth McGovern in *Ragtime* (1981).

About 50 feet in front of the crucifix, but about 250 feet on the opposite side, in Lot 304, you'll find the grave of one of the most honored American filmmakers, **John Ford (1895–1973)**, four-time winner of the Academy Award as Best Director.

After graduating from high school in 1913, Ford went to Hollywood to follow in the footsteps of his older brother, Francis, an actor and director. Francis changed his last name from O'Feeney to Ford, and his younger brother followed suit. The younger Ford started work as a set laborer, assistant prop man, and stuntman, often doubling for his brother. In one of his first film appearances, John Ford rode as one of the hooded Ku Klux Klan riders in D. W. Griffith's *The Birth of a Nation* (1915).

Ford began writing scripts, primarily for Westerns, beginning in 1917, and he made his debut as a director with *The Tornado* (1917). Ford directed scores of silent films, including *The Iron Horse* (1924), *The Blue Eagle* (1926), and *Four Sons* (1928), and worked with many of the top screen cowboys of the day, including Hoot Gibson, Buck Jones, and Tom Mix.

Ford won his first Academy Award for *The Informer* (1935), a story of deceit and betrayal set during the 1922 Irish Rebellion. He was also nominated for the award for *Stagecoach* (1939), starring John Wayne, who would become a Ford favorite and a leading player in the director's "stock company" of actors, which also included Ward Bond, Ben Johnson, Victor McLaglen, James Stewart, John Carradine, and Henry Fonda, among others. Another Ford trademark was the use of Monument Valley, Utah, for his outdoor scenes.

Ford won Academy Awards for *The Grapes of Wrath* (1940), *How Green Was My Valley* (1941)—both stories of tightly knit families struggling to survive in the face of adversity—and *The Quiet Man* (1952). During World War II, Ford was appointed chief of the Field Photographic Branch of the Office of Strategic Services, and he won two more Academy Awards for his documentaries *The Battle of Midway* (1942) and *December 7th* (1943).

Ford also directed *Wee Willie Winkie* (1937), *Young Mister Lincoln* (1939), *Drums Along the Mohawk* (1939), *The Long Voyage Home* (1940), *Tobacco Road* (1941), *My Darling Clementine* (1946), *Three Godfathers* (1948), *She Wore a Yellow Ribbon* (1949), *Rio Grande* (1950), *Wagonmaster* (1950), *What*

Price Glory (1952), *Mogambo* (1953), *The Long Gray Line* (1955), *The Searchers* (1956), *Two Rode Together* (1961), *The Man Who Shot Liberty Valance* (1962), *Donovan's Reef* (1963), and *Cheyenne Autumn* (1964).

In 1973, Ford was the first recipient of the American Film Institute's Life Achievement Award.

Ford's grave marker identifies him as Admiral John Ford, in honor of the rank he achieved in the U.S. Naval Reserves. He's buried with his wife, Mary Ford (1896–1979).

Ford was born Sean Aloysius O'Feeney on February 1, 1895 (some sources say 1894), in Cape Elizabeth, Maine. He died August 31, 1973, in Palm Desert, California.

Directly behind the crucifix is the large Holy Cross Mausoleum. Although there is parking available along the curb in front of the mausoleum, there is also a large parking lot behind the building. The main entrance of the mausoleum takes you directly into a large chapel, which features the mural *The Resurrection* behind the altar.

On the left side of the chapel, about halfway to the altar, in the first space up from the floor, you'll find the crypt of **Ray Bolger (1904–1987)**, the rubber-limbed singer, dancer, and comedian best known as the Scarecrow in *The Wizard of Oz* (1939).

Bolger worked a variety of jobs as a teenager, including bank clerk, accountant, and vacuum-cleaner salesman, while taking dance lessons and making plans to become an entertainer. Bolger made his professional debut in 1922 with a musical-comedy repertory company in New England, touring and performing in small towns. He began performing in vaudeville in 1924 as half of a dance act called, "Sanford and Bolger, a Pair of Nifties." After appearing in several successful Broadway shows, Bolger made his film debut playing himself in *The Great Ziegfeld* (1936), starring William Powell, Myrna Loy, and his future *Oz* costar, Frank Morgan. Bolger also appeared with Morgan in his next two films—*Rosalie* (1937), which starred Nelson Eddy and Eleanor Powell, and *Sweethearts* (1938), which starred Eddy and Jeanette MacDonald.

In 1938, Bolger was contacted by MGM and offered a role in *The Wizard of Oz*, but the studio wanted him to play the Tin Woodsman. "It's not my cup of tea," Bolger responded. "I'm not a tin performer. I'm fluid." Bolger wanted to appear in the film, but he desperately wanted the role of the Scarecrow, since it was that character that inspired him to become a performer in the first place. As a young boy, Bolger had seen a stage production of *The Wizard of Oz*, with Fred Stone in the role of the Scarecrow. Bolger later said that when he saw the Scarecrow leap out of a haystack onstage, it was a defining moment for him. "I've never forgotten it," he recalled. "That moment opened up a whole new world for me. Up until then, the theater had nothing to do with me. . . . I was just after survival, after making a living for myself. That moment in the theater changed all that."

MGM wanted lanky dancer Buddy Ebsen for the Scarecrow, and even had Ebsen fitted for the Scarecrow's costume. But Bolger persisted, and eventually won the role, with Ebsen given the role of the Tin Woodsman. But though Ebsen said he would be happy with any role in the film, it was not to be. He developed an allergic reaction to the chemicals used in the Woodsman's silver makeup, spent two weeks in the hospital, and was replaced by Jack Haley. Bolger and Haley were also the highest-paid among the *Oz* actors, making $3,000 per week. Morgan, who played the Wizard, among several roles, and Bert Lahr, who played the Cowardly Lion, both received $2,500 per week, and Judy Garland, who played Dorothy, received only $500 per week.

After *Oz*, Bolger's film career stalled. He returned to the stage, starring in a lengthy run on Broadway in *Charley's Aunt*, before returning to Hollywood to star in the filmed version of the play, *Where's Charley?* (1952). In 1953, Bolger starred in his own television sitcom, initially called *Where's Raymond?* but later re-titled *The Ray Bolger Show*. He also made regular appearances on television variety shows and sitcoms, including several memorable guest appearances on *The Partridge Family* in the early 1970s, playing the grandfather of the musical clan.

Bolger is buried with his wife, Gwendolyn Rickard Bolger (1909–1997). They were married in 1929, and celebrated their fifty-seventh anniversary a few months before he died.

Bolger was born Raymond Wallace Bulcao on January 10, 1904, in Dorchester, Massachusetts. He died January 15, 1987, in Los Angeles.

On the right side of the altar, you'll find the crypt of singer **Mario Lanza (1921–1959).** His short and sad life has all the makings of an epic tragedy.

A high school dropout, Lanza was working in his parents' grocery store when he auditioned for conductor Serge Koussevitzky in 1942. Lanza's commanding and powerful tenor voice won him a music scholarship, a spot at the Berkshire Summer Music Festival, and a nationwide concert tour. Young fans reacted to Lanza the way fans of future generations reacted to Elvis Presley or the Beatles. After serving in World War II, Lanza was signed by MGM studios and starred in four films that successfully exploited his powerful voice, rugged good looks, and dazzling smile—*That Midnight Kiss* (1949), *The Toast of New Orleans* (1950), *The Great Caruso* (1951), and *Because You're Mine* (1952). Lanza, equally effective singing popular songs or classical opera, was quickly becoming a fan favorite. In 1951, he won the *Photoplay* Award as Most Popular Male Star.

Lanza was scheduled to star in *The Student Prince* (1954), but his increasing weight caused MGM to replace him in the title role, although Lanza did provide the prince's singing voice. Crushed by the decision, he increased his consumption of alcohol and drugs. Lanza starred in *Serenade* (1956) for Warner Bros., then went to Italy to film *Arrivederci Roma* (1957) and *For the First Time* (1959). While in Rome, Lanza went on a rigorous diet, which may have contributed to the heart attack that killed him in 1959. Lanza was thirty-eight years old. Shortly after Lanza's death, rumors surfaced that he had actually been killed by Lucky Luciano for refusing to sing at a charity event in Naples hosted by the mobster.

Lanza's wife, Betty, returned to Hollywood, and died six months later of a drug overdose. One of the Lanzas' four children died of a heart attack in 1993 at the age of thirty-seven, another was killed in an automobile accident in 1997 at the age of fifty-nine.

Lanza is buried next to his wife, Betty Lanza (1922–1960).

Lanza was born Alfredo Cocozza on January 31, 1921, in Philadelphia, Pennsylvania. He died October 7, 1959, in Rome, Italy.

On the second floor of the mausoleum, behind and to the left of the altar, you'll find the crypt of Academy Award–winning choreographer **Hermes Pan (1909–1990)**, who often worked with Fred Astaire and Ginger Rogers on their films in the 1930s and 1940s.

Pan started his career as the assistant dance director on the first Astaire-Rogers film, *Flying Down to Rio* (1933), and worked with the pair on *The Gay Divorcee* (1934), *Roberta* (1935), *Top Hat* (1935), *Follow the Fleet* (1936), *Swing Time* (1936), *Shall We Dance?* (1937), *Carefree* (1938), *The Story of*

Vernon and Irene Castle (1939), and *The Barkleys of Broadway* (1949). Pan bore a striking physical resemblance to Astaire, and even doubled for the dancer in some long shots.

Pan was also the choreographer in *Kiss Me Kate* (1953), *Pal Joey* (1957), *Silk Stockings* (1957), *Can-Can* (1960), *My Fair Lady* (1964), and *Darling Lili* (1970), among dozens of other films. He also appeared in cameo roles, typically as a dancer, in *Moon Over Miami* (1941), *Footlight Serenade* (1942), *My Gal Sal* (1942), *Pin-Up Girl* (1944), *Kiss Me Kate,* and *Pal Joey.*

Pan was nominated for an Academy Award for Best Dance Direction for *Top Hat* and *Swing Time,* and won the award for *A Damsel in Distress* (1937).

> *Pan was born Hermes Panagiotopoulos on December 10, 1909 (some sources say 1910), in Memphis, Tennessee. He died September 19, 1990, in Beverly Hills, California.*

Now, head back to the main entrance of the mausoleum. Standing at the main entrance and facing the altar, turn right and walk about seventy-five feet down the hallway, toward a large statue. Make a short turn to the right in front of the statue, then turn left down another hallway. About seventy-five feet down, on the right, you'll see a small alcove labeled "Room 7." Inside that alcove, on the left, near the ceiling, you'll see the crypt of rotund actor and comedian **John Candy (1950–1994)**, who provided memorable comic moments in dozens of films during his short career.

Candy appeared in small roles in several films in the early 1970s, including *Hercules in New York* (1970), *Class of '44* (1973), *The Clown Murders* (1975), and *Tunnel Vision* (1976), before gaining fame as a writer and performer on

Actor and comedian John Candy is buried in the mausoleum at Holy Cross Cemetery.

the popular *SCTV* television series, which was produced in Canada and debuted in 1976. Candy created dozens of memorable characters on the sketch comedy show, including Johnny LaRue, Billy Sol Hurok, Mayor Tommy Shanks, and Yosh Schmenge. Candy came to Hollywood in the late 1970s, with supporting roles in *Lost and Found* (1979), *1941* (1979), *The Blues Brothers* (1980), *Stripes* (1981), *National Lampoon's Vacation* (1983), and *Splash!* (1984).

Candy was less successful in starring roles in the late 1980s, however, in films including *Summer Rental* (1985), *Armed and Dangerous* (1986), *The Great Outdoors* (1988), and *Who's Harry Crumb?* (1989). Candy successfully mixed sentiment with humor in *Planes, Trains and Automobiles* (1987), *Uncle Buck* (1989), and *Only the Lonely* (1991), and he even appeared in an effective cameo role in Oliver Stone's *JFK* (1991). In *Cool Runnings* (1993), Candy played the coach of the Jamaican bobsled team, and he finally proved that he was a talented actor as well as a comedian.

While filming *Wagons East* (1994) on location in Mexico, Candy suffered a fatal heart attack. He was forty-three.

Candy's crypt contains the inscription "One heart and one soul—We miss you dearly."

Candy was born John Franklin Candy on October 31, 1950, in Toronto, Canada. He died March 4, 1994, in Durango, Mexico.

Two spaces below Candy is the crypt of actor **Fred MacMurray (1908–1991).** Though younger audiences may remember MacMurray best as the kindly father in the long-running television sitcom *My Three Sons* in the 1960s, or his appearances in a series of light-entertainment Disney films, film fans remember MacMurray for his role as scheming insurance agent Walter Neff in the sexually charged film-noir classic, *Double Indemnity* (1944).

MacMurray started his entertainment career as a saxophone player who toured the country with various bands. On concert stops in Los Angeles in the late 1920s, MacMurray appeared as an extra in several silent films. After he appeared in the Broadway musical *Roberta*, MacMurray was signed by Paramount studios, and the tall, good-looking actor quickly proved his versatility as a leading man in a variety of films, including *The Gilded Lily* (1935), a romantic comedy with Claudette Colbert; *Alice Adams* (1935), a drama with Katharine Hepburn; *Hands Across the Table* (1935), a romantic comedy with Carole Lombard; and *The Forest Rangers* (1942), an action-adventure with

Paulette Goddard and Susan Hayward. He even got a chance to sing in *The Princess Comes Across* (1936).

In *Double Indemnity* (1944), MacMurray's murky insurance salesman plots a murder with Barbara Stanwyck while trying to keep one step ahead of his boss, played by Edward G. Robinson. The film received Academy Award nominations for Best Picture, Best Actress, Best Screenplay (Raymond Chandler and Billy Wilder), and Best Director (Wilder), but MacMurray's performance was overlooked. In 1998, the American Film Institute released its list of "100 Greatest American Movies," in commemoration of the first hundred years of American cinema, and *Double Indemnity* ranked thirty-eighth on the list.

MacMurray continued to move with ease between comedic and dramatic roles, starring in *Murder, He Says* (1945), *The Egg and I* (1947), *The Miracle of the Bells* (1948), *Father Was a Fullback* (1949), *Never a Dull Moment* (1950), *Fair Wind to Java* (1953), *The Caine Mutiny* (1954), *Pushover* (1954), *There's Always Tomorrow* (1956), and *The Apartment* (1960).

MacMurray's career took a different turn in 1959, when he starred in the first of several popular comedies for Disney, *The Shaggy Dog* (1959), followed by *The Absent-Minded Professor* (1961), *Son of Flubber* (1963), and *The Happiest Millionaire* (1967). From 1960 to 1972, MacMurray starred as Steven Douglas, widowed father of three boys in *My Three Sons*.

In 1954, MacMurray married actress June Haver, and her name also appears on his crypt (although, at this writing, she's not yet ready for her eternal rest). MacMurray and Haver met when they costarred in *Where Do We Go From Here?* (1945). Haver's mother, Maria Haver (1904–1992), and her sister, Evelyn Haver (1927–2000), occupy adjacent crypts.

MacMurray was born Fredrick Martin MacMurray on August 30, 1908, in Kankakee, Illinois. He died November 5, 1991, in Santa Monica, California.

Head back to the main entrance of the mausoleum and go outside. Southeast of the main entrance, you'll find Section N, Mother of Sorrows. Cross the road at the southeast corner of the mausoleum and walk about seventy-five feet into Section N. About fifteen feet west of a large pine tree, in Lot 523, you'll find the grave of actress **Mary Astor (1906–1987),** best known for her role as the femme fatale in *The Maltese Falcon* (1941).

After winning a beauty contest, Astor made her film debut at the age of fourteen, playing a bit part in *The Scarecrow* (1920), a comedy starring Buster Keaton. After appearing in small roles in dozens of films over the next few years, Astor got her first major role in *Beau Brummel* (1924), with John Barrymore, and there were rumors of an offscreen romance between the forty-two-year-old actor and his eighteen-year-old costar. Astor appeared in a number of costume dramas and swashbuckling adventures over the next few years, including *Don Q, Son of Zorro* (1925) and *Don Juan* (1926). Astor made a successful transition to talkies, and appeared in dozens of films in the early 1930s, including *Runaway Bride* (1930), *Behind Office Doors* (1931), *The Lost Squadron* (1932), *Red Dust* (1932), *The Kennel Murder Case* (1933), and *Dodsworth* (1936).

Astor made headlines in a different way in 1936, when she was in the midst of divorce and a custody battle with her second husband. Admitted as evidence at the trial was Astor's diary, which included a graphic and detailed account of Astor's sixteen-month affair with playwright George S. Kaufman, and the case became the most publicized and talked-about scandal in Hollywood in the 1930s. But rather than end Astor's career, the trial publicity seemed to energize it, and she next appeared in *The Prisoner of Zenda* (1937), *The Hurricane* (1937), *Midnight* (1939), and *Turnabout* (1940), before costarring with Humphrey Bogart in Dashiell Hammett's *The Maltese Falcon* (1941). For her performance in her next film, *The Great Lie* (1941), Astor won the Academy Award for Best Supporting Actress.

By the mid-1940s, Astor was making the transition from roles as the elegant and sophisticated leading lady to character and supporting parts, including roles in *The Palm Beach Story* (1942), *Thousands Cheer* (1943), *Meet Me in St. Louis* (1944), *Desert Fury* (1947), *Little Women* (1949), and *A Kiss Before Dying* (1956). Her last film was *Hush, Hush, Sweet Charlotte* (1965).

> *Astor was born Lucile Vasconcellos Langhanke on May 3, 1906, in Quincy, Illinois. She died September 25, 1987, in Woodland Hills, California.*

About one hundred feet southwest (left) of Astor's grave and one row farther from the road, in Lot 490, you'll find the grave of **Mack Sennett (1880–1960)**, silent film's undisputed King of Comedy.

Sennett grew up in Canada, the son of working-class Irish immigrants, with dreams of becoming an opera singer. His family moved to the East Coast when Sennett was a teenager, and he decided to try his luck on the stage, where he found work as a burlesque performer and Broadway chorus boy. Looking for more regular employment, Sennett went to Biograph studios in 1908 and began acting in films under the direction of D. W. Griffith, costarring with Florence Lawrence, Lionel Barrymore, Mary Pickford, and Mabel Normand. By 1910, Sennett was also directing.

In 1912, Sennett left Biograph and formed his own studio—Keystone—and began to specialize in slapstick comedies. The Keystone roster soon included comedy stars Roscoe "Fatty" Arbuckle, Edgar Kennedy, Slim Summerville, Chester Conklin, Charlie Chase, Mack Swain, and Normand, who left Biograph to work with Sennett. Wallace Beery and Gloria Swanson also got their starts working for Sennett at Keystone. In 1914, a British dance-hall comedian named Charlie Chaplin came to the United States and was signed by Keystone. Chaplin appeared in thirty-five comedies at the studio during 1914, most of them directed by Sennett.

The typical Keystone comedy featured a thin plot and a quick succession of visual gags and often-improvised physical comedy. Sennett was also a master at taking advantage of any real-life situation that might happen to occur, such as a parade, a fire, or the draining of a lake, and using it as the backdrop for one of his comedies. In his first year in business, Sennett produced 140 films, many of them featuring his famous Keystone Kops.

In 1915, Keystone became part of the newly formed Triangle Film Corporation. Two years later, Sennett left to again form his own company, Mack Sennett Comedies, working first for Paramount studios. Sennett continued to produce two-reel comedies and the occasional feature-length film. The end of the silent era in the late 1920s also marked the end of Sennett's reign as King of Comedy, with Hal Roach replacing him. In 1935, Sennett retired and moved to a farm in Canada, virtually penniless. He returned to Hollywood in 1937 to accept an honorary Academy Award. The citation read, in part, "for his lasting contribution to the comedy technique of the screen, the basic principles of which are as important today as when they were first put into practice, the Academy presents a special award to that master of fun, discoverer of stars, sympathetic, kindly, understanding comedy genius, Mack Sennett."

Sennett was portrayed by Robert Preston in the Broadway musical *Mack and Mabel,* in the mid-1970s, and by Dan Aykroyd in *Chaplin* (1992).

Sennett's grave marker identifies him as the "Beloved King of Comedy."

Sennett was born Mikall Sinnott on January 17, 1880, in Richmond, Canada. He died November 5, 1960, in Woodland Hills, California.

An etched silhouette of the bandleader adorns the grave marker of Lawrence Welk.

Northeast of Section N, behind and to the right of the mausoleum, is Section Y, St. Francis. Drive around to the southeast side of the section (the side opposite the mausoleum), and stop in front of the statue of St. Francis. About 50 feet in from the road, and about 175 feet directly in front of the statue, in Tier 9, Lot 110, you'll find the grave of accordionist, bandleader, and "Champagne Music" maker, **Lawrence Welk (1903–1992).**

Welk formed a popular dance band in the 1920s, playing at dancehalls and hotels across the country. The group was called "America's Biggest Little Band," since each band member could play several instruments. While critics cited the band's lack of imagination and simplistic arrangements, the dancers and listeners loved it, and Welk's band started performing on radio, beginning in Yankton, South Dakota, in late 1927. The band was renamed "Lawrence Welk and His Hotsy Totsy Boys," then "Lawrence Welk and His Honolulu Fruit Gum Orchestra," with band members wearing ruffled, multicolored shirts. Welk called his style "champagne music," insisting that he knew what America wanted to hear. And it seems that he was right.

In 1951, Welk and his orchestra smoothly made the transition to television, broadcasting live from the Aragon Ballroom. In 1955, Welk brought his show to ABC as *The Lawrence Welk Show,* and both the show and his recordings were popular. In 1961, two of Welk's albums were on the charts for the entire year, and he had a total of forty-two albums on the charts from 1956 to

1972. Featuring performances by Myron Floren, Norma Zimmer, and the Lennon Sisters, and dance numbers by Bobby Burgess, *The Lawrence Welk Show* provided dependable Saturday night entertainment until it was canceled in 1982.

Welk's trademarks were the bubble machine, beginning each musical number by counting down "a-one, and a-two," and describing the performances as "wunnerful, wunnerful."

Welk's grave marker includes an etched silhouette of the bandleader, his baton poised and ready, along with the phrase "Keep a song in your heart."

Welk was born March 11, 1903, in Strasburg, North Dakota.
He died May 17, 1992, in Santa Monica, California.

Northeast of Section Y, at the northeast edge of the cemetery, is Section CC, Holy Martyrs. About one hundred feet from the road and sixty feet in front of a statue of Jesus and two lambs, in Tier 52, Lot 58, you'll find the grave of actress **Mary Frann (1943–1998),** best known for her role as the wife of Bob Newhart on the long-running sitcom *Newhart,* from 1982 to 1990.

Frann was a child model who won the title of America's Junior Miss in 1961. With her Junior Miss scholarship, Frann studied drama at Northwestern University and later worked as a television weather reporter in her native St. Louis. She also hosted a morning television show in Chicago for four years before moving to Los Angeles to appear in the series *My Friend Tony,* in 1969. She also appeared in the series *Return to Peyton Place* from 1973 to 1974, and *Days of Our Lives* from 1974 to 1979.

In the 1960s and 1970s, Frann made guest appearances on various television series, including *The Wild, Wild West, That Girl, The Mary Tyler Moore Show, Bonanza, Hawaii Five-O, The Rockford Files, WKRP in Cincinnati,* and *The Incredible Hulk.*

In 1982, Frann starred as Joanna Louden, the wife of writer Dick Louden, played by Bob Newhart, in *Newhart.* The Loudens' Vermont inn was the meeting place for an assortment of quirky local characters, and the show was a popular series for eight years. After the series was canceled in 1990, Frann appeared in several made-for-television movies and was also active in charity work in Los Angeles, particularly the Los Angeles Mission, where she worked with women in rehabilitation from problems with drugs, alcohol, or prostitution. Frann also formed the Celebrity Women's Action Committee with other television stars.

In September 1998, after spending an evening working with homeless women at the Los Angeles Mission, Frann suffered a heart attack and was found dead in her bed by her longtime companion, John Cookman. An autopsy revealed that Frann was suffering from a previously undiagnosed condition that causes scarring of the heart muscle tissue. She was fifty-five.

The location of Frann's grave—which includes a currently unoccupied spot for Cookman—is one of the highest points in the cemetery, and is a good spot to look back toward the west and see the Pacific Ocean.

Frann was born Mary Frances Luecke on February 27, 1943, in St. Louis, Missouri. She died September 23, 1998, in Beverly Hills, California.

Head back toward the main entrance. As you pass Section Y on your right, you'll see Section AA, St. Patrick, on your left, then Section W, Holy Family. Turn down the road that separates Section AA and Section W, and look for the statue of the Holy Family in Section W, on your right. About fifty feet behind and a little to the right of the statue, about twenty feet from the road, in Tier 53, Lot 37, you'll find the grave of Owen Patrick McNulty, better known as singer **Dennis Day (1916–1988)**, a regular on *The Jack Benny Show* on both radio and television from the 1930s to the 1950s, also known as "America's favorite Irish tenor."

After graduating from college in New York City, Day was planning to enroll in law school when he decided to send a recording of his songs to Jack Benny's wife, Mary Livingstone, in 1939. Livingstone convinced Benny to give Day a two-week tryout on their radio show, and Day ended up working with Benny for nearly twenty-five years. Day's character, innocent but harebrained, would typically engage in comedically frustrating conversations with Benny, until the exasperated Benny would say, "Oh, for heaven's sake, Dennis, just sing!" And Day, with his smooth Irish tenor voice, would sing an Irish ballad or a foot-tapping rendition of "MacNamara's Band." Day also starred on his own radio program, *A Day in the Life of Dennis Day,* from 1946 to 1951, and his own television show, *The Dennis Day Show,* which debuted in 1953 and lasted for one season.

Day made his film debut in *Buck Benny Rides Again* (1940), costarring with Benny and many of the regular performers from his radio show. He also appeared in *The Powers Girl* (1942), *Sleepy Lagoon* (1943), *Music in Manhattan* (1944), *Make Mine Laughs* (1949), *I'll Get By* (1950), *Golden Girl*

(1951), and *The Girl Next Door* (1953). He also provided his voice in several animated films, including *Melody Time* (1948), *Johnny Appleseed* (1948), and *Frosty's Winter Wonderland* (1976).

Day continued to perform until shortly before his death, singing at conventions, fairs, and clubs. In his later years, he would sing from a wheelchair, and he also often performed with his sister-in-law, actress Ann Blyth.

Day legally changed his name from Owen Patrick McNulty in 1944, but changed it back three years later, though he always performed as Dennis Day. His grave marker includes both his birth name and his professional name.

Day was born Owen Patrick McNulty on May 21, 1916
(some sources say 1917), in New York City.
He died June 22, 1988, in Los Angeles.

6

Hillside Memorial Park

~

6001 West Centinela Avenue
Los Angeles, California 90045

~ *HISTORY*

In 1941, ten leaders of the Los Angeles–area Jewish community pooled their resources to finance the purchase of forty acres to be used as a cemetery. Hillside Memorial Park was officially opened for business five years later.

The most visible landmark at Hillside, one that can easily be seen by drivers passing on the nearby San Diego Freeway (405), is the memorial to singer Al Jolson, which features a large dome atop six white marble columns and a 120-foot water-fall. Jolson's body was moved here when the memorial was completed in 1951, nearly a year after his death. The three-story main mausoleum, located behind the Jolson memorial, was also completed in 1951. The north wing of the mausoleum was added in 1961.

In the early 1950s, the Garden of Memories, an outdoor garden mausoleum, was built at the western edge of the cemetery property. A few years later, the ceme-tery was purchased by Temple Israel of Hollywood, a reform congregation based in Los Angeles. During the 1960s and 1970s, Hillside added the first two-story garden mausoleum built in the United States, behind the main mausoleum. The cemetery's mortuary was opened in 1980.

The cemetery is currently making plans for a new five-thousand-crypt mau-soleum at the northeastern corner of the property. The project, to be called the Garden of the Matriarchs and covering more than two acres, will include a three-story, sky-lit mausoleum, surrounding gardens, a meditative pavilion, and a stone fountain. It is scheduled to be completed in 2005.

Hillside Memorial Park is also one of the friendliest cemeteries in Los Angeles for celebrity-hunters. Visitors who stop in the main office to ask for a map of the grounds will be assisted by a helpful receptionist, who will also hand you a two-page list of many of the cemetery's notable "permanent residents," along with brief biographies and grave locations. Are you listening, Forest Lawn?

~ *DIRECTIONS*

Hillside Memorial Park is located next to the San Diego Freeway (405), about four and a half miles south of the Santa Monica Freeway (10). From either direction on the San Diego Freeway, exit at Howard Hughes Parkway. Follow the exit road to Sepulveda Boulevard and turn right. After the turn, the second signal light will be Centinela Avenue. Turn right on Centinela, drive under the freeway, and look for the cemetery on your left.

~ *HOURS*

The cemetery is open from 8 A.M. to 5 P.M., Sunday through Friday. The mausoleum is open from 8 A.M. to 4:30 P.M. The cemetery is closed on Saturday.

~

The Tour

The tour starts with the spectacular memorial to singer **Al Jolson (1886–1950)**, located on the right as you pass through the main gates, just past the administrative offices. You literally can't miss it.

Jolson, the son of immigrants, first sang in front of an audience as a child in the synagogue where his father was a cantor. Jolson later performed with a circus, then in nightclubs and in vaudeville, often in blackface makeup. He quickly rose to stardom on Broadway. His first film appearance was in *Mammy's Boy* (1923), written and directed by D. W. Griffith, but the film was never completed. Jolson next appeared in *A Plantation Act* (1926), wearing overalls and blackface and singing three songs on the accompanying soundtrack. This film was thought to be lost for many years until it turned up, mislabeled, in the 1990s in the Library of Congress.

Jolson's next film appearance made history. In the mid-1920s, the Warner Bros. studio was making plans for the first film with synchronized sound. Up to this point, silent films were usually accompanied by an organist or other musicians in each theater. As an experiment, Warner Bros. added a musical score, performed by the New York Philharmonic orchestra, to *Don Juan* (1926), starring John Barrymore. The score was recorded on records and synchronized with the film projectors. After an overwhelmingly positive audience response, Warner Bros. paid $50,000 for the rights to a popular Broadway play about a singing rabbi called *The Jazz Singer*. Though George Jessel starred in the play, the Warners hired Jolson for the film version, and decided to record the performers actually singing instead of just adding music later to the film. *The Jazz Singer* was basically planned as a silent film, with occasional musical performances. During the filming, Jolson prefaced a song with the statement "Wait a minute, wait a minute. You ain't heard nothing yet!"—the first spoken words in a film. When *The Jazz Singer* (1927) was released, the "talking picture" was born. With the expensive sound equipment—and Jolson's $75,000 salary—*The Jazz Singer* cost $500,000 to make, but netted $3 million in profits.

Despite the financial and critical success of *The Jazz Singer*, other studios were slow to embrace the new technology. Even Warner Bros. didn't completely abandon their silent films. But Jolson had become an international sensation. He followed *The Jazz Singer* with appearances in *The Singing Fool*

Al Jolson's memorial at Hillside Memorial Park features a white marble dome and a 120-foot waterfall.

The inside of the dome above Jolson's grave features a mosaic of Moses and identifies Jolson as "The Sweet Singer of Israel."

(1928), *Sonny Boy* (1929), *Say It With Songs* (1929), *Big Boy* (1930), *Mammy* (1930), and *Hallelujah, I'm a Bum* (1933). Though a talented singer and entertainer, Jolson left something to be desired as an actor. When audiences grew tired of his thematic films, Jolson returned to the stage and radio perfor-mances. But in 1945 Jolson returned to the screen, play-ing himself, in the George Gershwin biography, *Rhap-sody in Blue* (1945).

When Columbia decided to make his biography the following year, Jolson was forced to take a screen test to see if he would be able to play himself. When the deci-sion was made that the fifty-nine-year-old Jolson was probably too old for the film, which focused on Jolson's early career, the part was given to Larry Parks. Jolson recorded the songs for the film and Parks lip-synched them, but Jolson did appear as himself onscreen in some long shots of stage performances. *The Jolson Story* (1946) was a huge success, and Parks was nominated for an Academy Award as Best Actor. Columbia released a sequel, *Jolson Sings Again* (1949), with Parks again in the title role and Jolson again supplying the vocals as well as making a brief appearance in the film.

During World War II and the Korean War, Jolson also kept busy enter-taining U.S. troops around the world. Shortly after returning from a trip to

Korea in October 1950, Jolson was playing gin rummy with friends in the St. Francis Hotel in San Francisco when he suffered a fatal heart attack. Jolson died in Room 1221 at the hotel—the same room where Virginia Rappe was allegedly attacked by comedian Roscoe "Fatty" Arbuckle in September 1921. (For more on Rappe and Arbuckle, see Chapter 3.)

An estimated twenty thousand people showed up at Temple Israel on Hollywood Boulevard for Jolson's funeral services. George Jessel delivered a memorable eulogy—despite the fact that Jolson had once told his wife that he specifically didn't want Jessel to speak at his funeral. Jolson was first buried at Beth Olam Cemetery, a small Jewish cemetery that was part of Hollywood Memorial Park, until a more appropriate burial site could be prepared. Jessel, Jack Benny, and Eddie Cantor were among Jolson's pallbearers—and all would eventually join him at Hillside Memorial Park.

Jolson's widow, Erle, purchased a plot at Hillside for $9,000 and paid another $75,000 for the monument, which was designed by architect Paul Williams. The six-pillar marble structure is topped by a dome, next to a three-quarter-size bronze statue of Jolson, eternally resting on one knee, arms outstretched, apparently ready to break into another verse of "Mammy." The inside of the dome features a huge mosaic of Moses holding the tablets containing the Ten Commandments, and identifies Jolson as "The Sweet Singer of Israel" and "The Man Raised Up High."

Erle said Jolson once told her that he wanted to be buried near a waterfall, so the cemetery management provided the 120-foot, blue-tiled cascade of water. There was some public discussion at the time as to whether Jolson's monument was a little too much, a little too ostentatious, even for the man who described himself as the "World's Greatest Entertainer." A columnist for the *Los Angeles Mirror* wrote that the memorial was in bad taste. But others have said the memorial was an appropriate match for Jolson's healthy ego.

It's also interesting to note that the memorial for Jolson, who often performed in blackface, was designed by one of the first well-known black architects in southern California. Though Paul Williams was best known for designing homes for celebrities—his client list included Lon Chaney, Lucille Ball and Desi Arnaz, Bert Lahr, Tyrone Power, Barbara Stanwyck, Zsa Zsa Gabor, and Frank Sinatra—he also designed the spider-shaped building at the center of Los Angeles International Airport, the Knickerbocker Hotel in Los Angeles, and the Pearl Harbor Memorial in Honolulu.

Jolson's body was moved to Hillside on September 23, 1951, nearly a year after his death, and another memorial service was held. This time, Jack Benny delivered the eulogy.

Because of his work entertaining U.S. troops, Jolson was posthumously awarded the Civilian Order of Merit by President Harry Truman.

Jolson was born Asa Yoelson on May 26, 1886, in Srednik, Lithuania. He died October 23, 1950, in San Francisco, California.

Directly behind the Jolson monument is a three-level mausoleum housing thousands of individual and family crypts. Inside the brightly lit and inviting structure are wide hallways decorated in marble and wood, with comfortable sofas and chairs to create a home-like atmosphere. The gold-and-white overhead lamps feature a Star of David design, and most of the crypts are decorated with artificial flowers.

Just inside the main doors of the mausoleum is the Rotunda of Adoration. On the opposite side of the rotunda are two doors leading to the Memorial Court, a small, open garden area. Walk through the door on the left. About twenty feet from the door on the left side, in the first space up from the ground, you'll find the crypt of **David Janssen (1931–1980),** best known as the star of the 1960s television series *The Fugitive.*

Fans who remember Janssen as the dark, brooding, gravelly voiced star of several television series from the 1950s through the 1970s might find it hard to believe that he actually started his career as a child actor. Janssen made his film debut in a bit part in *It's a Pleasure* (1945), starring Sonja Henie. He appeared in supporting roles in a series of films in the late 1940s and 1950s, usually playing a soldier or college student, including *Swamp Fire* (1946), *Yankee Buccaneer* (1952), *No Room for the Groom* (1952), *Bonzo Goes to College* (1952), *Chief Crazy Horse* (1955), *To Hell and Back* (1955), *The Private War of Major Benson* (1955), *The Square Jungle* (1955), and *The Toy Tiger* (1956). Janssen also appeared in three films starring Francis, the talking mule—*Francis Goes to West Point* (1952), *Francis in the Navy* (1955), and *Francis in the Haunted House* (1956).

In 1957, Janssen landed the title role as *Richard Diamond, Private Detective,* playing a suave private investigator, ably assisted by his unseen secretary, Sam, played by Mary Tyler Moore in her first television series. After three years as Richard Diamond, Janssen took the title role as Dr. Richard Kimble, an innocent man convicted of murdering his wife, in *The Fugitive,* which debuted in 1963. Loosely based on the case of Dr. Sam Shepard, the series followed Janssen as he searched for the one-armed man who killed his wife while eluding the police lieutenant obsessed with his capture. The series finale in August 1967, in which Janssen finally catches the one-armed man, attracted the highest ratings of any single episode of a television series in history; 72 percent of the viewing public tuned in—a record that stood for thirteen years before being topped by the "Who Shot J.R.?" episode of *Dallas* in 1980. The only other regularly scheduled series to attract a larger audience was the final episode of *M*A*S*H* in 1983.

Janssen also starred in the television series *O'Hara, U.S. Treasury* from 1971 to 1972, and *Harry O* from 1974 to 1976, as well as more than forty made-for-television movies. On the big screen, Janssen starred in *The Green Berets* (1968), *Marooned* (1969), *Two-Minute Warning* (1976), and *Inchon* (1982).

Janssen died of a sudden heart attack at the age of forty-eight. His black marble crypt contains the inscription "My love is with you always."

Janssen was born David Harold Meyer on March 27, 1931, in Naponee, Nebraska. He died February 13, 1980, in Malibu, California.

Four spaces above Janssen's crypt you'll find the crypt of entertainer **George Jessel (1898–1981),** known as America's "Toastmaster General."

Jessel began singing professionally at the age of nine and two years later he was performing in vaudeville with Eddie Cantor. Though he made a few appearances in silent comedies, Jessel gained fame in nightclubs and on Broadway, where he starred in *The Jazz Singer.* In the 1930s and 1940s, Jessel appeared in supporting roles in several musicals, usually playing himself, including *Happy Days* (1930), *Stage Door Canteen* (1943), *Four Jills in a Jeep* (1944), and *Show Business* (1944). Jessel also hosted several musical variety television series in the early 1950s.

Because of his frequent role as master of ceremonies at various entertainment and political gatherings, he was given the nickname "Toastmaster General," which appears on his crypt.

Jessel was born April 3, 1898, in New York City. He died May 24, 1981, in Los Angeles.

About thirty feet past Janssen and Jessel, in the very top row, you'll find the crypt of comedian **Dick Shawn (1923–1987).**

Shawn made his film debut in a small role as a singer in *The Opposite Sex* (1956) and gained fame for his role as Sylvester, the manic son of Ethel Merman, in *It's a Mad Mad Mad Mad World* (1963). Shawn also appeared in the Mel Brooks comedy *The Producers* (1968), playing an actor who stars in a musical based on the life of Adolf Hitler.

On April 17, 1987, Shawn was performing his one-man show, *The Second Funniest Man in the World,* at the University of California—San Diego when he suffered a heart attack and collapsed onstage. Many audience members thought it was part of his act, and Shawn lay on the stage for nearly five minutes before someone finally checked on him and called for an ambulance. He died less than an hour later.

Shawn's crypt contains this humble inscription: "The greatest entertainer, father and friend in the whole wide world."

Shawn was born Richard Schulefand on December 1, 1923
(some sources say 1929), in Buffalo, New York.
He died April 17, 1987, in San Diego, California.

At the far end of the Memorial Court is a doorway leading to another, smaller courtyard area with a small, gurgling fountain in the center and private alcoves along the walls. In this area, in the fourth alcove on the left, you'll find the crypt of producer, director, and actor **Michael Landon (1936–1991),** best known as Little Joe Cartwright on the long-running Western series *Bonanza.*

Landon, the son of a film publicist and a Broadway comedian, came to southern California after winning an athletic scholarship to the University of Southern California as a javelin thrower. When a torn ligament in his shoulder ended his athletic aspirations, he turned to acting and made his film debut in the title role in *I Was a Teenage Werewolf* (1957). After appearing in supporting roles in a handful of films, including *God's Little Acre* (1958) and *High School Confidential* (1958), he joined the cast of *Bonanza* in 1959, playing one of three sons in the Cartwright clan. *Bonanza* was among the top-ten most popular series from 1961 to 1970, including three seasons as the number one show on television.

When the *Bonanza* run ended in 1973, Landon immediately moved to another successful series, as executive producer, director, writer, and star of *Little House on the Prairie,* based on the popular *Little House* book series by Laura Ingalls-Wilder. After that series ended in 1983, Landon was executive producer, director, and star of *Highway to Heaven* from 1984 to 1989, making Landon the only actor to star in three consecutive long-running television series.

Landon died of liver and pancreatic cancer in 1991 at the age of fifty-four. His grave marker reads: "He seized life with joy. He gave to live generously. He leaves a legacy of love and laughter."

*Landon was born Eugene Maurice Orowitz on
October 31, 1936, in Forest Hills, New York.
He died July 1, 1991, in Malibu, California.*

Past the courtyard area is a larger, outdoor garden crypt area, known as the Courts of the Book. About sixty feet past Landon's alcove, on the right side, you'll find the crypts of **Max Factor Sr. (1877–1938),** who founded the makeup empire that bears his name, and his son **Max Factor Jr. (1904–1996),** the makeup artist to the stars who invented many popular cosmetic products still in use by women around the world. Together, they literally changed the face of the movies and the face of America.

The elder Factor started as an apprentice to a wig-maker in his native Russia. After serving four years in the Russian army, he opened a small cosmetics shop in a suburb of Moscow. By the time he was twenty, he had been appointed the official cosmetics expert for the Russian royal family and the Imperial Russian Grand Opera. In 1904, Factor came to the United States, settling in St. Louis and opening a cosmetics shop. He moved to Hollywood in 1908, where he developed special makeup for use in films. Factor discovered that the traditional greasepaint makeup used in theaters looked flat onscreen, so he developed special pancake makeup, false eyelashes, eyebrow pencil, and lip gloss to make actresses look more stylish. Factor's makeup was available in many shades, was lighter than greasepaint, and did not crack or peel under the hot studio lights. Many of the actresses were so impressed with their new look that they began wearing Factor's makeup offscreen. In 1927, Factor introduced the first line of cosmetics for non-theatrical consumers.

When Factor died in 1938, his son Francis—who changed his name to Max Factor Jr.—took over as president of the Max Factor Co. and continued to develop products for the screen as well as for the general public, including waterproof mascara and long-lasting lipstick. Factor used celebrities including Lana Turner, Veronica Lake, and Elizabeth Taylor in advertising to suggest that any women could look like a movie star with Max Factor makeup. Factor also developed special cosmetic formulas for use on television.

Max Sr. and Max Jr. were honored with a star on the Hollywood Walk of Fame in 1969. The Max Factor Co. continued to develop new consumer products through the 1960s and 1970s. Max Jr. and his brother, Davis, sold the company to Norton Simon Inc. in 1973 for $480 million. The company changed hands several more times before it was acquired by Procter & Gamble in 1991 as part of a $1 billion deal with Revlon.

Max Factor Sr. was originally buried in Hollywood Memorial Park, now known as Hollywood Forever, but his body was moved to its current location when family members were concerned about the deteriorating condition of the cemetery.

Max Factor Sr. was born Max Faktor in 1877 (some sources say 1872 or 1874), in Lodz, Russia—now part of Poland. He died August 30, 1938, in Beverly Hills, California.

Max Factor Jr. was born Francis Factor on August 18, 1904, in St. Louis, Missouri. He died June 7, 1996, in Los Angeles.

About 120 feet past the Factors' crypt, along the same wall, in the second space up from the floor, V-247, you'll find the crypt of singer **Dinah Shore (1916–1994).**

Shore began her career as a singer on the radio in Tennessee and went to New York City in 1938 to perform and record with bandleader Xavier Cugat. Shore attempted to make the transition to films in the early 1940s, appearing in *Thank Your Lucky Stars* (1943), *Up in Arms* (1944), *Follow the Boys* (1944), *Belle of the Yukon* (1944), and *Till the Clouds Roll By* (1947), but without much critical or commercial success. In 1951, she tried television, as host of *The Dinah Shore Show*—she was the first woman to host her own prime-time television variety show. She hosted various prime-time and daytime variety and music shows, and she was a popular fixture on television until 1980.

Shore was nominated for Emmy awards seventeen times between 1954 and 1981; she won eight of them.

Shore's crypt contains the inscription "Loved by all who knew her and millions who never did."

Shore was born Frances Rose Shore on February 29, 1916 (some sources say 1917), in Winchester, Tennessee. She died February 24, 1994, in Beverly Hills, California.

About thirty feet directly in front of Shore's crypt, on the lawn, you'll find the grave of actor **Lorne Greene (1915–1987)**, best known as Ben Cartwright, the patriarch of the Ponderosa ranch on the long-running Western series *Bonanza*.

After a successful career as the top newscaster in Canada, at radio station CBO in Ottawa, Greene came to Hollywood and made his film debut as Saint Peter in *The Silver Chalice* (1954). After appearing in supporting roles in *Autumn Leaves* (1956), *Peyton Place* (1957), and *The Buccaneer* (1958), Greene won the role of Ben Cartwright on *Bonanza*, which debuted in 1959. Greene was only thirteen years older than two of the actors who played his sons—Dan Blocker and Pernell Roberts—and only twenty-one years older than his third son—Michael Landon—but his deep, authoritative voice and silver hair made him convincing in the role. *Bonanza* wasn't a traditional Western in that problems weren't usually solved with gunfire. Instead, the show explored the relationships within the Cartwright family and the problems and issues they faced in the out-side world, and episodes usually ended with Greene helping his sons learn a valuable life lesson.

Lorne Greene's grave marker identifies him as the "world's best loved father—Ben Cartwright."

After *Bonanza* ended in 1973, Greene starred in the television series *Griff* from 1973 to 1974, *Battlestar Galactica* from 1978 to 1980, and *Code Red* from 1981 to 1982. Greene also had a relatively successful, if often ridiculed, recording career. His spoken-word recording of "Ringo" reached number one on the *Billboard* charts in 1964.

Greene's grave marker identifies him as "The world's best loved father, Ben Cartwright" and "The great voice of Canada."

Greene was born February 12, 1915, in Ottawa, Ontario, Canada.
He died September 11, 1987, in Santa Monica, California.

Go back to the courtyard containing Landon's alcove. On the opposite wall is a door leading back into the mausoleum. About ten feet past the door, on the left, in the second space up from the floor, you'll find the crypt of banjo-eyed singer and actor **Eddie Cantor (1892–1964).**

Cantor started performing as a teenager, including a stint as a singing waiter at Coney Island, New York. He became a popular vaudeville and Broadway performer with appearances in the Ziegfeld Follies and shows including *The Midnight Frolics, Kid Boots,* and *Whoopee.* Cantor made his screen debut in a filmed version of *Kid Boots* (1926), but he didn't achieve real screen stardom until talkies allowed him to sing. Cantor brought another of his Broadway shows to the screen with *Whoopee* (1930), a Technicolor spectacular featuring lavish Busby Berkeley–staged production numbers hung on a scant story line. Most of Cantor's subsequent films followed a similar theme, including *Palmy Days* (1931), *The Kid From Spain* (1932), *Roman Scandals* (1933), *Kid Millions* (1934), and *Strike Me Pink* (1936).

Cantor, who served as president of the Screen Actors Guild from 1933 to 1935, appeared in few films after the 1930s, but he did host a successful radio show and continued to perform onstage and occasionally on television from the early 1950s. Cantor is also credited with coming up with the name "March of Dimes" for the donation campaign for the National Foundation for Infantile Paralysis, a play on the popular "March of Time" newsreels. He launched the first campaign on his radio show in January 1938, asking people to mail a dime to the nation's most famous polio victim, President Franklin D. Roosevelt. Other entertainers joined the appeal on their own radio shows, and the White House mailroom was deluged with 2,680,000 dimes.

Cantor wrote four volumes of his memoirs—*My Life Is in Your Hands, Take My Life, The Way I See It,* and *As I Remember Them.* In 1957, he was given a special Academy Award, "for distinguished service to the film industry."

Cantor is buried with his wife, Ida Tobias Cantor (1892–1962), who was immortalized in the song "Ida, Sweet as Apple Cider," and their daughters, Marjorie Cantor (1915–1959) and Natalie Cantor Clary (1916–1997).

Cantor was born Edward Israel Iskowitz on January 31, 1892, in New York City, New York. He died October 10, 1964, in Beverly Hills, California.

About twenty feet past Cantor's crypt, you'll find the large black marble sarcophagus containing the remains of one of America's best-known and best-loved comedians, **Jack Benny (1894–1974).**

Benny was born in Chicago and grew up in the suburb of Waukegan, Illinois. When he started performing as a violinist in vaudeville under his real name, Benjamin Kubelsky, another violinist named Jan Kubelik asked him to change his name to avoid confusion. So Benny changed his name to Ben Benny, until bandleader and violinist Ben Bernie asked him to change it again for the same reason, and he became Jack Benny. In 1911, at the age of seventeen, Benny was playing the violin in the pit orchestra at a vaudeville theater in Waukegan for $7.50 per week, when the Marx Brothers brought their act to town. The Marxes offered to double Benny's salary if he would travel with them, playing the violin and conducting the pit orchestra. Benny initially accepted the offer, but his parents wouldn't allow him to go.

Though Benny was actually a talented violinist, he added comedy to his act during a performance in front of a group of sailors while serving in the navy. His audience wasn't too appreciative of classical music, so Benny ad-libbed a few jokes. Based on the response, he gradually replaced his music with comedy, even though he often used his violin as a comedy prop in his act, usually scratching out his theme song, "Love in Bloom." Benny also developed his image as a miserly penny pincher from his early vaudeville act. One of Benny's favorite jokes was based on that reputation: A hold-up man

Radio and television legend Jack Benny is buried with his wife, Mary, in the mausoleum at Hillside Memorial Park

approaches Benny, points a gun at him and demands, "Your money or your life." After a long pause, the hold-up man gets impatient. "C'mon, hurry up," he says. "I'm thinking it over," Benny replies. Despite his image, Benny was considered one of the most modest and generous men in show business.

Benny met Sadie Marks during his vaudeville years, and they were married in Waukegan in 1927. (Despite some reports to the contrary, Marks was not related to the Marx Brothers.) One night, when Benny's partner became ill, he persuaded Sadie to fill in onstage, even though she had no performing experience. She played a character named Mary Livingstone, which she later changed to her legal name, and she became a permanent part of Benny's act.

After performing on Broadway and in a few films—including *Chasing Rainbows* (1930), *The Medicine Man* (1930), and a handful of comedy shorts—Benny made his radio debut on Ed Sullivan's show in New York City in March 1932. A few months later, he had his own show, and he gradually added a supporting cast, including his wife, Mary; his valet, Eddie "Rochester" Anderson; bandleader Phil Harris; singer Dennis Day; announcer Don Wilson; and Mel Blanc as the "voice" of Benny's Maxwell automobile, among other characters. *The Jack Benny Show*, with various sponsors over the years, was a Sunday night radio staple for an incredible twenty-three years, finally ending its long run in 1955.

Benny's guests on the show included just about every major Hollywood star, including Humphrey Bogart, Lauren Bacall, George Jessel, Tony Curtis, James Stewart, Bing Crosby, Frank Sinatra, Groucho Marx, Bob Hope, Ronald Coleman, Al Jolson, Eddie Cantor, Red Skelton, Gene Kelly, Tyrone Power, Claudette Colbert, Edward G. Robinson, Peter Lorre, Ray Milland, Alan Ladd, Gary Cooper, Orson Welles, Barbara Stanwyck, and Joan Crawford. As a comedian, Benny was unique. With his ensemble cast and frequent guest stars, Benny usually played straight man and let his fellow performers get the biggest laughs.

While performing regularly on radio, Benny continued to make the occasional film appearance, including starring roles in *Artists and Models* (1937), *Charley's Aunt* (1941), *To Be or Not To Be* (1942), *George Washington Slept Here* (1942), and *The Horn Blows at Midnight* (1945). After a long and successful career on radio, Benny brought his show and supporting cast to television in 1950, and the series remained popular for fifteen years. In fact, his show was on both radio and television at the same time for five years. Benny also hosted dozens of television specials and variety shows from 1959 to 1974.

In 1961, Benny returned to his hometown of Waukegan to dedicate Jack Benny Junior High School, where the school sports teams are still known as the "'39ers" in his honor—one of Benny's long-running gags was insisting that he was never older than thirty-nine. Benny, a high school dropout, called the dedication of the school "the proudest moment of my life."

Benny continued to work through the 1960s and early 1970s, appearing regularly on television and making cameo appearances in films including *Gypsy* (1962), *It's a Mad Mad Mad Mad World* (1963), and *The Man* (1972). Benny was scheduled to costar with Red Skelton in the film version of Neil Simon's *The Sunshine Boys* (1975), as a pair of cantankerous old ex–vaudeville stars. Shortly after production was scheduled to begin, Skelton dropped out of the project and was replaced by Walter Matthau. When Benny died the day after Christmas 1974, his part was given to George Burns, who won the Academy Award as Best Supporting Actor for his performance.

The day after Benny died, a single, long-stemmed red rose was delivered to Mary Livingstone Benny, his wife of nearly forty-eight years. Another arrived the next day, and the next. Mary called the florist to find out who was sending them. The florist told her that Benny had made arrangements for a rose to be sent to her every day for the rest of her life, and he had included a provision in his will for the deliveries—a touching and romantic final gesture for a man born on Valentine's Day.

Benny's sarcophagus contains the simple inscription "A gentle man."

Buried with Benny is his wife, **Mary Livingstone Benny (1906–1983)**, his costar on both his radio and television shows.

Benny was born Benjamin Kubelsky on February 14, 1894, in Chicago, Illinois. He died December 26, 1974, in Los Angeles.

Mary Livingstone Benny was born Sadie Marks on June 23, 1906, in Seattle, Washington. She died June 30, 1983, in Los Angeles.

About twenty feet past the Bennys' sarcophagus, turn left just before the door heading back outside. On both sides of the hallway you'll see dozens of niches containing cremated remains. On the left side in the far right column, in the eighth space up from the floor, you'll find the remains of rubber-limbed, sad-faced comedian **Ben Blue (1901–1975)**.

A vaudeville dancer and comedian, Blue appeared in dozens of comedy shorts for various studios in the late 1920s and 1930s. Later, he provided the comic relief in dozens of films, usually musicals, including *For Me and My Gal* (1942), *Panama Hattie* (1942), *Thousands Cheer* (1943), *Two Girls and a Sailor* (1944), *Easy to Wed* (1946), *My Wild Irish Rose* (1947), *It's a Mad Mad Mad Mad World* (1963), *The Russians Are Coming, the Russians Are Coming* (1966), and *Where Were You When the Lights Went Out?* (1968).

Blue was born Benjamin Bernstein on September 12, 1901, in Montreal, Quebec, Canada. He died March 7, 1975, in Los Angeles.

Outside the mausoleum, at the far northern edge of the cemetery property, in the Canaan Section, is a long wall of garden crypts. Slightly to the left of the center of the wall, in space E-249, you'll find the crypt of animator **Isadore "Friz" Freleng (1906–1995).**

After working for several years as an animator for Walt Disney in the late 1920s, Freleng joined the animation staff at Warner Bros., where he remained for most of his career. Though Freleng wasn't known for his wild or wacky cartoons, he was a versatile animator who worked successfully with all the characters at Warner Bros., from Bugs Bunny and Daffy Duck, to Speedy Gonzales and Yosemite Sam—a character reportedly based on the diminutive and sometimes hot-tempered Freleng.

One of Freleng's specialties was musical cartoons, and his most popular was *Rhapsody in Rivits* (1941), which features a skyscraper being built to the musical accompaniment of Liszt's Second Hungarian Rhapsody. One of Freleng's most imaginative cartoons was *You Ought to Be in Pictures* (1940), which combined live action and animation as Daffy Duck convinces Porky Pig to quit his job as a cartoon actor to become a leading man. While Porky is off getting into trouble throughout the studio, Daffy tries to steal Porky's old job.

Freleng's crypt contains the inscription "He shared his talent with the world," and it features several of Warner Bros. best-known characters, including Bugs Bunny, Daffy Duck, Porky Pig, Elmer Fudd, Tweety Bird, Yosemite Sam, Sylvester, and Speedy Gonzales, all dressed in tuxedos in a high-kicking chorus line.

Freleng was born August 21, 1906, in Kansas City, Missouri. He died May 26, 1995, in Los Angeles.

North of the main entrance to the cemetery, along the western edge of the cemetery property, is the Garden of Memories, a large section of garden mausoleums. At the southern edge of this area, near the cemetery chapel, is a walkway into the Court of Love, which leads into a large courtyard area. At the opposite side of the courtyard is another walkway, leading to a smaller, triangular-shaped courtyard. On the far wall of this courtyard, in the second space up from the ground, space C-233, you'll find the crypt of the leader of the Three Stooges, **Moe Howard (1897–1975).**

In 1922, Howard and his brother Shemp teamed up with a boyhood friend, vaudeville comedian Ted Healy, in a slapstick comedy act called "Ted Healy and His Stooges." Violinist Larry Fine was added as the third Stooge in 1925. After appearing in several successful shows on Broadway, Healy and the Stooges came to Hollywood in 1930 to make two-reel comedies, and Shemp was replaced by another Howard brother, Jerome—better known as Curly.

Healy and the Stooges went their separate ways in 1934, with the Stooges signing a contract to make comedy shorts for Columbia Pictures. The Three Stooges made nearly 200 two-reelers for Columbia, and they were among the most popular and profitable film performers of the 1930s, 1940s, and 1950s, even though they were never able to convince Columbia to allow them to star in a feature-length film. The Stooges shorts basically consisted of any excuse for madcap, cartoonish violence, usually initiated by Moe Howard, including slaps, punches, and pokes in the eye, and hits on the head with everything from brooms and shovels to sledgehammers and crowbars. After Curly died in 1952, Shemp re-joined the act until his death three years later. Shemp was replaced by Joe Besser from 1956 to 1958, then Joe DeRita, who was known as Curly-Joe.

Columbia terminated the Stooges' contract in 1958, but the team enjoyed a popular revival with a new generation of fans when their shorts started to be shown on television in the late 1950s. With their new popularity, the Stooges finally got the chance to star in their first feature-length film—*Have Rocket, Will Travel* (1959). They followed that with *Snow White and the Three Stooges* (1961), *The Three Stooges Meet Hercules* (1962), *The Three Stooges Go Around the World in a Daze* (1963), and *The Outlaws Is Coming* (1965). The Stooges also appeared in bit parts in *Four for Texas* (1963), a Western starring Dean Martin and Frank Sinatra, and *It's a Mad Mad Mad Mad World* (1963).

The final Three Stooges film was *Kook's Tour* (1970), which featured the Stooges and their dog on a camping trip. During the final days of filming, Fine suffered a stroke and was unable to complete the film. Director Norman

Maurer attempted to salvage the film by adding additional scenes without Fine and narration by Moe Howard. The film was finally released on video in 1999.

Howard is buried with his wife, Helen Schonberger Howard (1899–1975). They were married in 1925.

Howard was born Moses Horwitz on June 19, 1897, in Brooklyn, New York. He died May 4, 1975, in Los Angeles.

7

Mount Sinai Memorial Park

~

5950 Forest Lawn Drive
Los Angeles, California 90068

~ HISTORY

Mount Sinai Memorial Park opened in 1953. It is adjacent to Forest Lawn–
Hollywood Hills, which opened in 1948. Mount Sinai, one of the largest Jewish
cemeteries in the Los Angeles area, covers eighty-two acres nestled against Griffith
Park and overlooking the nearby city of Burbank and the San Fernando Valley. The
cemetery is currently owned and operated by Sinai Temple of Los Angeles, which
purchased the property in 1964.

By the late 1990s, Mount Sinai was beginning to reach its capacity, with only a
few acres available for new burials. In response to this potential problem, a new
160-acre Mount Sinai Memorial Park was dedicated in Simi Valley, California, in
early 1997—the largest Jewish cemetery west of the Mississippi River.

Mount Sinai Memorial Park in Los Angeles was created to be an authentic
reflection of the Jewish experience, with the landscape designed to reflect images of
ancient Israel. The cemetery grounds are planted with cedars of Lebanon, acacia,
myrtle, and other trees and plants mentioned in the Bible.

The cemetery features a 146-foot-long, 28-foot-high "Heritage" mosaic mural,
depicting Jewish history in the United States from 1654 to the present day. The
mural, based on a painting by Neil Boyle, was completed in 1984. The cemetery
also includes a stark and dramatic "Memorial to the Six Million," in honor of the
victims of the Holocaust, which was created by Bernard Zakheim, a Jewish immigrant from Poland who came to the United States seeking political asylum in 1920.

Though he isn't buried here, Groucho Marx's remains made a brief visit to
Mount Sinai Memorial Park a few years after his death. Marx died in 1977, and his
ashes were placed in the mausoleum at Eden Memorial Park in Mission Hills,

A stark memorial to the six million victims of the Holocaust is located at Mount Sinai Memorial Park.

north of Los Angeles (see Chapter 11). In May 1982, his ashes were stolen from the mausoleum. They were discovered a few hours later at the gates of Mount Sinai, about twelve miles away.

~ DIRECTIONS

Mount Sinai Memorial Park is located next to Forest Lawn–Hollywood Hills, on Forest Lawn Drive. From downtown Los Angeles, take the Hollywood Freeway (101) north to Barham Boulevard. Take Barham north about a mile to Forest Lawn Drive and turn right. The cemetery gates are about a mile and a half down Forest Lawn Drive, on the right. Or take the Golden State Freeway (5) north, then west on the Ventura Freeway (134), and exit about a mile and a half down at Forest Lawn Drive. The cemetery gates are on Forest Lawn Drive, about a half-mile from the Ventura Freeway, on the left. Maps of the grounds are available at the main entrance.

~ HOURS

The grounds are open from 8:30 A.M. to 5 P.M., Sunday through Friday, and closed on Saturdays and all Jewish holidays.

~

The Tour

After you enter the main gates off Forest Lawn Drive, head south on Mount Sinai Drive toward the large mural in the Gardens of the Heritage, at the southwest corner of the cemetery property. Park in front of the mural, and walk up the sidewalk on the far right side of the Gardens of the Heritage area. About 150 feet from the road, 65 feet to the right of the mural and 10 feet to the left of the sidewalk, almost hidden behind a large sink and flower prepa- ration table, is the grave of **Phil Silvers (1911–1985),** best known as Sergeant Ernie Bilko in the long-running television series *The Phil Silvers Show* in the 1950s. His grave marker simply says, "Phil Silvers, Comedian."

Silvers started performing as a singer in vaudeville when he was eleven years old, then he joined Minsky's burlesque troupe as a comedian. He made his feature-film debut in *Hit Parade of 1941* (1940) and costarred with Jimmy Durante in *You're in the Army Now* (1941). Silvers typically played supporting roles in films for the next fifteen years, usually musicals or comedies, includ- ing *All Through the Night* (1942), *Roxie Hart* (1942), *A Lady Takes a Chance* (1943), *Coney Island* (1943), *Cover Girl* (1944), *Four Jills in a Jeep* (1944), *Diamond Horseshoe* (1945), *Summer Stock* (1950), *Top Banana* (1953), and *Lucky Me* (1954).

Silvers's career-defining break came when he landed the television role of Ernie Bilko, the lovable, backslapping con man who runs the motor pool at a small army base in Kansas. The show, which debuted in 1955, was originally called *You'll Never Get Rich.* After the first few episodes, it was renamed *The Phil Silvers Show.* In 1956, the series won Emmy Awards for Best Comedy Series, Best Writing, and Best Directing, and Silvers won Emmy Awards for Best Actor and Best Comedian.

After the series ended in 1959, Silvers played similar characters in films including *It's a Mad Mad Mad Mad World* (1963), *A Funny Thing Happened*

Phil Silvers left instruc- tions in his will for his grave marker to read simply, "Comedian."

on the Way to the Forum (1966), and *Buona Sera, Mrs. Campbell* (1968), as well as guest appearances on the television series *The Beverly Hillbillies* and *Gilligan's Island.*

In his will—a four-page, handwritten document signed less than two years before he died—Silvers requested that his funeral be held at Forest Lawn and that comedian Milton Berle deliver the eulogy. "I want a simple coffin and a small headstone inscribed 'Phil Silvers, Comedian,'" he wrote. "I request my funeral arrangements, coffin and headstone not to exceed the sum of $10,000. . . . I go to my God knowing at least as a comedian I was only one of a kind."

Silvers was born Philip Silversmith on May 11, 1911
(some sources say 1912), in Brooklyn, New York.
He died November 1, 1985, in Los Angeles.

From Silvers's grave, walk about twenty-five feet toward the mural and you'll see a wall filled with crypts and niches containing cremated remains. In the third column from the left and the seventh row up from the ground, just about at eye level, you'll find a small plaque marking the grave of **Norman Fell (1924–1998).** Though best known for playing the leering landlord, Stanley Roper, on the television series *Three's Company* and the short-lived spinoff series, *The Ropers,* in the late 1970s, Fell played supporting roles in dozens of dramatic and comedy films in the 1960s and early 1970s.

After studying at the prestigious Actors Studio in New York City, Fell's first roles were supporting parts on television drama series in the late 1950s, including *Perry Mason* and *The Untouchables.* Fell made his film debut in *Pork Chop Hill* (1959), and also appeared in *Ocean's Eleven* (1960), *Inherit the Wind* (1960), *PT 109* (1963), *It's a Mad Mad Mad Mad World* (1963), *The Killers* (1964), *Fitzwilly* (1967), *The Graduate* (1967), *Bullitt* (1968), *Catch-22* (1970), *Charley Varrick* (1973), and *Airport 1975* (1974).

In 1977, Fell took the role of Stanley Roper in the popular television comedy *Three's Company,* playing the landlord of roommates played by John Ritter, Joyce DeWitt, and Suzanne Somers. In 1979, Fell's character was popular enough to lead to a spinoff series, *The Ropers,* which lasted for only one season. Fell returned to *Three's Company* in 1981.

Throughout the 1970s, 1980s, and early 1990s, Fell appeared in several made-for-television movies, and also made guest appearances on dozens of dramatic and comedy television series, including, *Police Story; Rhoda; Starksy and Hutch; Cannon; The Streets of San Francisco; The Love Boat; Charlie's Angels; Murder, She Wrote; Matlock;* and *The Naked Truth,* and he even revived his Stanley Roper character for an episode of *Ellen* in 1997.

Fell's grave marker identifies him as "A greatly talented and romantic man."

Fell was born Norman Noah Fell on March 24, 1924, in Philadelphia, Pennsylvania. He died December 14, 1998, in Woodland Hills, California.

Walk back out toward the front of the mural, and walk all the way past it. Just beyond the mural is a walkway leading into a large courtyard area behind the mural, known as the Garden of the People of the Book. Turn right at the end of the mural, just past the picture of Albert Einstein, then turn right again. On the wall behind the mural in the fourth column from the right (column number 60), in the third space up from the bottom, you'll find the crypt of comedian **Totie Fields (1930–1978).**

Fields began her career as a singer on the radio when she was four years old, and by the time she was fourteen she was performing at resorts in New York's Catskill Mountains. After many years of playing in nightclubs and resorts on the East Coast, Fields was spotted by Ed Sullivan, who booked her for the first of more than forty appearances on his television show. In the early 1970s, Fields was a top nightclub act across the country, and made regular appearances on television variety shows, including 125 appearances on *The Mike Douglas Show.*

Her early act consisted primarily of the four-foot-ten, 190-pound Fields making jokes about her weight and appearance. In 1976, she entered a hospital for minor cosmetic surgery, and developed phlebitis in her leg; her leg had to be amputated. Shortly after, she suffered two heart attacks, breast cancer, and eye problems due to diabetes. But Fields continued to perform, first using a cane, then in a wheelchair, and the focus of her act switched to jokes about her medical problems.

Fields died after suffering a third heart attack at her home in Las Vegas in 1978 at the age of forty-eight—the day before she was scheduled to open a new show at the Sahara Hotel. She was originally buried in Las Vegas, but her body was moved to Mount Sinai in 1996, where she's buried next to her husband of twenty-seven years, George William Johnston, a former nightclub comedian who later became Fields's musical conductor. He died in 1995. The inscription on their crypt reads, "It Takes Two to Make One."

Fields was born Sophie Feldman on May 7, 1930, in Hartford, Connecticut. She died August 2, 1978, in Las Vegas, Nevada.

In the southeast corner of the courtyard is a stairway leading up to the second level. At the top of the stairs, go straight to the front of the courtyard area, then turn left. About seventy-five feet down on the right, directly above the main entrance in the middle of the courtyard, you'll see a section of white crypts with golden tiled borders. In this area, in column number 39, in the second row up from the bottom, you'll find the crypt of producer **Irwin Allen (1916–1991),** the "Master of Disaster."

Though most film producers have a few disasters on their professional résumés, Allen is best known as the producer of many *intentional* disaster films, including *The Poseidon Adventure* (1972) and *The Towering Inferno* (1974).

Allen started his career as a magazine editor and owner of an advertising agency before entering the film business in the late 1940s, writing, producing, and directing nature documentaries. Allen won the Academy Award for Best Documentary for *The Sea Around Us* (1951). Allen also produced and directed several science-based adventure films, including *The Story of Mankind* (1957), *The Lost World* (1960), *Voyage to the Bottom of the Sea* (1961), and *Five Weeks in a Balloon* (1962).

In 1964, Allen produced the television series based on *Voyage to the Bottom of the Sea,* and he followed that with three more adventure series—*Lost in Space* in 1965, *The Time Tunnel* in 1966, and *Land of the Giants* in 1968. Allen returned to the big screen with *The Poseidon Adventure,* the story of a luxury cruise ship capsized by a giant tidal wave, featuring an all-star cast, including Gene Hackman, Ernest Borgnine, Red Buttons, Carol Lynley, Shelley Winters, Jack Albertson, Roddy McDowall, Stella Stevens, and Leslie Nielsen. The film launched a series of disaster films in the 1970s, including another by Allen, *The Towering Inferno,* starring Paul Newman, Steve McQueen, William Holden, Faye Dunaway, Fred Astaire, Richard Chamberlain, Robert Wagner, Jennifer Jones, and Robert Vaughn. *The Towering Inferno* was nominated for an Academy Award for Best Picture.

Allen brought the disaster film to television with *Flood!* (1976) and *Fire!* (1977), but these films were generally considered disasters in more ways than one. Allen also produced and directed the equally unsuccessful big-screen disaster films *The Swarm* (1978) and *Beyond the Poseidon Adventure* (1979).

Allen's crypt includes a silhouette of a movie camera.

Allen was born June 12, 1916, in New York City.
He died November 2, 1991, in Santa Monica, California.

East of the Gardens of the Heritage area are two smaller enclosed courtyard areas known as the Courts of Tanach. In the first courtyard, in the far southeast corner of the lawn, you'll find the grave of Ellen Naomi Cohen, better known as singer **"Mama Cass" Elliot (1941–1974).**

Elliot started her singing career in the 1960s in the Greenwich Village area of New York City with folk groups including the Big Three and the Mugwumps. One of her fellow performers in the Mugwumps, Denny Doherty, introduced Elliot to John and Michelle Phillips, and they formed a new group called The Mamas and the Papas. The group, which mixed folk, rock, and pop music with a little touch of jazz, had a hit with their first song, "California Dreamin'," in 1965. The Mamas and the Papas had four gold albums, seven top-ten singles, and a 1966 Grammy Award for Best Single for "Monday, Monday." The group's other hits included, "I Saw Her Again," "Dedicated to the One I Love," "Go Where You Wanna Go," "Words of Love," "Dream a Little Dream of Me," "Words of Love," and "Creque Alley."

The Mamas and the Papas broke up in 1971, and Elliot launched a successful solo career. She released eight solo albums, appeared on numerous television shows, headlined in Las Vegas, and attempted to distance herself from her "Mama Cass" image and nickname.

While on a tour

Ellen Naomi Cohen's grave marker at Mount Sinai Memorial Park includes her professional name—Cass Elliot.

of the United Kingdom, after performing in two sold-out shows at the London Palladium, Elliot died at the age of thirty-two. Despite the oft-repeated story that Elliot choked to death on a ham sandwich, the actual, official cause of her death was a heart attack, probably caused by her lifelong obesity—she was five-foot-five and reportedly weighed 238 pounds at the time of her death— and several crash diets, which may have weakened her heart. A partially eaten ham sandwich was found by her bed, however, which led to the early specu- lation that she might have choked. By the time the official autopsy results were completed a week later, the ham sandwich story had become something of an urban legend.

Despite the fact that they were only together for a few years, The Mamas and the Papas were inducted into the Rock and Roll Hall of Fame in 1998.

Elliot's grave marker includes her birth name as well as her professional name—"Cass Elliot," not Mama Cass—flanked by musical notes.

Elliot was born Ellen Naomi Cohen on September 19, 1941, in Baltimore, Maryland. She died July 29, 1974, in London, England.

Walk out of the courtyard area and turn right, and you'll find a large open courtyard area between the two Courts of Tanach. In the southeast corner of this area, in the seventh column from the right, in the second row up from the bottom, in space 52250, you'll find the crypt of **Hershel Bernardi (1923–1986),** whose career ranged from Tony-nominated performances on Broadway, to a successful film and television career, to providing the voices for animated characters in television commercials.

Bernardi started his acting career performing with his parents in Yiddish stage productions, and he made his film debut in Yiddish productions of *The Singing Blacksmith* (1937) and *Green Fields* (1938). His English-speaking film debut was a small role in *Crime, Inc.* (1945). In the early 1950s, just as his film career was beginning, Bernardi was blacklisted in Hollywood for several years, due primarily to his enrollment in an actors' studio that also included some political radicals and Communists. Bernardi began working again in the late 1950s, taking the role of Lieutenant Jacoby on the *Peter Gunn* television series, which ran from 1958 to 1961. He starred in his own series, *Arnie*, from 1970 to 1972, playing a loading dock foreman who was promoted to a company executive. He was twice nominated for a Golden Globe Award as Best Actor for his performance in the series.

On the big screen, Bernardi played supporting roles in films including *The George Raft Story* (1961), *Irma la Douce* (1963), *Love With the Proper Stranger* (1963), *The Honey Pot* (1967), *No Deposit, No Return* (1976), and *The Front* (1976), a comedy about the Hollywood blacklists of the 1950s, which starred several other actors who were also real-life victims of the blacklist, including Zero Mostel. The film was written by Walter Bernstein and directed by Martin Ritt, who were also both blacklist victims.

On Broadway, Bernardi played Tevye in *Fiddler on the Roof* in more than 1,200 performances from 1965 to 1967, taking over the role from Mostel. In 1968, he starred in *Zorba!*, for which he received his first Tony Award nomination as Best Actor in a Musical. He was nominated again in 1982 for a revival of *Fiddler on the Roof*.

Bernardi also provided the voice for many animated commercial characters, including the Jolly Green Giant and Charlie, the StarKist tuna. Shortly before his death, Bernardi was honored by the tuna-canning company for his twenty-five years as the voice of Charlie.

Bernardi made guest appearances on various television series, including *Bonanza, Zorro, Naked City, The Untouchables, Route 66, The Fugitive,* and *Murder, She Wrote*. He made his final television appearance, appropriately enough, on an episode of *Highway to Heaven*, which aired less than two months before he died in 1986.

Bernardi was born October 20, 1923 (some sources say 1924), in New York City. He died May 9, 1986, in Los Angeles.

Directly north, across the road from the open courtyard, is a stairway leading down to the Garden of Shemot, a shady courtyard area with a large, Zodiac-themed tile mosaic in the center. Turn left at the bottom of the stairs and walk about 170 feet, nearly to the end of the courtyard area. Then turn right and walk about 60 feet across the lawn. Just before you reach the next sidewalk, next to a large tree, you'll find the grave of actor **Lee J. Cobb (1911–1976).**

Cobb was a child prodigy on the violin, but a broken wrist ended his plans for a musical career and he studied acting instead. At the age of seventeen, he left home in New York and headed to Hollywood to become a film actor. Cobb was unsuccessful in his first attempt at a film career, and he headed back to New York, where he performed in radio dramas and onstage.

Cobb returned to California a few years later and made his screen debut in an uncredited role in an adventure serial, *The Vanishing Shadow* (1934). Cobb next appeared as a villain in *North of the Rio Grande* (1937), a Western in the Hopalong Cassidy series. Cobb continued to land bit parts in minor adventures, mysteries, and Western serials, as well as a few major films, including *Golden Boy* (1939), *The Song of Bernadette* (1943), *Anna and the King of Siam* (1946), *Captain From Castile* (1947), *The Miracle of the Bells* (1948), and *Call Northside 777* (1948). Cobb returned to the New York stage in 1949, where he created the role of Willy Loman on Broadway in Arthur Miller's *Death of a Salesman*.

Cobb returned to Hollywood and was nominated for an Academy Award as Best Supporting Actor for his performance as union racketeer Johnny Friendly in *On the Waterfront* (1954). He was also nominated for the same award for his performance in *The Brothers Karamazov* (1958). Cobb often played villains and character roles in films throughout the 1950s and 1960s, including *The Man in the Gray Flannel Suit* (1956), *12 Angry Men* (1957), *The Three Faces of Eve* (1957), *Exodus* (1960), *How the West Was Won* (1962), *In Like Flint* (1967), and *Coogan's Bluff* (1968).

Cobb also was a regular on several television series, including *The Virginian* from 1962 to 1966, and *The Young Lawyers* from 1970 to 1971. One of his final film roles was in *The Exorcist* (1973).

Cobb's grave marker includes the inscription "Ay, every inch a king."

Cobb was born Leo Jacoby on December 8, 1911, in New York City. He died February 11, 1976, in Los Angeles.

Go back to Mount Sinai Drive and head east, toward the eastern edge of the cemetery. Past the large Courts of the Psalms area, on the right, you'll see a series of small, walled garden courtyards. Stop just past the intersection of Moriah Road. On the right side, look for a sidewalk located between the "Map C" and "D Map" markings on the curb. Walk about 50 feet up the sidewalk, turn right and walk about 10 feet, then turn left and walk about 170 feet, almost to the back wall of the garden area. On your left, you'll see a small waterfall. On your right, in the center of the final lawn section, you'll find the large marker over the grave of **Brandon Tartikoff (1949–1997)**, the golden boy of NBC television in the 1980s.

Tartikoff became the youngest entertainment president of a major network when he took over NBC in 1980 at the age of thirty. He brought the network from worst to first in the ratings in the 1980s with shows including *Hill Street*

Blues, Cheers, L.A. Law, The Cosby Show, St. Elsewhere, The A-Team, and *Miami Vice.* Under Tartikoff's leadership, NBC was the top-rated network for five consecutive seasons.

After graduating from Yale University, Tartikoff worked in a series of jobs in television and advertising on the East Coast before coming to Los Angeles to look for a job in network television. His big break came when Fred Silverman, head of programming at ABC, hired him as the network's director of dramatic development in 1976. A year later, he went to NBC to supervise comedy programming. Three years later, he was in charge of all of the network's entertainment offerings, and he remained in that position for eleven years. Tartikoff even played himself in episodes of the television series *Night Court* and *Saved by the Bell.*

After leaving NBC, Tartikoff became head of Paramount Pictures in 1991. A little more than a year after taking the job, Tartikoff suddenly resigned to spend more time with his family after his daughter was seriously injured in a car accident and was undergoing rehabilitation. After she recovered, Tartikoff became head of New World Entertainment from 1994 to 1996. He also ran his own production company, called H. Beale, named after a character in the movie *Network* (1976). Shortly before his death, Tartikoff was hired by America Online to oversee the development of original interactive entertainment for the online service.

Tartikoff was first diagnosed with Hodgkin's disease, a cancer of the lymph nodes, when he was twenty-three, but he kept his illness quiet while he was working at NBC. He was undergoing chemotherapy treatments when he died at the age of forty-eight.

Tartikoff's widow, Lilly—a former dancer with the New York City Ballet—has became one of the country's leading fundraisers for cancer research. She has raised tens of millions of dollars to fight breast and ovarian cancer, she created the National Women's Cancer Research Alliance, and she is the co-founder of the National Colorectal Cancer Research Alliance. Lilly Tartikoff also helped create the Revlon/UCLA Women's Cancer Research Program, which raises money with its annual "Fire and Ice Ball" and the Revlon Run/Walk in Los Angeles and New York City.

Tartikoff's grave marker includes the inscription: "The Last Great Ride—We miss your energy, fun, brilliance and love every minute."

Tartikoff was born January 13, 1949, in Freeport, New York. He died August 27, 1997, in Los Angeles.

Turn left down Moriah Road and stop at the intersection with Covenant Way, near the Holocaust Memorial. About fifteen feet north of the intersection is a pine tree, and directly on the other side of the pine tree you'll find the grave of **Ross Martin (1920–1981)**, best known for his role as Artemus Gordon in the television series *The Wild, Wild West* in the late 1960s.

Martin, who moved to the United States from Poland when he was just a few days old, studied business, science, and law in New York City, eventually earning a law degree. While he was in school, however, he was also studying acting and even performing as a stand-up comedian.

After working for several years in television, Martin made his screen debut in *Conquest of Space* (1955). He appeared in supporting roles in several films in the late 1950s and early 1960s, including *The Great Race* (1965), before taking the role of Artemus Gordon, a Secret Service agent in the Old West, in *The Wild, Wild West*, costarring with Robert Conrad. The series, which debuted in 1965 and lasted four seasons, featured Martin's character as a master of disguise and scientific gizmos. Though the series wasn't a ratings success, never even finishing among the top twenty, it had a loyal following and continues to find new fans in syndication. (A big-budget film was made in 1999 based on the series, starring Will Smith, with Kevin Kline in the Artemus Gordon role.)

After suffering a near-fatal heart attack in 1968, Martin made few film appearances other than reviving the role of Artemus Gordon in two made-for-television movies—*The Wild, Wild West Revisited* (1979) and *More Wild, Wild West* (1980). Martin also made guest appearances on nearly one hundred television series from 1950 through 1978, including *Peter Gunn, Bat Masterson, Gunsmoke, Sea Hunt, Richard Diamond, Private Detective, The Twilight Zone, Dr. Kildare, Bonanza, Wagon Train, Love, American Style, Night Gallery, Ironside, McCloud, Barnaby Jones, Ellery Queen, Sanford and Son, Baretta, Wonder Woman, Charlie's Angels, Vega$, Hawaii Five-O, Fantasy Island*, and *Mork & Mindy*.

Martin suffered a fatal heart attack while playing tennis in hundred-degree heat in July 1981.

Martin was born Martin Rosenblatt on March 22, 1920, in Grodek, Poland. He died July 3, 1981, in Ramona, California.

8

Oakwood Memorial Park

~

22601 Lassen Street
Chatsworth, California 91311

~ HISTORY

Located about twenty-five miles northwest of Hollywood, Oakwood Memorial Park has a long history as a cemetery, beginning as a Native American burial ground at the end of the nineteenth century. The property is at the western edge of the city of Chatsworth, at the foot of the Santa Susana Mountains. The Old Stagecoach Trail ran through the property, and a stagecoach relay station was located on the cemetery grounds. Rock was quarried here to be used for the Los Angeles Harbor breakwater, and a few large boulders remain on the property.

The site was originally established as Oakwood Memorial Park in 1924, and it has been operated by the Enderle family since 1943. Roy Rogers and Dale Evans lived for many years on a ranch near Andora Avenue, just south of the cemetery. Their ranch is now a residential subdivision known as Roy Rogers Estates, and it includes streets named Dale Court, Trigger Street, and Trigger Place.

Although the vast majority of the 230-acre grounds is used for belowground burials, two new mausoleums have been built at the western edge of the cemetery. Additional expansion is under way, with space being carved out of the rocky foothills of the mountains.

The Chatsworth Community Church, the oldest Protestant church in the San Fernando Valley, was moved to the cemetery in 1965. The seventy-five-seat, white frame building, built in the style of a classic New England church, was built in 1903 on Topanga Canyon Boulevard, about a mile from the cemetery. During the 1940s and 1950s, Roy Rogers and Dale Evans were active members of the church, which was also used as a high school. In 1963, the church was declared a Cultural Historical Monument by the Los Angeles Municipal Arts Department, and the Chatsworth Historical Society was formed to find a new location for the building.

In 1965, the church was moved to a rocky knoll at the north end of the cemetery. Currently, the congregation of St. Mary the Virgin Anglican Catholic Episcopal Church holds services in the church every Sunday at 10 A.M., and tours of the building are given the first Sunday of every month from 1 P.M. to 4 P.M. The church, which is available for wedding and funeral services, also houses a small museum, which displays artifacts from the history of Chatsworth.

Despite Oakwood's fairly remote location in the far northwest San Fernando Valley, and the relatively small number of celebrities buried there, it is significant as the final resting place for both Fred Astaire and Ginger Rogers, who are buried a few hundred yards apart.

About a mile north of the cemetery, just south of the Simi Valley Freeway, south of the intersection of Santa Susana Pass Road and Iverson Road, was the location of the Spahn Movie Ranch. The Spahn Ranch was located on land once owned by movie cowboy William S. Hart, and had been used as a movie set and tourist attraction until it burned down in the wildfires of September 1970, and the property was sold to a developer. But the Spahn Ranch is probably best known as one of the last hideouts of Charles Manson and his murderous followers.

∼ DIRECTIONS

From downtown Los Angeles, take the Hollywood Freeway (101) to the Ventura Freeway, west to Topanga Canyon Boulevard (Route 27). Take Topanga Canyon Boulevard north about five and a half miles, then turn left on Lassen Street. A little less than a mile through a residential area on Lassen, at the intersection with Valley Circle Boulevard, you'll find the main entrance of Oakwood Memorial Park. When you enter the cemetery grounds, stop at the office in the building on the left for a map of the property.

Another option is to take the Ventura Freeway west to the San Diego Freeway (405), then north on the 405 about seven miles to the Simi Valley Freeway (118). Take the Simi Valley Freeway west for about eight miles to Topanga Canyon Boulevard, then south about two miles to Lassen Street, and follow the directions listed above. This route may actually be a little longer, but since it's mostly on freeways, it might be quicker.

∼ HOURS

The cemetery grounds are open every day from 8:30 A.M. to 5 P.M.

∼

The Tour

Turn right just past the main entrance, on Valley Road, and continue about five hundred feet. Stop just before you reach a large drainage grate that crosses the road. Walk toward the left (northwest) into Section E, about fifty feet, to Plot 303, where you'll find the grave of **Ginger Rogers (1911–1995).** Her gravestone is by itself, located between two rows of grave markers.

Though best known as Fred Astaire's dancing partner in a series of musicals made in the 1930s, Rogers appeared in nearly one hundred films and was an excellent comedic and dramatic actress, and a talented singer. Rogers won the Academy Award for Best Actress for her dramatic performance in *Kitty Foyle* (1940), beating fellow nominees and more-established dramatic actresses Bette Davis, Martha Scott, Katharine Hepburn, and Joan Fontaine.

Rogers got her first experience on the stage in Forth Worth, Texas, where she appeared in various high school productions. She then moved on to Broadway and quickly to Hollywood, where she appeared in her first film, a small role in a musical-comedy short titled *A Night in a Dormitory* (1929), when she was only eighteen. Rogers appeared in a series of musical-comedy shorts for Paramount and RKO studios, costarring with Rudy Vallee, Jack Oakie, Ed Wynn, and Joe E. Brown, among others. Rogers quickly graduated to bigger parts in better musicals, including *42nd Street* (1933) with Warner Baxter and Ruby Keeler, and *Gold Diggers of 1933*, with Dick Powell, Joan

Ginger Rogers, best known as Fred Astaire's dance partner, is buried with her mother at Oakwood Memorial Park.

Blondell, and Keeler, which featured Rogers singing and dancing to "We're in the Money."

Later in 1933, Rogers was teamed with dancer Fred Astaire in *Flying Down to Rio*, the first of ten films the pair did together. The others included *The Gay Divorcee* (1934), *Top Hat* (1935), *Roberta* (1935), *Swing Time* (1936), *Follow the Fleet* (1936), *Shall We Dance?* (1937), and *Carefree* (1938). Rogers proved to be the perfect partner for Astaire, and their films were a popular combination of light comedy, marvelous music, and elegant dance numbers. Between films with Astaire, Rogers also appeared in romantic comedies on her own, including *Twenty Million Sweethearts* (1934) with Dick Powell and Pat O'Brien, *Star of Midnight* (1935), with William Powell; *Vivacious Lady* (1938), with Jimmy Stewart; *Having Wonderful Time* (1938), with Douglas Fairbanks Jr.; and *Bachelor Mother* (1939), with David Niven.

The next Astaire-Rogers film, *The Story of Vernon and Irene Castle* (1939), was critically acclaimed but a box-office failure, perhaps because of the more serious tone of the film. Astaire and Rogers would make one more film together, *The Barkleys of Broadway* (1949). Rogers headed in a different direction with *Kitty Foyle* (1940), in which she starred as an engaged working girl who falls in love with a wealthy married man and must wrestle with her conscience to decide what she should do. Rogers followed that film with a comedic look at the same theme in *Tom, Dick and Harry* (1941), in which she is pursued by three very different men, and imagines what life would be like with each of them.

Rogers worked steadily through the 1940s and early 1950s, appearing in comedies, dramas, and musicals, notably *Roxie Hart* (1942), with Adolph Menjou; *The Major and the Minor* (1942), with Ray Milland; *I'll Be Seeing You* (1944), with Joseph Cotton and Shirley Temple; and *Monkey Business* (1952), with Cary Grant and Marilyn Monroe. But she never again achieved the level of popularity she reached while "dancing cheek to cheek" with Fred Astaire. Her last film role was playing Jean Harlow's mother in *Harlow* (1965).

The most famous quote about Rogers—"She did everything Fred Astaire did, and she did it backwards and in high heels"—has been attributed to various sources, including Rogers herself. But in her autobiography, Rogers gives the credit for that line to cartoonist Bob Thaves and says the line first appeared in his *Frank and Ernest* cartoon strip.

Rogers is buried next to her mother, actress and writer Lela Rogers (1890–1977). They share a simple gravestone, decorated with two roses.

*Rogers was born Virginia Katherine McMath on July 16, 1911, in
Independence, Missouri. She died April 25, 1995, in
Rancho Mirage, California.*

Continue on Valley Road about 150 feet, and turn left on Laurel Lane, between Section C and Section D. Turn left again at the first crossroad, Vista Lane, then right at the next, Arcadia Lane. The Elm Section will be on your left, and the Arcadia Section will be on your right. Drive about halfway to the wall that separates the northeastern edge of the cemetery from an apartment complex.

On the left, in the Elm Section, is a large memorial inscribed with the Lord's Prayer. About one hundred feet directly in front of that memorial, near a tree directly in the center of the Elm Section, you'll find the grave of **Richard Reeves (1912–1967)**, in Plot 209. Reeves, who served as a sergeant in World War II, has a military-style grave marker.

Reeves is an actor whose name you might not recognize, but you'd certainly recognize his face. The tough-guy actor usually played cowboys, prison guards, convicts, or thugs in fifty-two films from 1947 until 1967, including five films with Elvis Presley. He made an almost equal number of television appearances, playing the same types of characters, in everything from *Wagon Train*, *Maverick*, and *Gunsmoke*, to *Mister Ed*, *I Dream of Jeannie*, and *The Munsters*.

*Reeves was born August 10, 1912, in New York City.
He died March 17, 1967, in Northridge, California.*

Continue toward the wall, then turn left (the only direction you can go) and follow the road around the Elm Section. Turn right at the first crossroad, Oak Drive, heading north. The road will turn left, toward the small, white church. Stop about halfway between the turn and the church.

The Pioneer Section will be on your left. About ten feet from the road, in Plot 242, you'll find the grave of **Gloria Grahame (1923–1981)**. Though she won an Academy Award for Best Supporting Actress for her performance in *The Bad and the Beautiful* in 1953, Grahame is probably best known as Violet Bick, the town temptress and "good bad girl" in the 1946 Christmas classic *It's a Wonderful Life*. Grahame had a long and varied film career, beginning with *Blonde Fever* in 1944. She appeared in a total of forty-four films, including *A Woman's Secret* (1949), *The Greatest Show on Earth* (1952), *Oklahoma!* (1955), and *Melvin and Howard* (1980).

Grahame was also nominated for an Academy Award as Best Supporting Actress for her performance in *Crossfire* (1947). She appeared in the 1976 television miniseries *Rich Man, Poor Man* and guest-starred on several television drama series in the 1960s, including *The Fugitive, Outer Limits, Burke's Law,* and *Mannix.*

Grahame's gravestone is decorated with the actor's masks of comedy and tragedy, and two small roses.

Grahame was born Gloria Hallward on November 28, 1923, in Los Angeles. She died October 5, 1981, in New York City.

Directly north of the church, about fifty feet north of the road in the Willows West Section, Plot 134, is the grave of **Montie Montana (1910–1998).** Montana appeared in seven films, all Westerns, but he was perhaps best known as a fixture in the annual Tournament of Roses Parade in Pasadena, California, where he made more than sixty appearances, performing rope tricks while he rode on a horse with a silver saddle. Montana also made headlines during Dwight Eisenhower's inaugural parade in 1953 when he tossed a lasso over the new president. Although Montana reportedly asked Ike for permission, he apparently neglected to mention the trick to the Secret Service agents who were protecting the president, and they were not amused by the stunt.

A week after Montana's death, more than four hundred friends, fans, and family members came to the cemetery for a memorial service, which included cowboy songs and a demonstration of rope tricks by Montana's grandson, Jess Montana.

Montana was buried in a wooden coffin branded with his initials. Montana's gravestone features his name spelled in rope, and two images of him, including one on horseback twirling a lasso.

Montana was born Owen Harlan Mickel on June 21, 1910, near Miles City, Montana. He died May 20, 1998, in Santa Clarita, California.

Continue west past the church on Oakwood Drive, which turns left toward two large mausoleums on the western edge of the cemetery. Across from the north mausoleum, in the Oak Knoll Section, **Bob Crane (1928–1978)** was originally buried in Plot 34B. Crane, the star of *Hogan's Heroes* in the late

1960s, was moved to Westwood Memorial Park in Los Angeles in 1999 (see Chapter 4).

In the south mausoleum, in the northeast corner of the building on the top row, is the crypt of **Stephen Boyd (1931–1977)**. Though he appeared in nearly fifty films, Boyd is best remembered for his role as Messala in the 1959 classic, *Ben-Hur*. Messala and Ben-Hur, played by Charlton Heston, battled in the film's climactic chariot race, and Messala is thrown from his chariot and killed. In 1960, Boyd won a Golden Globe Award as Best Supporting Actor for his role in *Ben-Hur*.

Boyd also appeared in *The Man Who Never Was* (1956), *Woman Obsessed* (1959), *Fall of the Roman Empire* (1964), *Ghengis Khan* (1965), *The Oscar* (1966), and *Fantastic Voyage* (1966). Throughout the 1970s, Boyd kept busy appearing in a series of largely forgettable films, including *Kill! Kill! Kill!* (1974), *Those Dirty Dogs* (1974), *Evil in the Deep* (1976), *Lady Dracula* (1977), and *The Squeeze* (1977), as well as several West German horror films.

> *Boyd was born William Millar on July 4, 1928, in Belfast, Northern Ireland. He died August 19, 1977, in Los Angeles.*

Continue south past the mausoleums. Just past a small rose garden on the left, turn left on Crescent Lane, a narrow, shaded road. Stop about sixty feet down the road. On your left, about fifty feet from the road in Section G, Plot 82, you'll find the grave of **Fred Astaire (1899–1987)**.

"Can't act. Can't sing. Balding. Can dance a little." Though that evaluation of Fred Astaire's first screen test may be more Hollywood legend than fact, Astaire proved them wrong by acting, singing, and dancing his way through some of the best-loved and most memorable musicals ever made. (And he wore a toupee, so he overcame that "balding" problem, too.)

The son of an Austrian immigrant, Astaire started in show business in vaudeville and on Broadway, dancing with his sister, Adele. From 1917 to 1932, the Astaires were a successful Broadway dance team, appearing in such musicals as *Over the Top, Lady Be Good,* and *Funny Face*. After Adele retired from the act in 1932 to marry Lord Charles Cavendish, Astaire headed to Hollywood. After his first film, *Dancing Lady* (1933), Astaire appeared in *Flying Down to Rio* (1933), which was his first pairing with Ginger Rogers. Astaire and Rogers made ten films together, usually light comedies with even lighter plots that followed a standard format. But the slim plots were just an excuse for Astaire and Rogers to do what they did best—him in top hat, white

Like his dancing, Fred Astaire's grave marker is simple, elegant, and timeless— and also dateless.

tie and tails; her in a flowing, feathery gown, combining the elements of ball-room, tap and other dance styles in a seamless picture of grace and elegance.

Astaire danced with many other partners in his film career, including Eleanor Powell in *Broadway Melody of 1940,* Rita Hayworth in *You'll Never Get Rich* (1941), Judy Garland in *Easter Parade* (1948), Cyd Charisse in *Silk Stockings* (1957), and Audrey Hepburn in *Funny Face* (1957). Taking nothing away from his human partners, but Astaire could even make the coat rack he danced with in *Royal Wedding* (1951) seem graceful and elegant. Altogether, Astaire appeared in fifty-four films. In 1975, he was nominated for an Academy Award for Best Supporting Actor for his performance in *The Towering Inferno.* Astaire was awarded an honorary Academy Award in 1950, "for his unique artistry and his contributions to the technique of musical pictures." He was also a three-time Emmy winner.

Astaire married his first wife, Phyllis, in 1933, and had two children, Fred Jr. and Ava. Phyllis also had another child, Peter, from a previous marriage. Phyllis died in 1954. In 1980, the eighty-one-year-old Astaire married jockey Robyn Smith—who, at thirty-five, was younger than both of his children.

Astaire's gravestone is as you might expect it to be, simple and elegant: "Fred Astaire, I Will Always Love You My Darling, Thank You." And, for an entertainer with endless and timeless talent, it does not include the dates of his birth or death.

Throughout his life, Astaire was known as a very private person who kept close ties to his family. So it's natural that he is surrounded by the people he loved most. Buried near Astaire is his sister Adele Astaire Douglas (1897–1981)—after her first husband died, she married Kingman Douglas. Next to Adele is Ann Astaire (1878–1975), Fred and Adele's mother. Next to Ann Astaire is Phyllis Livingston Astaire (1908–1954), Fred's first wife. Next to Phyllis are the graves of her aunt and uncle, Henry Worthington Bull (1874–1958) and Maud Livingston Bull (1875–1962). Fred had known Henry Bull for several years before he met Phyllis, due to their mutual interest in horseracing, and the two couples remained close throughout their lives.

In his will, which was signed less than two years before he died, Astaire requested "that my funeral be private and that there be no memorial service."

Astaire was born Frederick Austerlitz on May 10, 1899, in Omaha, Nebraska. He died June 22, 1987, in Los Angeles.

Continue about three hundred feet on Crescent Lane, as it turns back toward the cemetery office and main gate. On the right, in Section H, Plot 174, about ten feet off the road, is the grave of **Russell "Lucky" Hayden (1910–1981).**

Hayden got his start in show business working in the sound department at Paramount Studios, and he held various jobs at the studio before he moved in front of the cameras. He appeared in seventy-six films but was best known as "Lucky Jenkins" in the Hopalong Cassidy films in the 1940s. He also appeared in dozens of other films, usually Westerns, and usually playing a character named Lucky. In later years, he worked as a producer and director of television Westerns.

Hayden's small gravestone includes the phrase "To the Big Director in the Sky."

Next to Hayden is the grave of his second wife, **Lillian M. "Mousie" Hayden (1917–1997),** the former Lillian Porter, who appeared in nineteen films in the 1930s and 1940s as a contract player at 20th Century-Fox studios, usually in small, uncredited roles. The diminutive actress played a Munchkin in the 1939 film *The Wizard of Oz*. She received her nickname when studio executive Darryl F. Zanuck saw her and reportedly commented, "You're a cute little mouse."

To the left of Hayden is the grave of his daughter Sandra Jane "DeDe" Hayden (1940–1956). Her mother was Hayden's first wife, actress Jan Clayton—who played the first mother in the long-running television series

Lassie. Sixteen-year-old Sandra Hayden was killed in an automobile accident on Coldwater Canyon Road in Los Angeles.

Hayden was born Pate Lucid on June 12, 1912, in Chico, California. He died June 9, 1981, in Palm Springs, California.

From Hayden's grave, you can see the main entrance and office of the cemetery. Walk about a hundred feet south, directly toward the office, and you'll find, in Plot 223, the grave of composer **Ted Snyder (1881–1965)**.

Snyder is best known for giving Irving Berlin his first break in show business when he hired the twenty-one-year-old in 1909 as a staff pianist with the Ted Snyder Company, a music publishing house in New York City. With Snyder writing the music and Berlin writing the lyrics, the pair became a successful songwriting team. By 1913, the company was re-named Waterson, Berlin and Snyder.

Snyder wrote the music for such hits as "The Sheik of Araby" and "Who's Sorry Now?" In 1930, Snyder retired from songwriting and went into the restaurant business in Hollywood.

And, of course, his young protégé, Irving Berlin, went on to become one of the best-known and most successful songwriters in history. Berlin wrote, among his many other hits, the songs for the Fred Astaire and Ginger Rogers film *Top Hat* (1935). Which brings us, historically and literally, back to the beginning of the tour.

Snyder was born August 15, 1881, in Freeport, Illinois. He died July 16, 1965, in Woodland Hills, California.

9

Calvary Cemetery

~

4201 Whittier Boulevard
Los Angeles, California 90023

~ HISTORY

The original Calvary Cemetery was one of the first burial grounds to open in Los Angeles. The plot for the Roman Catholic cemetery was laid out in early 1844, northwest of the city, near the current location of Dodger Stadium. The road leading from the city to the cemetery—the "last mile" for the dearly departed—was originally called Calle de Eternidad, or Eternity Street. The name was later changed to Buena Vista Street, and is now known as North Broadway.

The small cemetery grounds were blessed by a parish priest in November 1844, but the site was not formally consecrated until 1866, with Bishop Thaddeus Amat doing the honors. There was a minor scandal at the cemetery in 1856 when someone forced open the lock on the main cemetery gate and illegally buried a body that was not officially eligible for burial in a Catholic cemetery—perhaps the only recorded case of "reverse grave-robbing."

The cemetery quickly filled and was officially closed to new burials in 1896, when the new Calvary Cemetery was opened on a 137-acre site on Whittier Boulevard in East Los Angeles. But the old cemetery site remained, neglected and crumbling. The fence surrounding the property was falling, monuments were broken, and tall weeds covered the grounds. In 1925, the city of Los Angeles passed an ordinance requiring that all bodies be removed from the old Calvary Cemetery and re-interred in the new cemetery by January 1, 1928. But it wasn't until the early 1930s when the last body was finally removed and relocated.

Cathedral High School, the first all-boys Catholic high school in Los Angeles, opened on the site of the old cemetery in 1925. In honor of the location's previous occupants, the high school's teams are known as the "Phantoms." The Pasadena

Freeway (110), which opened in 1940, runs through part of the old cemetery grounds.

The new Calvary Cemetery is located at 4201 Whittier Boulevard in East Los Angeles, bounded by Third Street on the north, Eastern Avenue on the east, and Downey Road on the west. At the far north end of the cemetery is a twelve-foot-high concrete obelisk, a memorial to the Old Calvary Cemetery.

As a Catholic cemetery, Calvary features a display of colorful, hand-painted, glass-enclosed Stations of the Cross around the property. Calvary also contains the mortal remains of many high-ranking church officials,

Most of the celebrities at Calvary Cemetery are located in the Main Mausoleum, which was built in 1929.

including cardinals, archbishops, and bishops. Hundreds of priests and nuns are buried around the All Souls Chapel in the middle of the cemetery. This ornate Gothic chapel, which was built in 1902, is a replica of a rural church in Buckinghamshire, England.

Calvary Cemetery is also the current home for the remains of the patron saint of the Archdiocese of Los Angeles, St. Vibiana. In 1853, her remains were unearthed in Rome, along with a marble slab inscribed, "To the soul of the innocent and pure Vibiana." The church determined that her remains were 1,500 years old, and that she had died a violent death for her faith, so Vibiana was declared a virgin-martyr and saint. Meanwhile, the Archdiocese of Los Angeles wanted the remains of an honest-to-goodness saint to display in the cathedral they were planning to build, so they petitioned to have St. Vibiana's holy remains shipped to California. In 1854, Pope Pius IX agreed to send the remains to Los Angeles, with the requirement that the new cathedral be named in her honor. On the way to Los Angeles, St. Vibiana's remains were placed in the Church of Our Lady of Sorrows in Santa Barbara, California, until the new cathedral was completed. In 1865, the church was destroyed by fire, but the remains of St. Vibiana were untouched by the flames.

St. Vibiana's Cathedral was completed at Second and Main Streets in downtown Los Angeles in 1876, at a cost of $80,000, and the saint's remains were placed in a wax statue inside a glass crypt above the high altar of the cathedral. When the cathedral was damaged by an earthquake in 1994, St. Vibiana's remains were temporarily moved to a crypt in the Calvary Mausoleum, in a secret location. When the new Cathedral of Our Lady of the Angels is completed at Temple and Hill Streets in Los Angeles in the spring of 2002, at an estimated cost of more than $100 million, St. Vibiana's remains will be moved to a crypt in the Chapel of St. Vibiana, beneath the main cathedral.

∿ DIRECTIONS

From downtown Los Angeles, take the Santa Ana Freeway (5) south, to the Indiana Street exit, just before the Long Beach Freeway (710). Take Indiana Street north about a quarter-mile to Whittier Boulevard, then turn right. The entrance to the cemetery is about a mile down on Whittier Boulevard, between Downey Road and Eastern Avenue, on the left side of the street.

∿ HOURS

The cemetery grounds are open from 8 A.M. to 6 P.M. every day. The Main Mausoleum is open from 8 A.M. to 4 P.M. on weekdays and Holy Days, and 9 A.M. to 4 P.M. on Sundays and holidays.

∿

The Tour

Stop in the cemetery office at the southwest corner of the property and get a map of the grounds, which identifies the sections of the cemetery. As you drive through the cemetery, you'll see that each section is identified by letter, as shown on the map, and also by a name printed on the curb along the road. Though the main cemetery sections are clearly marked and easy to find, the specific gravesites are a different matter. The lot markers are few and far between, difficult to find, and the numbering system is almost impossible to follow.

Luckily, most of the celebrities at Calvary Cemetery are located in the Main Mausoleum, a large, three-level building built in 1929 and located in Section Q, in the center of the cemetery. There are signs at the entrances and throughout the grounds to help you find the mausoleum. The main entrance to the mausoleum is on the south side of the building, at the end of a wide stone courtyard. The door is flanked by ten pillars, each about twenty-five feet high, and topped by ten-foot-tall stone angels. The entire scene around the mausoleum entrance looks like a movie set from *Cleopatra* or *Ben-Hur*.

Inside, the mausoleum has the look and feel of a catacomb, with cool marble floors and walls and high arched ceilings. The numbers identifying the sections in the mausoleum can also be very difficult to find, and just as difficult to see. In some, but not all, areas, there are small numbers etched very lightly into the marble, at about eye level.

Immediately inside the main entrance, head upstairs to the second level, where you'll see a small chapel. At the top of the stairs, turn right toward a stained-glass window depicting the Last Supper. In that alcove, Number 352, on the left side, in the bottom row, you'll find a crypt with the name of **John Barrymore (1882–1942),** and the inscription "Good Night, Sweet Prince." But Barrymore's body isn't here. His cremated remains are more than two thousand miles away, in the family plot in Mount Vernon Cemetery in Philadelphia. In fact, Barrymore's body did a fair share of traveling after his death, and its story has become an enduring Hollywood legend.

For the Barrymores, the theater was the family profession. John Barrymore's father, Maurice Barrymore, was a dashing leading man (who changed the family name from Blyth); his mother, Georgiana Drew, was a popular comedian; one uncle, John Drew, was known as the "First Gentleman of the American Stage"; and another uncle, Sidney Drew, was also a popular comedian. Though John Barrymore initially resisted the family business, working for a while as a painter and commercial illustrator, he eventually joined his brother Lionel and sister Ethel onstage in New York. Barrymore quickly became a popular comedic actor, and it was several years before he attempted a dramatic role. The elegant and handsome Barrymore was also quickly developing a strong interest in nightclubs and the company of attractive chorus girls—tastes that would stay with him for the rest of his life.

In 1920, Barrymore first attempted Shakespeare, playing the title role in *Richard III* on Broadway. The theater critics were nearly unanimous in their praise of Barrymore's performance in this physically difficult and emotionally complex role. Two years later, Barrymore took on *Hamlet*, and the critics and the public were even more enthusiastic. Barrymore brought Hamlet into the twentieth century, they said, presenting him less the genteel "sweet prince" and "melancholy Dane," and more of a vibrant, forceful, complicated, sexually charged modern man. Barrymore even took his Hamlet to London, where he received equally glowing reviews from the British press.

Barrymore moved to Hollywood and appeared in more than twenty silent films, usually swashbuckling costume melodramas or romantic comedies. With the introduction of sound, Barrymore's talents were even more in demand, and he appeared in more than thirty films during the 1930s, costarring with the top leading ladies of the day, including Greta Garbo, Katharine Hepburn, Carole Lombard, and Jean Harlow. *Rasputin and the Empress,* released in 1932, was the only film in which John, Lionel, and Ethel Barrymore appeared together.

By the mid-1930s, however, Barrymore's years of hard living and hard drinking were beginning to take their toll. Barrymore had slipped significantly from his status as the "Great Profile" and one of the greatest Shakespearean actors who ever walked on an American stage. His performances had become caricatures and shadows of his former greatness, even to the point that he was lampooning his own image. And he was also spending much of his time drinking and carousing with a group of like-minded Hollywood pals, including Errol Flynn and director Raoul Walsh, known collectively as the "Bundy Drive Boys."

On May 19, 1942, Barrymore collapsed and was taken to Hollywood Presbyterian Hospital, where he was diagnosed with bronchial pneumonia, hardening of the arteries, hemorrhaging ulcers, and cirrhosis of the liver. He died ten days later.

But Barrymore's journey was far from over—at least according to a popular Hollywood legend. In their autobiographies, Bundy Drive Boys Flynn and Walsh each tell slightly different versions of the story.

Flynn recalls that after Barrymore's death, several of the Bundy Drive Boys were mourning their loss at the Cock and Bull tavern on Sunset Boulevard when Walsh claimed to be overcome by grief and left early. While the others stayed behind, Walsh and a few friends went to the Pierce Brothers Mortuary, where they bribed a mortuary employee with $200—though in later versions of the story, also told by Flynn, the bribe amount increased to $500. Walsh took Barrymore's body and brought it to Flynn's home, where he propped it in a chair near the door. Walsh and the others then hid outside and waited for Flynn to come home.

Lionel Barrymore's crypt is above the empty crypt that once housed the body of his brother, John.

In Walsh's version of the story, they were drinking at Flynn's home when Flynn received an urgent telephone call from his lawyer and had to leave. While Flynn was gone, Walsh went to the Malloy Brothers mortuary, where Dick Malloy, a former actor who had worked with Walsh, agreed to let him take Barrymore's body for an hour. Walsh said he propped Barrymore's body on the sofa near the fireplace, and put a drink in front of it.

Both agree that when Flynn came home and saw the body, he screamed and ran out of the house. Several Barrymore biographers, however, are just as adamant that the incident never happened and that Barrymore's body was closely guarded at the mortuary until the time of the funeral services. James Kotsilibas-Davis, author of *The Barrymores: The Royal Family in Hollywood*, called the story a "gaudy legend" and "Raoul Walsh's cruel boast. . . . Actually, quiet dignity prevailed as America mourned its tragic prince." John Kobler, author of *Damned in Paradise: The Life of John Barrymore*, said the legendary visit to Flynn's house "is an ugly story. . . . The truth is nobody kidnapped the body."

Is this just another colorful Hollywood legend? Perhaps an attempt by Flynn and Walsh to perpetuate their reputations as wild bad boys who were willing to do anything for a joke? Or an attempt by the later biographers to recover some of John Barrymore's lost dignity? The truth will probably never be known.

Thirty-eight years later, Barrymore's body took another journey and this story, though just as bizarre, is definitely true. In his will, Barrymore had left specific instructions that he wanted his body to be cremated and his ashes buried next to his parents in Philadelphia. At the time of his death, however, cremation was not allowed by the Catholic Church. And, since both brother Lionel and sister Ethel were Catholic, and Lionel was executor of his brother's will, they decided that John would be buried in a crypt in Calvary Cemetery. By 1980, however, both Lionel and Ethel were dead, and the church had changed its stance on cremation, so Barrymore's son, John Jr., and his grandson, John Blyth Barrymore, decided to finally honor Barrymore's last request.

After obtaining all the proper documents and permission, the surviving Barrymores returned to Calvary Cemetery. The first step, recalled John Blyth Barrymore, was to pry off the marble front of the crypt. "Once they got it off the smell of the thing assaulted us," he recalled. "He had been dead for thirty-eight years, and in spite of the fact that the body was embalmed it had still been decomposing. The casket was solid bronze, and although it had a glass liner, it must have cracked or something, because the fluids from the body had leaked out and had formed a kind of glue between the casket and the floor of the crypt. The burly grave diggers pulled with all their weight on the end handle, but they couldn't seem to move the casket."

Once they got Barrymore's casket out of the crypt, they loaded it on a hand truck, and wheeled it down a long ramp to the first floor, "and out to the plain brown Ford van we had waiting outside," the younger Barrymore recalled. "The body fluids were leaking out all the way."

Barrymore's body was taken to the nearest crematorium at the Odd Fellows Cemetery, down the street at 3640 Whittier Boulevard. The next day, John Blyth Barrymore picked up the remains of his grandfather in a small, square package wrapped in plain, brown paper. John Barrymore Jr. took the package to Philadelphia, where the ashes were buried in Mt. Vernon Cemetery. Barrymore's grave in Philadelphia is also inscribed with a quote from Shakespeare's *Hamlet*—"Alas, Poor Yorick." Back at Calvary Cemetery, the marble monument was replaced over Barrymore's now-empty tomb.

Barrymore was born John Sidney Blyth on February 15, 1882, in Philadelphia, Pennsylvania. He died May 29, 1942, in Los Angeles.

Directly above John Barrymore's empty crypt are the remains of his older brother, **Lionel Barrymore (1878–1954)**.

Lionel Barrymore was one of the early pioneers of the film business, acting in one-reel dramas and Westerns for director D. W. Griffith's Biograph Company in New York City as early as 1908, at a salary of $10 per week. After appearing in nearly forty short films for Griffith, playing tough cowboys, lovable grandfathers, evil villains, or anything else Griffith needed, Barrymore began to try his hand at writing and directing.

Lionel left Biograph in 1914, and for the next several years bounced back and forth between Hollywood films and the stage, including a lightly praised performance as *MacBeth* in New York in 1920, shortly after his younger brother John had received raves as *Richard III*. After a few more flops on Broadway, Lionel moved to Hollywood for good in 1925.

Lionel wrote, acted, directed, and even composed music for the films he made for several studios in the early 1920s. In 1926, he signed a contract with Metro-Goldwyn-Mayer studios, where he remained for the rest of his career, working as both an actor and director. Even as a young actor, Lionel seemed to find the most success playing menacing villains and much older men. At MGM, Lionel continued that specialty, playing a murderous sea captain in *The Barrier* (1926), a homicidal sideshow performer in *The Show* (1927), a disreputable surgeon in *Body and Soul* (1927), a criminal mastermind in *The Thirteenth Hour* (1927), an ugly hunchback who kills his wife and brother in *Drums of Love* (1928), and a sanctimonious lecher in *Sadie Thompson* (1928).

While the careers of many silent-screen actors ended when "talkies" became popular in the late 1920s, Lionel's popularity took off when he started to speak in films. As an experienced stage actor, Lionel even assisted the studio executives with the transition to spoken dialogue. Lionel was recognized as one of the experts in all phases of filmmaking, and he was asked to try his hand behind the camera. His first assignment as a director in a feature-length film, *Madame X* (1929), earned him an Academy Award nomination as Best Director. After directing several more films for MGM, Lionel was feeling the pressure of the time-consuming responsibilities required of a director, leaving him little time for his hobbies of music and sketching. Lionel asked the studio to allow him to return to acting, and he quickly proved his expertise in front of the camera, winning the Academy Award as Best Actor for his performance in *A Free Soul* (1931), in which he played Norma Shearer's alcoholic father.

Lionel and John Barrymore worked together in the classic *Grand Hotel* (1932), featuring Greta Garbo, Joan Crawford, Wallace Beery, Lewis Stone, and Jean Hersholt. Sister Ethel was coaxed off the Broadway stage long enough for all three Barrymores to costar in *Rasputin and the Empress* (1932).

Lionel and John followed that with the star-studded *Dinner at Eight* (1933).

Though John and Ethel may have eclipsed Lionel's talents as a stage actor, he was the most accomplished and successful of the three Barrymore siblings in the film business. In addition to his award-winning accomplishments as an actor and director, many performers who worked with him during his years at MGM recall Lionel giving guidance to young actors to help them create a character or play a scene.

Lionel continued to play villains, scoundrels, and rogues in dozens of films through the 1930s and 1940s, often nearly unrecognizable under heavy make-up, even the wig and dress he wore to play a diabolical old woman in *The Devil Doll* (1936). While filming *Saratoga* (1937), Lionel, who already suffered from severe rheumatism, fell at the studio and fractured his hip. Because of the injury, he missed out on playing a part in *Gone With the Wind* (1939) and played most of his roles after that with the help of a cane, crutches or, in later years, in a wheelchair.

Some of Lionel's best-known performances were done from his wheelchair. He portrayed Dr. Gillespie in fifteen films in the *Dr. Kildare* series from 1938 to 1947. And he's still seen on television every holiday season as mean old Mr. Potter, the Scrooge of Bedford Falls, in Frank Capra's *It's a Wonderful Life* (1946).

In his later years, music and sketching took up more of Lionel's attention. His musical compositions were performed in concerts by the United States Military Academy Band and the Philadelphia Orchestra, among others, and his artwork was displayed in galleries across the country. In the year before he died, Lionel also published a novel, started writing a regular newspaper column, and was the host of the weekly *Hallmark Hall of Fame* show on CBS radio. After he died, more than seven hundred mourners packed into the chapel at Calvary Cemetery for his funeral services.

Buried next to Barrymore is his second wife, Irene Fenwick Barrymore (1887–1936), a former stage actress from Chicago who came to Hollywood, made a handful of silent films from 1915 to 1917, then retired.

Barrymore was born Lionel Herbert Blyth on April 28, 1878, in Philadelphia, Pennsylvania. He died November 15, 1954, in Van Nuys, California.

As you come out of the alcove that houses the Barrymore crypts, walk toward the altar. In the next alcove, number 354, on the left side, first column in, fifth space up from the floor, is the crypt of Louis Francis Cristillo, better known as comedian **Lou Costello (1906–1959).**

Costello and his partner, Bud Abbott, formed one of the most popular and enduring comedy teams of all time. Abbott was the tall, streetwise sharpie who always had a scheme. Costello was short, plump, innocent, slow-witted, and clumsy, best known for his trademark catchphrases, "Hey, Abbott!" and "I'm a ba-a-a-a-ad boy."

Though he was born in New Jersey, Costello came to Los Angeles after graduating high school and worked as a carpenter, stuntman, and extra at MGM and Warner Bros. studios. After this taste of show business, Costello returned to the East Coast and started working the vaudeville circuit as part of a comedy team. Costello was working at a theater in Brooklyn in 1931 when his straight man became ill and Abbott filled in for him. The team clicked. Abbott and Costello worked together in burlesque and vaudeville houses until the late 1930s, when they gained national popularity after an appearance on the *Kate Smith Hour* radio show, where they performed their famous "Who's On First?" routine.

Abbott and Costello signed with Universal Studios and made their movie debut in 1940, in *One Night in the Tropics.* It wasn't very successful, but their second film, *Buck Privates* (1941), costarring the Andrews Sisters, was a smash hit, grossing what was then a studio record of $10 million. The team continued to be one of Universal's top attractions through the 1940s and early 1950s, starring in films like *Hold That Ghost* (1941), *Lost in a Harem* (1944), *Buck Privates Come Home* (1947), and *The Naughty Nineties* (1945), in which the pair did their "Who's On First?" routine. Due to the popularity of that routine, Abbott and Costello became the first non-baseball celebrities to be inducted into the Baseball Hall of Fame in Cooperstown, New York, in 1957.

The team also did a popular series of *Abbott and Costello Meet . . .* films, in which they encountered *Frankenstein* (1948), *The Killer* (1949), *The Invisible Man* (1951), *Captain Kidd* (1952), *Dr. Jekyll and Mr. Hyde* (1953), and *The Mummy* (1955). In 1952, Abbott and Costello tackled the new medium of television with *The Abbott and Costello Show,* which ran for two seasons on the CBS network.

Based on an annual nationwide survey of theater owners, Abbott and Costello were ranked among the top ten box-office attractions from 1941 to 1944, and again from 1948 to 1951—they were number one in 1942, ahead of Clark Gable and Gary Cooper. *People* magazine analyzed sixty-six years of these annual box-office surveys, from 1933 to 1999, and ranked Abbott and Costello as the fifteenth-biggest box-office draw of all time, finishing ahead of such stars as Jimmy Stewart, Shirley Temple, Elizabeth Taylor, and Jack Nicholson.

Costello is buried next to his wife, Anne Cristillo (1912–1959).

As you stand facing the alcove where Lou Costello is buried, turn to your right, looking back toward the alcove containing the Barrymore crypts. About seventy feet down the hall, you'll see two columns of crypts, containing mostly infants and children. In the column on the right side, in the second space up from the floor, is the crypt of Costello's son, Louis Francis Cristillo Jr. (1942–1943). Lou Jr., known to the family as Butch, accidentally drowned in the family swimming pool just two days before his first birthday.

Costello was born Louis Francis Cristillo on March 6, 1908,
in Paterson, New Jersey. He died March 3, 1959, in Los Angeles.

Go back to the top of the stairs and cross over to the left side of the altar. Directly opposite the Barrymore alcove, in Number 353, on the right side in the second row from the right, second space up from the bottom, is the crypt of **Irene Dunne Griffin (1901–1990).**

While growing up in Kentucky and Indiana, Irene Dunne studied voice, took piano lessons, and dreamed of a career in music. She was rejected by the Metropolitan Opera Company in New York because she was too young and inexperienced, so she decided to take her musical talents to the stage and appeared in several plays and musicals on Broadway while she was studying at the Chicago Music College.

Dunne was noticed by Hollywood scouts, and she was signed to a contract by RKO Studios in 1930. The next year, she appeared in *Cimarron* (1931), for which she received the first of five Acadamy Award nominations for Best Actress. She was nominated again for *Theodora Goes Wild* (1936) and *The Awful Truth* (1937), in which she costarred with Cary Grant. Dunne and Grant also shared top billing in *My Favorite Wife* (1940) and *Penny Seranade* (1941).

As an actress, Dunne was equally adept in screwball comedies, melodramas, musicals, and romantic dramas. She is probably best remembered for her roles in *Showboat* (1936), in which she re-created the role of Magnolia Hawks, which she had performed on Broadway in the 1920s; *Love Affair* (1939), in which she costarred with Charles Boyer and was again nominated for an

Academy Award (and which was remade as *An Affair to Remember* in 1957 with Cary Grant and Deborah Kerr); *Life With Father* (1947), with William Powell; and *I Remember Mama* (1948), in which her performance as Mama Hansen, the loving, self-sacrificing Norwegian mother, earned her a fifth Academy Award nomination.

After retiring as a performer in the early 1950s, Dunne became more involved in volunteer work for the United Nations and several charitable organizations, including the Red Cross and the American Cancer Society. In 1957, she was appointed as a special delegate to the United Nations by President Dwight Eisenhower. The emblems on her crypt note that she was also honored as a Knight of Malta and a Knight of the Order of the Holy Sepulchre. Though she never won an Academy Award, Dunne received a Lifetime Achievement Award in 1985 from the Kennedy Center.

Buried next to Dunne is her husband, Dr. Francis D. Griffin (1883–1965), whom she married in 1928.

Irene Dunne was born Irene Marie Dunn on December 20, 1901
(some sources say 1898), in Louisville, Kentucky.
She died September 4, 1990, in Los Angeles.

Leave Irene Dunne's alcove and head up toward the altar, passing on your left the ornate crypts of some of the highest-ranking officials of the Catholic Church in Los Angeles, including Bishop Thaddeus Amat, who served from 1854 to 1878 (and consecrated the first Calvary Cemetery in 1866); Bishop Francis Mora (1878 to 1896); Bishop Thomas Conaty (1903 to 1915); Archbishop John J. Cantwell (1917 to 1947); and Cardinal J. Francis McIntyre (1948 to 1970). Cardinal Timothy Manning (1970 to 1985) is buried outside the mausoleum, near the All Souls Chapel.

Continue behind the altar into what looks like a newer section of the mausoleum. Turn left down the first hallway and walk about twenty-five feet. On your left, in the first space above the floor, you'll find the crypt of **Ethel Barrymore Colt (1879–1959)**.

Best known as a distinguished and regal stage actress, Ethel Barrymore appeared in about a dozen silent films from 1914 to 1919—including *Life's Whirlpool* (1917), written and directed by brother Lionel—before heading back to Broadway, where she remained onstage for the next twenty-five years. Her only venture into films during that time was an appearance in *Rasputin and the Empress* (1932), the only film that features all three Barrymores. Ethel played Russian empress Alexandra; brother Lionel played Rasputin, the mad monk; and brother John played Prince Paul Chegodieff. The production was difficult for Ethel; she had disputes with the director and felt she was being upstaged by her brothers, who were both more experienced film actors. After three months in Hollywood, as soon as the filming was completed, Ethel boarded a train and returned to Broadway.

In 1944, Ethel returned to Hollywood for good, appearing with Cary Grant and Barry Fitzgerald in *None But the Lonely Heart,* for which she received the first of her four Academy Award nominations as Best Supporting Actress, and her only Oscar.

But Ethel was not as comfortable in front of a camera as she was onstage. She was distracted by the activity going on behind the scenes, and she was terrified of microphones. Nevertheless, being the professional that she was and needing the income from film work, Ethel overcame her fears and was again nominated for an Academy Award as Best Supporting Actress for *The Spiral Staircase* (1946), *The Paradine Case* (1947), and *Pinky* (1949).

In her films of the late 1940s and early 1950s, Ethel typically played a strong-willed matriarch. In her private life, Ethel tried to bring some of the refinement and glamour of Broadway society to Hollywood, often hosting spectacular dinner parties for the elite of the entertainment industry, as well as the top names from the world of art, music, politics, and sports. Her guest lists included authors Somerset Maugham and Aldous Huxley, composers Irving Berlin and Cole Porter, musicians Artur Rubenstein and Vladimir Horowitz, California senator Richard Nixon, and New York Yankees outfielder Joe DiMaggio, among many others.

In 1949, shortly before her seventieth birthday, Ethel signed a contract with MGM and appeared in four films during her first year at the studio. She was loaned to 20th Century-Fox studios for *Deadline, USA* (1952), playing a newspaper publisher's widow who joins forces with a crime-fighting editor, played by Humphrey Bogart, to save the paper.

Ethel made a few appearances in television dramas and won an Emmy nomination for her role in *The Thirteenth Chair* in 1954. She also hosted a weekly half-hour drama series called *The Ethel Barrymore Theater.* Her last film was *Johnny Trouble* (1957). She died two years later, just two months shy of her eightieth birthday.

In 1909, Ethel married Russell G. Colt, whose grandfather invented the Colt revolver. She divorced her philandering, violent husband in 1923. A devout Catholic, Ethel said the divorce was a legal separation, but since divorce was not recognized by the church, she didn't consider it official, either, and she never remarried.

Ethel Barrymore was born Ethel Mae Blyth on August 15, 1879, in Philadelphia, Pennsylvania. She died June 18, 1959, in Beverly Hills, California.

A few feet past Ethyl Barrymore's crypt, turn right into the Saint Paul alcove. On the left in the fifth column from the door, the second space up from the floor, is the crypt of silent-film star **Pola Negri (1899–1987).**

Negri was born in Poland and studied acting at the Warsaw Imperial Academy of Dramatic Arts. While still a teenager, Negri was a success onstage in Warsaw and went to Berlin to work with German director Ernst Lubitsch, who featured her as a lusty, earthy, exotic woman. One of their films, *Madame Du Barry* (1919), was re-titled *Passion* and released in the United States with great success, and both Negri and Lubitsch signed contracts and came to work in Hollywood. Negri went to work for Paramount Pictures and among her most popular films were *Vendetta* (1921), with Emil Jannings; *Forbidden Paradise* (1924), with Adolph Menjou; *Barbed Wire* (1927), with Clive Brook; and *Three Sinners* (1928), with Warner Baxter.

The quintessential screen vamp, with large gray eyes and thick black hair, Negri was romantically linked with Rudolph Valentino, Howard Hughes, and Charlie Chaplin, among many others. When Valentino died in 1926, Negri said she and the screen shiek had been engaged to be married. During his funeral services, she flung herself on his coffin and swooned—though most witnesses said she did it as a stunt for the press. In fact, she did it several times, they said, whenever a camera was pointed at her.

Two main factors helped bring an end to Negri's screen career. One was the Hays Office Production Code, which was instituted in 1934 to restrict the amount of sex, violence, and immorality being shown in films. The Hays Code severely limited the studios' need for a sultry sex siren like Negri, especially considering her very public offscreen reputation. But perhaps the main reason for Negri's decline and early retirement was the growing popularity of sound pictures in the late 1920s and early 1930s. Negri's thick European accent made her difficult for audiences to understand.

Negri went back to Europe, but she returned to the United States when Adolf Hitler began to gain power in Germany, even though Hitler was one of Negri's biggest fans. Negri became a U.S. citizen in 1951, but she rarely worked in films after her return. Her last film was a small part in *The Moon-Spinners* (1964), a Disney film starring Hayley Mills. Negri retired to her home in Texas, where she died.

Negri was born Apolonia Chalupec on December 31, 1899
(though some sources say 1894), in Janowa, Poland.
She died August 1, 1987, in San Antonio, Texas.

Retrace your route back toward Irene Dunne's crypt, near the top of the main stairs. Go to the right of the main stairs and continue down the hallway until you reach another stairwell, with stairs going up and down. Turn right and walk about twenty feet down the hallway. On the left side, in the second space up from the floor, you'll find the crypt of **Mabel Normand Cody (1894–1930),** the silent screen's undisputed Queen of Comedy, and later Hollywood's Queen of Scandal.

After working as an advertising model in New York City, Normand took a job as a bit player for Biograph studios. Normand's first screen appearance was a small role in *A Tale of Two Cities* (1911), the first filmed version of the Dickens novel. Normand appeared in dozens of short films during the next few years, usually working for Biograph or the Vitagraph Company of America, with directors D. W. Griffith and Mack Sennett.

Though Griffith usually used Normand in dramatic roles, Sennett saw her talent for comedy, and he brought her to California to appear in a series of short comedies. In 1912, Sennett opened his Keystone Film Company and convinced Normand to leave Biograph and come to work for him. Normand's first film for Keystone was *The Water Nymph* (1912), directed by and costarring Sennett and generally regarded as Sennett's first "bathing beauty" film. Over the next few years, Normand appeared in dozens of short one-reel comedies for Sennett.

The crypt of silent-film comedian Mabel Normand, in the Main Mausoleum at Calvary Cemetery.

Normand also wrote and directed several comedy shorts for Keystone, including *Caught in a Cabaret* (1914)—one of the first film appearances by a young comedian named Charlie Chaplin. Normand, Chaplin, and Marie Dressler costarred in *Tillie's Punctured Romance* (1914), the full-length comedy feature film, and Normand and Chaplin starred together in many more films for Keystone. Normand also costarred with Roscoe "Fatty" Arbuckle in a popular series of *Fatty and Mabel* films in 1915 and 1916. In the Keystone films, Normand usually played a debutante or a damsel in distress, but she did so with reckless abandon, performing a variety of physically challenging and wildly dangerous stunts, including riding horses, flying in airplanes, and fighting with villains. Normand has even been credited with being the first silent-film performer to throw a pie. These slapstick skills, coupled with Normand's talent as a comedian and her "bathing beauty" good looks, made her an audience favorite. Normand was a sexy clown, and in a survey of filmgoers conducted by *Motion Picture Magazine* in 1915, Chaplin was voted Best Male Comedian and Normand was voted Best Female Comedian.

Despite her success as a comedian, Normand wanted more control over her films, and she wanted to try a wider range of roles than Sennett was willing to allow her to do at Keystone. To keep his star happy, Sennett offered Normand her own film company and studio—the Mabel Normand Feature Film Company. One of the first projects of the new film company was *Mickey* (1918), starring Normand in the title role as a girl from the wilds of California who is sent to live with her high-society relatives in the East. The film effectively combined comedy with melodrama and showed audiences another side of Normand's talent as an actress. But the pressure of running her own film company and studio, in addition to starring in the films, proved to be too much for Normand. She left Sennett and went to work for the Goldwyn Pictures Corporation for a few years, but returned to Sennett to star in *Molly O'* (1921).

Over the next three years, Normand's name was linked to several major scandals that had a severe impact on her popularity and ultimately ended her film career, even though she was never a proven participant or officially accused of any crime. The first incident happened in September 1921, about a month before Sennett planned to release *Molly O'*, when Normand's friend and former costar, Roscoe "Fatty" Arbuckle, was arrested and charged with the rape and murder of a young starlet, Virginia Rappe (see Chapter 3), during a wild party at a hotel in San Francisco. After three sensational trials, Arbuckle was acquitted, but his career as a comedian was over. Sennett delayed the release of *Molly O'* until the storm of publicity surrounding Arbuckle had subsided.

The second scandal happened in February 1922, when Normand went to visit a friend, director William Desmond Taylor. After spending less than an hour with Taylor in his apartment, Normand left. The next morning, Taylor was found dead, shot once in the back. (The Taylor murder has never been solved, and it remains a popular discussion topic among Hollywood historians and mystery fans. For more information on Taylor, see Chapter 3.)

Though Normand was questioned by police, she was never considered a serious suspect in the shooting. But her friendship with Taylor—which she always claimed was nothing more than platonic, even though love letters from her were found in Taylor's apartment—further tarnished her reputation. The police investigation also uncovered Normand's $2,000-per-month cocaine habit. The press gleefully jumped on the story as yet another example of the evil and sinful side of Hollywood, and Normand's relationship with Taylor was often mentioned in the stories. To escape the spotlight, Normand took an extended vacation in Europe in the summer of 1922, and Sennett delayed for nearly a year the release of Normand's next film, *Suzanna* (1923), until the Taylor publicity cooled down.

Suzanna was a box-office success, as was Normand's next film, *The Extra Girl* (1923), until yet another incident brought Normand's name back into the headlines. On New Year's Day 1924, Normand was visiting actress Edna Purviance and her boyfriend, millionaire oil tycoon Courtland S. Dines, at Dines's apartment. Normand's chauffeur got into an argument with Dines, then returned with a pistol owned by Normand and shot Dines twice. Though Dines recovered and didn't press charges against the chauffeur, who claimed the shooting was in self-defense, Normand's name was linked to yet another scandal. After the Dines shooting, the Ohio Board of Film Censorship banned the showing of all films featuring Normand. The state of Kansas and the cities of Boston and Detroit were considering taking similar action. In response, Normand went on a nationwide publicity tour, promoting *The Extra Girl* and attempting to clear her name. Although Normand was somewhat successful in turning public opinion to her side, Sennett decided to drop her, and *The Extra Girl* was the last film she did for him.

Later in 1924, Normand was named in the divorce proceedings of a wealthy California couple, Norman and Georgia Church. Mrs. Church, in the complaint she filed against her husband, said Mr. Church told her that he had been involved in an affair with Normand while they were both patients at the same hospital in late 1923. Normand attempted to clear her name by becoming involved in the divorce proceedings. But the judge ruled that although her name was mentioned in the complaint, she did not have direct personal interest in the proceedings, and her statements were not relevant in the divorce.

By this point, after being dropped by Sennett, and with her popularity fading fast, Normand's film career was nearly over. With her involvement in the Taylor and Dines shootings, the Church divorce case, and her well-known drug habit, Normand was quickly becoming the poster girl for immorality and scandal in Hollywood. Normand appeared in several stage productions on the East Coast and attempted a brief comeback to films in 1926 and 1927 in a series of short comedies produced by Hal Roach.

In September 1926, Normand married actor Lew Cody, her costar in *Mickey*. The following year, Normand was hospitalized several times with pneumonia and, in December 1928, she was diagnosed with tuberculosis. The thirty-five-year-old actress died in the Pottenger Sanitarium in Monrovia, California, on February 23, 1930.

Above Normand's crypt is that of her mother, Mary J. Normand (1869–1932).

Normand was born Mabel Ethelreid Normand on November 16, 1894, in New York City. She died February 23, 1930, in Monrovia, California.

Go back down the stairs and out the main entrance of the Mausoleum. Drive around behind the Mausoleum to Section R, Immaculate Conception. Drive along the east side of the section and look for the number 51 painted on the curb. At that point, walk west into Section R, about one hundred feet. Directly in front of a large tree, in Plot 306, you'll find the graves and the simple headstones of **John Edward Reagan (1883–1941)** and **Nelle Wilson Reagan (1883–1962)**, the parents of former actor and President Ronald Reagan.

Turn around and head back toward the south. Just as you pass the Mausoleum on your right, turn left between Section H, Sacred Heart, and Section G, Divine Savior. Continue toward a small stone church in Section F, Good Shepherd. The church is the All Souls Chapel, and it's surrounded by the graves of dozens of priests, nuns, and other church officials from the Los Angeles area, including Cardinal Timothy Manning, who served the Archdiocese of Los Angeles from 1970 to 1985.

Park in front of the chapel. In the middle of Section F, about 100 feet northeast of the chapel, in Plot 1693, is the grave of comedian and former leader of the Three Stooges **Ted Healy (1896–1937).**

After an unsuccessful career as a businessman, Healy became a successful comedian in vaudeville, telling jokes and doing impressions. For a time, Healy was the highest-paid entertainer on the vaudeville circuit, earning as much as $8,500 per week in the early 1920s. In 1922, Healy decided to add a "stooge" to his act, to help him with the physical slapstick comedy, so he called on his boyhood friend Moe Howard. Later, Howard's brother Shemp was added to the act, which was now known as "Ted Healy and His Stooges." As the act gained notoriety and success, a third Stooge—violinist Larry Fine—was added to the group in 1925. With his trio of Stooges, Healy appeared in a string of successful Broadway shows before heading west to Hollywood to make short, two-reel comedies.

After their first film, *From Soup to Nuts,* was made in 1930, Shemp left the act and was replaced by another Howard brother, Jerome—better known as Curly. After appearing in ten films with Healy, Moe, Larry, and Curly left the act in 1934, and Healy went on to play supporting roles in about two dozen films during the next few years. Surprisingly, most were dramas or mysteries, not comedies, including *Reckless* (1935), with Jean Harlow and William Powell; *San Francisco* (1936), with Clark Gable and Spencer Tracy; and *Speed* (1936), with Jimmy Stewart. Healy also played Harlow's brother in *Bombshell* (1933). His last film was *Hollywood Hotel* (1938), a Busby Berkeley musical starring Dick Powell.

The generally accepted story behind the cause of Healy's death in 1937 is that he was out celebrating the birth of his first child when he got involved in a fight at the Trocadero nightclub on Sunset Boulevard in Los Angeles. Healy suffered serious head injuries in the fight and died later in his apartment, a few weeks before his forty-first birthday. The official autopsy report, however, showed that Healy died of a heart attack, and attributed his death to natural causes.

Healy was born Charles Earnest Lee Nash on October 1, 1896, in Kaufman, Texas. He died September 12, 1937, in Los Angeles.

Continue past the church on the circular roadway, following the road as it turns back toward the west. Turn left at the first crossroads, and head south. Section H, Sacred Heart, will be on your right, and Section C, St. Christopher, will be on your left. Continue until you see the number 35 painted on the curb in Section C, on your left. From that spot, walk east into Section C, about 125 feet to Plot 586, and you'll find the grave of silent-film star **Ramon Novarro (1899–1968).**

Novarro was the son of a prosperous Mexican dentist, but his family left the country at the outbreak of the Mexican Revolution in 1910 and settled in Los Angeles. Novarro worked several jobs, including grocery clerk, singing waiter, piano teacher, usher in a movie house, and busboy at the elegant Alexandria Hotel, where he met a young dancer named Rodolfo Guglielmi, later known as Rudolph Valentino. During this time, Novarro also worked as a film extra. His first screen appearance was a small part in *Joan the Woman* (1916), directed by Cecil B. De Mille.

But Novarro's big break happened when his friend Rudolph Valentino set the screen on fire in *The Sheik* (1921), and film fans fell in love with Valentino's slick black hair, smoldering eyes, and swarthy sensuality. Almost immediately, every studio needed a "Latin lover," and Novarro fit the bill. Novarro's first starring roles were in *The Prisoner of Zenda* (1922), *Scaramouche* (1923), and a *Shiek* copy called *The Arab* (1923), all directed by Rex Ingram. Novarro quickly became known as "Ravishing Ramon" and the "Second Valentino." Novarro and Francis X. Bushman costarred in *Ben-Hur* (1925), the silent epic filmed partially on location in Italy.

In addition to playing the sexy leading man roles in high-adventure films, Novarro also tried his hand at light comedy and romantic roles, including *The Student Prince in Old Heidelberg* (1927), with Norma Shearer; *Across to Singapore* (1928), with Joan Crawford; and *Forbidden Hours* (1928), with Renée Adorée. Novarro was one of the few silent-film stars who successfully made the transition to "talkies," and he starred in several musicals, including *In Gay Madrid* (1930) and *Call of the Flesh* (1930), both with Dorothy Jordan.

Novarro continued to make adventures, musicals, and comedies through the early 1930s, costarring with

The career of silent-film star Ramon Novarro has been overshadowed by his brutal murder in his home in 1968.

some of the top actresses in Hollywood, including *Mata Hari* (1931), with Greta Garbo; *The Son-Daughter* (1932), with Helen Hayes; *The Barbarian* (1933), with Myrna Loy; *The Cat and the Fiddle* (1934), with Jeanette MacDonald; and *Laughing Boy* (1934), with Lupe Velez. By the end of the 1930s, however, Novarro had been replaced by the next wave of romantic leading men, and he retired from films. He made a brief comeback with a small role in *We Were Strangers* (1949), starring John Garfield and Jennifer Jones. In the 1960s, Novarro had moved to the small screen, making guest appearances on such television series as *Combat!, Rawhide, Bonanza*, and *Dr. Kildare.*

Unfortunately, Novarro's career has been somewhat overshadowed by his violent murder. In his later years, he was known to hire the services of male prostitutes. In 1968, two teenage brothers, Paul and Tom Ferguson, heard a rumor that Novarro had $5,000 in cash hidden in his house, so they decided to rob him. The brothers went to Novarro's home, pretending to be interested in a sexual encounter. They drank with Novarro and then brutally beat the sixty-nine-year-old actor to death before ransacking his home in an unsuccessful search for the money. Although both brothers were convicted of murder and sentenced to life in prison, they were paroled after serving only seven years.

Novarro was born José Ramón Samaniegos on February 6, 1899, in Durango, Mexico. He died October 31, 1968, in Los Angeles.

Continue south and follow the road as it curves toward the left, around Section A, St. Vibiana. Continue all the way around Section A until you reach Section D, St. Christopher, on your left. (To add to the confusion and difficulty in finding specific graves, Section C and Section D are both named St. Christopher.) Stop when you see the number 1109 painted on the curb on your left. From that spot, walk into Section C about 150 feet, heading northwest. Between two small trees you'll find a tan tombstone about four feet high and three feet wide. On the side of the tombstone facing away from the road is a relief carving of an angel standing with two small children.

The stone marks the grave of Mae Costello (1882–1929). Next to it is the small stone marking the grave of her husband, actor Maurice Costello (1879–1950), who appeared in more than one hundred films from 1908 to 1943. Though Maurice Costello was a popular matinee idol in the beginning of his career, he was nearly forgotten by the early 1920s and ended up playing small or uncredited parts.

Directly in front of those markers is the grave of their daughter **Dolores Costello Barrymore (1903–1979),** who was once known as the "Goddess of the Silent Screen," but is probably best remembered today as the ex-wife of actor John Barrymore and the grandmother of actress Drew Barrymore.

When Maurice Costello was working for Vitagraph studios in New York City, he often found roles in his short comedies for his two daughters, Dolores and Helen (later known as Helene), who both made their screen debuts in 1911. In 1924, the sisters both signed contracts with Warner Bros. Studios, and the entire family moved to Los Angeles. In one of her first films, Dolores costarred with John Barrymore in *The Sea Beast* (1926). They were married two years later.

John and Dolores had two children—DeDe, born in 1931, and John Blyth Barrymore Jr., born in 1932—and Dolores put her acting career on hold. Due primarily to John Barrymore's excessive drinking, Dolores filed for divorce in 1935. After the divorce, Dolores attempted to revive her acting career and appeared in *Little Lord Fauntleroy* (1936), *The Magnificent Ambersons* (1942), and *This Is the Army* (1943), her last film. Harsh makeup used by the studio scarred the delicate skin on her face, and Dolores, at age forty, was forced into early retirement. She lived the rest of her live in semi-seclusion on her avocado ranch in Fallbrook, California, near San Diego.

Her son, John Blyth Barrymore Jr. (who changed his name to John Drew Barrymore in 1958), is the father of actress Drew Barrymore, who was born in Los Angeles in 1975, and rose to stardom in *E.T.* (1982).

*Dolores Costello Barrymore was born September 12, 1903, in
Pittsburgh, Pennsylvania. She died March 1, 1979,
in Fallbrook, California.*

10

Home of Peace Memorial Park

~

4334 Whittier Boulevard
Los Angeles, California 90023

~ HISTORY

Like that of Calvary Cemetery across Whittier Boulevard, the history of the Home of Peace Memorial Park begins in the middle of the nineteenth century, at a location northwest of Los Angeles, near the current site of Dodger Stadium.

The Hebrew Benevolent Society of Los Angeles was formed in 1854 with its prime objective being the creation of a cemetery to serve the city's small but growing Jewish population. The group selected a three-acre site near the current intersection of Lilac Terrace and Lookout Drive in the Chavez Ravine area, just a few hundred yards from the first Calvary Cemetery, which had opened ten years earlier. The site, which was purchased from the city for $1, was officially known as the Hebrew Benevolent Society Burial Ground, but more commonly referred to as simply the Jewish Cemetery.

The cemetery was fenced and officially opened in April 1855, but the first burial didn't take place there until 1858. In 1861, the Home of Peace Society—an organization of Jewish women—was formed to assist with the upkeep and maintenance at the cemetery. This location was the city's only Jewish cemetery for forty-four years, and a total of 360 people were buried here.

In 1902, when the cemetery reached its capacity, Congregation B'nai B'rith—now known as the Wilshire Boulevard Temple—opened the Home of Peace Cemetery on a thirty-five-acre site on Whittier Boulevard in East Los Angeles, and the remains buried in the original cemetery were moved there between 1902 to 1910. Part of the site of the old Jewish Cemetery was sold to the city of Los Angeles in 1905. In the 1930s, some of the area was used as a trash dump and, in 1943, it

317

FIRST JEWISH SITE IN LOS ANGELES

THE HEBREW BENEVOLENT SOCIETY OF LOS ANGELES
(1854), FIRST CHARITABLE ORGANIZATION IN THE
CITY, ACQUIRED THIS SITE BY DEED ON APRIL 9, 1855
FROM THE CITY COUNCIL FOR A SACRED BURIAL
GROUND. THIS PROPERTY REPRESENTED THE FIRST
ORGANIZED COMMUNITY EFFORT BY THE PIONEER
JEWISH SETTLERS.

CALIFORNIA REGISTERED HISTORICAL LANDMARK NO. 822

PLAQUE PLACED BY THE STATE DEPARTMENT OF PARKS
AND RECREATION IN COOPERATION WITH THE JEWISH
FEDERATION COUNCIL OF GREATER LOS ANGELES
SEPTEMBER 25, 1968

A historical plaque near Dodger Stadium marks the site of the first Jewish cemetery in Los Angeles.

was sold to the U.S. Government. The U.S. Naval and Marine Corps Reserve Center now occupies part of the old cemetery site.

A historical plaque marking the site of the old cemetery is located near the intersection of Lilac Terrace and Lookout Drive, about a quarter-mile west of Stadium Way. The plaque is next to a tall, narrow pine tree in a weed-choked area behind the parking lot of the Los Angeles City Fire Department Training Center, and identifies the cemetery as "the first organized community effort by pioneer Jewish settlers."

A small section on the western edge of the Home of Peace Memorial Park along Downey Road was once a separate cemetery known as the Beth David Cemetery. Operated by a Sephardic congregation in Los Angeles, that cemetery became part of Home of Peace in the early 1960s. Home of Peace Memorial Park is still owned and operated by the Wilshire Boulevard Temple.

In many Jewish communities, it's a cemetery custom to place a small stone on top of a tombstone as a sign of respect for the deceased. In addition to the stones, some visitors leave other small items, such as coins, keys, or toys. Many celebrity graves, in fact, can be easily found by the piles of mementos on top of their tombstones.

Far from the bright lights and glamour of Hollywood, Home of Peace Memorial Park is the final resting place of the biggest and best-known Hollywood studio executives from MGM, Universal, and Warner Bros., as well as two of the Three Stooges.

∼ DIRECTIONS

From downtown Los Angeles, take the Santa Ana Freeway (5) south, to the Indiana Street exit, just before the Long Beach Freeway (710). Take Indiana

Street north about a quarter-mile to Whittier Boulevard, then turn right. The entrance to the cemetery is about a mile down on Whittier Boulevard, between Downey Road and Eastern Avenue, on the right side of the street.

∿ HOURS

The cemetery is open Sunday through Friday from 9 A.M. to 4:30 P.M. It is closed on Saturday.

∿

The Tour

Most of the celebrities at Home of Peace Memorial Park are located in or near the mausoleum and chapel in the center of the property, directly south of the main entrance. The mausoleum, which was dedicated in 1934, has a decidedly eastern, almost mosque-like appearance, with a large dome and minarets, and even minaret-shaped stained-glass windows and archways.

From the main entrance of the mausoleum, walk into the rotunda toward the chapel, and turn right down the first corridor—the Corridor of Love. At the very end of the corridor, on the right side, is a small room with the name "Laemmle" on the small brass door. Inside is the crypt of **Carl Laemmle (1867–1939),** founder of Universal Pictures.

Laemmle was working as a bookkeeper and office manager in a small town in Germany when he set out to make his fortune in America in 1884. After settling in Chicago, Laemmle bought a small nickelodeon theater in 1906—the White Front Theatre. Within a few years, the young entrepreneur owned a chain of nickelodeons and his own film distribution business, Laemmle Film Service, which quickly became the largest film distributor in the country. After his distribution company was boycotted by the major studios, Laemmle started producing his own films under the banner of IMP (Independent Motion Picture Co.) in New York. (Laemmle's personal secretary at IMP was Irving Thalberg, who later became the "boy wonder" production chief at Universal at the age of twenty, then creative director at MGM Studios when he was twenty-four.)

Among his many innovations, Laemmle is credited with inventing the idea of a "movie star" by promoting the names and faces of the performers in his films. Before that time, studios were afraid to feature or even identify any specific individual performers for fear that they would become too popular and start to ask for more money. D. W. Griffith's Biograph studios promoted films

The mausoleum at Home of Peace Memorial Park has a Middle Eastern appearance.

starring the "Biograph Girl" but never identified her by name. Laemmle realized that audiences would return to the theaters week after week to see their favorite performers. So in 1910, he hired away the "Biograph Girl" and re-named her the "IMP Girl." He also told audiences, for the first time, her real name—Florence Lawrence. Griffith, meanwhile, replaced Lawrence with Mary Pickford as the new "Biograph Girl." (On her gravestone, Lawrence is identified as "The First Movie Star." For more information on Lawrence, see Chapter 3.)

In 1912, Laemmle moved to California and merged his Independent Motion Picture Co. with several other production companies to form Universal Pictures—one of the first studios in the Los Angeles area. Two years later, Universal purchased a 240-acre chicken ranch in the San Fernando Valley north of Los Angeles for $165,000 and, in 1915, opened the Universal City studio complex, where 250 films were produced in the first year of operation. The new lot boasted a zoo, horse corrals, police station, fire company, restaurant, hospital, and all the departmental studio facilities needed to make motion pictures.

In the early years, Universal was best known for producing two-reel Westerns and serials—Laemmle's experience with the nickelodeon theaters in Chicago showed him the business sense in producing films that would encourage people to return every week to see the next episode. In the 1920s and 1930s, Universal became known as the horror movie studio, producing such classics as *The Hunchback of Notre Dame* (1923) and *The Phantom of the Opera* (1925), both starring Lon Chaney Sr.; *Dracula* (1931) and *Murders in the Rue Morgue* (1932), both starring Bela Lugosi; *Frankenstein* (1931) and *The Mummy* (1932), both starring Boris Karloff; and *The Invisible Man* (1933), starring Claude Rains.

In 1929, Laemmle put his twenty-one-year-old son, Carl Jr., in charge of production at Universal. Though the elder Laemmle was well known for hiring friends and relatives—at one time, he had seventy relatives on the Universal payroll—Carl Jr. scored an almost immediate success when one of his first projects, *All Quiet on the Western Front* (1930), won the Academy Award for Best Picture, and Lewis Milestone was nominated for Best Director. Carl Jr. also produced *Showboat* (1936), as well as most of the Universal horror films.

"Uncle Carl," as Laemmle was affectionately known, suffered the same fate that befell many studio owners during the depression. Due to his financial extravagances and increasing pressure from creditors, Laemmle was forced to sell Universal in 1935 for a mere $4.5 million—a fraction of what the studio was actually worth.

The Laemmle room in the Home of Peace Mausoleum also contains the remains of Laemmle's mother Recha Laemmle (1876–1919), his son Carl Jr. (1908–1979), his daughter Rosabelle Laemmle Bergerman (1903–1965), and his granddaughters Carol Laemmle Bergerman (1930–1994) and Laura Lee Bergerman.

Laemmle was born January 17, 1867, in Laupheim, Germany.
He died September 24, 1939, in Beverly Hills, California.

Go back to the main rotunda, walk toward the chapel, then turn right down the second corridor on the right side of the chapel—the Corridor of Devotion. Take the first left and walk all the way to the end of the hall, to the Corridor of Immortality. Turn right, and walk almost to the end of the corridor. On the left side in the last row, the fourth space up from the floor, you'll find the crypt of another studio executive, **Louis B. Mayer (1885–1957).**

Mayer was the stereotypical Hollywood studio mogul—a short, feisty, cigar-chomping czar who ruled his kingdom with an iron fist. His studios were true film factories, with the stars treated like assembly-line workers and "L. B." in charge of everything for twenty-seven years—equally respected and feared, part father figure, part tyrant.

Mayer was born in a small town in the Minsk district of Russia, although the exact date is not certain. Mayer knew only that he was born in the summer, so he picked July 4 for his birthday. The family came to North America, living for a while in New Brunswick, Canada. Mayer's father worked as a peddler and a scrap metal dealer, and Mayer made several trips to Boston to arrange for the sale of scrap metal. In 1904, the nineteen-year-old Mayer moved to Boston, leaving his family behind in New Brunswick.

With the scrap metal business failing, Mayer purchased a small, dilapidated, six-hundred-seat theater called the Gem in the Boston suburb of Haverhill in 1907. Mayer re-named the theater the Orpheum and promised the public that he would present only "high-class films." When the Orpheum became a success, Mayer expanded into film distribution by opening the Louis B. Mayer Film Company. In 1913, Mayer entered into an arrangement with Jesse Lasky, who was producing films in California, and some other film producers. Two years later, Mayer and several partners formed the Metro Pictures Corporation, and one of the first films they acquired for distribution was D. W. Griffith's classic *The Birth of a Nation* (1915).

Following the enormous financial success of that film, Mayer formed a series of distribution companies—Master Photoplays, Serial Producing Company, and American Feature Film Company. In 1918, Mayer lured actress Anita Stewart away from Vitagraph, formed Louis B. Mayer Pictures, and moved to Los Angeles to start making his own films. His first production, *Virtuous Wives* (1918), starring Stewart and Hedda Hopper, was a success.

Beginning with his promise of presenting only "high-class films" in Haverhill, Mayer continued his policy of making films that stuck to the themes of honor, fidelity, decency, and virtue. His early films followed a similar formula—poor but decent girl faces severe temptations, and triumphs over all in the end. "I will only make pictures that I won't be ashamed to have my children see," Mayer said. And the filmgoing public seemed to enjoy these themes as much as Mayer did.

While building his studio, Mayer hired twenty-four-year-old Irving Thalberg away from Universal Studios to be his vice president and production assistant in 1923. Later that year, Marcus Loew, president of the powerful Metro Pictures Corp. and the Loew theater chain; Frank Joseph Godsol, president of the Goldwyn Company; and Mayer met to discuss a merger of the three companies. Loew had a large and successful chain of theaters, but he was unhappy with the way his film-production studio was being operated. Godsol had a large and well-stocked studio in Culver City, but he lacked the distribution and exhibition facilities. And Mayer and Thalberg could provide the successful studio management. The deal was signed in 1924, and Metro-Goldwyn-Mayer was born.

Mayer moved to the Goldwyn lot in Culver City, a forty-acre facility with a three-story office building and six large stages. With the facilities and talent of the three combined studios at their disposal, Mayer and Thalberg built an entertainment empire. One of their first big productions was the epic *Ben-Hur*

(1925), starring Ramon Novarro and Francis X. Bushman, which was filmed partially on location in Italy.

For a time, the MGM film factory released an average of one feature film per week. In 1936, Mayer was the first business executive in the country to make $1 million per year, and he remained the highest-paid executive through 1944. Thalberg felt entitled to an equal share, but Mayer had begun to resent the prevailing opinion that Thalberg was the real genius behind MGM's success. An angry Thalberg threatened to leave MGM. Their conflict was finally ended when the sickly Thalberg died of pneumonia in 1936.

Some of the films made by MGM during Mayer's twenty-seven-year tenure include *Anna Christie* (1930), *Grand Hotel* (1932), *Dinner at Eight* (1933), *Mutiny on the Bounty* (1935), *A Night at the Opera* (1935), *Romeo and Juliet* (1936), *The Good Earth* (1937), *Captains Courageous* (1937), *Marie Antoinette* (1938), *Boys Town* (1938), *The Wizard of Oz* (1939), *Ninotchka* (1939), *Gone With the Wind* (1939), *The Philadelphia Story* (1940), *Dr. Jekyll and Mr. Hyde* (1941), *Mrs. Miniver* (1942), *The Human Comedy* (1943), *Gaslight* (1944), *Anchors Aweigh* (1945), *The Yearling* (1946), *Adam's Rib* (1949), and *Father of the Bride* (1950), as well as the *Broadway Melody* series, the *Thin Man* series, the *Lassie* series, and the *Andy Hardy* series—which Mayer was always watching over to keep the kissing and romance between young Andy Hardy and Polly Benedict to an absolute minimum.

On the MGM payroll, according to the well-known studio slogan, were "more stars than there are in heaven," including, at various times, Clark Gable, Joan Crawford, Cary Grant, Spencer Tracy, Elizabeth Taylor, Buster Keaton, Katharine Hepburn, Lana Turner, Judy Garland, Mickey Rooney, the Marx Brothers, Laurel and Hardy, William Powell, John Barrymore, Lionel Barrymore, Myrna Loy, Ava Gardner, and one of Mayer's personal discoveries, Greta Garbo. Mayer was often personally involved in the private lives of his employees, usually to make sure their public reputation matched the studio's image for wholesomeness and decency. When MGM executive and writer Paul Bern, recently married to MGM starlet Jean Harlow, committed suicide, Mayer arrived on the scene before the police and took Bern's suicide note. He feared the incident might reflect poorly on the studio, but he was eventually convinced to turn the note over to the police. When Mickey Rooney, star of the *Andy Hardy* series and a well-known womanizer and partygoer, started to get a little too much press, Mayer took him aside and gave him the Mayer version of a Judge Hardy lecture: "You're Andy Hardy! You're the United States! You're Stars and Stripes! You're a symbol! Behave yourself!" There are even reports that when one of MGM's biggest stars was driving drunk on Hollywood Boulevard and killed a pedestrian, Mayer arranged for a low-level studio employee to take the blame in exchange for a lifetime job guarantee.

Mayer ruled over MGM as a big family—with Mayer as the paternalistic authority, rewarding loyalty and obedience, punishing insubordination, and regarding opposition as personal betrayal.

By the late 1940s, the golden years for studio moguls were coming to an end. The government was forcing the film industry to divest its lucrative theater chains, and top stars and directors were demanding a share of the profits that Mayer had always denied them. Dore Schary, head of production at RKO Studios and former Academy Award–winning writer at MGM (for *Boys Town*) was hired to replace Thalberg. Schary and Mayer battled from the very start. When the slumping financial situation at MGM began to improve almost as soon as Schary returned to the studio lot, rumors began circulating that Mayer would either resign or be forced out by Nick Schenck, president of Loew's, Inc., which controlled MGM. After yet another battle with Schary, Mayer called Schenck with an ultimatum—"It's either me or Schary." To Mayer's shock, Schenck chose Schary, and Mayer submitted his resignation in 1951. After Schenck retired in 1955, Mayer made an attempt to convince the major Loew's stockholders to allow him back to control the studio again, but he was rejected just weeks before he died.

In 1950, Mayer was given a special Academy Award, "for distinguished service to the motion picture industry."

At Mayer's funeral, Jeanette MacDonald sang, "Ah, Sweet Mystery of Life," and Samuel Goldwyn, the founder and former head of the Goldwyn Company, reportedly quipped, "The reason so many people showed up at his funeral was because they wanted to make sure he was dead."

Above Mayer's crypt is that of his sister, Ida Mayer Cummings (1883–1968).

Mayer was born Ezemiel Mayer on July 4, 1882, in Vilme, Russia. He died October 29, 1957, in Los Angeles.

Now, retrace your route and go back to the rotunda just inside the main entrance. This time, go to the left side of the chapel and turn left down the second corridor—the Corridor of Memory. Turn right down the first corridor and walk about twenty-five feet to a small hallway between the Corridor of Harmony and the Corridor of Benevolence. (The corridor names are marked with signs on the floor.) The wall on the left contains a series of niches for cremated remains. **Fanny Brice (1891–1951)** was originally interred in this area, in Niche E1109, but her ashes were moved to the new Memorial Gardens area at Westwood Memorial Park in May 1999 (see Chapter 4).

Turn left down the Corridor of Benevolence, then right into the Corridor of Eternal Life—a brightly lit area with stained-glass windows running the length of the ceiling. On the right, in the fifth column in, second space up from the floor, you'll find the crypt of **Shemp Howard (1895–1955)**, best known as one of the Three Stooges.

Shemp, who was born Samuel Horwitz, received his nickname at an early age. When his mother would call to him, her thick European accent made the name "Sam" sound like "Shemp," so that's what the rest of the family started to call him. Shemp, with his long black hair slicked back behind his large ears, was one of the original Stooges when the group made their debut in 1922 as a vaudeville act called "Ted Healy and His Stooges." (For more information on Ted Healy, see Chapter 9.) Shemp and his brother Moe were joined by violinist Larry Fine in 1925, and Healy and his Stooges moved to Hollywood to make two-reel comedies.

Shemp appeared in the first Stooges film, *From Soup to Nuts* (1930), but then left the act and was replaced by his younger brother, Jerome, better known as "Curly." While Healy and the Stooges were making dozens of comedies, Shemp was appearing in more than seventy films on his own, usually in small, supporting roles, including *In the Dough* (1932), with Roscoe "Fatty" Arbuckle; *Another Thin Man* (1939), with William Powell and Myrna Loy; *The Bank Dick* (1940), with W. C. Fields; several Abbott and Costello comedies; and even a few films in the *Charlie Chan* and *Blondie* series.

When Curly suffered a stroke in 1946, Shemp rejoined the act and appeared in seventy-three short comedies with the Stooges until his death in 1955. As with many celebrity graves and crypts, fans like to leave souvenirs or other items behind. The narrow ledge in front of Shemp's crypt, which is inscribed "Shemp Howard, Beloved Husband and Father," is usually covered with coins and small stones.

Shemp Howard was born Samuel Horwitz on March 17, 1895, in Brooklyn, New York. He died November 23, 1955, in Los Angeles.

Retrace your route again, and go back out to the front of the mausoleum. Directly in front is the large, private mausoleum of **Rabbi Edgar Fogel**

Magnin (1890–1984). Magnin started his career as a twenty-five-year-old associate rabbi at Temple B'nai B'rith in Los Angeles—renamed Wilshire Boulevard Temple in 1929. In 1919, Magnin was named rabbi when his predecessor retired, and he served in that position for sixty-five years, until his death.

Magnin quickly developed a reputation as a vigorous and outspoken religious leader, frequently speaking on radio, at the Hollywood Bowl, and to groups outside of traditional Jewish circles. He became well-known and well-respected throughout Los Angeles and across the country. For many years, he was seen as the unofficial Jewish spokesman to the Christian community.

Magnin was actively involved in many religious, civic, and community organizations in Los Angeles. He served as president of the Los Angeles Rabbinical Association, chairman of the local Jewish Welfare Board, vice president of Cedars of Lebanon Hospital, and director of the Los Angeles Chapter of the American Red Cross. He was one of the founders of the National Council on Alcoholism, and he also served as a member of the advisory committee of the Los Angeles Philharmonic Orchestra Association and the advisory board of the National Academy of American Literature. For many years, he lectured on history at the University of Southern California and wrote a weekly column in the *Los Angeles Herald Examiner.*

During Magnin's tenure, his congregation grew from 400 families to more than 2,700 families, and Magnin gained a reputation as the "rabbi to the stars." As such, he officiated at the funerals of many of the biggest names in entertainment, from MGM studio head Louis B. Mayer in 1957 to comedian Jack Benny in 1974.

Magnin was born July 1, 1890, in San Francisco, California.
He died July 17, 1984, in Los Angeles.

About 150 feet in front of the Mausoleum, in Section D at the southeast corner of the circular drive, you'll find the first Warner family mausoleum. This large but simple mausoleum contains the remains of Benjamin Warner (1857–1935) and his wife, Pearl Leah Warner (1857–1934)—the parents of twelve children, including the famous moviemaking Warner brothers—Harry, Albert, Sam, and Jack—who founded the Warner Bros. studio in 1923.

The Warner parents were from the small village of Krasnashiltz in Poland, near the German border. They married in 1876, when they were both nineteen years old. Their first child, Cecilia, died when she was four years old. In addition to the Warner parents, the family mausoleum also contains their daughter Anna Warner Robins (1879–1958), son **Samuel L. Warner (1885–1927),** daughter Rosa Warner Charnas (1889–1955), son David Warner (1893–1939), daughter Sadie Warner Halper (1895–1959) and her husband, Louis J. Halper (1894–1957).

Hidden behind that mausoleum and a few large evergreen trees is a smaller Warner family mausoleum. This one contains the remains of son **Harry Morris Warner (1881–1958),** his wife Rea E. Warner (1888–1970), their son Lewis Joseph Warner (1908–1931), their daughter Doris Ruth Warner Vidor (1912–1978), and her husband, director Charles Vidor (1899–1959).

Notable by his absence from the Warner family mausoleums is brother Jack, but he's not far away. About two hundred feet west of the Warner mausoleums, northwest of the main mausoleum, in the Joshua Section, is the grave of **Jack Warner (1892–1978)** and his wife Ann Warner (1908–1990). Beneath Jack Warner's name is the inscription "In Memory of Years of Devotion." Their graves are just off the road in a lush and colorful garden. Behind their graves is a fountain, a small granite bench, and a low, black granite wall with the name "Warner" written in gold.

Some have suggested that the reason Jack wasn't entombed in the family mausoleums was because of a split among the brothers when Jack wrested control of the Warner Bros. studio from his older brother, Harry. But it's more likely that the flamboyant Jack wanted a more lavish and ornate burial spot, and he didn't want to share the spotlight, even after death.

The Warner family came to America from Poland in 1883, settling first in Baltimore, where Benjamin worked as a cobbler, then in Ontario, Canada, where he traded furs. When Harry, the eldest son, moved to Youngstown, Ohio, and set up his own successful shoe repair shop, the rest of the family quickly followed. Four of the Warner boys—Harry, Albert, Sam, and Jack—were eager entrepreneurs, and they opened a series of businesses in Youngstown, including a grocery store, a bicycle repair shop, and a bowling alley. In 1903, they purchased a projector and a print of *The Great Train Robbery*, one of the most popular attractions in the nickelodeons at the time, and took their traveling show throughout Ohio and Pennsylvania. The following year, with the profits they made, they bought their own theater in New Castle, Pennsylvania, and named it the Cascade. They opened another theater in New Castle, the Bijou, but quickly realized that the economic future of the film business was in distribution, not exhibition. Harry Warner suggested that the brothers sell the theaters and open a "film exchange" business, which would allow theater owners to buy films and exchange them with other theater owners. The Warners' business—the Duquesne Amusement Supply Company—would facilitate those exchanges, for a fee.

The next step was for the four Warners to begin making their own films. In 1912, they began to produce films in New York City. They shifted their operation to Los Angeles in 1918, and, five years later, they opened their own studio. Warner Bros. Pictures was established in 1923, with Harry as president, Sam and Jack as vice presidents in charge of production, and Albert as treasurer. As the company was originally set up, Harry and Albert would stay in New York City to deal with distributors and financiers—the business end— while Sam and Jack would produce the films in Hollywood.

After working in several locations in the Los Angeles area, Sam and Jack found a ten-acre lot at Sunset Boulevard and Bronson Avenue, in the heart of Hollywood, which they bought for $25,000 and quickly outfitted with an office building and a stage. Back in New York, Harry was making arrangements to purchase theaters or enter into exchange agreements with existing theaters to show Warner Bros. films, and buying up the rights to literary works by F. Scott Fitzgerald, Sinclair Lewis, and other prominent authors. But the first big Warner Bros. star was a German shepherd dog named Rin-Tin-Tin, who starred in *Where the North Begins* (1923) and won the heart of the nation. More than twelve thousand pieces of fan mail for the dog poured into the studio every week, and a young writer named Darryl F. Zanuck was hired to write a series of Rin-Tin-Tin adventures.

Though the studio was succeeding, tension was growing between the four Warner brothers. Harry and Albert were primarily focused on the bottom line and interested in keeping company costs low and profits high. Sam was more of a visionary who wanted to raise the quality of a Warner Bros. film to something that couldn't be achieved when the studio's biggest attraction was a German shepherd—it was Sam's idea to bring Shakespearean stage actor John Barrymore to Warner Bros., over his brothers' objections. And Jack was happiest when he was running the studio and cranking out two-reelers and cheaply made serials.

The Warner brothers purchased a radio station in Los Angeles, which they set up on their Sunset Boulevard lot with the call letters KWBC, which stood for Warner Bros. Classics. The station was used primarily to promote Warner Bros. films and give Jack, a frustrated entertainer, the chance to sing to an audience. The call letters were later changed to KFWB. It was in the

One of the Warner Brothers is buried in this family mausoleum at Home of Peace Memorial Park. Two others are buried nearby.

radio station offices in 1925 that Sam and Jack first heard of a new invention recently demonstrated in New York—"talking pictures." The films were shown with two synchronized motors running side by side. One motor operated the film projector, and the other ran a wax recording of the sound, which was broadcast through a speaker behind the screen. Of all the Warners, Sam was the most excited about the idea, but he had a difficult time convincing his brothers that there was any future in presenting films with synchronized sound.

Sam finally convinced Harry to see a demonstration of the new process in New York, and the brothers entered into a contract with Western Electric, which had developed the synchronized sound process. The Warners' first plan was to add a musical score to *Don Juan,* which was already being filmed with Barrymore at the Warner studios. The film debuted in 1926 in New York City with a musical score recorded by the New York Philharmonic Orchestra, and the audience response was overwhelming. Although the Warners had an exclusive contract to use the synchronized sound process, the costs to record the sound and properly outfit their theaters with sound equipment was staggering. The studio was forced to renegotiate their contract with Western Electric, which gave other studios an opportunity to use the sound system.

Meanwhile, the Warners were proceeding with their next ambitious project. Harry paid $50,000 for the rights to a popular Broadway play about a singing rabbi called *The Jazz Singer.* Though George Jessel starred in the play, the Warners hired Al Jolson for the film version, and they decided to try their sound process again, this time recording the actors singing instead of just adding music to the film. During the filming, Jolson prefaced a song with the statement "Wait a minute. You ain't heard nothing yet!" And, with that, the "talking picture" was born.

Though it was not the first film to use synchronized sound, and even though title cards were still used for most of the dialogue, *The Jazz Singer* (1927) was the first feature-length film in which spoken dialogue was used as part of the dramatic action. The film cost $500,000 to make but netted $3 million in profits. Unfortunately, Sam Warner, the driving force behind the sound process, wasn't around to enjoy the results of his efforts. He died in Los Angeles on October 5, 1927—the day before *The Jazz Singer*'s New York City premiere.

Despite the success of *The Jazz Singer*, other studios were slow to embrace the new technology. Even the Warner brothers didn't drop their silent films. In 1928, the Warner studio schedule included twelve "talkies" and twenty-eight silent films. But the profits from *The Jazz Singer* allowed the Warners to start buying movie theaters across the country—for a time at the rate of one new theater per day. Within a year, Warner Bros. Pictures owned five hundred theaters. The brothers also bought First National Pictures, a film production company with a 110-acre studio complex in Burbank, California.

The grave of Jack Warner, the most well-known of the four famous Warner brothers, includes a small fountain.

Jack Warner was now running two studios, and he enjoyed his role as a powerful and successful entertainment mogul, even though he didn't like the word *mogul*—"It reminds me of some bad Turkish cigarettes I used to smoke," he quipped. In 1930, Jack moved all major production facilities to the Burbank studios and used the Sunset Boulevard location for B pictures and shorts. Zanuck, the former Rin-Tin-Tin writer, was named Warner Bros. head of production.

The only thing that the other major studios had that Warner Bros. didn't was star power. To remedy that situation, the Warners broke an unwritten code of conduct in Hollywood—they raided another studio. William Powell, Kay Francis, and Ruth Chatterson—three of the top stars at Paramount Pictures—were lured to Warner Bros. at double their salaries. Warner Bros. made another course-defining move when they produced *Little Caesar* (1930), starring Broadway actor Edward G. Robinson. From that moment on, Warner Bros. became known as the home of the gangster film, with such films as *Sinner's Holiday* (1930), marking the film debuts of James Cagney and Joan Blondell; *Doorway to Hell* (1931) and *The Public Enemy* (1931), both with Cagney; *I Am a Fugitive from a Chain Gang* (1932), with Paul Muni; *The Petrified Forest* (1936), which made a star out of Humphrey Bogart; *Angels With Dirty Faces* (1938), with Cagney, Bogart, and Pat O'Brien; *The Roaring Twenties* (1939), with Cagney and Bogart; and *Each Dawn I Die* (1939), with Cagney and George Raft. With these popular actors, plus Bette Davis, Joan Crawford, Olivia de Havilland, Errol Flynn, Ingrid Bergman, Barbara Stanwyck, Dick Powell, George Raft, Loretta Young, Douglas Fairbanks Jr., Burt Lancaster, Carole Lombard, Lauren Bacall, Peter Lorre, and Ronald Reagan on the payroll, Warner Bros. finally had star power.

Warner Bros. was one of the top studios in Hollywood during the 1940s, usually sticking with gritty realism in black-and-white productions, such as *The Maltese Falcon* (1941), *Casablanca* (1942), *To Have and Have Not* (1945), *The Big Sleep* (1946), *Key Largo* (1948), *The Treasure of the Sierra Madre* (1948), and *White Heat* (1949). The screen's ultimate moody rebel, James Dean, played all three of his starring roles at Warner Bros.—*Rebel Without a Cause* (1955), *East of Eden* (1955), and *Giant* (1956). During this time, Warner Bros. made a few musicals, but with mixed results, from the failure of *A Midsummer Night's Dream* (1935), to the huge success of *Yankee Doodle Dandy* (1942). In fact, it wasn't until the late 1950s that Warner Bros. finally started making big-production, full-color musicals, such as *Damn Yankees* (1958), *The Music Man* (1962), and *My Fair Lady* (1964).

Jack Warner often clashed with his actors, having famously public and long-running feuds with Bogart, Cagney, Flynn, and Davis, as well as with directors John Huston and Michael Curtiz, with the battles occasionally ending up in court. Warner hired and fired employees at will—sometimes the same ones over and over—and he never failed to point out to any troublesome workers that his name was painted on the studio's water tower. Jack even fired the studio's first big star, Rin-Tin-Tin, with a letter to the dog's owner and trainer stating that making another film starring a dog "is not in keeping with the policy that has been adopted by us for talking pictures, very obviously, of course, because dogs don't talk." Jack even fired his own son, Jack Jr., from his position as the studio's vice president in charge of commercial and industrial films.

In the late 1940s, Harry moved from New York to California, and Jack wasn't happy with his older brother looking over his shoulder. And Harry didn't like the idea that all the Warner Bros. employees in Burbank—including Jack—acted as if Jack were running the company. Little by little, Harry spent less time at the studio and more time with his horses at his San Fernando Valley ranch.

By the mid-1950s, both Harry and Albert Warner were in their seventies and becoming less involved in the day-to-day operations of the company. In 1956, Jack told his brothers that the studio's profits were slumping and they needed a major influx of capital if they were to remain competitive with the other studios. Over Harry's strong objections, Warner Bros. sold the rights to all of their films made before 1949 to United Artists Television for $21 million. Next, Jack convinced his brothers that they should all sell their stock in the company for $22 million to a group of investment bankers Jack knew in Boston. The Warners would remain on the company board of trustees, but a new administration would run the company, according to Jack's plan. Harry and Albert agreed to join Jack in selling their stock. But Jack immediately bought back his shares, announced that he was now the primary stockholder in the company, and took Harry's old title as president of Warner Bros.

Harry was stunned and vowed never to speak to Jack again. When Harry died in 1958, Rea, his widow, said bitterly, "Harry didn't die; Jack killed him." Jack did not attend Harry's funeral. Albert wasn't nearly so upset with Jack's deception. He was just happy to be out of the business and happy to retire to his home in Miami Beach, Florida, where he died in 1967.

Jack Warner remained active at the studio through the 1960s, overseeing production of such hits as *My Fair Lady* (1964)—the first Warner Bros. film to win an Academy Award for Best Picture since *Casablanca*, nineteen years earlier. In 1966, forty-three years after the founding of Warner Bros. Pictures, Jack announced that he was selling his interest in the company to Seven Arts Productions for $32 million, and this time he didn't plan to buy it back.

But Jack wasn't done working. After leaving Warner Bros., he opened an office in Century City and, at the age of seventy-four, started work as an independent producer. Unfortunately, he had little success, and he died in 1978.

In 1958, Jack Warner was given the Irving G. Thalberg Memorial Award, which is presented by the Academy of Motion Picture Arts and Sciences "for consistently high quality of production." Previously, Warner had made no secret of his disappointment that the Academy had given the Thalberg Award to Hal Wallis twice and to Darryl Zanuck three times but hadn't seen fit to honor the man who hired them both.

Harry Warner was born Hirsch Warner on December 12, 1881, in Krasnashiltz, Poland. He died July 25, 1958, in Los Angeles.

Albert Warner was born Abraham Warner on July 23, 1884, in Baltimore, Maryland (some sources say he was born in Poland). He died November 26, 1967, in Miami Beach, Florida.

Sam Warner was born in Baltimore, Maryland, on August 10, 1885. He died October 5, 1927, in Los Angeles.

Jack L. Warner was born Jacob Warner on August 2, 1892, in London, Ontario, Canada. He died September 9, 1978, in Los Angeles.

Behind the Home of Peace Mausoleum, in the far southwest corner of the cemetery, in the Western Jewish Institute Section, is the most visited spot in the cemetery—the grave of **Jerome Howard (1903–1952),** better known as "Curly" of the Three Stooges. Curly's grave is about 50 feet west of the road and about 225 feet from the fence at the southern edge of the cemetery.

Curly was the rotund, bald Stooge who was on the receiving end of most of the physical abuse from his fellow Stooge and older brother, Moe Howard, whether being hit on the head by a sledgehammer, poked in the eyes, or grabbed by the nose with a pair of pliers.

Curly joined "Ted Healy and His Stooges" in 1932, replacing his older brother, Shemp Howard. Before joining the Stooges, Curly had thick, wavy brown hair and a mustache, which Healy insisted he shave off. Curly always felt self-conscious about his shiny scalp, and he usually wore a hat when he was in public. He was adept at both physical and verbal comedy, and many of today's top comedians and actors credit him as their inspiration.

In 1934, Columbia Pictures offered a long-term contract to the Stooges if they left Ted Healy, which they did. The Three Stooges made more than 100 two-reelers for Columbia, and they were among the most popular and most profitable film performers of the 1930s, 1940s, and 1950s, though they were

Fans use pennies to spell out one of the catchphrases of Jerome Howard, better known as Curly of the Three Stooges.

never able to convince Columbia to allow them to star in a feature-length film.

Despite his onscreen image as an ill-mannered buffoon, Curly was a fine athlete and an accomplished ballroom dancer, and he loved to sing. Considered quite a lady's man, he was married four times. Throughout his life, Curly had a weakness for wine, women, and song, and his wild life eventually did him in. He appeared in more than one hundred Stooge shorts until he suffered a stroke on the set of *Half-Wits Holiday* in 1946. Shemp returned to the act to replace him. Curly suffered several more strokes between 1949 and 1952, and he was confined for long periods in hospitals and convalescence homes. In early 1952, he was admitted to the ironically named Baldy View Sanitarium, where he died at the age of forty-eight.

Unlike his brother Shemp, Curly's grave marker does not include his well-known Stooges nickname, or any other indication of his career. The inscription simply states, "Jerome Howard—Beloved Husband, Father and Brother."

Curly's grave is by far the most popular spot in the cemetery, according to cemetery employees. His tombstone is usually covered with flowers, coins, stones, notes, and other items left behind by fans. On a recent visit, someone had spelled out his well-known catchphrase, "Nyuk, nyuk, nyuk," in pennies in front of his gravestone.

Curly was born Jerome Lester Horwitz on October 22, 1903,
in Brooklyn, New York. He died January 18, 1952, in
San Gabriel, California.

In front of Curly's grave is the slightly larger memorial marking the graves of his parents—Solomon and Jennie Horwitz. Other than the family name on the stone, the rest of the inscription is written in Hebrew.

an inside corner, is a metal gate. Behind the gate is a small room, about ten feet by twelve feet. In the center of the back wall you'll find the remains of comedian **Groucho Marx (1890–1977),** behind a six-inch-square bronze plaque.

With his trademark swallowtail coat, greasepaint mustache, and ever-present cigar, Groucho's entertainment career spanned more than seventy years, and included success in vaudeville, films, radio, and television. He also wrote six popular books, including *Groucho and Me, The Groucho Letters, Beds,* and *Memoirs of a Mangy Lover.*

Groucho—born Julius Henry Marx—was the master of the ad-libbed insult and the hilarious non sequitur, usually delivered with rolling eyes and arched eyebrows. With his brothers Harpo (Adolph), Chico (Leonard), and sometimes Zeppo (Herbert), Groucho created a comedy world of slapstick farce, rapid-fire repartee, and free-spirited anarchy, usually aimed at deflating the pompous and the upper class. A fifth brother, Gummo (Milton), performed with his brothers during their early vaudeville days but left the act to become a theatrical agent. (A sixth brother, Manfred Marx, died in infancy.)

The Marx brothers got their names from Art Fisher, a comedian who specialized in making up nicknames—Adolph played the harp and became Harpo, Leonard had a reputation as a woman-chaser and became Chico, Milton wore gum-soled shoes and became Gummo, and Herbert was named after a popular performing monkey named Zippo. And, of course, because of his typically sardonic disposition, Julius became Groucho.

Groucho's father, Sam, was a struggling immigrant tailor in New York City and their mother, the former Minnie Schoenberg, was the stage-struck sister of Al Shean, of the popular comedy team of Gallagher and Shean. Minnie Marx pushed all of her five sons into show business, even joining them for a while in an act called "The Six Musical Mascots," which consisted of Groucho, Harpo, Gummo, a young singer named Janie O'Reilly, Minnie, and her sister, Hannah. When Minnie and Hannah left the act, it became "The Four Nightingales," then "The Marx Brothers and Company." While touring through small towns in the South and Midwest, the Marxes began to add more comedy to the act, including a wide assortment of jokes, puns, and ad-libbed comments, usually made up for their own entertainment in the small-town theaters, and often at the expense of their audience.

Groucho was also gradually creating his familiar look. The swallowtail coat was added when he played a teacher in a classroom sketch. The cigar was a useful comedy prop to make him look older, and also helpful to puff on while

If you look very closely you can see the remains of come-dian Groucho Marx in the center of this wall of niches.

trying to remember a line. Even Groucho's distinctive walk came from a sketch that required him to portray an older man. Groucho hunched his shoulders and leaned forward, but when he walked quickly across the stage, the audience laughed, so he continued to do it. His painted-on mustache was born when he arrived late at the theater and didn't have time to apply his fake mustache, so he just smeared greasepaint under his nose.

The Marx Brothers' first appearance on film was in a silent comedy short titled *Humor Risk* (1921). The film was previewed once and shown again five years later, but it was never widely released and is believed to have been lost.

Eventually, the Marx Brothers returned to the stage in New York City, and by 1924 they were a hit on Broadway with their musical comedy show, *I'll Say She Is*. They followed that with two more Broadway hits—*The Cocoanuts* and *Animal Crackers*. When talking pictures were introduced in the late 1920s, studios came to Broadway looking for comedians, and the Marxes were signed by Paramount Pictures to appear in the filmed version of *The Cocoanuts* (1929), which they worked on during the day, while appearing onstage in *Animal Crackers* every evening.

Animal Crackers was filmed in 1930, with Groucho in one his most popular roles as celebrated big-game hunter Captain Jeffrey T. Spaulding. Groucho arrives as the guest of honor at a high-society soiree, and greets the guests with the song "Hello, I Must Be Going." He then delivers a lengthy discussion of his adventures in Africa, in typical Groucho fashion—"One morning I shot an elephant in my pajamas. How he got in my pajamas, I'll never know. . . . While shooting elephants in Africa, I found the tusks were very difficult to remove. But in Alabama, the Tuscaloosa."

Although the Marx Brothers films were officially written by some of the top comedy writers of the time, including George S. Kaufman, Morrie Ryskind, S. J. Perelman, Nat Perrin, Bert Kalmar, and Harry Ruby, the versions that finally appeared on the screen were often more ad-lib and rewrites by the brothers than the original script. Kaufman once jumped to his feet during a rehearsal, apparently shocked at something he had heard. When asked if there was a problem, Kaufman said, "I think I just heard one of the original lines."

Animal Crackers was followed by *Monkey Business* (1931), *Horse Feathers* (1932), and two films that most Marx Brothers fans agree are the brothers' best work—*Duck Soup* (1933) and *A Night at the Opera* (1935), which was their first film at MGM studios. Irving Thalberg, the vice president and head of production at MGM, was given the responsibility of controlling the Marxes, but he quickly discovered that they couldn't be controlled. According to one popular story, the Marxes were called to Thalberg's office for a meeting but were kept waiting for more than two hours. When Thalberg finally arrived, he discovered the brothers sitting in front of his fireplace, nude, roasting potatoes over the open fire.

A Night at the Opera was also the brothers' first film without Zeppo, although there were four members of the family in the film. Sam Marx, their father, appeared in two scenes as an extra. The three remaining Marx Brothers—Groucho, Harpo, and Chico—made five more films at MGM: *A Day at the Races* (1937), *Room Service* (1938), *At*

A much closer view of Groucho Marx's simple plaque at Eden Memorial Park.

the Circus (1939), Go West (1940), and The Big Store (1941). After taking several years off, they returned to the screen in A Night in Casablanca (1946) and Love Happy (1950)—which is perhaps less significant as the Marx Brothers' final film together than it is as one of the first film appearances of a young actress named Marilyn Monroe.

With his film career essentially over, the sixty-year-old Groucho moved to a new medium—television—as the host of You Bet Your Life, a comedy and quiz show that premiered in 1950 and ran for more than ten years. Groucho started hosting You Bet Your Life on radio in 1947, and the show was popular more for Groucho's interviews with the contestants than for the actual question-and-answer portion of the show. Though Groucho never received any major awards during his film career, he won an Emmy in 1951 as "Most Outstanding Personality" for his work on You Bet Your Life. The show itself was also nominated for five Emmy Awards, first as Best Comedy Show, and later as Best Quiz Show. In 1948, You Bet Your Life won a Peabody Award, which honors distinguished achievement and meritorious service in radio and television.

In the 1960s and 1970s, a new generation of fans discovered the Marx Brothers. In May 1972, Groucho appeared in An Evening With Groucho, a sold-out performance at Carnegie Hall in New York City. In 1974, Groucho was given an honorary Academy Award "in recognition of his brilliant creativity and for the unequaled achievements of the Marx Brothers in the art of motion picture comedy."

Recently, the American Film Institute selected a ranked list of "America's 100 funniest movies" of the past century. Even though the Marx Brothers made only thirteen films together, they placed five in the top hundred, including Duck Soup (ranked 5th on the list), A Night at the Opera (12th), A Day at the Races (59th), Horse Feathers (65th), and Monkey Business (73rd). Duck Soup also appeared in the 85th spot on AFI's list of the top one hundred films of all time.

Groucho was married three times and had three children. His son, Arthur Marx, is a successful scriptwriter and author of several Hollywood biographies.

Marx was born Julius Henry Marx on October 2, 1890, in New York City. He died August 19, 1977, in Los Angeles.

Drive around on the road directly behind the mausoleum. On the south side of the road, directly behind the center of the mausoleum, you'll find a sign identifying the "Mount Nebo Section." Walk about forty feet directly south of that sign, toward the back of the mausoleum, and you'll find the grave of comedian **Lenny Bruce (1925–1966)**, who spent most of his career battling arrests for obscenity and drug possession, and who was a major influence on many of today's comedians.

After serving in the navy for four years, from 1942 to 1946, Bruce found work as a comedian in nightclubs in New York City. He got his first big break in October 1948, with an appearance on *Arthur Godfrey's Talent Scouts*. Based on the success of that performance, Bruce toured the country and appeared on several television shows. His act consisted of observations and comments on social issues, rather than the typical stand-up comedian's stream of mother-in-law jokes and snappy one-liners.

Comedian Lenny Bruce may have found "peace at last" at Eden Memorial Park.

Bruce seemed to enjoy shocking his audiences by the issues he liked to discuss, which included topics that were rarely discussed in public, let alone made fun of by comedians—race, sex, and religion were some of his favorite subjects—and by his language, which included most of the standard four-letter profanities and other language never before used on a nightclub stage. Offstage, Bruce was developing a strong relationship with drugs, both prescription and illegal narcotics, particularly heroin. Beginning in the early 1960s, Bruce was often arrested both for the contents of his act and for his drug use.

Though his supporters praised his role as a contemporary social satirist in the tradition of Jonathan Swift and Mark Twain, others called him simply a "sick comic."

Bruce was arrested in Philadelphia on September 29, 1961, for possession of narcotics, a charge that would later be dropped when he produced prescriptions for the drugs. He was arrested again at a comedy club in San

Francisco, and a week later in Los Angeles for violating the California Obscenity Code, but he was acquitted of the charges. In 1962, after one performance in Australia, he was banned from the country. The following year, he was twice denied admittance to Great Britain, which declared him "an undesirable alien."

At this point, the police were closely watching Bruce wherever he worked, ready to arrest him for either drugs or obscenity. And Bruce didn't disappoint them. He was arrested on October 6, 1962, in Los Angeles for possessing narcotics, and on October 24, 1962, for using obscenity during a performance at the Troubadour on Santa Monica Boulevard. After he was acquitted again, Bruce's act began to turn into an unstructured monologue on race, religion, sex, drugs, the police, and any other sacred cows he could find to skewer, as well as commentary on his many legal battles. Bruce was arrested and charged with obscenity in Chicago in December 1962, charged with possession of narcotics in Los Angeles in January 1963, and charged with obscenity in New York City in April 1964. After a six-week trial in New York City, Bruce was found guilty. Bruce responded by filing a complaint with the FBI in October 1965, charging that the government was conspiring to violate his rights of free speech. (In February 1968, eighteen months after Bruce's death, a state court in New York reversed the obscenity conviction.)

Bruce published his autobiography, *How to Talk Dirty and Influence People,* in 1965, but due to his many arrests he had increasing difficulty finding work in comedy clubs, and he began to spend more time and money on his legal battles. When Bruce did find work, he had become so obsessed with his First Amendment struggles that he would bring transcripts from his trials to the stage and read them to his ever-shrinking audience. In late 1965, he filed for bankruptcy, claiming that he had earned only $2,000 in the past year. In April 1966, the Los Angeles Municipal Court sentenced Bruce for his 1962 drug arrest—one-year suspended jail term, a $260 fine, and two years' probation.

Bruce's last performance was on June 26, 1966, in San Francisco. On August 3, 1966, he was found dead in his apartment on Hollywood Boulevard in Los Angeles. He was forty. The coroner ruled that his death was caused by an accidental overdose of heroin.

Lenny, a musical based on his life and including much of his comic material, was a hit on Broadway in 1971. Bruce was introduced to a new generation in the biographical film *Lenny* (1974), directed by Bob Fosse and starring Dustin Hoffman in the title role. The film was nominated for Academy

Awards for Best Picture, Best Director, Best Actor, Best Actress (Valerie Perrine as Bruce's wife, Honey), and Best Screenplay, but it did not win any awards.

Today, when comedians on television can pretty much discuss any topic, and comedians in concert and on cable television can pretty much say anything and use any language they want, it's difficult to believe that Lenny Bruce was arrested so recently for using particular words or discussing particular topics. But, on freedom-of-speech issues for entertainers, Bruce was the trailblazer. If not for him, his legal struggles and his ultimate victory—even though it came too late for him to enjoy—we probably wouldn't have comedians like Richard Pryor, George Carlin, and Chris Rock. Whether Bruce gets the credit or the blame for the current state of comedy is certainly up to each person to decide.

Bruce's grave marker identifies him as "Lenny 'Bruce' Schneider—Beloved father, Devoted son—Peace at Last."

Lenny Bruce was born Leonard Alfred Schneider on October 13, 1925, in Mineola, New York. He died August 3, 1966, in Los Angeles.

At the top of the hill on the north end of the cemetery property are two large, newer garden mausoleums. Drive up to the larger of the two mausoleums, and park on the south side of the structure. Walk up the sidewalk that heads toward the center of the mausoleum. There are several small, white stone benches on either side of the sidewalk. Just before you reach the mausoleum, turn right. In front of the third bench from the sidewalk, you'll find the grave of actor and acting teacher **Harvey Lembeck (1923–1982).**

Lembeck started his acting career on Broadway. He appeared in *Mister Roberts* in 1948, *Stalag 17* in 1951, and played Sancho Panza in the touring company of *Man of La Mancha.*

As a film actor, Lembeck is best remembered for playing two basic characters. He started his career playing a series of Brooklyn-accented, low-level military grunts in World War II films such as *You're in the Navy Now* (1951), *The Frogmen* (1951), *Back at the Front* (1952), *Stalag 17* (1953), *Mission Over Korea* (1953), *The Command* (1954), *Between Heaven and Hell* (1956), and *The Last Time I Saw Archie* (1961), as well as on *The Phil Silvers Show.*

Then, beginning with *Beach Party* (1963), Lembeck played Eric Von Zipper, the sanitized, slightly goofy version of a leather-jacketed motorcycle gang leader in a series of teen beach movies starring Frankie Avalon and Annette Funicello, including *Bikini Beach* (1964), *Pajama Party* (1964), *Beach Blanket Bingo* (1965), *Dr. Goldfoot and the Bikini Machine* (1965), *How to Stuff a Wild Bikini* (1965), and *The Ghost in the Invisible Bikini* (1966).

Lembeck had two children—Michael Lembeck, who appeared as an actor in several situation comedies and films in the 1970s and 1980s and is currently an Emmy-winning sitcom director, and Helaine Lembeck, an actress who was a regular on the TV series *Welcome Back, Kotter* in the 1970s and has also appeared in a handful of made-for-TV movies.

After the beach films, Lembeck opened a successful acting school in Los Angeles, which is currently operated by his children.

The inscription on Lembeck's grave marker reads, "He loved, he laughed, he lives."

Lembeck was born April 15, 1923, in Brooklyn, New York.
He died January 5, 1982, in Los Angeles.

12

San Fernando Mission Cemetery

~

11160 Stranwood Avenue
Mission Hills, California 91345

~ HISTORY

The San Fernando Mission was established in 1797, one of many Christian missions built throughout California. Like most missions, the San Fernando Mission contained a small chapel and a graveyard. The burial grounds at the San Fernando Mission were originally intended for "Christianized Indians," but many European settlers and at least five priests are also buried here. Many of the graves are unmarked, and many of the deceased were buried directly in the ground without a coffin, sometimes wrapped in blankets. There were also multiple burials, with more than one person buried in a single grave space.

According to mission records, the first burial was in 1800, and the last at the old mission graveyard was in 1852. In between, nearly 2,500 people were buried at the mission.

The current San Fernando Mission Cemetery, one of eleven Catholic cemeteries in the Archdiocese of Los Angeles, was opened in 1952, adjacent to the old mission churchyard. The total property includes eighty-six acres, with nearly thirty acres currently undeveloped.

~ DIRECTIONS

San Fernando Mission Cemetery is located on the northern edge of the San Fernando Valley, in a triangle of property bounded by the Simi Valley Freeway (118) on the south, the San Diego Freeway (405) on the west, and the Golden State Freeway (5) on the east. From downtown Los Angeles, take the Hollywood Freeway (101 and 170) north to the Golden State Freeway (5), then northwest about three miles to the Simi Valley Freeway (118). Take the Simi Valley Freeway west for a little more than a mile, to Sepulveda Boulevard. Take Sepulveda north about a half-mile to Stranwood Avenue and turn right.

From the west side of Los Angeles, take the San Diego Freeway (405) north, about eight miles past the Ventura Freeway (101), and take the Rinaldi Street exit. Turn right on Sepulveda Boulevard, then south about a block to Stranwood Avenue.

~ *Hours*

The cemetery grounds are open every day from 8 A.M. to 5 P.M. during the fall and winter seasons, and from 8 A.M. to 6 P.M. during the spring and summer.

~

The Tour

As you enter the cemetery through the main gate on the west side of the property, you'll see the administrative offices on your right. Turn right at the first intersection, then follow the road as it curves toward the east. Stop when you see the number 247 on the curb on the left side of the road. About fifteen feet north of that number, you'll find the grave of the first Hispanic rock star, **Ritchie Valens (1941–1959).**

Valens began performing while he was still in junior high school, singing and playing the guitar at school assemblies. He was discovered by record producer Bob Keane in 1958 and was signed to Keane's Del-Fi label. Valens's first song, "Come On, Let's Go," sold 750,000 copies and reached number forty-two on the record charts, and his next release, "Donna," a ballad Valens wrote to his girlfriend, Donna Ludwig, reached number two in early 1959. Over the objections of record company executives who questioned the marketability of a rock song sung entirely in Spanish, Valens recorded "La Bamba" on the flip side. "La Bamba" was a traditional Spanish folk song that Valens learned from his mother, but he added a rock beat.

The seventeen-year-old Valens was quickly becoming a rock superstar and was sent out on a national concert tour called "The Winter Dance Party" with Buddy Holly, twenty-two, and J. P. Richardson, twenty-four, better known as the "Big Bopper." All three performers were rising stars—together they had sold more than ten million records in the past year. After a performance in Clear Lake, Iowa, on February 3, 1959, all three boarded a small, single-engine plane to take them to their next show, but the plane crashed shortly

The music from two of his popular songs is etched into the grave marker of Ritchie Valens, who died in a plane crash at seventeen.

after takeoff in a blinding snowstorm, killing the three musicians and their twenty-one-year-old pilot.

The crash was immortalized by singer Don McLean's 1971 song, "American Pie" as "the day the music died." Valens was introduced to a new generation of fans through the film biography *La Bamba* (1987), in which the singer was played by Lou Diamond Phillips, and the song "La Bamba," this time performed by the group Los Lobos, became a hit all over again. Valens was inducted into the Rock and Roll Hall of Fame in 2001.

Valens's grave marker includes an etched photograph of him and a picture of an electric guitar, as well as a few notes from his first song, "Come On, Let's Go." He is buried next to his mother, Concepcion Reyes Valenzuela (1915–1987), and her marker includes a few notes from "La Bamba."

Ritchie Valens was born Richard Steven Valenzuela on May 13, 1941, in Pacoima, California. He died February 3, 1959, near Clear Lake, Iowa.

About 150 feet north of Valens's grave, just before you reach a large tree, you'll find the grave of **Alice Joyce Brown (1890–1955)**, a silent-film star known as the "Madonna of the Screen."

After working as a telephone operator and a fashion model, Joyce started her acting career with the Kalem production company in New York in 1910. She quickly gained popularity as the charming, well-mannered leading lady in numerous silent shorts. When Kalem was purchased by the Vitagraph production company in 1916, Joyce became one of the first "Vitagraph Girls." As her popularity skyrocketed, Joyce was billed as the "Madonna of the Screen."

Joyce appeared in nearly two hundred films, including *The Green Goddess* (1923), *Stella Dallas* (1925), *Beau Geste* (1926), *Dancing Mothers* (1926), and *The Squall* (1929). After appearing in a handful of early talkies, including a remake of *The Green Goddess* (1930), Joyce retired. She married director Clarence Brown in 1933, and they were divorced twelve years later.

Joyce is buried next to her mother, Vallie Olive Joyce (1873–1938).

Alice Joyce was born October 1, 1890 (some sources say 1889), in Kansas City, Missouri. She died October 9, 1955, in Los Angeles.

Continue back on the road, past the next intersection, and look for the number 121 on the curb on the left side of the road. Walk north about 250 feet from that point, until you're about 80 feet in front of a large statue of the Virgin Mary. There, you'll find the grave of veteran character actor **Edward Arnold (1890–1956).**

Arnold's acting career started on Broadway, where he appeared with Ethel Barrymore in *Dream of a Summer Night* in 1907. His film career started when he went to work for the Essanay production company in Chicago in 1915, and he appeared in numerous two-reel Westerns and adventure films. In 1920, Arnold returned to the stage, before coming to Hollywood in 1932. With his commanding presence and authoritative baritone voice, Arnold appeared in more than 150 films, usually playing judges, senators, lawyers, businessmen, and other authority figures, but often with a twist of deceit. Among his best-known roles were those in several Frank Capra films, including *You Can't Take It With You* (1938), *Mr. Smith Goes to Washington* (1939), and *Meet John Doe* (1941). Arnold also appeared in *I Am a Fugitive From a Chain Gang* (1932), *Rasputin and the Empress* (1932), *Diamond Jim* (1935), *The Great Ziegfeld* (1936), and *The Devil and Daniel Webster* (1941). He served as president of the Screen Actors Guild from 1940 to 1942.

Arnold was born Gunther Edward Arnold Schneider on February 18, 1890, in New York City. He died April 26, 1956, in Encino, California.

About twenty feet directly south of the statue of the Virgin Mary, you'll find a military tombstone marking the grave of flat-topped, self-deprecating, Emmy-winning comedian **George Gobel (1919–1991).**

Gobel started his entertainment career as a singer, performing as "Little George Gobel" on the *National Barn Dance* radio show when he was only eleven. Later, when he played his guitar and sang sad cowboy ballads, he was billed as "Lonesome George"—a nickname that would stay with him throughout his career as a comedian.

After serving as a flight instructor in the army air corps during World War II, Gobel began performing his comedy act in Chicago nightclubs. After making several appearances on television variety shows, Gobel was given his own show in late 1954. *The George Gobel Show* was an immediate success, winning an Emmy award for best comedy writing, and Gobel won the Emmy for "Most Outstanding New Personality," beating fellow nominees Walt Disney and Tennessee Ernie Ford, among others. *The George Gobel Show* ran for six years.

Gobel appeared in supporting roles in several films during the 1970s and early 1980s, including *Rabbit Test* (1978), *The Day It Came to Earth* (1979), and *Ellie* (1984). Gobel was also a regular guest on *The Hollywood Squares* television game show from 1974 to 1981.

Gobel has a military grave marker, which recognizes his rank as a first lieutenant in the U.S. Army Air Corps.

Gobel was born George Leslie Gobel on May 20, 1919, in Chicago, Illinois. He died February 24, 1991, in Encino, California.

Continue on the road, heading east, and look for the number 241 on the curb on the left side of the road. About one hundred feet north of that spot, near a large tree, you'll find the grave of actor **William Bendix (1906–1964),** best known for playing Chester A. Riley in the comedy series *The Life of Riley,* first on film, then on radio, then on television from 1953 to 1958.

Throughout his film career, Bendix typically played either dumb and brutish thugs or dense and lovable lugs. Born in New York City, Bendix worked as a New York Yankees batboy when he was a teenager, and he became a favorite of slugger Babe Ruth. Their friendship may have helped Bendix when he played the title role in *The Babe Ruth Story* (1948). After leaving New York, Bendix moved to New Jersey, where he played minor-league baseball and managed a grocery store. He also performed with the New Jersey

Federal Theater, then moved back to New York as a member of the New York Theater Guild.

Bendix made his debut on Broadway playing an Irish police officer in *The Time of Your Life* in 1939, then he moved to Hollywood. His first film appearance was in *Woman of the Year* (1942), starring Spencer Tracy and Katharine Hepburn. After several years playing supporting roles, particularly war films like *Wake Island* (1942) and *Guadalcanal Diary* (1943), Bendix turned in a sparkling and heart-wrenching performance in Alfred Hitchcock's *Lifeboat* (1942), as Gus, the shipwreck survivor and dance-contest winner who discovers that his gangrenous leg has to be amputated.

In 1949, Bendix played the title role in *The Life of Riley,* and continued the role in the radio program and long-running television series.

Bendix appeared in more than fifty films during his career, and was equally adept at action, melodrama, and light comedy. He appeared in *Sentimental Journey* (1946), *Two Years Before the Mast* (1946), *The Web* (1947), *Streets of Laredo* (1949), *A Connecticut Yankee in King Arthur's Court* (1949), *Kill the Umpire* (1950), and *Detective Story* (1951).

Bendix was nominated for an Academy Award as Best Supporting Actor for his performance in *Wake Island.*

William Bendix was born January 4, 1906, in New York City.
He died December 14, 1964, in Los Angeles.

Continue on the road, heading east, then turn left at the first cross street. Continue to the next intersection, and turn right. Look for the number 1089 on the curb on the left side of the road. From that point, walk north about 150 feet, and you'll find the grave of **Scott Beckett (1929–1968),** one of the child stars in the *Our Gang* comedies.

Scotty Beckett started his acting career when he was only three years old, appearing in *I Am Suzanne* (1933) and *Gallant Lady* (1933). Later that year, he joined the *Our Gang* troupe, first appearing in *Hi, Neighbor* (1934). With his dark hair and large, expressive eyes, Beckett was perhaps the cutest of the *Our Gang* actors. And, unlike many of his fellow *Our Gang* members, Beckett also appeared in other films while making the comedy shorts, including *Stand Up and Cheer* (1934), starring Shirley Temple; *Pursuit* (1935), starring Chester Morris; *Dante's Inferno* (1935), starring Spencer Tracy and Claire Trevor; *Old Hutch* (1936), starring Wallace Beery; *Wells Fargo* (1937), starring Joel McCrea; *Love Affair* (1939), starring Irene Dunne and Charles Boyer; *My*

Favorite Wife (1940), starring Cary Grant and Irene Dunne; *Kings Row* (1942), starring Ann Sheridan, Robert Cummings, and Ronald Reagan; and *Heaven Can Wait* (1943), starring Don Ameche and Gene Tierney. In 1946, Beckett played the young Al Jolson in *The Jolson Story,* which starred Larry Parks.

Like many child stars, Beckett had difficulty finding work after he grew up. By the early 1950s, the roles were becoming few and far between. Beckett appeared as Winky in several episodes of the *Rocky Jones, Space Ranger* television series in the mid-1950s, and his last film role was a small part in *The Oklahoman* (1957), starring Joel McCrea. About that time, Beckett began his relationship with alcohol and drugs and started his lengthy arrest record, which included drunk driving, drug possession, carrying a concealed weapon, and assaulting his stepdaughter with a crutch.

Beckett finally gave up acting and took a job as a car salesman in 1962. Four years later, he was found dead at the Royal Palms Hotel in Los Angeles, after taking an overdose of sleeping pills. His gravestone reads, "Actor and Father, Scott H. Beckett."

Scotty Beckett was born Scott Hastings Beckett on October 4, 1929, in Oakland, California. He died May 10, 1968, in Los Angeles.

Turn around and head west, back toward the cemetery entrance. Continue until you see the number 445 on the curb on the left side of the road. About ten feet from that spot, you'll find the grave of actor and three-time Academy Award winner **Walter Brennan (1894–1974).**

While studying engineering in Massachusetts, Brennan also became involved in the school's acting club. After serving in France during World War I, and against the wishes of his family, Brennan moved from the East Coast to Hollywood to pursue his dream of becoming an actor. Brennan first started working on Westerns in the late 1920s, usually playing supporting roles or doing stunts. During one of the films, he was involved in a fight scene in which another actor accidentally kicked Brennan in the face, knocking out all his front teeth. Brennan later described the incident as "the luckiest break in the world. I got a set of false choppers, so I looked all right off the set. But when necessary, I could take them out and suddenly look about forty years older."

With that skill, Brennan quickly developed a career as a character actor, winning Academy Awards as Best Supporting Actor for his work in *Come and Get It* (1936), *Kentucky* (1938), and *The Westerner* (1940). He was the first actor to win three Oscars, and is the only actor to pick up three awards for supporting roles. He was also nominated for his work in *Sergeant York* (1941).

Though best known for his roles as a grizzled old man, Brennan could also play melodrama and light comedy with equal success. He even had small roles in the horror films *The Invisible Man* (1933) and *The Bride of Frankenstein* (1935), and he appeared with the Three Stooges in *Woman Haters* (1934). Brennan often worked with his offscreen friend Gary Cooper, appearing with him in *The Wedding Night* (1935), *The Cowboy and the Lady* (1938), *The Westerner* (1940), *Sergeant York* (1941), *Meet John Doe* (1941), *Pride of the Yankees* (1942), and *Task Force* (1949). Brennan appeared in more than two hundred films, including *Barbary Coast* (1935), *Three Godfathers* (1936), *The Adventures of Tom Sawyer* (1938), *The Story of Verne and Irene Castle* (1939), *Northwest Passage* (1940), *To Have and Have Not* (1944), *My Darling Clementine* (1946), *Red River* (1948), *Bad Day at Black Rock* (1955), *Tammy and the Bachelor* (1957), *Rio Bravo* (1959), *How the West Was Won* (1962), and *The Gnome-Mobile* (1967).

In 1957, Brennan accepted his first role in a television series, playing Grandpa Amos McCoy in the long-running series *The Real McCoys*. He also starred in the series *The Tycoon* in 1964, and *The Guns of Will Sonnett* from 1967 to 1969.

Brennan was born Walter Andrew Brennan on July 25, 1894, in Swampscott, Massachusetts. He died September 21, 1974, in Oxnard, California.

Directly across the road from Brennan's grave, you'll find the number 842 on the curb. Walk about fifty feet north from that point, and you'll find the grave of another star of the *Our Gang* comedies, actress **June (Marlowe) Sprigg (1903–1984)**, best known for her role as teacher Miss June Crabtree.

Marlowe was discovered while appearing in a school play at Hollywood High School by director Malcolm St. Clair. She made her first screen appearance in 1923 and quickly began working at several studios in Hollywood. In 1924, she costarred with one of the biggest stars at Warner Bros.—Rin-Tin-Tin—in *Find Your Man*, the first of several films she made with the popular canine star. Warner Bros. promoted Marlowe as the "Most Beautiful Girl on the Screen" and the "Girl With the Soulful Eyes." Marlowe also starred in *Don Juan* (1926) with John Barrymore.

In the late 1920s, Marlowe made a few films in Germany and became a popular radio star in that country, where listeners were impressed by the American actress who spoke their language fluently. When she returned to Hollywood in 1930, Marlowe appeared in the comedies *Fast Work* (1930) with Charley Chase and *Pardon Us* (1931), the first feature-length film starring Stan Laurel and Oliver Hardy. While working at the Hal Roach Studios, the dark-haired Marlowe dyed her hair blonde and was given the role of Miss June Crabtree in the *Our Gang* comedies, and she appeared in six films in the series—*Teacher's Pet* (1930), *School's Out* (1930), *Love Business* (1931), *Little Daddy* (1931), *Shiver My Timbers* (1931), and *Readin' and Writin'* (1932).

In 1932, before she turned thirty, Marlowe retired from films. The following year, she married businessman Rodney Sprigg. Her gravestone reads, "Beloved Sister, June Sprigg." She is buried next to her brother, Louis J. Goetten (1906–1991), who worked as a prop man and assistant director for many years at Warner Bros. as "Louis Marlowe," and her parents, John P. Goetten (1874–1967) and Hedwig "Hattie" Goetten (1880–1952).

> *Marlowe was born Gisela Goetten on November 6, 1903, in St. Cloud, Minnesota. She died March 10, 1984, in Burbank, California.*

About fifty feet north of Sprigg's grave you'll find the grave of comedian **Jerry Colonna (1904–1986),** best known as comedian Bob Hope's sidekick for more than thirty years. Colonna, with his six-inch-long walrus mustache and large rolling eyes, was a popular radio and film performer who often traveled with Hope on his annual Christmas trips to entertain U.S. troops overseas.

Colonna started his career as a trombone player, and he was performing with his own orchestra by the time he was fourteen years old. While working with many of the popular Big Band leaders, including Benny Goodman, Artie Shaw, and Tommy and Jimmy Dorsey, Colonna gradually added comedy to his musical act. In the late 1930s, he was often a guest on the Fred Allen and Bing Crosby radio shows. In 1938, he signed a contract to be a regular performer on Hope's radio show, which started a lifelong personal and professional relationship between the two performers.

Colonna made his film debut in the musical *57th Street* (1937), which showcased his musical and comedic talents. He also appeared with Hope in the comedy *College Swing* (1938), as well as three *Road* films with Hope and Bing Crosby—*Road to Singapore* (1940), *Road to Rio* (1947), and *Road to Hong*

Kong (1962). Colonna hosted *The Jerry Colonna Show*, a music and variety series that ran for one season on television in 1951. He also provided the voice of the March Hare in Walt Disney's animated version of *Alice in Wonderland* (1951).

In the early 1960s, Colonna made several guest appearances on television series, including *The Monkees* and *McHale's Navy*.

Colonna was born Gerardo Luigi Colonna on September 17, 1904, in Boston, Massachusetts. He died November 21, 1986, in Woodland Hills, California.

Continue on the road, past the next intersection, and look for the number 395 on the curb on the left side of the road. Walk about 110 feet south from that point, toward a large statue of Jesus in the center of the section, and you'll find the grave of Academy Award–winning actor **Ed Begley Sr. (1901–1970).** Begley appeared in more than forty films during his career, and almost an equal number of television series.

When he was only eleven years old, Begley ran away from home and joined a traveling carnival. He worked a variety of jobs and served in the U.S. Navy before starting his show business career as a radio announcer in 1931. After performing for several years on Broadway, Begley made his film debut in *Boomerang!* (1947). In films, Begley often played the villain, usually a corrupt businessman or politician. Among his more memorable roles was as one of the jurors in *12 Angry Men* (1957).

Begley also appeared in *Sorry, Wrong Number* (1948), *It Happens Every Spring* (1949), *Deadline, USA (1952), The Unsinkable Molly Brown* (1964), and *Firecreek* (1968). Begley was nominated for an Emmy in 1956 for his performance on the *Kraft Television Theater,* and he won an Academy Award as Best Supporting Actor for his performance in *Sweet Bird of Youth* (1962). Begley is the father of actor Ed Begley Jr.

Begley was born Edward James Begley on March 25, 1901, in Hartford, Connecticut. He died April 28, 1970, in Los Angeles.

Just past curb number 395, turn right at the next intersection, heading north. Turn right again at the next intersection, and look for the number 120 on the curb on the left side of the road. Walk about 125 feet north of that point, toward a statue of the Madonna and child, and you'll find the grave of

Chuck Connors (1921–1992), who was "discovered" while playing minor-league baseball in Los Angeles and became much more successful as an actor than he ever was as an athlete.

The six-foot-five Connors played at the professional level in two sports—basketball and baseball. After serving in the military during World War II, Connors played for the Rochester Royals in the National Basketball League during the 1945–46 season. Connors played in fourteen games and scored a total of twenty-eight points, as the Royals won the league championship. The following season, Connors played for the newly formed Boston Celtics during the first season of the Basketball Association of America, which later became the National Basketball Association. Connors played in forty-nine games for the Celtics during the 1946–47 season, and averaged 4.6 points per game. And he also claimed a piece of basketball history, even though it was accidental. On November 5, 1946, the Celtics were scheduled to play their first home game ever in the Boston Garden, against the Chicago Stags. But, during warm-ups before the game, Connors splintered the wooden backboard with a dunk—the first broken backboard in professional basketball history. The game was delayed an hour for the backboard to be replaced, and the Celtics lost, 57–55.

The following season, Connors played only four games for the Celtics, averaging 3.0 points per game. After his basketball career ended, Connors turned his attention to baseball. Although he spent most of his professional baseball career in the minor leagues, he did have one unsuccessful at bat as

Chuck Connors's grave marker includes symbols of his early athletic career as well as his television role as the Rifleman.

a pinch hitter for the Brooklyn Dodgers in 1949, and he played sixty-six games as a first baseman for the Chicago Cubs in 1951, hitting .239 with two home runs in 201 at bats.

After the 1951 season, the Cubs sent Connors to one of their minor-league teams, the Los Angeles Angels. Connors was an enthusiastic and fun-loving player, and he often entertained his teammates and the fans by doing things like reciting "Casey at the Bat" and turning cartwheels while rounding the bases. A Hollywood director noticed Connors's on-field antics and offered him an opportunity to perform in front of a larger crowd. He was given a one-line role as a highway patrolman in the film *Pat and Mike* (1952), starring Spencer Tracy and Katharine Hepburn. That experience, coupled with his doubtful future as a professional baseball player, convinced Connors to change careers again, and he gave up sports for acting. For the next few years, Connors played small roles in several films, usually as a police officer, soldier, or some other man in uniform.

Though his rugged good looks and chiseled features made Connors a natural for action and adventure films, one of his first major roles was as Sylvester J. Superman in the *Adventures of Superman* television series in 1955, in an episode titled "Flight to the North." Connors played a country bumpkin with an unusual name who visits Metropolis and gets caught in the middle of a case of mistaken identity with the real Superman. This role was the first opportunity for Connors to show his comedic skills, which he didn't really get a chance to use again until *Airplane II: The Sequel* (1982).

For most of the late 1950s, Connors played a variety of villains and tough guys in the movies, including roles in *Designing Women* (1957) and *The Big Country* (1958). In 1958, he became a good guy again, playing the title role in the television series *The Rifleman*. Connors played Lucas McCain, the frontiersman and single parent trying to raise his son while dealing with the dangers of life in the Old West.

After *The Rifleman* ended in 1963, Connors starred in another television series, *Branded,* in which he played an army officer in the 1880s falsely accused of cowardice, trying to restore his good name and reputation. Though critically acclaimed, *Branded* lasted only one season. For the rest of his career, Connors regularly appeared in films and on television, though much of his film work was little seen and quickly forgotten. Connors played slave owner Tom Moore in the groundbreaking television miniseries *Roots* in 1977.

Connors's gravestone includes most of his sports and acting history. The marker, which identifies him as "Kevin 'Chuck' Connors," includes the logos of the Boston Celtics, the Brooklyn Dodgers, the Chicago Cubs, and an etched photograph of Connors as the *Rifleman*.

*Connors was born Kevin Joseph Aloysius Connors
on April 10, 1921, in Brooklyn, New York. He died
November 10, 1992, in Los Angeles.*

Retrace your route back toward Ed Begley's grave and turn right toward the main entrance. Follow the road as it curves to the left and look for the number 64 on the curb on the left side of the road. Walk about forty feet east of that point, and you'll find the grave of actor **William Frawley (1887–1966)**, best known as neighbor and landlord Fred Mertz on the television series *I Love Lucy*.

Frawley started his professional career as a comedian in a vaudeville act with his younger brother, Paul. In 1914, Frawley and his wife, Edna Louise Broedt, toured the country with their comedy act, "Frawley and Louise." But the act—and their marriage—ended in 1927. Though Frawley never re-married, he never stopped performing. He worked on Broadway for several years before moving to Hollywood in 1932. He was a popular film actor in the 1930s and 1940s, appearing in *Roberta* (1935), *The General Died at Dawn* (1936), *Gentleman Jim* (1942), *Going My Way* (1944), and *Miracle on 34th Street* (1947). Frawley appeared in more than one hundred films, often playing gruff but lovable bartenders, bar patrons, police officers, or other stereotypically Irish roles.

In 1951, he took the role of Fred Mertz in the *I Love Lucy* television series, with Lucille Ball, Desi Arnaz, and Vivian Vance. When the show was canceled in 1960, Frawley moved to the *My Three Sons* television series, with Fred MacMurray. He retired in 1965 due to ill health. He died March 3, 1966, after suffering a heart attack and collapsing while walking along Hollywood Boulevard.

Frawley was nominated for an Emmy Award as Best Supporting Actor three times for his work on *I Love Lucy*, in 1954, 1955, and 1956, but lost each time to Art Carney.

Frawley is buried next to his brothers, John Frawley (1884–1968) and Paul Frawley (1889–1973).

*William Frawley was born February 26, 1887, in Burlington,
Iowa. He died March 3, 1966, in Los Angeles.*

13

Pierce Brothers Valhalla Memorial Park

~

10621 Victory Boulevard
North Hollywood, California 91606

~ HISTORY

Founded in 1923 and located near the border between Los Angeles and Burbank, just south of the Burbank Glendale Pasadena Airport, Valhalla Memorial Park is more closely associated with aviation than entertainment, although a few popular celebrities are buried there.

Valhalla Memorial Park is home to the Portal of the Folded Wings museum and shrine to aviation pioneers. The structure, which was built in 1924 by architect Kenneth MacDonald Jr. and sculptor Federico Giorgi, was originally known as the Valhalla Memorial Rotunda and was built as the entrance to the cemetery on Valhalla Drive, off North Hollywood Way on the eastern edge of the cemetery grounds.

The Memorial Rotunda, with its graceful garden walls and three reflecting pools, became a tourist attraction and was used as the setting for concerts, radio broadcasts, and other public events. In 1930, the airport—first known as Union Airport—was opened north of the cemetery across Vanowen Street, and aircraft noise over the rotunda prompted cemetery management to close the east entrance. The main entrance to the cemetery was moved to Cahuenga and Victory Boulevards at the south end of the cemetery, and vehicle traffic through the rotunda ceased. The area beneath the rotunda dome was enclosed with an iron fence, and the three reflecting pools were filled in.

But cemetery employee and aviation enthusiast James Gillette, noting the rotunda's close proximity to the airport and the Lockheed Aircraft Co., as well as the growing aviation industry in the area, came up with a plan to use the rotunda as a shrine to aviation, to honor the pioneers of flight. Gillette worked on his plan for nearly twenty years. Finally, at ceremonies held on December 17, 1953—the fiftieth anniversary of the Wright brothers' first powered airplane flight at Kitty Hawk, North Carolina—the rotunda was officially renamed the "Portal of the Folded Wings." The shrine has become well-known in the world of aviation, and it is sometimes referred to as the "Arlington of the Air."

These thirteen aviation pioneers are buried beneath the floor of the Portal dome:

- Bertrand Acosta (1895–1954), who served as U.S. Navy Adm. Richard Byrd's copilot on an unsuccessful flight from New York to France in 1927
- Walter R. Brookings (1889–1953), the Wright brothers' first student and later a flight instructor
- Mark M. Campbell (1897–1963), an aircraft designer, stunt pilot, and parachute expert
- Col. Warren S. Eaton (1891–1966), aircraft designer and builder
- W. Bertrum Kinner (1882–1957), aircraft company executive and inventor of the compound folded wing
- A. Roy Knabenshue (1876–1960), America's first dirigible pilot
- Elizabeth L. McQueen (1878–1958), one of the first women pilots in Los Angeles and the founder and first president of the Women's International Aeronautical Association
- John B. Moisant (1868–1910), designer of the first all-metal aircraft and the first pilot to carry a passenger across the English Channel
- Matilde J. Moisant (1878–1964), sister of John Moisant, the second licensed female pilot in the United States, and the holder of many altitude records
- J. Floyd Smith (1884–1956), test pilot and parachute designer
- Hilder F. Smith (1890–1977), wife of J. Floyd Smith and aerial acrobat who parachute-jumped over Los Angeles Harbor in 1914
- Carl B. Squier (1893–1967), cofounder of Lockheed Aircraft, test pilot, and winner of the Croix de Guerre as an army aviator in France during World War I
- Charles E. Taylor (1868–1956), machinist for the Wright Brothers who helped design and build the motor they used to fly at Kitty Hawk

The Portal also includes plaques honoring Amelia Earhart, Admiral Richard Byrd, General William Mitchell, the Wright brothers, and Harriet Quimby, the first female pilot licensed in the United States. The Portal was added to the National Register of Historic Places in 1998.

The Burbank Glendale Pasadena Airport control tower is visible from the

A plane taking off from a nearby airport flies over the Portal of the Folded Wings at Valhalla Memorial Park.

Portal, and planes taking off from the airport fly directly over the structure. All around the Portal are buried professional pilots and employees of the aviation industry, as well as weekend flyers and others involved in all aspects of flight.

∼ DIRECTIONS

From downtown Los Angeles, take the Golden State Freeway (5) north to the Burbank Boulevard exit, about three miles north of the Ventura Freeway (134). Head west on Burbank Boulevard a few hundred yards until Victory Boulevard angles off toward the right. Continue west on Victory Boulevard for a little more than two miles, to the intersection with Cahuenga Boulevard. Turn right on Cahuenga, which will take you right into the cemetery's main entrance.

∼ HOURS

The cemetery is open every day from 8 A.M. to 7 P.M., and the Portal of the Folded Wings is open every day from 9 A.M. to 4 P.M.

∼

The Tour

After coming in the main entrance at the south end of the property, near the intersection of Victory and Cahuenga Boulevards, you'll drive past the mortuary and chapel on your left. Just inside the cemetery gates, at the first cross road, turn right, toward the Veterans Memorial statue.

Follow the road as it turns toward the left, past the Veterans Memorial. About twenty-five feet past the turn, stop just before you reach the Garden of Rest, a small walled area for the interment of cremated remains. About twelve feet south of the Garden of Rest and about fifteen feet east of the road, in Section 338, Plot 19, you'll find the grave of **Curly-Joe DeRita (1909–1993).**

When the Three Stooges first formed as a comedy act in the 1920s, the members of the group were Moe Howard, his brother Shemp, and Larry Fine. Shemp Howard left the act in 1930 and was replaced by another Howard brother—Jerome, better known as Curly. When Curly suffered a stroke in 1946, Shemp rejoined the Stooges until his death in 1955. Shemp was replaced by Joe Besser, who lasted until 1958, when DeRita joined the group.

DeRita was born into a show business family and began performing when he was only eight years old, as one of the Dancing DeRitas. He toured in vaudeville until 1942 and performed in USO shows around the world during World War II. He appeared in about a dozen films from 1943 to 1958, usually playing small, often uncredited parts.

Curly-Joe DeRita's grave marker identifies him as "The Last Stooge."

By the time DeRita joined the Stooges in 1958 as "Curly-Joe," the comedy team was beginning to show its age. Larry Fine was fifty-five years old and Moe Howard was sixty-one. DeRita was fifty when he made his Stooges debut in *Have Rocket, Will Travel* (1959), the Stooges' first feature-length film. DeRita appeared in a total of eight films with the Stooges, including *Snow White and the Three Stooges* (1961), *The Three Stooges Meet Hercules* (1962), *The Three Stooges Go Around the World in a Daze* (1963), and *The Outlaws Is Coming* (1965). DeRita also appeared with the Stooges in bit parts in *Four for Texas* (1963), a Western starring Dean Martin and Frank Sinatra, and *It's a Mad Mad Mad Mad World* (1963).

As a Stooge, DeRita was reminiscent of Curly, in that he could be delicate and graceful despite his weight, and the Stooges revived many of their early routines. When Moe Howard died in 1975, DeRita retired.

DeRita's gravestone includes an etched portrait of him, and the inscription "The Last Stooge." DeRita is the only one of the Stooges to include any reference to the comedy team on his grave marker.

DeRita was born Joseph Wardell on July 12, 1909, in Philadelphia, Pennsylvania. He died July 3, 1993, in Woodland Hills, California.

Continue north along the road for a few hundred feet until you see a small wall along the road on the right side, identified as the Garden of Hope. On the inside of the wall is a bronze memorial plaque to **Oliver Hardy (1892–1957)**, Stan Laurel's partner in one of the most popular comedy teams ever to appear in films. The plaque, which describes Hardy as "A genius of comedy—his talent brought joy and laughter to all the world," was added to the wall in 1977 by the Sons of the Desert, an international Laurel and Hardy fan club.

About eight feet in front of the plaque is a more modest marker over Hardy's buried ashes, which reads, "Oliver N. Hardy, Beloved Husband."

Hardy was born Norvell Hardy in Harlem, Georgia. His father, attorney and politician Oliver Hardy, died shortly after his son was born and, in his honor, Hardy changed his name to Oliver Norvell Hardy, and he often refered to himself by his full name in his films. As a child, Hardy's mother encouraged his interest in music. When he was only eight, Hardy toured the South as a boy soprano with Colburn's Minstrels. Hardy's musical interests surfaced in his later film performances, when he would often find an excuse to sing or play an instrument.

By 1910, Hardy was studying to become a lawyer, perhaps with an idea of following in his father's footsteps, but he was also running a movie theater in Milledgeville, Georgia, and he decided that he preferred the world of entertainment to the world of law. When he saw the level of acting in the comedies being shown in his theater, the eighteen-year-old Hardy decided that he could do at least that well, and he set off for Jacksonville, Florida, the film capital of the South. From 1914 to 1917, Hardy appeared in more than one hundred short comedies for the Lubin and Vin film companies, usually in supporting roles as the star's pal or the villain. While in Jacksonville, Hardy also acquired his lifelong nickname, Babe.

In 1922, Hardy had a bit part in a comedy short titled *Lucky Dog,* which starred a young vaudeville comedian from England named Stan Laurel. The pair didn't work together again until *Forty-Five Minutes from Hollywood* (1926). Though Hardy and Laurel appeared in several more films together, it wasn't until Hal Roach paired them as a comedy team that the "Laurel and Hardy" characters emerged— the Mutt and Jeff pair, in suits and bowler hats, full of dignity and self-importance, set to take on the world. The only problem is, they always lose. They are innocent, simple, and unswervingly dedicated to each other. And through more than two hundred films together for Hal Roach Studios, they never finished better off than when they started.

This memorial to Oliver Hardy was installed at Valhalla by the Sons of the Desert fan club.

Though the Laurel and Hardy characters evolved slowly, *Do Detectives Think?* (1927) is generally accepted at the first official "Laurel and Hardy" film. The pair were both masters at every form of comedy, from broad physical humor and slapstick, to verbal sparring, to more subtle humor. Audiences would laugh just as hard at the pair being chased down a flight of stairs by a runaway piano as at Hardy's delicate "slow burn" after yet another of Laurel's well-meaning but misguided efforts. Few other comedians were as successful in so many different ways.

For a large man—at his peak, he weighed nearly 350 pounds—Hardy was athletic and extremely agile. Which was fortunate, since he was the one who usually ended up falling out of boats, slipping on banana peels, or tumbling out of windows.

Laurel and Hardy entered into sound films without missing a beat, or losing any of their comedy. In fact, their verbal exchanges became the more memorable parts of their films, starting with Hardy's oft-repeated comment to Laurel, "Well, here's another fine mess you've gotten me into." The duo also progressed from two-reel comedies to full-length features, though they won an Academy Award in 1932 for *The Music Box*, the first Oscar presented for a live-action short comedy. *The Music Box* was the simple story of Laurel and Hardy trying to haul a piano up a lengthy flight of stairs. The stairs are still there, virtually unchanged, at 923 North Vendome Street, near Del Monte Drive in Los Angeles, in the Silver Lake neighborhood. They are a popular spot for Laurel and Hardy fans, and a commemorative plaque has been added to the site.

Laurel and Hardy were at their creative and popular peak in the 1930s, with films like *Pardon Us* (1931), *Beau Hunks* (1931), *Towed in a Hole* (1932), *The Devil's Brother* (1933), *Busy Bodies* (1933), *Sons of the Desert* (1933), *Them Thar Hills* (1934), *Tit for Tat* (1935), *Way Out West* (1937), *Swiss Miss* (1938), and *Block Heads* (1938). In the 1940s, Laurel and Hardy continued to work, but their advancing ages necessitated a slower pace and less physical comedy. Hardy made a few films without Laurel, including *The Fighting Kentuckian* (1949), a Western starring John Wayne. Laurel and Hardy's last film together was *Utopia* (1950).

Hardy was born Norvell Hardy on January 18, 1892, in Harlem, Georgia. He died August 7, 1957, in North Hollywood, California.

Continue toward the center of the cemetery, toward the large Heritage Fountain, which was added to the grounds in 1925 and is surrounded by the George Washington and Abraham Lincoln memorial gardens. Turn right at the cross street just before the fountain, then turn right again, following the sign pointing toward the Portal of the Folded Wings.

Stop about thirty feet past the second turn, about halfway to the next cross street. On the left side, about twenty feet from the road, you'll find the grave of the first big name in professional wrestling and a true pioneer of television, **Gorgeous George (1915–1963).**

Milton Berle wasn't the only entertainer who had families crowded around their television sets in the 1950s. He wasn't even the first. Gorgeous George combined the arrogance of Muhammad Ali, the "bad boy" image of Dennis Rodman, and the wardrobe of Liberace to create a character that was more well known than the president of the United States.

Beginning his career in the late 1940s, Gorgeous George was the first true celebrity of professional wrestling, and he deserves all the credit—or blame— for transforming the sport from simple athletic competition into entertainment and spectacle. Before Gorgeous George, wrestlers were just wrestlers. There were no "good guys" and no "villians." Fans cheered for a good match, and rooted for their favorites. Then Gorgeous George entered the ring, with his long, curly, platinum-blond hair held in place with gold-plated pins, sometimes adorned with an orchid. He would wear one of his collection of frilly, sequined, lace-and-fur-trimmed, floor-length dressing gowns, and he would be escorted by one of his "ring butlers," who would spread rose petals in front of him and spray the wrestling mat with perfume, while "Pomp and Circumstance" played over loudspeakers. (His ring butlers even carried candelabras into the ring, until wrestling officials, fearing a fire hazard, made him stop. Gorgeous George claimed that Liberace stole the candelabra idea from him.)

Gorgeous George would stroll daintily around the ring, preening and fussing with his hair. He would sneer disdainfully at the crowd, taunting them with a shout of, "Peasants!" And, once the match started, Gorgeous George would break every rule in the book to gain an upper hand against his opponent. He was the first true "villain" in professional wrestling, and even though wrestling fans booed and screamed for his opponents to tear him apart, golden lock by golden lock, they couldn't get enough of "The Gorgeous One." He was the man the audience loved to hate.

Gorgeous George was born George Wagner in Seward, Nebraska, and his family moved throughout the Midwest, eventually settling in Houston, Texas, where George caught the wrestling bug and also cultivated his desire to be noticed. "Even as a boy, I didn't want to look like anyone else when I walked down the street," he once said. "I wanted people to notice me. I used to wear knickers so the other kids would tease me and pick a fight."

George started wrestling at the Houston YMCA. When he was seventeen, he wrestled at a carnival and was paid thirty-five cents. When his wrestling coach found out about the payment, he told George that he was now a professional, and kicked him out of the wrestling class. So George became a professional wrestler. He won his first title—the northwest middleweight crown—in 1938, in Eugene, Oregon. In the next few years, he added the Pacific Coast light-heavyweight title and the world light-heavyweight title.

Along the way, George was also indulging his desire to be noticed. Relatively short for a wrestler—he was only five-foot-nine—he grew his hair long, dyed it blond, and started wearing fancy robes and wrestling tights. According to legend, a woman sitting near the ring saw him and commented, "Isn't he gorgeous?" The ring announcer heard her and introduced the wrestler as "Gorgeous George Wagner." He started using the name professionally in 1941 and had his name legally changed to Gorgeous George in 1950, though friends called him "G.G."

Gorgeous George and television were made for each other. Wrestling was one of the few spectator sports the early television cameras could capture, and Gorgeous George was a dream come true for the new medium. With his theatrics and high drama, fans watched in record numbers. Even people who would never consider attending a wrestling match tuned in to watch the spectacle of this perfumed fop in the sweaty, violent world of wrestling.

People bought television sets just so they could follow his antics. According to the Wrestling Hall of Fame, "Gorgeous George single-handedly established the unproven new technology of television as a viable, entertaining medium that could reach millions of homes across the country. Pro wrestling was TV's first real hit with the public, the first programs that drew any real numbers for the new technology and Gorgeous George was responsible for all the commotion."

George reached his professional peak when he won the American Wrestling Association World Title in 1950. By the mid-1950s, in addition to his title belt, Gorgeous George also owned 127 flamboyant dressing gowns and was making more than $150,000 per year. He wrestled for another ten years before being defeated in one of his last matches by a young Bruno Sammartino.

After his wrestling career ended, Gorgeous George retired to the role of "gentleman farmer" on his turkey ranch in Beaumont, California. He died of a heart attack at the age of forty-eight. The free-spending Gorgeous George had lost most of his money, but he still had enough to be buried in an orchid-colored coffin—flamboyant to the very end.

His tombstone reads, "Love to our daddy, Gorgeous George, 1915–1963, Carol and Don."

*Gorgeous George was born George Raymond Wagner on
March 24, 1915, in Seward, Nebraska. He died
December 26, 1963, in Los Angeles.*

Continue straight about a quarter-mile, passing a small fountain in the middle of an intersection. The fountain is officially known as the Harriet Quimby Compass Rose Fountain, named in honor of Harriet Quimby. On August 1, 1911, Quimby became the first licensed female pilot in the United States, and she was later the first woman to fly across the English Channel. Stop when you reach the Portal of the Folded Wings, at the eastern edge of the cemetery.

Behind the Portal is the Garden of Remembrance, which contains a white wall with eight large bronze tablets, each containing about one hundred names. On the second tablet from the left, in the second column, the twelfth name up from the bottom is **Yakima Canutt (1895–1986)**, Hollywood's best-known stuntman.

Canutt grew up riding and roping; he entered his first rodeo at the age of sixteen. While appearing at a rodeo in Los Angeles, Canutt met film cowboy Tom Mix, who got him a job working as an extra in Westerns. Although Canutt occasionally played villains in the films, he concentrated his efforts on stunt work and gained a reputation as one of the top stuntmen in Hollywood in the 1930s, when he worked as the stunt double for John Wayne, Roy Rogers, Gene Autry, and Clark Gable, among others. Canutt and Wayne are credited with creating new techniques and camera angles to make filmed fight scenes look more realistic, and Canutt created or refined most of the stunt techniques used in Westerns and action films.

After suffering severe injuries while working on *Boom Town* (1940) and *In Old Oklahoma* (1943), Canutt retired from active stunt work, but he continued to work behind the camera, directing action scenes, supervising stunts, and creating new stunt techniques.

Canutt was the stunt coordinator for *Stagecoach* (1939), *Gone With the Wind* (1939), *Dark Command* (1940), *Boom Town* (1940), and *Spartacus* (1960), among many others. Canutt also worked as the second-unit director— usually responsible for the action scenes—on many films, including *Knights of the Round Table* (1953), *Old Yeller* (1957), *Ben-Hur* (1959), *Spartacus* (1960), *El*

Cid (1961), *Where Eagles Dare* (1969), *Rio Lobo* (1970), and *A Man Called Horse* (1970). Canutt's direction of the chariot race in *Ben-Hur* is still one of the most exciting and dramatic action sequences ever filmed.

Though Canutt seemed daring and fearless as a stuntman—jumping off cliffs into lakes on horseback, leaping from a speeding stagecoach onto the team of horses—a fearless stuntman doesn't usually live very long. He was careful and precise in his planning, leaving little room for error. The chariot race in *Ben-Hur*, for example, took two years to plan and film.

In 1966, Canutt was given an honorary Academy Award, "for achievements as a stunt man and for developing safety devices to protect stunt men everywhere."

Canutt was born Enos Edward Canutt on November 29, 1896, in Colfax, Washington. He died May 24, 1986, in North Hollywood, California.

Turn back the way you came, down the main road, heading west toward the Quimby Fountain. Stop about 140 feet past the fountain, when you reach a red-brick planter on the right side of the road. One row east of the planter, about 75 feet north of the road, you'll find the grave of **Nels P. Nelson (1918–1994).**

Nelson's main claim to fame is his role as a munchkin in the classic film *The Wizard of Oz* (1939). His next film appearance was a supporting role in *The Court Jester* (1956), starring Danny Kaye. Nelson appeared on television in an episode of *The Twilight Zone* in 1959.

Nelson also appeared in *I Married a Munchkin*, a short documentary film produced in 1994.

Continue heading west toward the Heritage Fountain. Turn right at the first cross street and follow the road as it turns toward the right, back east toward the Portal. About one hundred feet past the turn, stop when you see the number 6812 stenciled on the curb on the right side of the road. About eighty feet to the right of that number, you'll find the grave of boxer **Slapsie Maxie Rosenbloom (1907–1976).**

Rosenbloom was the world light-heavyweight boxing champion from 1930 to 1934, and one of the busiest title-holders in ring history. Rosenbloom defeated Jimmy Slattery to win the crown on June 25, 1930, and he held the title until he was defeated by Bob Olin on November 16, 1934. During his four and a half years as champ, Rosenbloom fought 106 times—an average of one fight every fifteen days. Rosenbloom was elected to the Boxing Hall of Fame in 1972 and to the International Boxing Hall of Fame in 1993.

Rosenbloom was not an overpowering boxer, and he usually kept a safe distance between himself and his opponent. He appeared to hit his opponents with an open glove, inspiring journalist Damon Runyon to give him the nickname "Slapsie Maxie."

Like many early boxers, Rosenbloom started fighting as a youngster on the street. According to legend, actor George Raft saw Rosenbloom in a street brawl in New York City and suggested that the youngster pursue a career as a boxer. In 1923, the sixteen-year-old Rosenbloom turned professional and won his first eight fights. (His young age at the time of his professional debut may be the reason some sources claim he was born in 1904 and turned pro as a nineteen-year-old.)

In 1925, Rosenbloom was ranked among the top ten light-heavyweights in the world. In 1927, he fought Slattery for the title but was defeated. Three years later, they met in the ring again, and this time Rosenbloom won a fifteen-round decision.

A popular character among boxing fans, Rosenbloom didn't devote much time to training. Although he wasn't a drinker, Rosenbloom was a colorful personality who enjoyed gambling, the company of women, and late-night celebrations. When he retired from boxing in 1939, after a total of 299 fights, Rosenbloom's record was 223 wins (though only 19 were by knockout), 42 losses, 32 draws, and 2 no-contest rulings. Even before his boxing career was over, Rosenbloom was appearing in films, usually playing himself or a fictionalized version of himself. His film debut was in *Mr. Broadway* (1933), which featured New York City newspaper columnist Ed Sullivan taking viewers on a tour of New York nightspots. Rosenbloom appeared in more than sixty films, often playing a punch-drunk boxer, gangster, or some other tough guy, including *Punch Drunks* (1934), with the Three Stooges; *Nothing Sacred* (1937), with Carole Lombard and Fredric March; *Each Dawn I Die* (1939), with James Cagney and George Raft; and *Hollywood or Bust* (1956), with Dean Martin and Jerry Lewis. In the early 1950s, Rosenbloom and fellow boxer Max Baer appeared in five comedies together, including *Two Roaming Champs* (1950), *Skipalong Rosenbloom* (1951), and *Rootin' Tootin' Tenderfeet* (1952).

Rosenbloom also made a few television appearances, including an episode of *The Munsters* in 1964 and *I Dream of Jeannie* in 1965. Rosenbloom was such a popular and well-liked celebrity, he even inspired cartoon characters, including a fighting feline named "Slapsie Catsy" in *Pied Piper Porky* (1939), and a bull named "Slapsie Maxie Rosenbull" in *The Timid Toreador* (1940).

> *Rosenbloom was born September 6, 1907 (some sources say 1904), in Leonard's Bridge, Connecticut. He died March 6, 1976, in South Pasadena, California.*

Continue east for a few hundred feet, turn left at the first intersection, then left again at the next cross street. You should be heading back toward the west again. About two hundred feet past the second turn, stop between the numbers 6325 and 6346 stenciled on the curb on the right side of the road. Walk about twenty feet to the north, toward the back of a red-brick building, and you'll find the grave of silent-film actress **Mae Murray (1889–1965)**, known as "The Girl with the Bee-Stung Lips." Murray was a major star of silent films, but like many of her colleagues, she never made the transition to talkies.

Murray started as a dancer on Broadway, then with the Ziegfeld Follies in New York City. In 1915, Murray's dance number, in which she appeared as a bejeweled and dazzling Persian princess, had audiences leaping to their feet and literally stopped the show. The following year, Murray made her first appearance on film, starring in *To Have and To Hold*. Film audiences were impressed with Murray's frizzy blonde hair, delicate features, and radiant appearance, as well as her dancer's grace. Though she was initially billed as "The Gardenia of the Screen," she quickly became known as "The Girl With the Bee-Stung Lips."

Murray starred in thirty-three films from 1916 to 1924, usually elaborately costumed romances, and usually directed by Robert Z. Leonard, whom Murray married in 1918—her third marriage. Several of these films also starred a young dancer friend of Murray's named Rudolph Valentino.

Murray's crowning achievement as an actress was her starring role in *The Merry Widow* (1925), directed by Erich von Stroheim. Though the temperamental Murray battled with von Stroheim, often walking off the set and stopping production for days at a time, she later admitted that this was her best screen performance. When the film broke box-office records, and the Merry Widow Waltz became a nationwide dance craze, Murray's ego got the better of her. She divorced Leonard, who had become a top director at MGM studios, and married Prince David Mdivani, who took control of her career and her bank account. Mdivani convinced Murray to break her contract with MGM.

Murray left MGM in 1928 and made only three films after that—*Peacock*

Alley (1930), *Bachelor Apartment* (1931), and *High Stakes* (1931). None were as successful as her earlier efforts, and Murray quickly faded into obscurity. After Mdivani spent most of her money and then divorced her, Murray declared bankruptcy and lived her final days in relative poverty.

Mae Murray was born Marie Adrienne Koenig on May 10, 1889 (some sources say 1883 or 1885), in Portsmouth, Virginia. She died March 23, 1965, in Woodland Hills, California.

Walk about twenty-five feet west of Murray's grave, and you'll find the grave of **Cliff Edwards (1895–1971),** better known as "Ukulele Ike," but probably best known as the voice of Jiminy Cricket in the Walt Disney film *Pinocchio* (1940).

Edwards began his musical career singing and playing the ukulele in saloons in St. Louis when he was still a teenager. He was a popular and successful vaudeville musician in the early 1920s and appeared in several Broadway musicals, including "Lady Be Good" with Adele and Fred Astaire in 1924. Edwards had a series of musical hits in the late 1920s, including "It Had To Be You," "If You Knew Susie," "I Can't Give You Anything But Love," "Dinah," and "Paddlin' Madelin Home." When sound films became popular in the late 1920s and early 1930s, Edwards moved to Hollywood and appeared in more than eighty films, usually playing supporting roles in musicals and comedies. Edwards appeared in *Saratoga* (1937), starring Clark Gable and Jean Harlow, and *His Girl Friday* (1940), starring Cary Grant and Rosalind Russell. He even had a small role as a soldier in *Gone With the Wind* (1939).

In 1940, Edwards provided the voice of Jiminy Cricket for Walt Disney's *Pinocchio*, and sang two of the film's most popular songs—"Give a Little Whistle" and "When You Wish Upon a Star," which won the Academy Award for Best Song. Despite declining health, Edwards continued to work for Walt Disney Productions, recording children's songs and making television appearances on the *Mickey Mouse Club.*

In 1971, Edwards died a welfare patient in a convalescent hospital in Los Angeles. Problems with two failed marriages, alcohol, and gambling took a toll on Edwards, although he was never forgotten by Walt Disney Productions. Studio officials regularly visited him in the hospital, helped pay for most of his medical expenses, and even took him on visits to Disneyland. But, like his cemetery neighbor Mae Murray, Edwards died broke and forgotten by his fans.

The Motion Picture and Television Relief Fund donated the burial plot for Edwards, and the Disney studio paid for his funeral expenses and grave marker, which reads, "In Loving Memory of Ukulele Ike."

Cliff Edwards was born Clifton A. Edwards on June 14, 1895, in Hannibal, Missouri. He died July 17, 1971, in Los Angeles.

Walk another twenty-five feet past Edwards's grave, and cross to the other side of the street. Right next to the stenciled number 6583 on the curb is the grave of actress **Aneta L. Corsaut (1933–1995),** best known for her television role as Helen Crump, Opie's teacher and the longtime girlfriend of Sheriff Andy Taylor on *The Andy Griffith Show* in the 1960s.

Before moving to Mayberry, Corsaut started her television career almost exclusively in Westerns, appearing in a few episodes of *Gunsmoke, The Real McCoys, Johnny Ringo, Black Saddle,* and *Bonanza.* Her first film role was as Steve McQueen's girlfriend in *The Blob* (1958), a low-budget but memorable horror movie featuring McQueen and Corsaut trying to warn the local townspeople about a gelatinous alien mass that's gobbling up their neighbors.

Although *The Andy Griffith Show* debuted in 1960, Corsaut didn't join the cast until 1964. Before that, Andy's girlfriend was Ellie Walker, played by Elinor Donahue. Andy and Helen Crump dated for four years, while Helen taught Andy's son, Opie. In 1968, Griffith left the show and it was re-named *Mayberry R.F.D.,* with Ken Berry as the star. Griffith and Corsaut appeared in the debut episode of the revised show, when they were married and left Mayberry.

After *The Andy Griffith Show,* Corsaut appeared in a few made-for-TV movies and appeared on the *House Calls* television series from 1979 to 1982. In 1986, Griffith, Corsaut, and the rest of the original cast appeared in the made-for-TV movie *Return to Mayberry.* Corsaut made two guest appearances on Griffith's next television series, *Matlock,* in 1987 and 1990. Those were her last acting appearances.

Corsaut's gravestone identifies her as "Actor—trouper." She is buried next to her mother, Opal J. Corsaut (1900–1963).

Corsaut was born November 3, 1933, in Hutchinson, Kansas. She died November 6, 1995, in Los Angeles.

Follow the road back toward the Heritage Fountain. Go past the fountain, to the mausoleums at the far western edge of the cemetery. Between the

Mausoleum of Remembrance and the Mausoleum of Devotion is a large wall containing plaques marking cremated remains. As you face the wall, in the fifth column from the right about six feet up from the ground, you'll find a small plaque with the inscription "Criswell Predicts." This marks the final resting place for the first television psychic, **Charles Criswell King (1907–1982).**

Criswell was born in the backroom of a mortuary in a small town in Indiana. As Criswell describes it in his first book, *Criswell Predicts,* published in 1968, his gift of prognostication started at a very young age. Criswell's uncle offered him 25 cents to write brief personal items for his *Daily Democrat* newspaper. "My personal items were exclusive," Criswell recalled. "I would write what people were going to do," including announcing that a woman in town would be attending her sister's funeral—the day before the woman's sister died.

Criswell pursued several careers, first studying music and medicine, then working as a teacher, ambulance driver, newspaper reporter, and television newscaster. He continued to make predictions and began writing a syndicated newspaper column titled "Criswell Predicts." As his fame grew, Criswell became a popular television guest, often appearing with Jack Paar and Johnny Carson.

Criswell claimed that his predictions were 86 percent accurate, including his predictions of the assassination of President John Kennedy, the death of Jayne Mansfield, and the election of Ronald Reagan as governor of California. Criswell also predicted that the world would end on August 18, 1999—Criswell's birthday—when the earth would be covered by a black rainbow. The rainbow, Criswell wrote, "will seemingly bring about, through some mysterious force beyond our comprehension, a lack of oxygen. It will draw the oxygen from our atmosphere, as a huge snake encircling the world and feeding upon the oxygen which we need to exist. Hour after hour, it will grow worse. And we will grow weaker. It is through this that we will be so weakened that when the final end arrives, we will go silently, we will go gasping for breath, and then there will be only silence on the earth." Luckily, that prediction must've fallen into Criswell's 14 percent error margin.

To Criswell's credit, however, many of his predictions were eerily accurate. For example, he predicted an end to the use of money, and everyone would use "punch cards" to make purchases. Credit and debit cards, perhaps? He predicted the assassination of "one of the leaders of the Negro Civil Rights movement" in 1968. He also predicted "a set of septuplets, all boys, will be born in Cedar Rapids, Iowa, on January 19, 1973." Criswell was only off by twenty-four years and about a hundred miles, but the world's first surviving set of septuplets—four boys and three girls—was born in Iowa in 1997.

Among Criswell's other predictions, made in 1968:

- "I predict the assassination of Fidel Castro by a woman, on August 9, 1970."
- "By 1988, there will be substantiated records of visits to earth from other planets."
- "I predict that by 1982, a full medical education will require six months of study. The reason for the shortening of medical education is simple: Everything in medicine will be automated, and a course to qualify one as a medical doctor will require only knowledge of how to operate the proper computers and other equipment."
- "I predict that the District of Columbia within the next fifteen years will cease to exist as the capital of the United States. The seat of government will be moved to Wichita, Kansas, in the caverns beneath the city."

Criswell predicted that a large meteor would strike London on October 18, 1988, and that people would be able to perform do-it-yourself face-lifts for only $5. Criswell also predicted a ten-month worldwide drought in 1977, then a massive deluge that would destroy coastal regions around the world. Even Criswell admitted that he wasn't right all the time.

With his theatrical presentations, piercing eyes, and wavy, snowy-white hair, Criswell was a popular television performer—whether his predictions were accurate or not. Criswell hosted a television program called *Criswell Predicts,* which was recorded in Los Angeles and syndicated to stations across the country.

Criswell was also a close friend of film director Ed Wood, and he narrated and appeared in several Wood films, including *Night of the Ghouls* (1959), *Orgy of the Dead* (1965), and the film generally regarded as the worst film of all time, *Plan 9 From Outer Space* (1958). A new generation discovered Criswell in 1994, thanks to the film *Ed Wood,* in which Criswell was played by Jeffrey Jones.

Criswell was born Charles Jeron Criswell Konig on August 18, 1907, in Princeton, Indiana. He died October 4, 1982, in Burbank, California.

About two hundred feet south of the Mausoleum of Devotion is the Mausoleum of Hope. On the north side of the Mausoleum of Hope, in the first column on the left, in the third space up from the bottom, you'll find the crypt of actress **Bea Benaderet (1908–1963),** best known to television viewers as Kate Bradley, owner of the Shady Rest Hotel on *Petticoat Junction,* and the voice of Betty Rubble on the television cartoon series *The Flintstones.*

Benaderet made her professional debut at the age of twelve in San Francisco, in a production of the *Beggar's Opera.* The manager of a local radio station saw her and offered her a job as a singer. While she attended acting school in San Francisco, she also performed on various radio stations as an actress, singer, announcer, writer, and producer.

In 1936, Benaderet became a regular radio performer on Orson Welles's *Campbell Playhouse* and began her comedy career three years later on *The Jack Benny Show,* where she created the character of telephone operator Gertrude Gearshift. She also appeared on *The Great Gildersleeve, Fibber McGee and Molly,* and *The Adventures of Ozzie and Harriet.*

Benaderet provided the voices for dozens of cartoon characters in films throughout the 1940s, usually working at Warner Bros. with Mel Blanc. Her first appearance on film was an uncredited role as a file clerk in Alfred Hitchcock's *Notorious* (1946), starring Cary Grant and Ingrid Bergman.

Benaderet first appeared on television as Blanche Morton, the next-door neighbor on the *The George Burns and Gracie Allen Show* in 1950. Benaderet was twice nominated for an Emmy Award as Best Supporting Actress for her work on the Burns and Allen show, in 1954 and 1955, but lost both times. Benaderet was Lucille Ball's original choice to play the part of Ethel Mertz in *I Love Lucy,* which debuted in 1951, but Benaderet was unable to break her contract with the Burns and Allen show, so Vivian Vance got the part. Benaderet also provided the voice of Betty Rubble in *The Flintstones,* which debuted in 1960 and was the first full-length animated television program in prime time.

In 1962, Benaderet was considered for the role of Granny in *The Beverly Hillbillies,* but she lost the part to Irene Ryan. The show's producers were impressed with Benaderet, however, and created the role of Cousin Pearl Bodine for her. The following year, Benaderet starred in *Petticoat Junction* as Kate Bradley, a hotel owner and mother of three daughters—Billie Jo, Betty Jo, and Bobbie Jo.

During this time, Benaderet continued to do voice work for the Looney Tunes and Merrie Melodies cartoons at Warner Bros., including the voice of Granny in the Sylvester and Tweety cartoons.

Benaderet is buried next to her husband, Eugene Tracy Twombly (1914–1968), who worked as a radio and movie sound technician, and who died four days after his wife.

Benaderet was born April 4, 1908 (some sources say 1906), in New York City. She died October 13, 1968, in Los Angeles.

14

Inglewood Park Cemetery

~

720 East Florence Avenue
Inglewood, California 90301

~ HISTORY

Inglewood Park Cemetery is one of the largest cemeteries in the Los Angeles area, located on 340 acres a few miles northwest of Los Angeles International Airport. The nondenominational cemetery currently has more "permanent residents" than any other cemetery in California.

The cemetery was founded in 1905 when five businessmen in the Centinela Valley pooled their resources and formed the Inglewood Park Cemetery Association. At the time, the area was a sparsely populated farming region, and there were only thirty-two burials the first year.

In 1911, the Inglewood Mausoleum was built on the property, the first public mausoleum in California, and the first of many mausoleums to be built at Inglewood Park Cemetery. In the 1930s, construction began on the Mausoleum of the Golden West, which contains a beautiful collection of stained-glass scenes from California's early history. The Del Prado Mausoleum, built in the late 1950s, was designed to reflect the Spanish influence on the development of the state, and the Manchester Garden Mausoleum was added in the 1970s. The Sunset Mission Mausoleum, which contains the remains of former Los Angeles mayor Tom Bradley and singer Ella Fitzgerald, is being expanded to include nearly thirty-thousand interment spaces, which will make it the largest mausoleum in the country.

Inglewood Park is located across Manchester Boulevard from the Great Western Forum and a few blocks north of the Hollywood Park racetrack. The neighborhood surrounding the cemetery has seen better days, but the cemetery itself is an impressive and beautiful location. Although most of the southern half of the property contains primarily ground-level grave markers, the northern part of the cemetery features dozens of old private mausoleums, impressive statues, and a small lake.

∼ DIRECTIONS

From downtown Los Angeles, head west to the San Diego Freeway (405). Take the San Diego Freeway south. About six miles south of the Santa Monica Freeway (10), exit at Florence Avenue. Turn left on Florence and head east for about two miles. Look for the cemetery entrance just past Prairie Avenue (Avenue of the Champions). The cemetery gates are on the south side of Florence Avenue.

∼ HOURS

The cemetery grounds are open every day from 8 A.M. to 5:30 P.M. The mausoleums are open every day from 8 A.M. to 4:30 P.M.

∼

The Tour

Like at many older cemeteries, the numbered plot markers at Inglewood Park can be difficult or impossible to find. The small markers, which are used to identify the plot numbers within a specific section, settle with time and can be covered by dirt or grass. At Inglewood, particularly in the older sections of the cemetery, you'll see few, if any, plot markers, so knowing the number of a particular plot won't be very helpful. Luckily, most of the sections are identified with a stenciled name along the curb, and maps to the property are available in the cemetery offices.

Once inside the main gates on Florence Avenue, turn left past the cemetery offices—after stopping to pick up a map of the grounds—and follow the signs to the Mausoleum of the Golden West, located on the northern edge of the cemetery grounds. Look for the Cenotaph Entrance at the eastern end of the mausoleum. A detailed map of the building is located on the wall on the right, just inside the entrance.

From the Cenotaph Entrance, head down the corridor on your right, labeled Sanctuary of Hope (the corridor names are printed on the floor). Turn right down the second corridor, labeled Sanctuary of Faith. About halfway to the end of the corridor, it becomes the Sanctuary of Dawn. About fifty feet farther down on your right, in the third space up from the floor, you'll find the crypt of actress **Betty Grable (1916–1973)**, the World War II pinup girl with the "million-dollar legs."

Flowers and her popular pinup poster adorn the crypt of Betty Grable.

Grable's mother, Lillian, was determined to have one of her daughters in show business. When her oldest child, Marjorie, exhibited neither the talent nor the inclination, Lillian turned her efforts to her next child. Grable began her training at an early age, taking dance, voice, and saxophone lessons. She appeared as a dancer in several films while she was still a teenager, making her screen debut in *Let's Go Places* (1930). Grable spoke her first words onscreen in the Eddie Cantor comedy *Whoopee!* (1930), which was also Busby Berkeley's first film as a choreographer. Grable appeared in small parts in several more musicals and comedies during the early 1930s, including a brief appearance as a party guest in *The Gay Divorcee* (1934) and a singer in a trio in *Follow the Fleet* (1936), both starring Fred Astaire and Ginger Rogers. To supplement her acting income during this time, Grable also worked as a band singer.

Since Grable was just barely out of her teens, she was young enough to be believable in a series of "campus films," including *Sweetheart of Sigma Chi* (1933), *Student Tour* (1934), *Collegiate* (1936), *Pigskin Parade* (1936), *Campus Confessions* (1938), and *College Swing* (1938). In 1937, while still a struggling actress, Grable married former child star Jackie Coogan, who was still a popular performer, and the marriage helped to give Grable's career a needed boost. Grable got her big break with a starring role in *Million Dollar Legs* (1939), and even though the title referred to a horse, Grable ended up with the nickname for the rest of her career.

Darryl Zanuck brought Grable to Fox studios in the early 1940s, and she starred in a series of musicals that highlighted her impressive limbs, and also featured the studio's new Technicolor process—*Down Argentine Way* (1940), *Tin Pan Alley* (1940), *Moon Over Miami* (1941), *Song of the Islands* (1942), *Springtime in the Rockies* (1942), *Coney Island* (1943), *Sweet Rosie O'Grady* (1943), *Pin-Up Girl* (1944), and *The Dolly Sisters* (1945).

In 1942, Grable was ranked eighth on the list of the top ten box-office attractions; the following year, she was number one, and she remained on the list until 1951. In 1947, the U.S. Treasury Department reported that Grable's annual salary of $300,000 made her the highest-paid woman in the country. Fox studios even insured her legs for $1 million with Lloyd's of London, making that popular nickname official. During World War II, Grable was the favorite pinup girl of U.S. servicemen. The classic photograph of her in high heels and a one-piece white bathing suit, looking back over her shoulder, was posted in countless military barracks around the world. After the war, Grable starred in *The Shocking Miss Pilgrim* (1946), a musical comedy set in the 1800s. The biggest shock to Grable's fans was the lack of screen time in the film devoted to her legs, and they flooded the studio with letters of complaint. Grable returned to her previous form in *Mother Wore Tights* (1947), and her fans were happy again. She kept to the successful formula with *When My Baby Smiles at Me* (1948), *The Beautiful Blonde From Bashful Bend* (1949), *Wabash Avenue* (1950)—a remake of *Coney Island*—*My Blue Heaven* (1950), *Call Me Mister* (1951), and *Meet Me After the Show* (1951). By the time Grable appeared in *How to Marry a Millionaire* (1953), costarring with Marilyn Monroe and Lauren Bacall, her star was fading, and Zanuck was focusing the studio's attention on new performers. Her last film was *How to Be Very, Very Popular* (1955).

When her film career ended, Grable appeared often on television, in nightclubs, and on stages across the country. She starred in performances of *Guys and Dolls, Hello, Dolly,* and other musicals through the 1960s.

Grable is buried with her mother, Lillian Grable (1889–1964), and near her father, Conn Grable (1883–1954), and sister, Marjorie Grable Arnold (1909–1930).

Grable was married to actor Jackie Coogan from 1937 to 1940, and to bandleader Harry James from 1943 to 1965. The name on her crypt is "Betty Grable James." Although Harry James, who died in 1983, is buried in Las Vegas, his father, Everette James (1884–1955), is buried in the crypt next to Grable.

Grable was born Elizabeth Ruth Grable on December 18, 1916,
in St. Louis, Missouri. She died July 2, 1973, in
Santa Monica, California.

Retrace your steps back to the Sanctuary of Hope. Turn right and walk down a few steps, then turn right into the Sanctuary of Reverence. About half-way to the end of the corridor, turn left down a short hallway labeled Sanctuary of Dreams. Immediately on your left, you'll see a sign identifying the Alcove of Music. Just below that sign, behind a glass window, you'll see a lyre-shaped urn containing the remains of actor **Cesar Romero (1907–1994),** known to one generation as the tall, handsome "Latin lover" in more than one hundred films from the 1930s to the early 1960s, and to the next generation as the green-haired, white-faced Joker from the *Batman* television series of the late 1960s.

Romero was born into a distinguished Cuban family—his grandfather was Cuban writer and revolutionary Jose Marti. Romero started his career as a nightclub dancer before landing roles in several Broadway plays, including *All Points West* and *Dinner at Eight.* He was spotted by a talent scout for MGM studios and brought to Hollywood in 1933. Romero's first film role was in *The Shadow Laughs* (1933), and he followed that by playing a gigolo and murder suspect in *The Thin Man* (1934).

For the next few decades, Romero alternated between smooth romantic roles that highlighted his good looks and dancing ability, and sinister villains. Romero was an Afghan leader who counsels Shirley Temple in *Wee Willie Winkie* (1935) and a luckless lover in hot pursuit of Marlene Dietrich in *The Devil Is a Woman* (1935), and he had the chance to show off his dancing skills with Betty Grable in *Springtime in the Rockies* (1942). He also played the Cisco Kid in a series of Westerns in the early 1940s. Romero seemed equally comfortable in Westerns, dramas, comedies, adventures, romances, or musicals, though he typically played supporting roles.

The ashes of actor Cesar Romero are buried in this lyre-shaped urn at Inglewood Park Cemetery.

After returning from military service in the Coast Guard during World War II, Romero played Hernando Cortez in *Captain From Castile* (1947), one of his strongest performances and a role he later described as his favorite. In the early 1950s, Romero started working more in television, hosting *Your Chevrolet Showroom,* a musical comedy variety show, from 1953 to 1954, and starring as suave courier Steve McQuinn in the adventure series *Passport to Danger* from 1954 to 1955. In addition to guest appearances in television Westerns, Romero continued his regular appearances in films, including his roles as Marquis de Labordere in *Vera Cruz* (1954), gangster Duke Santos in *Ocean's Eleven* (1960), Adam Wright in *If a Man Answers* (1962), and Marquis Andre de Lage in *Donovan's Reef* (1963).

Romero played the Joker, Batman's nemesis, in the *Batman* television series from 1966 to 1968. When Romero agreed to play the role, he refused to shave off his mustache—which you can see if you look closely under his thick white makeup. He returned to television from 1985 to 1987, playing the wealthy and elegantly sexy Peter Stavros on the prime-time drama *Falcon's Crest,* and he hosted several television specials until the early 1990s.

Though Romero made regular appearances on the Hollywood social circuit, usually in the company of an attractive actress, he never married, and he was almost always described in interviews and articles as a "confirmed bachelor."

Romero is interred with his father, Cesar Romero Sr. (1872–1931); his mother, Maria (1880–1962); and his two sisters, Maria (1905–1991) and Graciela (1911–1996). Romero's mother was the daughter of Cuban writer and patriot Jose Marti, whose death in a battle with Spanish troops in 1895 made him the martyred symbol of Cuban independence from Spain.

Romero was born Cesar Julio Romero Jr. on February 15, 1907, in New York City. He died January 1, 1994, in Santa Monica, California.

Head back again to the Sanctuary of Hope and back to the main entrance. This time, walk down the corridor on the left side of the entrance and turn left down the second corridor, labeled the Sanctuary of Faith. About 150 feet down this corridor, on the right side, you'll find two columns of niches, with urns containing cremated remains. In the column on the right, in the second niche from the top, in space F-96, is the urn containing the remains of **Paul Bern (1889–1932),** screenwriter, producer, director, and assistant to Irving

Thalberg at MGM studios, but probably best remembered as the husband of actress Jean Harlow who killed himself shortly after their wedding.

Bern was educated at the American Academy of Dramatic Arts in New York City, and he started working in film as an editor, then as a screenwriter and director in 1920. He wrote and directed several films in the early 1920s before joining MGM studios as production assistant and Thalberg's story consultant. Berg was also instrumental in bringing Harlow to MGM, and helping to advance her career as she moved from small roles as an attractive background character to starring roles in comedies and dramas. Around the MGM studio, Bern was known as the "father confessor," the man sought out for advice by people in trouble or looking for sage advice.

But it was a surprise in the summer of 1932, even in Hollywood, when the forty-two-year-old Bern married the twenty-one-year-old Harlow. She was the "Platinum Blonde," the smoldering embodiment of screen sexuality. Bern, though talented and successful, was quiet, studious, bookish, and almost mousy in appearance, in addition to being twice Harlow's age. The questions about their marriage were quickly replaced by more serious, tragic questions. Two months after they were married, Bern was found dead in their Beverly Hills home, lying nude on the floor of Harlow's upstairs bedroom, shot once in the head with a .38-caliber pistol, an apparent suicide. After a butler discovered Bern's body, the first phone calls he made were to MGM studio chief Louis B. Mayer and Thalberg, who arrived at the scene, looking for anything that might be harmful to either the studio or Harlow's career. Mayer found Bern's suicide note and stuffed it in his pocket, but he was convinced later to turn it over to the police. The note didn't provide much information as to why Bern might take his own life: "Dearest Dear, Unfortunately this is the only way to make good the frightful wrong I have done you and to wipe out my abject humiliation. I love you, Paul. You understand that last night was only a comedy."

Initially, the stories surrounding Bern's suicide pointed to several possible causes for his action—he was deeply in debt, he and Harlow had argued about her domineering mother, or he was concerned about the discovery of his first wife, who was mentally ill and living in a sanatorium in northern California. But the story that eventually came out was that Bern was impotent and was unable to consummate their marriage. He had mistakenly hoped that Harlow, the screen sex goddess, could help him, but she could not. Less than five years later, Harlow was also dead.

According to Hollywood legend, the ghosts of Bern and Harlow still haunt the house where he killed himself. Subsequent owners of the property near Benedict Canyon Drive, about three miles north of Sunset Boulevard, have reported hearing the sound of a gunshot and a body falling in the upstairs bedroom, and the voice of a woman crying. In one notable incident, after the house was purchased in 1966 by hairstylist Jay Sebring, actress Sharon Tate was house-sitting when she thought she heard an intruder. She saw the image of a man who looked like Bern in the upstairs bedroom, running around and cursing, while blood spurted from a wound in his head. As Tate ran back downstairs, she saw the image of Sebring tied to the railing of the stairs, his throat slashed.

Three years later, in a house less than a mile away, Tate and Sebring were murdered by Charles Manson and his followers. Sebring and Tate were tied together, and Sebring's throat was slashed.

Paul Bern was born Paul Levy on December 3, 1889, in Wandsbek, Germany. He died September 5, 1932, in Beverly Hills, California.

Continue along the Sanctuary of Faith until you reach a small chapel area. Turn right toward the front of the chapel, then left into the Sanctuary of Eternity. About seventy-five feet down the corridor, on the right side, in the second space up from the floor, Space L-133, you'll find the crypt of Academy Award–winning screenwriter **Robert Riskin (1897–1955).**

Though director Frank Capra gets most of the credit for a string of depression-era social commentary comedies, including *Lady for a Day* (1933), *It Happened One Night* (1934), *Broadway Bill* (1934), *Mr. Deeds Goes to Town* (1936), *You Can't Take It With You* (1938), and *Meet John Doe* (1941), all of those films were written by Riskin, who was often described as Capra's "social conscience."

Riskin started writing for Paramount studios while he was still a teenager, then he returned to New York City, to write plays. He returned to Hollywood in 1931, working as a dialogue writer on *Platinum Blonde* (1931), which starred Jean Harlow and Loretta Young and was directed by Capra. After contributing to several more films, Riskin worked again with Capra on *American Madness* (1932), the story of a depression-era bank president, played by Walter Huston, who faces professional and personal scandal after his bank is robbed. Riskin and Capra worked again on *Lady for a Day* (1933), the story of a gang of big-city thugs who transform a sidewalk apple peddler into a high-society lady to impress her daughter. For their work on that film, both Riskin and Capra received their first Acadamy Award nominations, for Best Screenplay and Best Director, respectively.

Riskin wrote the screenplay for and Capra directed *It Happened One Night* (1934), the story of a spoiled heiress, played by Claudette Colbert, who runs away from an arranged marriage. She encounters a helpful stranger, played by Clark Gable, who turns out to be a reporter secretly planning to write a story about her. The film swept the Academy Awards, winning Oscars for Best Screenplay, Best Director, Best Actor, Best Actress, and Best Picture.

The films of Riskin and Capra centered on themes of raw idealism and evangelical faith in the common man, wrapped in a package of warm-hearted comedy. Riskin also worked with Capra on *Lost Horizon* (1937) and *Riding High* (1950). In addition to his films with Capra, Riskin wrote *The Whole Town's Talking* (1935), *The Thin Man Goes Home* (1945), *Mister 880* (1950), and *Here Comes the Groom* (1951). Riskin was nominated for the Academy Award five times, and in 1955, shortly before his death, he was awarded the Laurel Award for Screenwriting Achievement by the Writers Guild of America, which recognizes writers who have "advanced the literature of the motion picture through the years."

During World War II, Riskin served for three years as chief of the Office of War Information's overseas film division. Riskin was married to actress Fay Wray from 1942 until his death.

Robert Riskin was born March 30, 1897, in New York City.
He died September 20, 1955, in Beverly Hills, California.

South of the Mausoleum of the Golden West, across the lawn, is the smaller Inglewood Mausoleum. South of the Inglewood Mausoleum, in the Alta Section, is the Alta Mesa Mausoleum, surrounded by several large, private mausoleums. South of the Alta Section, at the western tip of the Miramar Section, is a seventeen-foot-tall statue of an angel reaching down to embrace a woman. The hauntingly beautiful statue marks the graves of two of the most famous—and most tragic—circus aerialists, **Lillian Leitzel (1892–1931)** and **Alfredo Codona (1893–1937).**

The diminutive Leitzel—she was only four-foot-nine and weighed just ninety-five pounds—was one of the early stars of the Ringling Bros. and Barnum & Bailey circus in the 1920s. She was promoted on circus posters as "The Queen of the Air" and "The World's Most Marvelous Lady Gymnast."

An angelic statue soars over the graves of circus aerialists Lillian Leitzel and Alfredo Codona. Note the broken rope at the base of the statue.

Leitzel was best known for a feat called the one-arm plunge, or swing-over, in which she would perform a nearly vertical rotation while hanging from a ring by only one arm.

Leitzel came from a European circus family. Her mother and two aunts were famous throughout Europe with their trapeze act known as the Leamy Ladies; her grandmother, Julia Pelikan, was still swinging from the trapeze at the age of eighty-four; and her uncle, Adolph Pelikan, was a popular circus clown. Although Leitzel received an extensive education in Germany at schools in Breslau and Berlin—she was fluent in six languages and was a talented pianist—she built a trapeze bar in her backyard and spent her free time practicing the tricks she saw her mother and aunts perform. Leitzel eventually joined her mother's act, and she first visited the United States in 1908, appearing with the Barnum & Bailey show in New York City. The Leamy Ladies returned to the United States again in 1911, but when they went home to Europe at the end of their tour, Leitzel stayed behind and became a popular performer on the vaudeville circuit.

In 1914, Leitzel joined the Ringling Bros. circus, and by the time the circus merged with Barnum & Bailey five years later to become "The Greatest Show on Earth," Leitzel was the undisputed star. When Leitzel was announced by the ringmaster, all the lights in the three-ring tent would be turned off. She was the only performer in the circus who did her act alone. The highlight of her act came when Leitzel would grab a padded rope loop attached to a swivel, and would repeatedly throw herself over the loop. While she was swinging high over their heads, the audience would keep count of her rotations. Her record was 249 revolutions, which is an incredible feat, considering that each time Leitzel completed a swing-over, her shoulder would become partially dislocated, then snap back into place. Once asked why she would put herself through such a difficult and painful routine, Leitzel gave a prophetic response: "I'd rather be a racehorse and last a minute than be a plow horse and last forever."

Outside the circus tent, Leitzel had a reputation as a temperamental prima donna, unpredictable and demanding. She was known to curse or slap circus employees, and she was the first circus performer to travel in her own private Pullman railcar, complete with a baby grand piano. In 1928, Leitzel married another hot-tempered circus performer, trapeze artist Alfredo Codona of the Flying Codonas, a stylish and graceful performer known for his daring triple somersault. Although Codona wasn't the first aerialist to perform the triple somersault, he was the first to include it as a regular part of his act. Leitzel and Codona shared similar temperaments, and their tumultuous marriage featured numerous arguments, public shouting matches, breakups, and reconciliations.

Alfredo Codona also came from a circus family. His father, Eduardo, owned and operated a small circus in southern Mexico, and several members of the family performed as aerialists. Alfredo joined the act before he was a year old, with his father balancing him on his hand as the opening act. In 1917, the Flying Codonas joined the Ringling Bros. circus, where Leitzel was already a star. When Eduardo retired, the Flying Codonas became the Three Codonas, with Alfredo, his brother, Lalo, and sister, Victoria. When Victoria quit the act, she was replaced by Vera Bruce. The Three Codonas appeared in a short film called *Swing High* (1931), which was nominated for an Academy Award as Best Short Subject. Alfredo Codona also performed most of the aerial stunts for the early *Tarzan* films starring Johnny Weissmuller in the early 1930s.

In addition to their combustible personalities, Leitzel and Alfredo Codona were also both tireless performers. Both craved the spotlight and the attention they received, and they often scheduled performances during their winter breaks from the circus. During one of these outside performances, on February 13, 1931, in Copenhagen, Denmark, one of the brass connections on Leitzel's rope broke, and she fell forty-five feet to a concrete floor, suffering a concussion and spinal injuries. Codona, who was performing in Berlin at the time, rushed to Copenhagen, but Leitzel insisted that her injuries weren't serious, and she urged Codona to return to Berlin to finish his engagement. Two days later, and a few hours after Codona left her side, Leitzel's condition worsened and she died.

Codona was devastated by Leitzel's death. He built the memorial to her, "In everlasting memory of my beloved, Leitzel Codona . . . Erected by her devoted husband, Alfredo Codona." At first glance, it appears that the statue, titled *Reunion*, represents an angel embracing Leitzel and taking her to heaven. But if the figure of the woman on the statue is supposed to represent Leitzel, the handsome, wavy-haired angel looks amazingly like Codona, based on the small photograph of him on his grave marker. Perhaps the angel is not really an angel at all, and the statue is merely a representation of Codona's love for Leitzel, with the wings as a symbol of his life as an aerialist. Just below the woman's feet on the statue are carved two small rings—the same type of rings Leitzel used in her famous swing-over routine. One of the rings is firmly attached to a rope, but above the other ring, the rope is broken.

After Leitzel's death, Codona married Vera Bruce in September 1932 and started to become increasingly reckless in his act. When he was seriously injured in a fall in 1933, doctors told him that torn ligaments in his shoulder would prevent him from ever performing again, and he was permanently "grounded." Still mourning Leitzel's death, and now faced with the end of his own career, Codona lost interest in his marriage to Bruce. He was working at a garage in Long Beach, California, when Bruce filed for divorce in 1937. In July 1937, the couple were in Bruce's attorney's office, along with Bruce's mother, to discuss divorce proceedings. Codona asked to speak to his wife in private. Bruce's mother refused to leave. After the attorney left the room, Codona locked the door, pulled a pistol from his coat pocket, shot his wife four times as her horrified mother watched, then shot himself once in the head. Codona died instantly, and Bruce died the next day. After the shooting, Codona's family found a suicide note containing his last request—to be buried beside Leitzel.

On one side of Codona's grave is a large marker over the grave of his brother, Lalo Codona (1895–1951), and on the other side is a small marker over the grave of his sister, Victoria Codona Adolph (1891–1983). Behind the angel statue are the graves of Codona's parents, Eduardo (1859–1934) and Hortensia (1869–1931).

Leitzel was born Leopoldina Alitza Pelikan on January 2, 1892, in Breslau, Germany (some sources say Bohemia). She died February 15, 1931, in Copenhagen, Denmark.

Codona was born October 7, 1893, in Sonora, Mexico. He died July 30, 1937, in Long Beach, California.

Drive around between the Miramar Section and the Crescent Section, until you reach an intersection that separates the Myrtle, Vista, Montcrest, and Miramar Sections. From that intersection, walk about fifty feet into the Miramar Section and you'll find a three-foot-high gray marble stone marking the grave of ventriloquist **Edgar Bergen (1903–1978)**.

Bergen came up with the idea of his most famous partner, the tuxedoed, top-hatted Charlie McCarthy, while he was still a high school student in Chicago. For twenty-five cents, he purchased a booklet to teach himself magic and ventriloquism, and he paid thirty-six dollars to a carpenter to carve a pine head for his dummy. After impressing his classmates and teachers with his ventriloquism, Bergen took his act to an amateur night at a Chicago theater and impressed the manager with his ventriloquism, but not with his magic. The manager said Bergen could continue to perform, but only if he dropped the magic from the act. Bergen's ventriloquism act helped pay for his first year in the premed program at Northwestern University, and then he took his act to the vaudeville circuit throughout the Midwest. Bergen dropped out of college before he graduated and became a full-time performer in 1925. After five years of playing small towns and theaters across the country, Bergen and Charlie finally made it to the big time in 1930—the Palace theater in New York City, where Bergen became the first ventriloquist act ever booked there.

Bergen and Charlie appeared in dozens of comedy shorts, beginning with *The Operation* (1930), in which Bergen plays a doctor and Charlie is his patient, as well as providing comic relief in other films through the 1930s and early 1940s, including *You Can't Cheat an Honest Man* (1939), *Look Who's Laughing* (1941), *Here We Go Again* (1942), and *Stage Door Canteen* (1943). Bergen even played a serious role, without Charlie, in *I Remember Mama* (1948).

After his success at the Palace, Bergen took Charlie on a world tour, performing in Europe, Asia, and South America, before he returned to the United

States and began performing in nightclubs. Bergen got his next big break when he appeared on singer Rudy Vallee's radio show in December 1936 and was so popular that his one-time guest appearance was extended to a three-month run. The following year, Bergen got his own radio show, which lasted for three years. The fact that a ventriloquist could be so popular on radio was a tribute to Bergen's talent as a performer and a comedian, and his ability to make Charlie McCarthy and his other characters, Mortimer Snerd and Effie Klinker, appear to be performers on their own, instead of just ventriloquist's puppets. In fact, for many fans, Charlie was the real star of the show, trading quips with guests and reciting memorable lines like, "Hard work never killed anybody, but why take a chance?" and "Ambition is a poor excuse for not having sense enough to be lazy." Bergen had some of the top stars of the day appear as guests on his program, including Mae West, Jack Benny, Betty Hutton, and Charles Boyer. Charlie also had a long-running, on-air feud with comedian W. C. Fields, who would threaten to carve Charlie up into a table leg or venetian blinds, but Charlie's quick comebacks usually got the best of Fields. Here's a sample exchange:

> *Fields:* "Tell me, Charles, is it true that your father was a gateleg table?"
> *Charlie:* "Well, if it is, your father was under it."
> *Fields:* "Quiet, you flophouse for termites, or I'll sic a beaver on you."
> *Charlie:* "Mr. Fields, is that a flamethrower I see, or is it your nose?"

In 1938, Bergen received an honorary Academy Award, "for his outstanding comedy creation, Charlie McCarthy." In recognition of Charlie's beginnings on a carpenter's bench, Bergen was awarded the first and only wooden Oscar statuette, complete with a movable jaw.

When the Academy of Television Arts and Sciences was formed in 1946, with its initial responsibility to be a central library to archive and preserve early television broadcasts, Bergen served as the group's first president. Today, the Academy is best known for handing out Emmy Awards for excellence in television production and performance.

Bergen continued on radio, moving from network to network through the 1940s and early 1950s. He continued to attract the top celebrities to appear on his shows, including actress Marilyn Monroe, who announced her engagement to Charlie. When the popularity of radio was replaced by television in the mid-1950s, Bergen easily made the transition, making guest appearances on variety and comedy shows. From 1956 to 1962, he even hosted a daytime television game show, *Do You Trust Your Wife?* While making his radio, television and film appearances, Bergen continued to appear onstage and in nightclubs. He was performing in Las Vegas with singer Andy Williams in 1978 when he died in his hotel room.

Bergen was the father of actress Candice Bergen, winner of five Emmy Awards as Outstanding Lead Actress in a Comedy Series for her work on the television sitcom *Murphy Brown*. When she won her first Emmy in 1989, she clutched the statuette, looked up, and said, "Dad, this is for you."

Bergen was born Edgar John Berggren on February 16, 1903, in Chicago, Illinois. He died September 30, 1978, in Las Vegas, Nevada.

Head west from Bergen's grave toward a small lake in the center of the cemetery grounds. On the opposite side of the lake is the Pinecrest Section. Go to the eastern edge of the Pinecrest Section, to the intersection that separates the Pinecrest, Utopia, and Cascade Gardens Sections. About fifteen feet west of that intersection and fifteen feet south of a large pine tree, in the Pinecrest Section, you'll find the grave of perhaps the most well-known stripper of all time, **Gypsy Rose Lee (1914–1970).**

Lee was born Rose Louise Hovick in Seattle, Washington, the eldest daughter of a mild-mannered newspaper reporter and a restless, fiery woman named Rose, who was determined to get out of Seattle and get one of her two daughters into show business. When her early efforts with her first daughter, who was known as Louise, weren't successful, she turned her attention to her youngest daughter, June, who seemed to be more talented and more interested in a career in entertainment than her older sister.

When Louise was seven and June was five, Rose put together an act with her daughters and six young chorus boys called "Baby June and Her Farmboys," which was moderately successful on the vaudeville circuit. June was the star, and Louise played one of the farmboys. After performing for nearly ten years, June was getting a little old to be called "Baby June," so she became "Dainty June," and the act continued as "Dainty June and Her Newsboy Songsters," with Louise as one of the newsboys. But June was getting tired of performing, so she ran off with one of the chorus boys from the act when she was thirteen and they got married. Rose put Louise in the spotlight, replaced the chorus boys with chorus girls, and re-named the act "Rose Louise and Her Hollywood Blondes."

By the late 1920s, vaudeville theaters were being transformed into movie

A small rose adorns the grave marker of author, actress, and stripper Gypsy Rose Lee.

houses, but the bawdy burlesque houses were still popular, so that's where Rose brought her daughter and their act. One evening in Toledo, Ohio, after one of the theater's star strippers had been arrested for assaulting a hotel manager and was unable to perform, the opportunistic Rose volunteered fifteen-year-old Louise to take her place. Louise's first striptease act was more "tease" than "strip"—she just danced and didn't take much off—but the audience enjoyed her performance. Louise changed her name to Gypsy Rose Lee, and she changed the typical striptease act, adding comedy, songs, flashy costumes, and a little sophistication. Lee became popular in burlesque houses across the country, setting attendance records wherever she performed, and she also become a well-known celebrity in mainstream America. She attended the best parties, her name was often mentioned in gossip columns, and even if people hadn't seen her act, they knew who she was. With her fame growing, Lee decided to try performing in films.

But even though Lee was popular, studio heads were afraid that putting a well-known stripper in films might hurt their image and reputation, so Lee made her film debut in *Ali Baba Goes to Town* (1937) under her real name, Louise Hovick. She appeared in four more films as Louise Hovick—*You Can't Have Everything* (1937), *My Lucky Star* (1938), *Battle of Broadway* (1938), and *Sally, Irene and Mary* (1938)—before she put her performing career on hold and turned to writing. Her first book, a mystery novel titled *The G-String Murders* and published in 1941, was made into a film, *Lady of Burlesque* (1943), starring Barbara Stanwyck.

By this time, Lee's sister, June, had become a successful actress and dancer, changing her name slightly to June Havoc. In 1957, after her mother died, Lee wrote her autobiography, *Gypsy*, and it became an immediate best-seller, appearing on the *New York Times* bestseller list for ten weeks. Excerpts were printed in *Harper's*, *Town and Country*, and other popular magazines, and the book was translated and published around the world. Broadway producers saw potential in the story, and the book was transformed into a musical, *Gypsy*, which premiered in May 1959 and was an instant success. The musical, which focuses on the tough and domineering Mama Rose and starred Ethel Merman in the original production, has been revived frequently over the years and was made into a popular film in 1962, with Rosalind Russell as Mama Rose and Natalie Wood as Gypsy. Another version, made in 1993, starred Bette Midler as Mama Rose, and Cynthia Gibb as Gypsy.

Following this newfound success, Lee returned to films, appearing in small roles in *Wind Across the Everglades* (1958), *The Stripper* (1963), and *The Trouble With Angels* (1966). She also hosted two short-lived television talk shows—*The Gypsy Rose Lee Show* in 1958, and *Gypsy* in 1965.

Lee's simple grave marker features a single rose.

Lee was born Rose Louise Hovick on February 9, 1914, in Seattle, Washington. She died April 26, 1970, in Los Angeles.

West of Lee's grave, in the center of the Pinecrest Section, there is a single row of tall memorial markers. In the center of that row, the tallest marker, made of red granite, marks the grave of the man recently voted the "Fighter of the Century," **Sugar Ray Robinson (1921–1989).**

Robinson was born Walker Smith Jr. in Detroit, Michigan. After his parents moved to New York City, Robinson began training at a local gym and traveling with amateur boxers to fights throughout the state. At one fight, the promoter needed a flyweight; Robinson was available, but he was too young to legally fight. So the promoter gave him the Amateur Athletic Union boxing card of a recently retired fighter named Ray Robinson, and he kept that name throughout his career. He also won his first amateur fight, earning ten dollars. In the late 1930s, a sportswriter said his fighting style was "sweet as sugar," and so he became Sugar Ray Robinson. Robinson later said he preferred the name to his own, since "Sugar Walker Smith doesn't have the same ring."

As an amateur boxer, Robinson was undefeated in 125 fights. After winning the 1939 New York Golden Gloves featherweight championship, Robinson turned professional at the age of nineteen, winning his first professional fight with a second-round knockout on October 4, 1940, and earning $150. By the end of 1942, Robinson was undefeated after forty fights, with twenty-nine victories by knockout. Robinson's first loss was to Jake LaMotta in early 1943—his only loss to LaMotta in six fights.

In 1946, when Robinson won the world welterweight championship, he had a record of seventy-four wins—including forty-nine by knockout—one loss and one draw. On February 14, 1951, Robinson beat LaMotta to win the world middleweight championship—Robinson's 121st victory, with still only one defeat. The fight with LaMotta was called the "St. Valentine's Day Massacre," the raging Robinson against the "Raging Bull," as LaMotta was known. By the thirteenth round, both fighters were battered and bloody, and following a barrage of unanswered punches from Robinson, the referee stopped the fight.

During his career, Robinson was the world welterweight champion from 1946 until 1951 (when he vacated the title to become a middleweight), and he won the world middleweight championship five times. Robinson was forty-four years old when he retired in 1965. Over his twenty-five-year career in the ring, Robinson fought 200 times, with 175 wins—109 of them by knockout–19 losses and 6 draws. Fifteen of Robinson's losses came after he turned thirty-five, and ten were after he turned forty.

In the ring, Robinson had all the tools. He was both a fighter and a boxer, with lightning-quick hands and power behind his punches. At the end of 1999, the Associated Press assembled a special panel of boxing experts to pick the top fighters of the century in each weight class, as well as a top over-all fighter. Robinson was named the best middleweight and the best welter-weight of the past hundred years, as well as topping Muhammad Ali for the title of "Fighter of the Century." (To compare records, Ali fought sixty-one times, with fifty-six wins—thirty-seven by knockout—and five losses.) *Ring* magazine named Robinson the best boxer in its seventy-five years of publication, and when ESPN, the cable sports channel, selected the top one hundred North American athletes of the century, Robinson finished in the twenty-fourth spot.

Outside of the ring, Robinson was one of boxing's first real personalities, and one of the first black athletes to become a major star outside of sports. He was the first to travel with a personal entourage, including trainers, secretary, barber, masseur, drama coach, golf pro, assorted female fans, and even his own mascot. Although Robinson earned an estimated $4 million during his boxing career, by the time he retired he was broke. So he revived his career by getting into show business, acting and even singing and dancing in nightclubs and on television. In 1986, Robinson made his final public appearance—as the best man at Jake LaMotta's wedding.

Robinson is buried with his wife, Mildred Robinson (1919–1995).

Robinson was born Walker Smith Jr. on May 3, 1921, in Detroit, Michigan. He died April 12, 1989, in Culver City, California.

Continue south from the Pinecrest Section and turn left between the Sylvan Section and the Sycamore Section. Stop at the next intersection, with the Acacia Slope Section on your left. At the southeast corner of the Acacia Slope Section, just a few feet from the curb, you'll find a military marker over the grave of **William B. Thomas (1931–1980)**, better known as "Buckwheat" in nearly one hundred *Our Gang* comedy shorts from the early 1930s to the early 1940s.

Thomas, who performed under the name of Billie Thomas, joined the *Our Gang* cast when he was only three years old. Though Thomas wasn't the first to play the character of Buckwheat, he was certainly the most memorable.

Thomas appeared in a few films outside the *Our Gang* series, including *Mokey* (1942), starring Dan Dailey, Donna Reed, and Robert Blake; *Honeymoon Lodge* (1943); and *Heavenly Music* (1943). After his *Our Gang* contract expired in 1944, Thomas appeared in *Colorado Pioneers* (1945), a Western in the Red Ryder series, then retired from the screen.

Unlike some of his fellow *Our Gang* actors, notably Carl "Alfalfa" Switzer and Scotty Beckett, Thomas led a fairly normal, stable life after his *Our Gang* days were over. He enrolled in public school, served in the U.S. Army during World War II, and worked for twenty years as a film lab technician for Technicolor in Los Angeles. He died of a heart attack at the age of forty-nine. And, despite Eddie Murphy's popular impression of an older Buckwheat on *Saturday Night Live,* Buckwheat wasn't actually the one who said, "O-tay!" That was Eugene "Porky" Lee, who was often teamed with Buckwheat in the comedies.

Thomas was born William B. Thomas Jr. on March 12, 1931, in Los Angeles. He died October 10, 1980, in Los Angeles.

Turn around and head back toward the west. Turn right between the Pleasant View Section and the Maple Section. Stop when you reach a T-shaped intersection, with the Cedars Section in front of you. On your right, in the Rosehill Section, just about fifteen feet in from the corner of the section, you'll find the grave of actor **Allan "Rocky" Lane (1909–1973),** who appeared in more than one hundred films, mostly Western serials, but is best remembered as the voice of *Mister Ed,* the talking horse, in the television series from 1961 to 1966.

Lane was a football player and model who occasionally worked on the stage in the late 1920s. He made his film debut in *Not Quite Decent* (1929) and also played a supporting role in *The Forward Pass* (1929), starring Douglas Fairbanks Jr. and Loretta Young. Lane's first appearance in a Western was playing a robber in *Law West of Tombstone* (1938), starring Harry Carey. Lane appeared in small roles in several more films through the 1940s before donning his cowboy hat and six-shooter as Sergeant Dave King, RCMP, in *King of the Royal Mounted* (1940). He starred in several more films in the *Sergeant King* series and other Westerns before playing Red Ryder in *Stagecoach to Denver* (1946), his first appearance in the *Red Ryder* series. The following year, Lane took the nickname Rocky, jumped on his faithful stallion, Black Jack, and appeared in the first of dozens of Westerns over the next several years, usually playing a character named Rocky Lane but sometimes promoting himself to Ranger Rocky Lane, Sergeant Rocky Lane, or Lieutenant Rocky Lane.

Lane appeared in a new Western every few months for the next several years for Republic Pictures, with titles that can almost make you hear the thunder of hoofbeats, including *Frontier Investigator* (1949), *Navajo Trail Raiders* (1949), *Powder River Rustlers* (1949), *Bandit King of Texas* (1949), *The Wyoming Bandit* (1949), *Death Valley Gunfighter* (1949), *Sheriff of Wichita* (1949), *Salt Lake Raiders* (1950), *Vigilante Hideout* (1950), *Rustlers on Horseback* (1950), *Frisco Tornado* (1950), *Covered Wagon Raid* (1950), *Code of the Silver Sage* (1950), *Gunmen of Abilene* (1950), *Fort Dodge Stampede* (1951), *Rough Riders of Durango* (1951), *Wells Fargo Gunmaster* (1951), *Desert of Lost Men* (1951), *Night Riders of Montana* (1951), *Black Hills Ambush* (1952), *Leadville Gunslinger* (1952), *El Paso Stampede* (1953), *Bandits of the West* (1953), and *Marshal of Cedar Rock* (1953). Through the early 1950s, Lane was one of the most popular film cowboys, but his film career ended quickly a few years later.

Many of Lane's costars and coworkers on these films described him as an egotistical perfectionist with no sense of humor, who always made sure everyone knew that he was the star of the film. Others said that once the cameras stopped rolling, Lane was a warm and friendly person who often made unpublicized visits to children's hospitals.

When *Mister Ed* started in 1961, Lane provided the voice for the talking horse. Initially, there was a great deal of secrecy about who was providing the voice, and the credits at the end of the show simply stated that the horse was played by "himself." Later, when the show became more popular—believe it or not, *Mister Ed* won a Golden Globe Award in 1963 as Best Television Show—Lane wanted to be listed in the credits, but the producers wanted to maintain the mystery and offered Lane a raise in salary instead.

Lane's grave marker features his real name and his screen name.

Lane was born Harry Leonard Albershart on September 22, 1909 (some sources say 1904), in Mishawaka, Indiana. He died October 27, 1973, in Woodland Hills, California.

Turn left in front of the Cedars Section, then turn right between the Cedars Section and the M Plot Section. Continue traveling straight past a few sections until you turn right between the Sunrise Section and the Del Ivy Section. Turn at the first left, between the Del Ivy Section and the Charter Oak Section.

Stop when you see a large memorial on your right, in the Charter Oak Section. The ten-foot-high, black granite memorial to "our British boys and nurses" who died during World War I was erected by the Canadian Women's Club of Los Angeles. Across the road from the memorial, in the Del Ivy Section, look for the name of the section stenciled on the curb. From that point, walk about fifty feet toward a tall pine tree. About fifteen feet in front of the tree, you'll find a small grave marker, inscribed only with "The Little Mouse, July 7–July 10, 1919." The marker identifies the grave of **Norman Spencer Chaplin**, the infant son of comedian Charlie Chaplin and his first wife, actress Mildred Harris. When the baby was born, possibly prematurely, his digestive system was improperly formed, and he died three days later. The death certificate listed the cause of death as "rudimentary development of the large intestine."

Chaplin was not at the hospital when his son was born, so Harris gave him the name "Charles Spencer Chaplin Jr." on his birth certificate, which Chaplin objected to. On his death certificate, the baby was identified as "Norman Spencer Chaplin." Chaplin also objected to his wife's choice of funeral director, and he was also unhappy about the artificial smile placed on the baby's face prior to the funeral services. Chaplin and Harris were divorced in November 1920.

Charlie Chaplin's infant son is identified only as "The Little Mouse" on his grave marker.

The baby's short life gets even shorter attention in Chaplin's autobiography, published in 1964. "After we had been married a year, a child was born but lived only three days," he wrote. "This began the withering of our marriage." And that was all he wrote about the child.

EXIT LINES

Entertainers and celebrities don't usually have writers working for them in real life, so their last words often aren't as dramatic or memorable as famous parting lines from the movies, like Edward G. Robinson's "Mother of mercy, is this the end of Rico?" from *Little Caesar* (1930); James Cagney's defiant "I made it, Ma! Top of the world!" from *White Heat* (1949); Orson Welles's gasping "Rosebud," from *Citizen Kane* (1941), or even Boris Karloff's creepy "We belong dead," from *The Bride of Frankenstein* (1935).

Still, a few celebrities were able to come up with some fairly noteworthy lines just before they pulled down the final curtain (though some may have been embellished just a little bit by their publicists):

Don't pull down the blinds. I feel fine. I want the sunlight to greet me.

~ RUDOLPH VALENTINO—AUGUST 23, 1926

I never felt better in my life!

~ DOUGLAS FAIRBANKS SR.—DECEMBER 12, 1939

Well, boys, this is it . . . I'm going . . . I'm going.

~ AL JOLSON—OCTOBER 23, 1950

Don't let them worry you. Nothing matters, nothing matters.

~ LOUIS B. MAYER—OCTOBER 29, 1957

Don't worry. The same thing happened about a week ago.

~ TYRONE POWER (AFTER SUFFERING A HEART ATTACK WHILE ON LOCATION IN SPAIN)—NOVEMBER 15, 1958

That was the best ice-cream soda I ever tasted.

~ LOU COSTELLO (BEFORE SUFFERING A FATAL STROKE)—MARCH 3, 1959

I'm tired. I'm going back to bed.

~ GEORGE "SUPERMAN" REEVES—JUNE 6, 1959

I'm happy. I want everyone to be happy.

~ ETHEL BARRYMORE—JUNE 18, 1959

*Dear World, I am leaving because I am bored. I feel I have lived long enough.
I am leaving you with your worries in this sweet cesspool. Good luck.*

~ GEORGE SANDERS (SUICIDE NOTE)—APRIL 25, 1972

Oh, God! No! Help! Someone, help!

~ SAL MINEO (WHILE BEING ATTACKED AND
STABBED IN A PARKING LOT)—
FEBRUARY 12, 1976

Damn it, don't you dare ask God to help me!

~ JOAN CRAWFORD (TO HER PRAYING
HOUSEKEEPER)—MAY 10, 1977

That was a great game of golf, fellas.

~ BING CROSBY (BEFORE COLLAPSING WHILE
WALKING OFF A GOLF COURSE IN
SPAIN)—OCTOBER 14, 1977

Don't worry. It's not loaded.

~ TERRY KATH (WHILE PLAYING WITH A
HANDGUN)—JANUARY 23, 1978

I'll finally get to see Marilyn.

~ JOE DIMAGGIO—MARCH 8, 1999

GLOSSARY

These are commonly accepted terms in the funeral and cemetery business. Though in common usage the words *grave, crypt,* and *tomb* might be interchangeable, in actuality they have very different meanings, and knowing those differences will help you understand the directions and navigate through the cemeteries.

In recent years, many commonly accepted words associated with funerals and cemeteries have been replaced by modern versions, usually at the insistence of the funeral directors or cemetery owners, apparently in an effort to improve their image. Cemeteries have become "memorial parks," funerals have become "memorial services," coffins are now called "caskets," hearses are "coaches," morticians are "funeral directors" or "grief counselors," graves are "interment spaces" or "lawn crypts," and those spaces are no longer dug up and filled in, but rather "opened" and "closed."

Burial—Although this usually refers to the placement of a body below ground, it can also refer to the placement of a body in an aboveground crypt.

Cenotaph—A memorial placed in honor of a person who is buried elsewhere. These are used especially if someone was born in one place, lived most of their life somewhere else, and was then buried near their hometown. The cenotaph memorial would be placed where they lived, to give mourners and fans a place to go to pay their respects. In Hollywood, for example, one of the best-known cenotaphs is Jayne Mansfield's memorial at Hollywood Forever cemetery, even though Mansfield is buried near her birthplace in Plainfield, Pennsylvania.

Coffin—A container for the burial of human remains, sometimes called a casket.

Columbarium—A room or other location used for the placement of cremated remains. The individual locations for the remains are called niches.

Cremation—The process of reducing human remains to ash through the use of high heat and evaporation.

Crematory—A building containing the furnace or other device used to cremate human remains.

Crypt—An enclosed structure for the final placement of human remains. These can include mausoleum crypts, which are generally above ground, or lawn crypts, which are generally below ground.

Epitaph—An inscription on a memorial.

Garden mausoleum—An outdoor mausoleum; a building or structure with the crypt spaces on the outer walls. These crypts are sometimes referred to as garden crypts or wall crypts.

Interment—The final placement of the human remains, either below ground in a lawn crypt or above ground in a mausoleum or columbarium.

Lawn crypt—A belowground burial site, commonly known as a grave.

Mausoleum—An enclosed building or structure intended for aboveground interment. A large, community mausoleum can contain a large number of crypts and niches. A private or family mausoleum is generally used for just one person or a small number of family members.

Mausoleum crypt—An aboveground interment site.

Memorial—A marker identifying a burial or interment space. These can be simple markers, listing the name, date of birth, and date of death, or larger, more elaborate memorials with commemorative statements, lists of accomplishments, and pictures. Memorials can also include statues, benches, or other identifying markers or monuments. Memorials can be referred to as gravestones, tombstones, headstones, or plaques.

Memorial park—A phrase coined by Hubert Eaton, the driving force behind the Forest Lawn cemeteries; a memorial park restricts or prohibits the use of large, upright memorials or monuments to create a park-like setting with large, open lawn areas. A cynic might suggest that this arrangement makes it much more difficult to find a particular grave location but much easier to cut the lawn with large mowers. Many cemeteries are officially called memorial parks even though they still allow large, upright memorials. Perhaps they just feel that "memorial park" sounds friendlier and more modern than "cemetery."

Monument—A large, upright memorial.

Niche—An individual space in a columbarium for the interment of cremated remains.

Pre-need—Making plans for funeral and burial before death.

Private mausoleum—A small mausoleum, intended for one person or family.

Sarcophagus—An aboveground structure, usually made of marble or stone, that usually contains one coffin. A typical sarcophagus often looks like a large, elaborate coffin.

Scattering garden—A small common area of the cemetery grounds, usually full of flowers, for the scattering of cremated remains.

Urn garden—An area where cremated remains are buried, usually with very small grave markers.

REFERENCES

~ BOOKS

Alleman, Richard. *The Movie Lover's Guide to Hollywood.* New York: Harper & Row, 1985.

Amburn, Ellis. *Dark Star: The Roy Orbison Story.* New York: Carol Publishing Group, 1990.

Anger, Kenneth. *Hollywood Babylon.* New York: Dell Publishing, 1975.

Arce, Hector. *Groucho.* New York: G. P. Putnam's Sons, 1979.

Astaire, Fred. *Steps in Time.* New York: Harper & Brothers, 1959.

Bahr, Robert. *Least of All Saints: The Story of Aimee Semple McPherson.* Englewood Cliffs, N.J.: Prentice-Hall, 1979.

Behlmer, Rudy. *Inside Warner Brothers.* New York: Viking Penguin, 1985.

Benny, Jack and Joan Benny. *Sunday Nights at Seven: The Jack Benny Story.* New York: Warner Books, 1990.

Benny, Mary Livingstone and Hilliard Marks. *Jack Benny.* Garden City, N.Y.: Doubleday, 1978.

Bergen, Candice. *Knock Wood.* New York City: Simon and Schuster, Linden Press, 1984.

Blanche, Tony and Brad Schreiber. *Death in Paradise.* Los Angeles, Calif.: General Publishing Group, Inc., 1998.

Bogdanovich, Peter. *The Killing of the Unicorn.* New York: William Morrow and Co., 1984.

Brook, Stephen. *L.A. Days, L.A. Nights.* New York: St. Martin's Press, 1992.

Brown, Joe E. *Laughter Is a Wonderful Thing.* New York: A. S. Barnes and Company, 1956.

Brown, Peter Harry and Patte B. Barnum. *Marilyn: The Last Take.* New York: Dutton, 1992.

Buford, Kate. *Burt Lancaster: An American Life.* New York: Alfred A. Knopf, 2000.

Burk, Margaret and Gary Hudson. *Final Curtain,*. Santa Ana, Calif.: Seven Locks Press, 1996.

Carpenter, Edwin H. *Early Cemeteries of the City of Los Angeles.* Los Angeles: Dawson's Book Shop, 1973.

Carrick, Peter. *A Tribute to Fred Astaire.* Salem, N.H.: Salem House, 1985.

Chaplin, Charles. *My Autobiography.* New York: Simon and Schuster, 1964.

Conrad, Barnaby. *Famous Last Words.* Garden City, N.Y.: Doubleday, 1961.

Costello, Chris and Raymond Strait. *Lou's on First.* New York: St. Martin's Press, 1981.

Criswell, Jeron. *Criswell Predicts.* Anderson, S.C.: Droke House Publishers, 1968.

———. *Criswell's Forbidden Predictions.* Anderson, S.C.: Droke House Publishers, 1972.

Crotty, James and Michael Lane. *The Mad Monks' Guide to California.* New York: Macmillan Travel, 2000.

Crowther, Bosley. *Hollywood Rajah—The Life and Times of Louis B. Mayer.* New York: Holt, Rinehart and Winston, 1960.

Culbertson, Judi and Tom Randall. *Permanent Californians.* Chelsea, Vt.: Chelsea Green Publishing Company, 1989.

Davies, Marion. *The Times We Had: Life With William Randolph Hearst.* New York: Bobbs–Merrill Company, 1975.

Dewey, Donald. *James Stewart—A Biography.* Atlanta, Ga.: Turner Publishing, 1996.

Dunning, John. *The Encyclopedia of Old-Time Radio.* New York: Oxford University Press, 1998.

Eberts, Mike. *Griffith Park: A Centennial History.* Los Angeles: The Historical Society of Southern California, 1996.

Eckley, Wilson. *The American Circus.* Boston: Twayne Publishers, 1984.

Fishgall, Gary. *Pieces of Time: The Life of Jimmy Stewart.* New York: Scribner, 1997.

Flynn, Errol. *My Wicked, Wicked Ways.* New York: G. P. Putnam's Sons, 1959.

Freeland, Michael. *Jolson.* New York: Stein and Day, 1972.

Gipe, George. *The Last Time When.* New York: World Almanac Publications, 1981.

Goldman, Herbert G. *Jolson: The Legend Comes to Life.* New York: Oxford University Press, 1988.

———. *Fanny Brice: The Original Funny Girl.* New York: Oxford University Press, 1992.

Gomery, Douglas. *The Hollywood Studio System.* New York: St. Martin's Press, 1986.

Gordon, William A. *The Ultimate Hollywood Tour Book.* El Toro, Calif.: North Ridge Books, 1998.

Grenier, Judson. *A Guide to Historic Places in Los Angeles County.* Dubuque, Iowa: Kendall/Hunt Publishing, 1978.

Grossman, Barbara W. *Funny Woman: The Life and Times of Fanny Brice.* Bloomington, Ind.: Indiana University Press, 1991.

Guiles, Fred Lawrence. *Marion Davies.* New York: McGraw-Hill, 1972.

———. *Tyrone Power: The Last Idol.* San Francisco: Mercury House, 1979.

Halliwell, Leslie. *Halliwell's Filmgoer's Companion.* New York: Charles Scribner's Sons, 1984.

Hancock, Ralph and Letitia Fairbanks. *Douglas Fairbanks: The Fourth Musketeer.* New York: Henry Holt and Company, 1953.

Hancock, Ralph. *The Forest Lawn Story.* Los Angeles: Academy Publishers, 1955.

Harmetz, Aljean. *The Making of* The Wizard of Oz. New York: Alfred A. Knopf, 1977.

Jacobson, Laurie. *Hollywood Heartbreak.* New York: Simon and Schuster, 1984.

Jarvis, Everett G. and Lois A. Johe. *Final Curtain.* Secaucus, N.J.: Carol Publishing Group, 1998.

Jillette, Penn and Teller. *Penn and Teller's How to Play in Traffic.* New York: Boulevard Books, 1997.

Josefsberg, Milt. *The Jack Benny Show.* New Rochelle, N.Y.: Arlington House Publishers, 1977.

Katz, Ephriam. *The Film Encyclopedia, Third Edition.* New York: Harper Perennial, 1998.

Kobler, John. *Damned in Paradise: The Life of John Barrymore.* New York: Atheneum, 1977.

Kotsilibas-Davis, James. *The Barrymores: The Royal Family in Hollywood.* New York: Crown Publishers, 1981.

Lackmann, Ron. *The Encyclopedia of American Radio*. New York: Facts on File, 1996.

Lawford, Patricia Seaton. *The Peter Lawford Story*. New York: Carroll & Graf Publishers, 1988.

Lawson, Kristan and Anneli Rufus. *California Babylon: A Guide to Sites of Scandal, Mayhem, and Celluloid in the Golden State*. New York: St. Martin's Griffin, 2000.

Lee, Gypsy Rose. *Gypsy: Memoirs of America's Most Celebrated Stripper*. Berkeley, Calif.: Frog, Ltd., 1999.

Llewellyn, John F. *A Cemetery Should Be Forever*. Glendale, Calif.: Tropico Press, 1998.

Lynn, Kenneth S. *Charlie Chaplin and His Times*. New York: Simon and Schuster, 1997.

Manvell, Roger. *Chaplin*. New York: Little, Brown and Company, 1974.

Marx, Maxine. *Growing Up With Chico*. Englewood Cliffs, N.J.: Prentice Hall, 1980.

McCabe, John. *Laurel and Hardy*. New York: Ballantine Books, 1975.

Milton, Joyce. *Tramp: The Life of Charlie Chaplin*. New York: HarperCollins Publishers, 1996.

Mitford, Jessica. *The American Way of Death Revisited*. New York: Vintage Books, 1998.

Mordden, Ethan. *The Hollywood Musical*. New York: St. Martin's Press, 1981.

Moses, Robert, ed. *American Movie Classics Classic Movie Companion*. New York: Hyperion, 1999.

Nass, Herbert E. *Wills of the Rich and Famous*. New York: Gramercy Books, 1991.

Noguchi, Thomas and Joseph DiMona. *Coroner*. New York: Simon and Schuster, 1983.

Osborne, Robert. *70 Years of Oscar; The Official History of the Academy Awards*. New York: Abbeville Press, 1999.

Poundstone, William. *Biggest Secrets*. New York: William Morrow and Co., 1993.

Rasmussen, Cecilia. *Curbside L.A.* Los Angeles: Los Angeles Times Syndicate, 1996.

Rogers, Ginger. *Ginger: My Story*. New York: HarperCollins Publishers, 1991.

Rubin, Barbara, Robert Carlton, and Arnold Rubin. *L.A. in Installments*. Santa Monica, Calif.: Westside Publications, 1979.

Schatz, Thomas. *The Genius of the System*. New York: Pantheon Books, 1988.

Shulman, Irving. *Harlow*. New York: Bernard Geis Associates, 1964.

Siegel, Scott and Barbara Siegel. *American Film Comedy*. New York: Prentice Hall, 1994.

Skretvedt, Randy. *Laurel and Hardy*. Beverly Hills, Calif.: Moonstone Press, 1987.

Smith, Ronald L. *Who's Who in Comedy*. New York: Facts on File, Inc., 1992.

Spada, James. *Peter Lawford: The Man Who Kept the Secrets*. New York: Bantam Books, 1991.

Stenn, David. *Bombshell: The Life and Death of Jean Harlow*. New York: Doubleday, 1993.

Stephens, Autumn. *Drama Queens*. Berkeley, Calif.: Conari Press, 1998.

Stern, Norton B., ed. *The Jews of Los Angeles: Urban Pioneers*. Los Angeles: Southern California Jewish Historical Society, 1981.

Tosches, Nick. *Dino: Living High in the Dirty Business of Dreams*. New York: Doubleday, 1992.

Thomas, Bob. *King Cohn—The Life and Times of Hollywood Mogul Harry Cohn*. Beverly Hills, Calif.: New Millennium Press, 2000.

———. *The Clown Prince of Hollywood—The Antic Life and Times of Jack L. Warner*. New York: McGraw-Hill, 1990.

Thomas, Tony. *The Best of Universal*. Vestal, N.Y.: The Vestal Press, Ltd., 1990.

Victor, Adam. *The Marilyn Encyclopedia*. Woodstock, N.Y.: The Overlook Press, 1999.

Vorspan, Max and Lloyd P. Gartner. *History of the Jews in Los Angeles*. San Marino, Calif.: The Huntington Library, 1970.

Waldron, Vince. *The Official Dick Van Dyke Show Book*. New York: Applause Theater Books, 1994.

Walsh, Raoul. *Each Man in His Time*. New York: Farrar, Straus and Giroux, 1974.

Waugh, Evelyn. *The Loved One*. New York: Little, Brown and Company, 1948.

Wigoder, Geoffrey, ed. *The Encyclopedia of Judiasm*. New York: Macmillan Publishing Co., 1989.

Wolfe, Donald H. *The Last Days of Marilyn Monroe.* New York: William Morrow and Co., 1998.

Wood, Lana. *Natalie: A Memoir by Her Sister.* New York: G. P. Putnam's Sons, 1984.

∼ NEWSPAPERS

The Los Angeles Times
The New York Times
New Times

∼ WEB SITES

www.IMDb.com (The Internet Movie Database)
www.FindAGrave.com
www.Seeing-Stars.com
www.HollywoodUnderground.com
www.Oscars.org
www.LittleGoldenGuy.com
www.Grammy.org
www.CityMorgueGiftShop.com

CELEBRITY BURIALS BY CEMETERY

Chapter 1—Forest Lawn Memorial Park–Glendale

Alda, Robert
Allen, Gracie
Andrews, La Verne
Andrews, Maxene
Bara, Theda
Baum, L. Frank
Baxter, Warner
Beery, Wallace
Bell, Rex
Besser, Joe
Blandick, Clara
Blondell, Joan
Bogart, Humphrey
Bow, Clara
Boyd, William "Hopalong Cassidy"
Brown, Joe E.
Burns, George
Bushman, Francis X.
Canova, Judy
Carson, Jack
Chase, Charley
Cole, Nat "King"
Cukor, George
Cummings, Robert
Curtiz, Michael
Dailey, Dan
Dandridge, Dorothy
Davis, Sammy Jr.

Demarest, William
Disney, Walt
Dressler, Marie
Eaton, Hubert
Fields, W. C.
Fine, Larry
Flynn, Errol
Frye, Dwight
Gable, Clark
Gilmore, Ethel M.
Goldwyn, Samuel
Grapewin, Charles
Grauman, Sid
Gumm, Frank A.
Hale, Alan Sr.
Harlow, Jean
Head, Edith
Hersholt, Jean
Horton, Edward Everett
Kath, Terry Alan
Knight, Ted
Ladd, Alan
Ladd, Sue Carol
Landis, Carole
LeRoy, Mervyn
Lewis, Mitchell, J.
Lloyd, Harold
Lombard, Carole
Lubitsch, Ernst
MacDonald, Jeanette
Marx, Chico

Fleming, Victor
Gaynor, Janet
Hackett, Joan
Harris, Mildred
Hood, Darla
Huston, John
La Marr, Barbara
Lake, Arthur
Lasky, Jesse L. Jr.
Lasky, Jesse L. Sr.
Lawrence, Florence
Lehrman, Henry "Pathe"
Lincoln, Elmo
Lorre, Peter
Lyon, Ben
Mansfield, Jayne
McDaniel, Hattie
Menjou, Adolph
Muni, Paul
Powell, Eleanor
Power, Tyrone
Rappe, Virginia
Riddle, Nelson
Ritz, Al
Ritz, Harry
Ritz, Jimmy
Rosson, Harold
Scotti, Vito
Siegel, Benjamin "Bugsy"
Switzer, Carl "Alfalfa"
Talmadge, Constance
Talmadge, Natalie
Talmadge, Norma
Taylor, William Desmond
Valentino, Rudolph
Webb, Clifton

Chapter 4—Pierce Brothers Westwood Village Memorial Park

Arden, Eve
Ayres, Lew
Backus, Jim
Basehart, Richard
Brice, Fanny
Cabot, Sebastian
Cahn, Sammy
Capote, Truman
Cassavetes, John
Conte, Richard
Crane, Bob
Dunne, Dominique
Gabor, Eva
Hammer, Armand
Johnson, Nunnally
Keith, Brian
Lancaster, Burt
Lawford, Peter
Lazar, Irving "Swifty"
Lemmon, Jack
Levant, June Gale
Levant, Oscar
Martin, Dean
Matthau, Walter
Monroe, Marilyn
Nolan, Lloyd
O'Connor, Caroll
O'Rourke, Heather
Orbison, Roy
Reed, Donna
Rich, Buddy
Riperton, Minnie
Scott, George C.
Stratten, Dorothy
Torme, Mel
Tuttle, Frank
Wilde, Cornel

Barrymore, John
Barrymore, Lionel
Cody, Mabel Normand
Colt, Ethel Barrymore
Costello, Lou
Griffin, Irene Dunne
Healy, Ted
Negri, Pola
Novarro, Ramon
Reagan, John Edward
Reagan, Nelle Wilson

Chapter 10—Home of Peace Memorial Park

Howard, Jerome
Howard, Shemp
Laemmle, Carl
Magnin, Rabbi Edgar Fogel
Mayer, Louis B.
Warner, Albert
Warner, Harry Morris
Warner, Jack
Warner, Samuel L.

Chapter 11—Eden Memorial Park

Bruce, Lenny
Lembeck, Harvey
Marx, Groucho

Chapter 12—San Fernando Mission Cemetery

Arnold, Edward
Beckett, Scott
Begley, Ed Sr.
Bendix, William
Brennan, Walter
Brown, Alice Joyce

Colonna, Jerry
Connors, Chuck
Frawley, William
Gobel, George
Sprigg, June (Marlowe)
Valens, Ritchie

Chapter 13—Pierce Brothers Valhalla Memorial Park

Benaderet, Bea
Canutt, Yakima
Corsaut, Aneta L.
DeRita, Curly-Joe
Edwards, Cliff
George, Gorgeous
Hardy, Oliver
King, Charles Criswell
Murray, Mae
Nelson, Nels P.
Rosenbloom, Slapsie Maxie

Chapter 14—Inglewood Park Cemetery

Bergen, Edgar
Bern, Paul
Chaplin, Norman Spencer
Codona, Alfredo
Grable, Betty
Lane, Allan "Rocky"
Lee, Gypsy Rose
Leitzel, Lillian
Riskin, Robert
Robinson, Sugar Ray
Romero, Cesar
Thomas, William B.

INDEX

THE LAST WORD

Have I missed anyone?

Do you know of any favorite celebrities that should be included in this book but aren't? Or perhaps they should be included in new books in the series, focusing on other locations. Please contact me and let me know the name of the celebrity and, if possible, the cemetery where they're buried and the location, and I'll try to include them in future editions.

Thanks.

Mark Masek
c/o Cumberland House Publishing, Inc.
431 Harding Industrial Drive
Nashville, TN 37211

You can also contact me by e-mail, at mark@cemeteryguide.com, or visit my Web site, www.cemeteryguide.com.

ABOUT THE AUTHOR

Mark Masek is a travel writer with many feature stories published under his byline. A native of Chicago, Illinois, he lives in Pasadena, California, with his wife, Theresa. *Hollywood Remains to Be Seen* is his first book.